THE AESTHETIC THEORY OF
THOMAS HOBBES

THE AESTHETIC THEORY
OF THOMAS HOBBES

With Special Reference to His
Contribution to the Psychological Approach
in English Literary Criticism

BY

CLARENCE DeWITT THORPE

NEW YORK
RUSSELL & RUSSELL · INC
1964

University of Michigan Publications

LANGUAGE AND LITERATURE

VOLUME XVIII

COPYRIGHT, 1940,
BY THE UNIVERSITY OF MICHIGAN

REISSUED, 1964, BY RUSSELL & RUSSELL, INC.
BY ARRANGEMENT WITH THE UNIVERSITY OF MICHIGAN PRESS
L. C. CATALOG CARD NO: 64—13934

PRINTED IN THE UNITED STATES OF AMERICA

21793

PREFACE

THIS study was originally begun as a chapter in a book
on Addison. My materials soon outran the limits I had
set, however, and the intended chapter gradually expanded
into a volume. Now that I have finished I present the work
with some diffidence. For a mere literary man to presume to
write a book on such a philosopher as Hobbes argues, I fear,
no little temerity. But if I have rushed in where wiser men
have not ventured, I can only offer as justification that I have
not tried to write like a philosopher. That would have been
impossible even had I been so ambitious. I have tried, rather,
to stick to my last, attempting to say only what one interested
in literature and art would have to say about Hobbes: that
is, I have confined myself to a study of those phases of his
thought which have a bearing on his aesthetic theory and
which seem to have had certain effects on subsequent criticism
and literary practice. I have further restricted myself by
giving emphasis to but one aspect of Hobbes's aesthetics and
by indicating evidences of his influence only on English writers
of his own century. Even so it has been necessary at times to
enter the realms of more purely psychological and philosophical
discussion. Hobbes's aesthetic theory is bound up with his
philosophy, and much of his philosophy — virtually all of its
civil and moral parts — is founded in psychology. For my
shortcomings in these fields I beg the indulgence of any technical specialists who may chance to read this book.

As I have gone on, the sense of Hobbes's importance in the
evolution of aesthetic theory has steadily grown upon me. It is
difficult to understand why he was so long generally neglected
by students of aesthetics. In Bosanquet's standard history, for
instance, the name of Hobbes does not appear in the index;
in Saintsbury's three-volume magnum opus he fares no better;

v

Croce gives him only insignificant mention. There have lately been some amends. Professor Spingarn has increased the obligation students of criticism everywhere owe him by his discerning summaries of Hobbes's theory. Before Spingarn Hamelius had indicated something of Hobbes's place in criticism, and Gayley and Scott had commended *The Answer to Davenant* as especially worth study for "its attempt at classifying poetry on a new principle." More recently, Professors W. Lee Ustick and Hoyt Hudson, Professor Donald Bond, and Professor Ronald Crane have each added valuable data on various phases of Hobbes's aesthetics. But so far there has been published no extended study of this phase of his thought. Hobbes is worthy of more attention. To understand his ideas and to perceive the nature and force and extent of their influence on succeeding literary theory is, I confidently believe, to hold one of the most valuable clues to the development of late seventeenth- and eighteenth-century criticism. I have tried in this book to contribute something to such an understanding. Much more, I am quite aware, remains to be done; but if I have succeeded, even to a small degree, in my aim, I can think of no better service I could render to the history of aesthetics.

It is a pleasure to record obligations to numerous friends and colleagues who have assisted me in this work. My first and greatest debt is to Professor DeWitt H. Parker of the Department of Philosophy, University of Michigan, for his careful reading of my manuscript, his scholarly advice and criticism, particularly on difficult points in philosophy, and his continued generous encouragement. To my colleagues in the English Department, Professors Louis I. Bredvold, John R. Reinhard, and Norman L. Nelson, I owe similar thanks for their sympathetic interest in examining my manuscript and for their many discriminating and valuable suggestions. Grateful acknowledgments are also due Professors Hugo Thieme and Henry W. Nordmeyer, of the University of Michigan, for reading and criticizing the manuscript, to Professor Roger McCutcheon of Tulane University for helpful comment and certain references on Hobbes, to Professors W. Lee Ustick of Harvard University and Hoyt Hudson of Princeton

University for their interest and assistance in the early stages of my project, to the students in my seminars who have patiently sat through my trial expositions and have cheerfully contributed ideas and materials, and, finally, to Dr. Eugene S. McCartney for his expert advice and assistance in editing my book and piloting it safely through the press.

C. D. T.

Ann Arbor, Michigan
February 21, 1939

CONTENTS

THE AESTHETIC THEORY OF
THOMAS HOBBES

CHAPTER I

Introduction: Hobbes as Literary Man, Empiricist, and Psychological Aesthetician

I

THE name of Thomas Hobbes is associated in the minds of most students of literature and philosophy with such weighty things as "leviathan" and "behemoth." A careful reading of his life and works shows, however, that the Sage of Malmesbury was concerned with other aspects of culture than the "matter, forme, and power of commonwealth" and the history of the civil wars. Hobbes was something of a literary man in his own right and gave considerable thought to problems of artistic composition and appeal. Anthony à Wood, speaking for Hobbes's later contemporaries, rated him not only a philosopher and a mathematician, but "a great critic and poet." [1] Dryden said that he knew of no one so like Lucretius as "our poet and philosopher of Malmesbury." [2] A British scholar has recently written about him as a "philosopher, publicist, and man of letters." [3] Hobbes's interest in the aesthetic side of literature was not sporadic nor incidental; it began when he was a student and extended throughout his life. While he was at Oxford he found pleasure in escaping from lectures on physics and logic to the book shops, "where

[1] *Athenæ Oxonienses* (London, 1813), III, 1208.
[2] "Preface to *Sylvæ*" (1685), in *Essays of John Dryden*, ed. by W. P. Ker (Oxford, 1926), I, 259.
[3] George E. G. Catlin, *Thomas Hobbes as Philosopher, Publicist, and Man of Letters* (Oxford, 1922).

3

he could pore over books of travel and maps, and follow in imagination the voyages of the great Elizabethan buccaneers."[4] Of the period following his graduation, when, as tutor to the son of William Cavendish, he was traveling and perfecting himself in the classics, he was, in later life, to express regret that he had spent so much time reading romances and plays.[5] At fourteen he had turned Euripides' *Medea* into Latin verse. In 1628–29 he published a translation of Thucydides, the culmination of a long period of apprenticeship in English prose; the fact that he invited Ben Jonson and the poet Ayton to pass judgment on his manner of writing in this translation reveals his conscious interest in a mastery of style.[6] Sometime before 1628 the future philosopher wrote a poem in which he extolled in Latin hexameters the wonders of the Peak in Derbyshire and the beauties of Chatworth.[7] While he was tutor to the young Cavendish he dictated to his pupil a free translation of important parts of Aristotle's *Rhetoric*.[8]

[4] Alfred Edward Taylor, *Thomas Hobbes* (London, 1908), pp. 3–4. The authority for this statement is Hobbes's own account of his life in Latin verse, "Vita Tho. Hobbes" (in *Opera Philosophica Quae Latine Scripsit Omnia*, edited by G. Molesworth [London, 1839–45], I, lxxxvii), particularly this passage:

> Ergo ad amoena magis me verto, librosque revolvo,
> Queis prius instructus, non bene doctus eram.
> Pascebamque animum chartis imitantibus orbem,
> Telluris faciem, et sydera picta videns:
> Gaudebam soli comes ire, et cernere cunctis
> Terricolis justos qua facit arte dies.
> Quoque Dracus filo Neptunum, Candisiusque
> Cinxerunt medium; quaeque adiere loca:
> Atque hominum exiguos, si possem, cernere nidos
> Et picta ignotis monstra videre locis.

[5] "Before Thucydides, he spent two yeares in reading romances and playes, which he haz often repented and sayd that these two yeares were lost of him" (John Aubrey, '*Brief Lives,' Chiefly of Contemporaries*, ed. by Andrew Clark [Oxford, 1898], I, 361). See also John Laird, *Hobbes* (London, 1934), p. 6.

[6] Aubrey, *op. cit.*, I, 365. Aubrey definitely says Ayton and Jonson. Hobbes's own account ("To the Readers," prefatory to his translation of Thucydides) merely contains the statement that the book has passed the censure of "some, whose judgments I very much esteem."

[7] *De Mirabilibus Pecci* (in *The English Works of Sir Thomas Hobbes of Malmesbury*, ed. by Sir William Molesworth [London, 1839–45]), printed in 1636, a poem sufficiently popular to call for new editions in 1675 (Blaeu, Amsterdam, and Crooke, London) and a translation, by a "person of quality," printed with the Latin original in 1678.

[8] *A Briefe of the Art of Rhetorique. Containing in Substance all that Aristotle hath*

Hobbes numbered among his literary friends Bacon and Ben Jonson, Waller, Cowley, and Davenant. He served as amanuensis to Bacon, who preferred him above all others.[9] Waller admired him extremely, and had at one time arranged to translate the *De Cive*, but when Hobbes had begun to put the book into English, he refused to meddle with it, saying that nobody else could do so well.[10] Cowley's ode to Hobbes [11] is one of the finest tributes ever paid to the philosopher. It is a further significant indication of the regard in which Hobbes was held by contemporary literary folk and of his own interest in poetry that when Davenant was composing his *Gondibert* in Paris, in 1650, he showed him the poem "in parcels," and in the end addressed his Preface to him, "his much Honour'd Friend." It is of importance, too, that Hobbes troubled himself to write a reply to Davenant in which he discussed *Gondibert* and laid down some principles for the heroic poem in general. This interest in literary things continued into the philosopher's old age, finding expression in a long autobiographic poem in Latin elegiacs,[12] in 1672, and in a complete English version of the *Iliad* and the *Odyssey*, published in 1673 and 1675.

written in his Three Bookes of that Subject Except onely what is not applicable to the English Tongue (London, 1637 [?]).

[9] "The Lord Chancellour Bacon loved to converse with him. He assisted his lordship in translating severall of his Essayes into Latin, one, I well remember, is that *Of the Greatnes of Cities*: the rest I have forgott. His lordship was a very contemplative person, and was wont to contemplate in his delicious walkes at Gorambery, and dictate to Mr. Thomas Bushell, or some other of his gentlemen, that attended him with inke and paper ready to sett downe presently his thoughts. His lordship would often say that he better liked Mr. Hobbes's taking his thoughts, then any of the other, because he understood what he wrote, which the others not understanding, my Lord would many times have a hard taske to make sense of what they writt.

"It is to be remembered that about these times, Mr. T. H. was much addicted to musique, and practised on the base-violl" (Aubrey, *op. cit.*, I, 331).

[10] Aubrey, *op. cit.*, II, 277.

[11] "To Mr. Hobs," in *Poems: Miscellanies, etc.*, ed. by A. R. Waller (Cambridge, 1905), pp. 188–190. Cowley's ode is significant for its praise of Hobbes as one who, when the intellectual empire of Aristotle had dwindled and, finally, in the hands of the Schoolmen had perished, gave to Western learning a mighty and permanent rebirth. See pages 261–263 of this book for citations from this ode and a discussion of it in relation to Hobbes's influence on Cowley.

[12] I have quoted from this poem on page 4, note 4.

In approaching a study of Hobbes's aesthetics it is well to
have these facts before us to remind ourselves that the man
who gave to England what is perhaps the most consistently
mechanical philosophy ever formulated was at heart something
of an artist, a critic, and a lover of nature and literature, a
man of feeling, of imagination, and of recognized taste; that,
therefore, we are considering the theory of one who, no matter
how much he may have neglected belles-lettres in his busy
middle days of philosophical meditation and controversy,
had a rather wide and intimate experience of imaginative
literature.

With the exception of the reply to Davenant, the Preface
to the Homer, and the much less important Introduction to the
Thucydides, Hobbes's ideas on literary matters and artistic
processes are scattered incidentally throughout his works, occurring usually in connection with his analyses of the phenomena of man's mind.   Even so, they bulk much larger than
the casual reader would suspect, and are, as one might readily
believe, coming from so acute and so precise a thinker as
Hobbes, of unusual significance.

Professor Spingarn, in his study of Jacobean and Caroline
critics in England, has presented a summary of Hobbes's
general literary approach and has ventured a judgment of its
value:

> The theme of poetry, then, is the manners of men; its method is that
> of verisimilitude, or resemblance to the actual conditions of life; and
> Hobbes's scorn for ghosts and magic is the natural outcome of this insistence
> on *vraisemblance*.   From acquaintance with the manners of men, rather
> than from books, the poet is to obtain the elements of style, or 'expression.'
> To know human nature well, to retain images of it in the memory that
> are distinct and clear, are the sources of perspicuity and propriety of style,
> and of 'decorum' in character-drawing; to know much of it is the source
> of variety and novelty of expression.   Hobbes's aesthetic is consistent and
> logical throughout, the first of its kind in English literature.[13]

In this succinct statement we have a view of Hobbes's achievement in a synthetic interpretation of emerging neoclassic
theory.   It represents, however, what we may regard as only

---

[13] J. E. Spingarn, "Jacobean and Caroline Criticism," in *The Cambridge
History of English Literature* (Cambridge, 1911), VII, 267.

the surface elements of Hobbes's critical reflections. Other
and more important contributions were rooted more deeply.
They had their foundation in philosophic probings into the
nature of man's mind, the springs of its passions, the causes
and effects of its pleasures and pains.

Hobbes's application of his findings on these matters to
aesthetics, often indirect and incidental, led him to conclusions
and intimations that had significant bearing on the evolution
of critical theory, particularly as it is concerned with the two
vital phases of the constructive imagination and the aesthetic
experience. In this he derives from Aristotle, and links, through
Addison and Hutcheson, with the Romantic criticism of Coleridge and Wordsworth and with the psychological approach
of our own day as represented by H. S. Langfeld and I. A.
Richards.

Professor Spingarn himself notes Hobbes's influence in
broadening the scope of aesthetic discussion,[14] without, however, carrying his generalizations through to detailed presentation and analysis. Spingarn, moreover, sees Hobbes as important chiefly in relation to later seventeenth-century criticism,
rather than to the long and somewhat devious development of
the psychological approach that culminated in Coleridge and
Wordsworth — which is the point of view maintained in the
present study. Professor Spingarn writes:

> The seventeenth century first attempted to deal accurately with the
> relation between the creative mind and the work of art; it began to analyse
> the content of such terms as 'wit,' 'fancy,' and 'taste.' Hobbes is here a
> pioneer; he left an impress on critical terminology, and his psychology
> became the groundwork of restoration criticism. The relation of Descartes
> to French classicism suggests the position of Hobbes in Stewart [sic] Eng-
> land.[15]

There is a large measure of truth in this; but it is not the whole
truth. Attention to and analysis of such terms as "wit,"
"fancy," and "taste" were increasingly evident in seventeenth-
century criticism, but these matters, even in England, were

[14] *Ibid.*, p. 265.
[15] *Ibid.*, p. 266. See also *Critical Essays of the Seventeenth Century*, ed. by J. E.
Spingarn (Oxford, 1908), I, xxviii–xxxiii.

subordinate to considerations of form and substance in relation to the dogma of neoclassic interpreters of Aristotle and Horace. It was to take another three quarters of a century, even after Dryden and Addison, for the psychological attack to break down the tradition of form and rules. A careful study of this psychological development points to Hobbes as having a large share in giving it impetus and direction. To Hobbes, more than to any other single Englishman, later criticism may be said to have owed its distrust for tradition and dogma and its gradual return to the spirit of Aristotle in basing its judgments on a close study of works of literature and on an analysis of facts of mind in relation to literature. These may appear to be large claims, but in the pages that follow I hope to offer substantial evidence in their support.

Emphasis in seventeenth-century criticism in England and France was placed largely upon literature as a thing external to the mind. Problems of form and of convention in general were given far more attention than was the mind creating, or the mind receiving and responding. In the course of the next century all this was changed. Attention shifted from literature as external to man to literature as related to the mind, an organic product of the human spirit, with certain inherent powers to affect the emotions and intellect. Thus Romantic criticism was concerned primarily with two problems: the pleasures peculiar to art, embodied in the total aesthetic experience, and the mental processes through which art is created. The aesthetic writings of Coleridge and Wordsworth are notable for their preoccupation with the psychological phenomena that pertain to these problems. It seems reasonable to believe that Hobbes had a considerable part in bringing about this change. In spite of the fact that his materialistic approach was almost the antithesis of their idealistic bias, Wordsworth and Coleridge, and all their kind who came between, were much indebted to Hobbes for the spirit and method of their investigations; for in his speculations having to do with aesthetic matters Hobbes started with the facts of experience and sought to analyze them. He was impatient with outworn conventions. His inquiries began with a scrutiny of the moving forces of our constructive and responsive life, and he bent the power of his great analytical intellect to arrive at solutions.

II

Inasmuch as Hobbes is traditionally classified as a rationalist in philosophy the implications for empiricism in the preceding sentences obviously require justification. Hobbes's reputation for rationalism may be traced to certain prominent facts. Under the influence of a deep interest in and respect for the scientific achievements of his day,[16] he attempted to found his philosophy upon principles and definitions capable of mathematical demonstration. "The true intellectual progenitor of Hobbes," declares Albert G. A. Balz, "is Galileo." The problem Hobbes set for himself, says Balz, paraphrasing Tönnies, was "whether knowledge, attaining the level of the certainty of mathematics, of geometrical demonstration from axioms and definitions, was possible, and how it was possible." [17] Hobbes therefore exalted ratiocination, making causal relationships a cornerstone of his system; [18] and his final method in arriving at truth is deductive rather than inductive. So Hobbes is regarded by many historians of philosophy as in direct opposition to Bacon both in method and in the ends he seeks. Balz,[19] for example, quotes with approval Seth's judgment that Hobbes's quarrel with scholasticism

concerns the subject-matter, not the method, of that philosophy. He does not join in Bacon's protest against the scholastic habit of anticipating nature,

---

[16] "At Paris he was an intimate of Mersenne . . . center of a scientific circle that included Descartes and Gassendi; and at Florence he held discourse with Galileo" (William Ritchie Sorley, *A History of English Philosophy* [New York and London, 1921], p. 50).

[17] Albert George Adam Balz, "The Psychology of Ideas in Hobbes," in *Studies in the History of Ideas* (New York, 1918), I, 128.

[18] "Hobbes defines philosophy as the knowledge of the causes of effects or phenomena which is derived by correct thinking. Its aim is, as with Bacon and Descartes, to further our ends by giving us power over things: *scientiam propter potentiam*. Its main divisions are: Mathematics; natural science, which really begins with Copernicus, Galileo, and Harvey; and the *philosophia civilis*, which in Hobbes's opinion is not older than the book *De Cive*" (Friedrich Paulsen, *Introduction to Philosophy*, tr. by Frank Thilly [New York, 1895], p. 24).

[19] *Loc. cit.*

of deducing facts from theories; he has no thought of substituting a scientific induction for the deductive rationalism of Scholastic philosophy. So far as . . . method is concerned, he is the opponent rather of Bacon than of the Schoolmen; for him, science, as such, is rationalistic or deductive, not empirical and inductive. Rational insight, not empirical knowledge, is his scientific ideal.[20]

It is quite possible that Bacon's place in the development of the inductive method has been sometimes overrated. It seems even more likely that Hobbes's sanction and use of the inductive approach, and with it his emphasis on the materials of experience, have been as frequently overlooked. I have said that Hobbes's "final method" in philosophy was deductive; it is also true that his ideal was a classification of knowledge in the form of a "demonstrative system deduced from principles." Yet in conceding this we must not neglect to inquire whence the mind of the investigator derives its knowledge, whence its principles, and to what it must refer in testing the validity of its conclusions.

The answer is broadly contained in the fact that Hobbes was primarily a sensationalist, the father of the whole later tribe of British sensationalists. To Hobbes all knowledge originates in sense; all ideas, all conceptions, therefore, have their beginning in experience. He does, indeed, make a distinction between original perception produced by motion from external objects and the use of materials already received into the brain in the discriminations and conclusions reached through the processes of ratiocination. But both of these types have their genesis in experience:

. . . there be two sorts of knowledge, whereof the one is nothing else but sense, or knowledge original . . . and remembrance of the same; the other is called science or knowledge of the truth of propositions, and how things are called, and is derived from understanding. Both of these sorts are but experience; the former being the experience of the effects of things that work upon us from without; and the latter the experience men have of the proper use of names in language. And all experience being . . . but remembrance, all knowledge is remembrance . . . .[21]

[20] James Seth, *English Philosophers and Schools of Philosophy* (London and New York, 1912), p. 58.
[21] *The Elements of Law*, ed. by Ferdinand Tönnies (Cambridge, 1928), I, vi, 1.

By science, however, Hobbes means quite another kind of
remembrance from that of a mere perception.   Science is
derived from understanding, and understanding in turn is a
product of speech.   "When a man upon the hearing of any
Speech, hath those thoughts which the words of that Speech,
and their connexion, were ordained and constituted to signifye;
Then he is said to understand it: *Understanding* being nothing
else but conception caused by Speech." [22]   Science is explicitly
defined by Hobbes as "a knowledge of Consequences, and de-
pendence of one fact on another."   It is attained, "first in
apt imposing of Names; and secondly by getting a good and
orderly Method in proceeding from the Elements, which are
Names, to Assertions made by Connexion of one of them to
another; and so to Syllogismes, which are the Connexions of
one Assertion to another . . . ." [23]   Science thus differs materially from sense and memory, which "are but knowledge
of Fact, which is a thing past and irrevocable." [24]   Science is a
secondary knowledge achieved through the application of
reason to materials already registered in the mind and labeled
with names.

The teleological argument for science is that through the
gradation of particular fact, definition, and assertion the mind
is relieved from the necessity of continual reëxamination of
isolated fact and may proceed to universal principles.   Hence
in the statement "*Every triangle hath its three angles equall to two
right angles*, . . . the Consequence found in one particular,
comes to be registred and remembred, as an Universall rule;
and . . . delivers us from all labor of the mind, saving the
first; and makes that which was found true *here* and *now*, to
be true in *all times* and *places*." [25]

The beginning of science is the accurate use of language,
particularly in definitions: "So that in the right Definition of
Names, lyes the first use of speech; which is the Acquisition
of Science." [26]   This principle practitioners of geometry, the
one true science hitherto existing, have exemplified in "settling

---

[22] *Leviathan*, ed. by Ernest Rhys (London, Toronto, and New York, 1914), I,
iv.   This is in Everyman's Library.
[23] *Ibid.*, I, v.   [24] *Ibid.*   [25] *Ibid.*, I, iv.   [26] *Ibid.*

the significations of their words; which . . . they call *Definitions;* and place them in the beginning of their reckoning." [27] Truth in assertions exists only when definitions are valid. For example, the statement "*A man is a living creature*" can be true only if the name "*living creature*" signify all that the name "*man*" signifies.[28] False science exists where definitions, hence assertions, are false: "in wrong or no Definitions lyes the first abuse." [29] Hobbes therefore issues grave warning against accepting definitions and principles handed down from former authors or using any others which are not carefully subjected to the test of evidence or experience. "Knowledge, therefore, which we call SCIENCE," he explains, "I define to be evidence of truth, from some beginning or principle of sense." [30]

The *dogmatici*, or false teachers, differ from the *mathematici*, or true teachers, in that the first "willingly take for principles those opinions which are already vulgarly received . . . from the authority of men, or of custom" and "press to have their opinions pass everywhere for truth, without any evident demonstration either from experience, or from places of Scripture of uncontroverted interpretation," [31] while the second "beginneth at something from experience," thence "going on slowly . . . from the imposition of names" to an inference of "the truth of their first propositions" and so on to general principles.[32] Valid reasoning, Hobbes says clearly, must bear the test of experience. "Now when a man reasoneth from principles that are found indubitable by experience, all deceptions of sense and equivocation of words avoided, the conclusion he maketh is said to be according to right reason." Conversely, "when from his conclusion a man may, by good ratiocination, derive that which is contradictory to any evident truth whatsoever, then he is said to have concluded against reason: and such a conclusion is called absurdity." [33] I hope I am not overdrawing the case when I say that such evidence points strongly to the conclusion that Hobbes's initial approach to philosophic truth is firmly empirical.

---

[27] *Leviathan*, I, iv.   [28] *Ibid.*   [29] *Ibid.*, I, v.
[30] *The Elements of Law*, I, vi, 4.
[31] *Ibid.*, I, xiii, 3–4.   [32] *Ibid.*   [33] *Ibid.*, I, v, 12.

This is not, however, to deny his rationalism. To stop with mere experience was with Hobbes as complete folly as to reason independently of evidence acquired through experience. I shall show later in this book that in relation to the arts and to practical life Hobbes makes large concessions to "natural prudence," which is a product of experience only; but when he talks of science and philosophy he insists on full use of the reasoning process. Science, with its end to discover causes and the truth of propositions through the proper use of names and definitions and syllogisms, is alone infallible. "Experience concludes nothing universally," Hobbes declares. "If the sign hit twenty times for once missing, a man may lay a wager of twenty to one of the event; but may not conclude it for a truth." [34] There is, however, a wide gap between a rationalism which resorts to experience for the materials of its definitions and principles, continually submitting its findings to the test of experience, and a rationalism which begins either with opinion and authority or with abstractions.

It would therefore seem nearer the truth to call Hobbes, if the term may be allowed, an "empirical-rationalist." Aristotle was something of this sort. John Dewey explains Aristotle's reputation for empiricism on the ground that Aristotle held that,

historically and psychologically, reason can function only as the outcome of a series of graded steps up from sensation. For him there was no original, separate and independent rational intuition. The latter had to pass through the stage of experience so that even a scientist, dealing with demonstrable and rational matters, would, as a matter of his own development and education, need the preparation of an empirical stage.[35]

These words might be spoken with almost equal truth of Hobbes. The presentation of the steps in true philosophy in the early chapters of the "Logic" confirms this view. Hobbes here emphasizes ratiocination and essays a clear distinction between philosophy, which is gotten through reason, and "prudence," which is gotten through experience. Philosophy,

[34] *Ibid.*, I, iv, 10.
[35] John Dewey, "An Empirical Survey of Empiricisms," in *Studies in the History of Ideas* (New York, 1935), III, 8.

he says, "*is such knowledge of effects or appearances, as we may acquire by true ratiocination from the knowledge we have first of their causes or generation: And again, of such causes or generations as may be from knowing first their effects.*" [36]   That we may better understand this definition, Hobbes points out, we must recognize that, though sense and memory are knowledge, they are given to us immediately by nature and not attained by ratiocination; hence they are not philosophy.   By the same token, since experience is only memory, and prudence expectation of such things in the future as we have had experience of in the past, prudence is not philosophy.   An important point to note again, however, is that the materials of ratiocination are originally derived from experience.   Ratiocination in its simple form is but the addition or subtraction of original simple perceptions.   Thus by adding together simple concepts we have the total concept "man" or "square."   In its more complex forms it is the process of "*finding out effects by their known causes, or of causes by their known effects,*" [37] which is the method of philosophy.   But, let us remember, the only origin for known causes or known effects is experience.

Hobbes is never able in his philosophic speculations to get far from the experiential base.   The parts of philosophy are four in number, he tells us.   The first is inquiry into the question of "what motion begets such and such effects." [38]   And the method of this kind of inquiry is *compositive*.   That is, "we are to observe what effect a body moved produceth, when we consider nothing in it besides its motion . . . ."   From this kind of contemplation has sprung geometry.   From a study of simple motion we pass to a consideration of the effects of the motion of one body upon another: first, what effects will follow when one body invades another which is at rest or in motion; secondly, what effects this second body will produce on a third, the third on a fourth body, and so forth. This is the "philosophy of motion."   The third type of inquiry has to do with such effects as are made by the motions of the

---

[36] "Computation or Logic," I, i, 2, in *The Elements of Philosophy*, in *The English Works of Thomas Hobbes of Malmesbury*, ed. by Sir William Molesworth (London, 1839–45).   [37] *Ibid.*, I, vi, 1.   [38] *Ibid.*, I, vi, 6.

parts of any body, when things that are the same seem not to be the same, but changed. This includes a study of such sensible qualities as *"light, colour, transparency, opacity, sound, odour, savour, heat, cold,* and the like." Since these cannot be known without knowing the cause of sense itself, the consideration of seeing, hearing, smelling, tasting, and touching belongs here. The study of the qualities, changes, and causes belonging to the second and third parts is comprehended under the fourth part of philosophy, "which is called *physics.*" In all these parts of philosophy the beginning and much of what comes after is in observation. Such explanations strongly imply an empirical basis for even the severer sciences of geometry and physics.[39]

When Hobbes approaches the subject of moral and civil philosophy, he makes even more definite concessions to the principle of empiricism. Moral philosophy has to do with "the motions of the mind, namely, *appetite, aversion, love, benevolence, hope, fear, anger, emulation, envy,* &c; what causes they have, and of what they be causes." [40] Civil philosophy, or the knowledge of laws and commonwealths and the exercise of power, has its foundation in an understanding of the motions of the mind. A way to the attainment of such knowledge is through the *"synthetical method,* and from the very first principles of philosophy," that is, through the route of geometry and physics; the passions of the mind and the acts of men which arise from these passions "have their causes in sense and imagination, which are the subject of *physical* contemplation." [41] There is, however, another way — easier perhaps, but I see in Hobbes's words no suggestion that it is less efficacious than the first — namely, the way of generalizations from experience. "For the causes of the motions of the mind are known, not only by ratiocination, but also by the experience of every man that takes the pains to observe those motions within himself." Here Hobbes is suggesting the possibility of a purely intro-

[39] This is the more apparent when we recall that Hobbes has declared only a few pages earlier that "The first beginnings of knowledge, are the phantasms of sense and imagination," and that "It is common to all sorts of method to proceed from the known to the unknown" (*ibid.*, I, vi, 1).

[40] *Ibid.*, I, vi, 6.   [41] *Ibid.*

spective, analytical method for moral philosophy; similarly for civil philosophy:

> . . . even they also that have not learned the first part of philosophy, namely, *geometry* and *physics*, may, notwithstanding, attain the principles of civil philosophy, by the *analytical method.* For if a question be propounded, as, *whether such an action be just or unjust;* if that *unjust* be resolved into *fact against law,* and that notion *law* into the *command* of him or them that have *coercive power;* and that *power* be derived from the *wills* of men that constitute such power, to the end they may live in peace, they may at last come to this, that the appetites of men and the passions of their minds are such, that, unless they be restrained by some power, they will always be making war upon one another; which may be known to be so by any man's experience, that will but examine his own mind. And, therefore, from hence he may proceed, by compounding, to the determination of the justice or injustice of any propounded action.[42]

The implications for the empirical approach contained in this passage are substantiated by Hobbes's method in moral and civil philosophy in *The Elements of Law* and in *Leviathan,* which works are, it must be admitted even after making full allowance for the use of certain large axiomatic principles, mainly the product of generalization from observation.

It is not surprising, then, to find that certain close students of Hobbes have noted the empirical element in his method. Thus Herbert G. Lord speaks of the "acknowledged fact that he is the founder of empirical psychology," [43] and again he calls him "the founder of both empirical and social psychology." [44] Lewes emphasizes the introspective method and the trend toward sensationalism in Hobbes: "He proclaimed that psychology is a science of observation; that if we would understand the conditions and operations of our minds, we must patiently look inwards and see what passes there." [45] Lewes further points out that on the question of the origin of knowledge Hobbes "takes a decided stand upon experience; he is the precursor of modern sensationalists." And he quotes from *Leviathan,* I, i, on the primacy of sense in the formation of

---

[42] "Computation or Logic," I, vi, 7.

[43] Herbert G. Lord, " The Attempt of Hobbes to Base Ethics on Psychology," in *Studies in the History of Ideas* (New York, 1918), I, 117.

[44] *Ibid.,* p. 118.

[45] George Henry Lewes, *The History of Philosophy* (London, 1871), II, 230.

our conceptions, with the comment, "Here is stated in the broadest manner, the principle of sensationalism." [46]

It is instructive to find George S. Morris rather implying that Hobbes's empiricism was inimical to philosophical achievement. The attention of Hobbes and his celebrated successors, says Morris, is directed to man the *phenomenon*, man as a series of mental states, or a bundle of mental processes or perceptions. "This is identifying philosophy with empirical psychology, i.e. substantially suppressing philosophy." Morris regards such an approach as a denial of man the *noumenon*, "as a free, ideal, spiritual agency apprehended in philosophical self-consciousness," in other words, "man true to himself (i.e. man as he might be and ought to be, but never is, except approximately)." [47] Hobbes, Morris holds, is not to be considered as opposing but as supplementing the inductive method of Bacon. [48] He had a predilection for deductive thinking, but he began with experience. His method was to appeal to common experience for "simple principles of axiomatic validity and to deduce from them conclusions resting on unquestioned demonstration." "In his philosophy of man, the foundation of his political theory, he was the first one to follow the method, recommended by Bacon and since followed by Locke and his followers, of purely empirical observation, analysis, and description." [49]

Even Paulsen, who classes Hobbes with the rationalists, [50] calls him the leader of practical philosophy of modern times, [51] which should indicate, according to Paulsen's characterization of modern thought, a strongly empirical bent. For modern thought, Paulsen explains, has lost faith in the purely speculative method — a search for "*a priori* knowledge of reality by means of a dialectical development of concepts." [52] We know but one road to truth, that is the rationalizing of experience. Similarly, philosophy now owns but one subject matter, the special subject matter indicated by Kant as the vindication

---

[46] *Ibid.*, p. 231.
[47] George S. Morris, *British Thought and Thinkers* (Chicago, 1880), pp. 165–166.   [48] *Ibid.*, pp. 149–150.   [49] *Ibid.*, p. 165.
[50] *Op. cit.*, p. 379.   [51] *Ibid.*, p. 290.   [52] *Ibid.*, p. 16.

of philosophy as a science: namely, that of knowledge. In the words of Kuno Fischer, "Things constitute the object of experience; experience . . . constitutes the object of philosophy." [53] It may be remarked further that Paulsen's definition of empiricism corresponds much more closely to what we observe in Hobbes than does his definition of rationalism. [54]

It is worth noting, too, that, though John Dewey in his study of empiricisms does not mention Hobbes as an empiricist, in rating Locke as one he gives a list of tendencies almost all of which are equally applicable to Hobbes. Dewey points out that Locke's empiricism was made possible by the fact that in the preceding period there occurred a reversal of the classical conception which "identified experience with the beliefs and skills that were due to custom and consolidated memory" and came to regard it, in consequence, as only a means to the higher activities of rational thought. Men now began to connect reason with conventional dogma and tradition, and to look upon experience as something fresh and personal. With this came a new esteem for the individual as the seat of freedom and the source of all advance. [55] Locke himself, Dewey explains, was following the empirical method (1) when he defined experience as consisting essentially of observation — individual contact with nature through the

[53] *Loc. cit.* Paulsen is quoting Fischer's *Geschichte der neuern Philosophie* (Heidelberg, 1869), III, 16. Fischer, it may be remarked, definitely places Hobbes in the English empirical tradition. See *History of Modern Philosophy: Descartes and His School*, tr. by J. P. Gordy (London, 1887), p. 161, and *Francis Bacon und seine Nachfolger* (Leipzig, 1875), pp. 509 ff.

[54] *Op. cit.*, pp. 341–342. Paulsen's definitions are as follows: According to *Sensualism* or *Empiricism* "all knowledge springs from perception, that is from outer or inner perception; experience arises by combining percepts, science by collecting and arranging experiences." On the other hand, *Rationalism* asserts: "All real or scientific knowledge is derived from reason; it is the result of the immanent evolution of consequences from *a priori* certain principles which do not arise from experience" (p. 341).

Paulsen lists four forms of epistemology: (1) *Realistic Empiricism:* "We know things as they are in themselves by perception"; (2) *Idealistic Empiricism:* "We know of things only by perception, which, of course, gives no adequate knowledge . . . . Hume is its most consistent representative"; (3) *Realistic Rationalism:* "We know things as they are, not by the senses but by reason" (Plato, Spinoza, and Hegel); (4) *Idealistic Rationalism:* "We can know reality *a priori* by pure reason; however, not as it is in itself, but only as it appears to us, and only as to its form" (p. 342).

[55] *Op. cit.*, p. 12.

senses; (2) when he insisted that sense perception is the only test of valid knowledge of physical matters; (3) when he held that the characteristic of sensation, observation, and experience is coerciveness. Compulsion thus becomes a safeguard against vagaries of fancy and accidents of conventional belief — our own mental constructions to be suspect unless we can check them by "experience." [56] It is possibly true, as Lewes and others have insisted (though I do not myself believe it), that Locke got nothing directly from Hobbes, had, indeed, not read Hobbes when he wrote his great work; but it is remarkable at how many points their thought and method are related. Respect for empirical knowledge is one of these; and Hobbes should certainly be reckoned as among those seventeenth-century thinkers who made Locke's empiricism possible.

The case for Hobbes's empiricism is not a simple one. His position may be more readily understood, however, if we concede that a man may be an empiricist and a rationalist at the same time. There can be no question of Hobbes's conviction that ratiocination through the use of axioms and definitions is the way to scientific and philosophic truth; there can be as little doubt that he conceived of observation through sense experience as the way to valid axioms and definitions. Seth's conclusion that "rational insight, not empirical knowledge" is Hobbes's scientific ideal is undeniably valid; but it is also correct to say that Hobbes believed that rational insight is impossible without empirical knowledge.

Even in his general philosophy Hobbes acknowledged experience as the basis of valid speculation. It is, however, in his psychology and his "civil philosophy" that his trend toward empiricism is strongest. [57] Not only does he concede that ex-

---

[56] *Ibid.*, pp. 13–14.

[57] Psychologists are generally agreed in classing Hobbes as an empiricist. Thus Otto Klemm remarks in discussing Hobbes: "Here, too, the first influence of empiricism makes itself felt" (*A History of Psychology*, tr. by Emil Carl Wilm and Rudolph Pintner [New York, Chicago, and Boston, 1914], p. 37); James Mark Baldwin writes, "In Gassendi and Hobbes the empirical tendencies of the Pre-Cartesians, Vives and Roger Bacon, focussed themselves" (*History of Psychology* [New York and London, 1913], I, 156); and George Sidney Brett presents at some length Hobbes's claim to the title of "father of empirical psychology" (*A History of Psychology* [London, 1921], II, 220–222).

perience may here supplant the method of true philosophy, but in his speculations in these fields he everywhere exemplifies the empirical approach — observation and introspection for truths about the mind, observation for the principles which concern civil relationships.   And this method naturally extends into his thinking on aesthetic matters, which is really a portion of his psychology.   General principles reached through rational synthesis are, indeed, his final goal; but experience furnishes the background and materials for these principles and is the final authority for their truth.

III

It is appropriate, in making inquiry into Hobbes's aesthetic theory, to begin with a restatement of the general objective of his philosophic effort, which was, as George C. Robertson, in his article in the *Encyclopaedia Britannica* has expressed it, "nothing less than such a universal construction of human knowledge as would bring society and man . . . within the same principles of scientific explanation as were found applicable to the world of nature."   In the study of man and the varied phenomena of his complex being Hobbes found nothing more engrossing as a subject for investigation and explanation than the affective side of his nature, which he identified, in accord with the rather vague terminology of his day, with the "passions."

As early as 1635, speaking of a certain Mr. Payne, Hobbes wrote: "I would he could give good reasons for the faculties and passions of the soul, such as may be expressed in plain English, if he. can; he is the first — that I ever heard of — could speak sense in that subject. If he cannot I hope to be the first." [58]   So far as English philosophers are concerned, Hobbes lived to realize his hope. His studies of the faculties and passions of the soul are the first clear and comprehensive accounts of these subjects in our language. [59] Through these

[58] Quoted by Laird, *op. cit.*, p. 9.
[59] Or, in his own opinion, in any language since Aristotle. Countless volumes have been written concerning the faculties, passions, and manners of men,

inquiries, which led him, inevitably, to an examination of those phases of mental activity which are concerned with the creation and perception of art, he greatly advanced the day of a more adequate psychology of aesthetic processes.

The spirit in which Hobbes approached his study of the faculties and the passions had much to do with the value of his results. Let us consider for a moment his treatment of the passions. Putting aside traditional prejudices and moralistic prepossessions alike, Hobbes sets out to examine the passions as a natural phenomenon, a fact to be reckoned with like any other fact of life. What are the passions? What is their origin? What are their functions? What part in the program of social life do they perform? His approach is empirical and scientific. Where others had asked, How may the passions be subjugated and controlled? his query is, How may they be so known and managed as to be put to their legitimate uses?

Of those who have treated Hobbes George S. Brett has, I believe, written best on this point. Brett considers Thucydides and Aristotle important influences on Hobbes's attitude toward the passions. In translating Thucydides Hobbes found a "moving picture of strong personalities," a "frank realism," which appealed directly to his active nature.[60] Hobbes had early developed a deep interest in manifestations of influence and power. Indeed, throughout his works, he regards the passion for power as dominant in human nature. It is quite natural, then, that he should have been struck with the vivid portrayal in the history of men whose conduct revealed much of this passion, in an account which was itself charged with emotional power. The *Rhetoric* of Aristotle, which he also translated, "served as a useful commentary on the art of managing those passions." Here he found how the passions may be employed to gain desired ends, how words may be used to arouse and direct the passions.[61]

Hobbes carried these ideas into his psychology and his civil

he remarked, only to multiply rather than clear doubt: "nor doth any man at this day so much as pretend to know more than hath been delivered two thousand years ago by Aristotle" (*The Elements of Law*, I, xiii, 3).

[60] Brett, *op. cit.*, II, 221.   [61] *Ibid.*

philosophy. Here he found most interest in the passions of
men, their likes and dislikes, the modes in which they made
use of their passions. So he came very close to a social psychology based on this point of view. He sets down facts about
the emotions and desires and motives of men as he finds them,
"just the things that we know about one another"; [62] he gives
us, in other words, a sketch of the mental operations we expect
to find in the ordinary individual in an ordinary society.

Professor Brett sees in Hobbes that which sets him apart
from those who hold the traditional attitude toward the passions, specifically as it was established by Plato and the Stoics:

> The fundamental difference between Plato or the Stoics and Aristotle
> or the Epicureans lies in the estimate of the passions. For the genuine
> Stoic a passion is always a derangement of reason, not an access of power
> but a loss. For the Stoic pleasure is a passion as well as pain: they are
> disturbances of reason. Gassendi and Hobbes chose the other line of
> thought. They regard pleasure as something positive, something which
> is the object of desire, and good because it is desired. The psychology which
> led up to this ethical valuation is therefore the reverse of the traditional.
> It recognizes desire as both natural and good. It refuses to distinguish
> between the lower and the higher types of desire, but regards all desire
> as fundamentally the striving of the organism after its satisfaction. . . .
> This then is the new point of view, a fresh conception of the natural man,
> a dynamic standpoint that sees in every person an eternal striving which
> creates the ends it strives to attain.[63]

Desire and pleasure are alike legitimate functions of the human
spirit,[64] to be respected like any other functions, to be understood and utilized.

Aesthetic pleasures — and here I depart from Mr. Brett
into an aspect of Hobbes's thought which this able author
does not explore — are, then, valid functions of man's mind,
to be investigated and explained as a part of the natural
phenomena of the human cosmos. The nature and causes of
these pleasures cannot be ignored in any systematic treatment
that pretends to take into account the moving forces of life.
Like other pleasures, they are good, for, as we shall see more

---

[62] Brett, *op. cit.*, II, 222.   [63] *Ibid.*

[64] Exception must be taken to Brett's statement that Hobbes refused to distinguish between lower and higher types of desire. In *The Elements of Law* (I, vii–viii)
he sets purely sensual appetite (lust) apart from the healthful desires of the mind.

clearly in later discussion, Hobbes regards all pleasure (except the purely sensual) as associated with good or a promise of good.

Such reasoning may be extended to Hobbes's view of the fancy, or imagination. Plato and, to a less extent, the Stoics and their followers held the imagination suspect. It had certain valid functions, but it was constantly a threat to reason; there was continual danger that it would deceive the rational part or run away with it, or otherwise prove subversive to it. But to Hobbes the imagination is, like the passions, a natural phenomenon, inalienable to man's nature, to be understood and employed to its full extent. Hobbes's interest is not to legislate against imagination and its works, but to learn what the imagination is, how it operates, to what good ends it may be, and has been, put, what its functions are in the whole of man's individual and social economy. Imagination viewed in this way becomes an object of scientific investigation, about which facts are to be gathered and analyzed, whatever the logical conclusions may be.

Approaching his study of the human mind in this manner, Hobbes finds that the imagination and the passions, including the inventive and perceptive faculties, man's appetites and his pleasures, assume a very important rôle indeed. (The large proportion of space given to these subjects in *Leviathan*, *The Elements of Law*, and *The Elements of Philosophy* shows how important.) And he finds that the rôle they play may generally be turned to the good of man. The imagination — under the name "fancy" — is found to be responsible not only for poetry but for all the arts and institutions which have marked man's rise from barbarism. Poetry itself may so embody truth as to do the philosopher's part where philosophy fails. And the passions are shown to be the mother of pleasure and of knowledge and of all productive activity. There need be no enmity between the passions and the imagination and the understanding. So far from being antagonistic and subversive to the reason they are, indeed, when properly directed by judgment, fit instruments of reason. One of Hobbes's distinct services to thought is to show how the understanding may work in harmony with the emotions and the imagination.

Such facts help explain Hobbes's habitually tolerant attitude toward the passions and the imaginative faculty, and the
pleasures associated with them.   It is not only that, as phenomena native to man, they should be reckoned with and used,
but that they are good in themselves as a means to desired ends.
Thus Hobbes did much to break down inhibitions to natural
pleasures and weaken the old distrust of the imagination.   This
was a service to poetry, for poetry is a natural product of the
imaginative faculty in which men take pleasure.   Poetry is
thus brought more nearly into the realm of ordinary experience.
Wordsworth was at a later day to write of the poet that he
was a "man speaking to men" and of poetry as a means to
and a form of knowledge closely related to man's everyday
emotional experiences.   Hobbes lays a foundation for such
an attitude.   He dignifies the emotions and the imagination
as organic functions of the mind; he draws the imagination
and the judgment together in poetic works; he finds in poetry
a good which need not necessarily be related to a moral lesson;
he forwards the day when men may take unashamed delight
in nature and poetry without regard to ulterior ends.

It will be my object in the main part of this book to trace
the processes of psychological investigation through which
Hobbes attained such results and to show the more immediate
effects of his work upon some of his contemporaries and successors.   Before doing that, however, I must digress to give a
rough indication of what had gone on before Hobbes in the
way of a psychological approach to aesthetic problems.   For
it must not be supposed that he was first in this field — he
decisively was not; his contribution lies rather in the fact
that in certain respects his researches penetrated more deeply
and were more fruitful than those of his predecessors, that to
a considerable extent, through a synthesis achieved by a powerful mind working in its own way on an old problem, he made
freshly available to his successors much that had been discovered in the past.   A significant thing, too, is that his ideas
took hold of the English literary mind, and so began to bear
almost immediate results.

CHAPTER II

Some of Hobbes's Predecessors in the Psychological Approach

I

AS WAS indicated at the close of the last chapter, it is essential, if we are to understand Hobbes's place in the history of literary theory, to survey briefly the manifestations of interest in the psychological approach before his time. As is the case in nearly all things else in aesthetic matters such a procedure takes us at once back to Plato and Aristotle, both of whom advanced theories of the imagination and of the psychology of effects which had far-reaching influence on subsequent thought.

Fortunately the work of Professor Bundy in his thorough study of concepts of the imagination in Plato and Aristotle and their followers [1] makes quite unnecessary here more than passing mention of their contributions.

Plato's views on the imagination are not consistent, ranging from an earlier deep distrust of images as mere appearance or illusion and of fancy as flights of mind without reference to truth, to more tolerant conceptions in later essays, which made phantasy, through its memories of physical beauty, an agency for rising to a contemplation of Heavenly Beauty. He did, however, leave for his followers a fairly definite conception of the imagination as the art of making likenesses (of things as they are), and of the fancy as the art of making appearances. That is, the imagination is an instrument of perceiving and

---

[1] Murray Wright Bundy, *The Theory of Imagination in Classical and Mediaeval Thought* (Urbana, Illinois, 1927).

imitating physical form; the fancy, an instrument of subjective inner creations. These inner creations might, indeed, be creatures of the lower phantasy, mere chimerical and irresponsible fancies; but they might also be constructions embodying visions of highest truth.

Plato's teaching on the whole left a basis for deep-grounded suspicion of imagination and fancy. Aristotle, however, gave the imagination a place of unequivocal importance. His conception was of an inner faculty whereby impressions from the external world, transmitted through motion upon the sensory organs, are transmuted into images — or, to use his own word, phantasms.[2] These phantasms are, in Aristotle's view, essential to thought,[3] and, by implication at least, to all sorts of ideal construction,[4] such as the universal conceptions that make poetry more philosophical than history. Aristotle admitted the possibility of falsity in imagination,[5] but, in general, his theory tended to dignify it as a faculty which, though lower in rank than reason, was yet indispensable to intellectual processes.

It is notable that Plato and Aristotle between them advanced ideas upon which virtually all later theories of the imagination were to be built. In Plato's notion of the lower phantasy there was warrant for the tradition of fancy as a wild, lawless activity of mind to be avoided, or to be held sternly in subjection by reason; but his conception of the higher phantasy included ideas of inspiration and of art as ideal creation in which the real and the divine fuse into radiant unity. Aristotle, on the other hand, became authority for empirical, sensational traditions, in which the imagination was regarded as an image-receiving, image-retaining faculty through which the mind of the artist constructs more or less ideal forms from the materials garnered through sense percep-

[2] See *De Anima*, III, iii, 11; tr. by Robert Drew Hicks (Cambridge, 1907), p. 129.
[3] "And for this reason, as without sensation a man would not learn or understand anything, so at the very time he is actually thinking he must have an image before him" (*ibid.*, III, viii, 3; Hicks, p. 145).
[4] "Hence we have the power of constructing a single image out of a number of images" (*ibid.*, III, xi, 2; Hicks, p. 155).
[5] *Ibid.*, III, iii, 8–10; Hicks, pp. 125, 127.

tion. These strains of influence rarely occurred in pure form.
In their constant intermingling lies one of the most tantalizing
problems in the history of aesthetics.

The Stoics, emphasizing reason as a faculty of a priori power,
sharply distinguished between phantasies and actuality. Ideas
come from the senses; they represent, however, not an impression like the object, but a modification or state of mind. Sensation is an activity of the central reason; the phantasy shows
the object to the mind at the same time that it illuminates the
mind. The process of sensation is thus an affection occurring
in the soul. Experience is the result of impressions retained
in the mind. These impressions, or phantasies, become the
basis for numerous and varied activities, such as "incidence,"
"analogy," "transposition," "resemblance," and "composition." For example, in composition the mind may create a
centaur by combining phantasies gained separately in actual
experience. Phantasies are therefore useful in that they
furnish images for the use of the intellect. But, since they are
subjective — impressions of reality, and not reality itself —
they may be false to truth. Rational beings must, therefore,
always be on their guard against deception when phantasms
present themselves, and must employ them with discrimination.
Otherwise phantasy may outrun the intellect, to its infinite
harm. The Stoics are, then, psychologically in line with Aristotle, but in their moral preoccupation, in their stress on the
contrast between phantasy and reason, and in their partial
distrust of the imagination they lean to the side of Plato.[6]

Plutarch (c. 46—c. 120) supports the Stoics in emphasis on
the rule of phantasy by reason but departs from them in a
theory of inspiration evidently derived from Plato's *Timaeus*.
In moments of vision, a state holy and divine, possible only when
the physical conditions of the body and its environment are pro-
pitious, the inspired phantasy perceives and records images of
the future. In the recording of such visions, however, reason
must have its place to judge of what is acceptable and fitting.

[6] For fuller accounts of Stoic psychology see George Sidney Brett, *A History
of Psychology* (London, 1912), I, 161 ff.; William Leslie Davidson, *The Stoic
Creed* (Edinburgh, 1907); and Bundy, *op. cit.*

The views of imagination expressed by Cicero, Quintilian, and Longinus are quite generally related to a theory of the power of images to produce desired effects. All three appear to think of the imagination largely in terms of a capacity for vivid, concrete pictorial apprehension. Cicero's conception of ideal imitation, to be reviewed presently, must be taken into account in considering his complete view. For the rest his theory can hardly be said to go beyond a notion of reproductive imagination through which the orator or poet is able to picture the objects imitated as if they were before the eyes of his hearers.[7] To Quintilian the imagination was a means to vivid experiences in which things absent appear to the inner eye as if they were present. The Greeks call these φαντασίας, the Romans, "visions." Harking back to some unidentified distinction between good and bad phantasies — derived no doubt from Platonic and Stoic classification — he explains that "Some writers describe the possessor of this power of vivid imagination, whereby things, words, and actions are presented in the most realistic manner, by the Greek word εὐφαντασίω-τος." [8] This desirable power is to be fostered, it seems, by studying nature, by absorbing, through sensation, images in the memory for future use, turning these over in the mind in revery, indulging even in daydream and hallucination in which we seem to be seeing moving pictures or engaging in delightful actions. Quintilian distinctly implies that such power of imagining can and should be acquired and cultivated if the full powers of oratory are to be realized. Only so can one paint pictures that will stir the hearts of his auditors.[9]

Longinus spoke of images as mental representations. The word "image," or "imagination," he said, is, in a general way, "applied to every idea of the mind, in whatever form it presents itself, which gives birth to speech." More specifically, however, he found that in his own day the word was predominantly used in cases where, "carried away by enthusiasm

---

[7] *A Dialogue concerning Oratorical Partitions*, vi, in *The Orations of Marcus Tullius Cicero*, tr. by C. D. Yonge (London, 1870), IV, 491–492.

[8] *The Institutio Oratoria*, VI, ii, 29–30; tr. by H. E. Butler (London and New York, 1922), II, 435.

[9] *Ibid.*, VIII, iii; X, vii; Butler, III, 62–72; IV, 14–15.

and passion, you think you see what you describe, and you place it before the eyes of your hearers." [10]   Longinus's illustrations are from poetry.   Euripides in the scenes in Orestes "himself saw Furies, and the image in his mind he almost compelled his audience to behold." [11]   Quoting Homer's account of the sun handing the reins to Phaethon he exclaims: "Would you not say that the soul of the writer enters the chariot at the same instant as Phaethon and shares in his dangers and in the rapid flight of his steeds?   For it could never have conceived such a picture had it not been borne in no less swift career on that journey through the heavens." [12] Thus, like Quintilian, Longinus ascribes to the imagination the power to call pictures before the mind and to project oneself into fancied actions and experiences with all the force of actuality;   then in turn so vividly to present these pictures to readers and auditors as to make them see and respond as if the things themselves were before their eyes.   For orators Longinus prescribes the limitation of such imagery to an appearance of "reality and truth," but to poets he allows "a tendency to exaggeration in the way of the fabulous" and a transcendence of the credible.[13]   Longinus fails to develop his psychology, but to him such imagery is evidently different from any imitation of reality;   for he distinguishes between greatness of soul, imitation, and imagery as sources of the sublime.[14]   Imagery, particularly in poets, appears to be a form of ideal creation.   Quintilian seems to regard imaginative creation as a sort of wish fulfilment or dream: "When the mind is unoccupied or is absorbed by fantastic hopes or daydreams, we are haunted by these visions." [15]   To Longinus, it is more the result of enthusiastic, passionate self-projection into acts and situations which the daring imagination is able to conceive for itself.[16]

Philostratus, the Athenian (A.D. 170–245), is sometimes spoken of as having first assigned the function of creation to

---

[10] Longinus, *On the Sublime*, xv, 1; tr. by W. Rhys Roberts (Cambridge, 1907), p. 85.   [11] *Ibid.*, XV, 3; Roberts, p. 85.
[12] *Ibid.*, XV, 4; Roberts, p. 87.   [13] *Ibid.*, XV, 8; Roberts, p. 89.
[14] *Ibid.*, XV, 12; Roberts, p. 91.   [15] *Op. cit.*, VI, 30; Butler, II, 433.
[16] *Op. cit.*, XIV, 1; XV, 1, 3–5; Roberts, pp. 83, 85, 87.

the imagination. The advance in idea in Philostratus over Aristotle, Quintilian, and Longinus is, however, less distinctive than the emphasis and clarity with which he states his view. Philostratus denies the principle of mere imitation in art, opposing to this idea a theory of selective re-creation by the imagination in accordance with an ideal pattern which it has framed for itself. Figures in the clouds flit through the heavens without meaning and by mere chance, Apollonius tells Damis; but in our paintings we "rearrange and create them." [17] Arguing with Thespesion, Apollonius attacks the Egyptian representation of their gods as crass and grotesque. Nettled by the charge, Thespesion satirically remarks: "Your artists then like Phidias . . . and like Praxiteles, went up, I suppose, to heaven and took a copy of the forms of the gods, and then reproduced these by their art, or was there any other influence which presided over and guided their moulding?"

The reply of Apollonius is one of the clearest statements for the imagination in early criticism:

> . . . There was . . . an influence pregnant with wisdom and genius . . . . Imagination . . . wrought these works, a wiser and subtler artist by far than imitation; for imitation can only create as its handiwork what it has seen, but imagination equally what it has not seen; for it will conceive of its ideal with reference to the reality,[18] and imitation is often baffled by terror, but imagination by nothing; for it marches undismayed to the goal which it has itself laid down. When you entertain a notion of Zeus you must, I suppose, envisage him along with heaven and seasons and stars as Phidias in his day endeavoured to do, and if you would fashion an image of Athene you must image in your mind armies and cunning, and handicrafts, and how she leapt out of Zeus himself.[19]

Philostratus has here expressed what Longinus no doubt had in mind when he set off imagery from imitation, and what Quintilian meant by ascribing effective pictorial presentation to vivid imagery in the mind of the maker: that is, the power of imagination to construct its own reality, probably from

---

[17] Philostratus, *The Life of Apollonius of Tyana*, II, xxii; tr. by F. C. Conybeare (London, 1912), I, 175.

[18] This has also been translated as follows: "but imagination goes on to what it has not seen, which it will assume as the standard of the reality" (I. A. Richards, *Coleridge on the Imagination* [New York, 1935], p. 215).

[19] Philostratus, *op. cit.*, VI, xix; Conybeare, II, 77–79.

materials furnished by the senses, but in freedom from the restrictions of an exact copying of external objects. And in this he is perhaps not far from the Aristotelian notion of *mimesis* in the *Poetics*, of a representation of life as it ought to be rather than as it is.

Plotinus (A.D. 204-70) is even more emphatic than Philostratus in attributing to the artist a creative activity beyond the mere process of imitating material objects. He makes concessions to the imitation of nature as it ought to be, in the Aristotelian sense, but his main theory revolves about concepts of ideal being. He believes in an archetypical reality of which the cosmic mind is the first image, and the soul of man the second. Nature has no reality except as it is informed by the cosmic mind from which it emanates. Because visible objects are unreliable witnesses of true form, that is eternal reality, Plotinus distrusts the phantasms of sensuous perception.[20] Yet he admits that man's experience is extended through contact with nature; for, although nature is inferior to man and given to false appearances, she unconsciously carries within herself evidences of "Ideal-Form," impressed upon her in her making by the cosmic soul, and hence has power to arouse in man recollections of beauty and true greatness.[21] The artist, in whom the principle of All-Being has a dwelling, stands midway between the sense and the ideal worlds, drawing from both. His loftier phantasies are chiefly derived from the ideal sphere. But the lower phantasies of the sensible may become merged in the higher ones, in which case the artist may conceive and create existence which bears evidence of actuality, but which carries within itself and mirrors forth a better order of things than can be found in the imperfect world of nature.

[20] Plotinus, *Psychic and Physical Treatises*, II, 6, 7; tr. by Stephen Mackenna and B. S. Page (London, 1921), II, 77-78.

[21] "Now if the sight of Beauty excellently reproduced upon a face hurries the mind to that other Sphere, surely no one seeing the loveliness lavish in the world of sense — this vast orderliness, the Form which the stars even in their remoteness display — no one could be so dull-witted, so immoveable, as not to be carried by all this to recollection, and gripped by reverent awe in the thought of all this, so great, sprung from greatness" (*Enneads*, II, 9, 16; Mackenna, II, 239). Later ages were to call this experience sublimity; to Plotinus it is a vision of ideality.

To Plotinus the imagination is a seeing and recognizing power. Although it has some concern with the images of daily experience, it is essentially a mode of rising to apprehensions of eternal being. Plotinus asserts that memory is not the recall of stored-up sensuous impressions: it is rather "the mind awakening its powers in such a way as to possess something not present to it." [22] The something belongs to its original being, however; memory is but a means of recovery. Similarly, creative imaginative activity is in a sense a recapture of a portion of the ideal unity that was dissipated in pristine cosmic creation. It is an activity of the conceiving mind ascending to a renewed grasp of first principles.

Plotinus conceives of all productive acts as originating in vision. Even the vegetation of the earth acts in growth from the "Reason-Principle" within, the vision that belongs to its character.[23] Man's actions are set toward contemplation of the soul's vision of perfection. "This vision achieved, the acting instinct pauses." [24] The artist seeks to impress upon his materials the "Form-Idea" of his intuition of the perfect beauty to which his soul aspires. His end is so to manipulate his symbols that observers are "deeply stirred by recognizing in the objects depicted . . . the presentation of what lies in the idea, and so are called to recollection of the truth — the very experience out of which Love rises." [25]

In the *Fifth Ennead* Plotinus considers how "the Beauty of the divine Intellect and of the Intellectual Kosmos may be revealed to contemplation." [26] He invites us to compare with an untouched stone a second one "minutely wrought . . . into some statue . . . not a portrait but a creation in which the sculptor's art has concentrated all loveliness." The difference is great.

Now it must be seen that the stone thus brought under the artist's hand to the beauty of form is beautiful not as a stone — for so the crude block would be as pleasant — but in virtue of the form or idea introduced

---

[22] *Op. cit.*, III, 6, 2; Mackenna, II, 70.
[23] *Ibid.*, III, 8, 3; Mackenna, II, 121–123.
[24] *Ibid.*, III, 8, 6; Mackenna, II, 126.
[25] *Ibid.*, II, 9, 16; Mackenna, II, 239.
[26] "On the Intellectual Beauty," V, 8, 1; Mackenna, IV, 73.

by the art. This form is not in the material; it is in the designer before ever it enters the stone; and the artificer holds it not by his equipment of eyes and hands but by his participation in his art. The beauty, therefore, exists in a far higher state in the art; for it does not come over integrally into the work; that original beauty is not transferred; what comes over is a derivative and a minor: and even that shows itself upon the statue not integrally and with entire realisation of intention but only in so far as it has subdued the resistance of the material.

Art, then, creating in the image of its own nature and content, and working by the Idea or Reason-Principle of the beautiful object it is to produce, must itself be beautiful in a far higher and purer degree, since it is the seat and source of that beauty, indwelling in the art, which must naturally be more complete than any comeliness of the external. In the degree in which the beauty is diffused by entering into matter, it is so much the weaker than that concentrated in unity; everything that reaches outwards is the less for it, strength less strong, heat less hot, every power less potent, and so beauty less beautiful.

The reasoning of Plotinus here is that prime causes must be greater than their effects can be; hence the art to be observed in a material work must be regarded as inferior to a yet higher art. Even so the material part is to be justified.

Still the arts are not to be slighted on the ground that they create by imitation of natural objects; for, to begin with, these natural objects are themselves imitations; then we must recognize that they [the arts] give no bare reproduction of the thing seen but go back to the Ideas from which Nature itself derives, and, furthermore, that much of their work is all their own; they are holders of beauty and add where nature is lacking. Thus Pheidias wrought the Zeus upon no model among things of sense but by apprehending what form Zeus must take if he chose to become manifest to sight.[27]

---

[27] *Ibid.*; Mackenna, IV, 73–74. This passage has been variously translated. I. A. Richards prints the following condensation, which in some respects is probably truer to the meaning of Plotinus than Mackenna's more literal rendition:

"This essence or character was not in the material, but it *was in the conceiving mind, even before it entered into the stone.* But it was in the artist not by virtue of his having eyes and hands, but by virtue of his imagination (τέχνη). And this beauty, already *comprehended in his imagination,* was far greater. For it went not out of him into the stone, but abode with him and gave birth to a lesser beauty . . . .

"The arts do not merely copy the visible world but *ascend to the principles on which nature is built up;* and, further, many of their creations are original. For they certainly make good the defects of things, as having the source of beauty in themselves. Thus Pheidias did not use any visible model for his Zeus, but apprehended him as he would appear if he deigned to show himself to our eyes" (Richards, *op. cit.,* p. 27).

The work of the artist, according to this instructive account, is somewhat analogous to the process by which the Divine Intelligence first created man and the visible world. As the Divine gave of his own high nature but in weakened and imperfect form to material objects, so the conceiving soul of the artist, through modified reproductions of these objects, seeks to impart its visions (or imaginative apprehensions) of the ideal unity. So the work of art becomes a sort of second nature. Like nature herself it is at best an inadequate means for conveying the intuitions of its creator — for "beauty is diffused by entering into matter": yet it is in respects better than nature, because the artist supplies from the beautiful form in his own mind that which nature lacks. Thus the artist confers upon his creation a perfection of truth not to be found in the world of material objects. Through such ideas, we may add, Plotinus furnishes elements for a theory of creative imagination as a repetition of the acts of the *Infinite I Am* which was to reach fulfilment in the capacious intellect of Coleridge. It furnishes a basis for a view of art which, though in some respects akin to Plato's, has advanced quite beyond the notion of a mere imitation of an imitation.

II

The hybrid theory of ideal imitation set forth by Cicero, obviously as an already established tradition, and maintained in one form or another up to the time of Du Fresnoy and Dryden, is a notable example of the crisscrossing of Platonism and Aristotelianism. Cicero, it will be recalled, cites the oft-repeated story of the painting of Helen by Zeuxis in illustration of the artist's method of constructing ideal beauty from a selection of details from experience; [28] but, elsewhere, he also

---

[28] " . . . Give me, then, said he, I beg you, the most beautiful of these virgins, while I paint the picture which I promised you, so that the reality may be transferred from the breathing model to the mute likeness. Then the citizens of Crotona, in accordance with a public vote, collected the virgins into one place, and gave the painter the opportunity of selecting whom he chose. But he selected five, whose names many poets have handed down to tradition, because they had been approved by the judgment of the man who was bound to have the most

shows that the guiding principle in such a selection is a perfect idea of beauty implanted — Platonic-wise, we judge — in the mind of the artist.[29]

Modifications of this theory run through Renaissance criticism. Leon Battista Alberti, Leonardo da Vinci, Raphael, Firenzuola, Daniello, Dolce, Minturno, Fracastoro, Lomazzo, Scaliger,[30] all subscribe in one way or another, with varying proportions of the Aristotelian and Platonic elements, to a doctrine of ideal imitation. The Aristotelian conception of an imitation more universal than can be found in an individual, of life as it ought to be rather than as it is,[31] which led him to think of a painter as making a "likeness which is true to life and yet more beautiful," [32] furnishes a basis for the theory; the Platonic conception of "Ideas" forms its main structure; while the notion of working from models that will provide details from which to construct a tangible lifelike imitation of the painter's vision of "ideal beauty" is a leaf from the notebook of practical artists attempting to accommodate a

---

accurate judgment respecting beauty. For he did not think that he could find all the component parts of perfect beauty in one person, because nature has made nothing of any class absolutely perfect in every part. Therefore as if nature would not have enough to give to everybody if it had given everything to one, it balances one advantage bestowed upon a person by another disadvantage" (*The Second Treatise on Rhetorical Invention*, i; Yonge, IV, 308).

[29] "But I lay down this position, that there is nothing of any kind so beautiful which has not something more beautiful still from which it is copied, — as a portrait is from a person's face, — though it can neither be perceived by the eyes or ears, or by any other of the senses; it is in the mind only, and by our thoughts that we embrace it. Therefore, though we have never seen anything of any kind more beautiful than the statues of Phidias and than those pictures which I have named, still we can imagine something more beautiful. Nor did that great artist, when he was making the statue of Jupiter or of Minerva, keep in his mind any particular person of whom he was making a likeness; but there dwelt in his mind a certain perfect idea of beauty, which he looked upon, and guided his art and his hand with reference to the likeness of that model" (*The Orator*, ii; Yonge, IV, 383).

[30] I wish to acknowledge the considerable debt I owe in this summary to Professor William Guild Howard's "*Ut Pictura Poesis,*" *PMLA*, XXIV (1909), 40 ff.

[31] *The Poetics*, II, 4; IX, 1–4; XV, 8; tr. by S. H. Butcher (London, 1922), pp. 12–13, 35–36, 57.

[32] *Ibid.*, XV, 8; Butcher, p. 57. The passage in which this idea occurs is notable not only for its further explication of Aristotle's view of ideal imitation, but for its probable influence on the development of the theory of *ut pictura poesis*.

doctrine of idealism to the necessities of realistic representation. The result is a sort of bastard Platonism (or Aristotelianism, as you please), exemplified in its generic form in Cicero.

The more empirical (or Aristotelian) phase of the theory is expressed by Alberti, who tells us, according to Bellori, "that we ought not so much to love the likeness as the beauty, and to choose from the fairest bodies severally the fairest parts." [33]   The less empirical occurs in Raphael, when he writes: "To paint a fair one, it is necessary for me to see many fair ones; but because there is so great a scarcity of lovely women, I am constrained to make use of one certain idea which I have formed to myself in my own fancy." [34]   The Aristotelian Scaliger accepts the Platonic notion of inspiration in a conception of the poet as a godlike creator able to construct a nature more perfect than reality.   "The poets invoke the Muses, that the divine madness may imbue them to do their work," Scaliger says. [35]   The work that they do, thus inspired, excels that of oratory, philosophy, and history, for while these arts "represent things just as they are, in some sense like a speaking picture, the poet depicts quite another sort of nature, and a variety of fortunes; in fact in so doing he transforms himself almost into a second deity . . . ; since poetry fashions images of those things which are not, as well as images more beautiful than life of those things which are, it seems . . . to be another god and to create." [36]   This is as positive a statement of the claims of the constructive imagination in ideal creation as is to be found in critical literature up to Francis Bacon, of whom I shall presently speak at some length.

III

A similar mingling of strands of influence from the two great philosophers runs through the late Latin, the Medieval,

[33] Quoted by Dryden in *A Parallel of Poetry and Painting*, in *Essays of John Dryden*, ed. by W. P. Ker (Oxford, 1926), II, 120.
[34] Letter to Castiglione. Quoted by Dryden, *op. cit.*, II, 120.
[35] J. G. Scaliger, *Select Translations from Scaliger's Poetics*, I, 2; tr. by F. M. Padelford (New York, 1905), p. 15.
[36] *Ibid.*, I, i; Padelford, pp. 7–8.

and the Renaissance periods. Scholastic psychology shows definite evidence of an interweaving of the two traditions, with some effort to accommodate them to Christian theology. In scholastic thought the imagination and fancy are in general assigned places in an elaborate hierarchy of faculties, with functions of receiving, retaining, and reproducing, or creating. Imagination, as the recipient and storehouse of images, is usually identified, or associated, with the memory. Phantasy, as in Avicenna and Albertus Magnus, is quite consistently the constructive faculty. Relying upon the imagination for its images, it may construct forms based on reality; or it may flee from reality and give birth to chimerical form with no relation to experience. In the latter function it is to be feared and repressed. In either case it must be kept under the firm control of reason.

Albertus Magnus (A.D. 1206?–80) may be taken as representative of the medieval faculty psychology. He conceived of organs of apprehension and organs of reason. The organs of apprehension are common sense, imagination, opinion, phantasy, and memory. Imagination he called the "*virtus imaginativa*, because the forms impressed on it are images of external objects." It has power to retain, is a depository. The memory is like imagination with the notion of time added. It furnishes images to the reason. Imaginations are combined to produce the effect of the terrible, the helpful, and the harmful — hence the imagination is the source of opinions. Phantasy has for its function to compare, to unite, to divide; it is a function operating between imagination and memory. Phantasy must be subservient to reason. (Albertus admits that the terms "imagination" and "phantasy" are often used interchangeably.) [37]

A more comprehensive theory of the imagination is to be found in St. Thomas Aquinas (A.D. 1225–74?). His system is eclectic, combining the empiricism of Aristotle, with its emphasis on phantasms (images) for activities of the intellect, and the supernaturalism of Plato, with its belief in the possi-

[37] For a more complete statement of the view of Albertus Magnus see Bundy, *op. cit.*, pp. 187 ff.

bilities of phantasms derived from supersensible sources. This, however, is to speak only roughly, for the Platonism of Aquinas is substantially modified by a liberal admixture of Christian theology, and his Aristotelianism by centuries of intervening interpretation, particularly by the medieval faculty psychology. Accepting, in general, current psychological views, he nevertheless redefines and limits them in important particulars. His most significant divergence from the schemes of immediate predecessors like Avicenna and Albertus is to deny the validity of accepted distinctions between the fancy and the imagination. He reduces the interior powers of the soul to four: namely, sense, the imagination (or phantasy), the estimative power, and the memorative power.[38]   The imagination (or phantasy) is the faculty for the retention and preservation of sensible forms received through the *proper sense* and the *common sense:* The imagination, then, becomes a "storehouse of forms received through the senses." [39]   But the imagination is also the power which "combines and divides imaginary forms: as when from the imaginary form of gold, and the imaginary form of a mountain, we compose the one form of a golden mountain, which we have never seen." [40]   The imagination here takes over the functions assigned by Avicenna, Albertus, and others to the fancy. The estimative faculty, according to Aquinas, is for the "apprehension of intentions which are not received through the senses" [41] — supersensible forms, in other words; and the memorative power is "a storehouse for such-like intentions." [42]   Moreover, "Although the operation of the intellect has its origin in the senses: yet, in the thing apprehended

---

[38] *Summa Theologica*, tr. by Fathers of the English Dominican Province (London, 1911–25), Part I, Third Number, Q. 78, A. 4, p. 85. For an able summary of the Aquinas theory of imagination see Bundy, *op. cit.*, pp. 216–224; and for an illuminating treatment of the phantasm in Aquinas see H. Carr, "The Function of the Phantasm in St. Thomas Aquinas," in *Philosophical Essays Presented to John Watson* (Kingston, Ontario, 1923), pp. 179 ff.

[39] *Sum. Theol., loc. cit.*   [40] *Ibid.*, p. 86.   [41] *Ibid.*, p. 85.

[42] *Ibid.* It will be observed that Aquinas suggests no power for the fusion of the materials received and preserved through these parallel faculties operating respectively upon impressions from the material and the immaterial worlds. Presumably, he assumed that union and fusion are accomplished through the active intellect, though his *imagination* might conceivably have been extended to cover this function.

through the senses, the intellect knows many things which the senses cannot perceive." [43]

The interweaving of Christian with Platonic influence in Aquinas appears in his ascription of sources of supersensible "intentions" to God and angels. The angels may be good or bad.[44] If bad (they are then demons), they may implant false visions, as in sleepers and lunatics. Such an evil can be guarded against only by a strict exercise of right judgment; hence the necessity of careful rule of the imagination by the intellect.

IV

Continental theories of imagination during the Renaissance, apart from the conventional notions of ideal imitation, are best represented in a group of Italian and Spanish thinkers of the naturalistic school who stemmed from Galen, and the thirteenth-century Paduans. It will be enough to mention here the names of Cardanus, Telesio, Huarte, and Campanella. So far as these men were aestheticians they belong primarily to the physiopsychological tradition, which was later to include Hobbes.

Cardanus [45] owes his claim to distinction largely to the fact that he was, in the words of Brett, "the author of the . . .

---

[43] *Ibid.*, p. 87.

[44] "Both a good and a bad angel by their own natural power can move the human imagination," says Aquinas. They do not accomplish this directly, however, but operate through the sensitive appetite, creating such internal commotions and impulses that the appearances resulting may be mistaken for products of external objects. Here Aquinas makes a fine distinction: "For we cannot imagine what we have never perceived by the senses . . . . Sometimes, however, the imagination is informed in such a way that the act of the imaginative movement arises from the impression preserved within." Thus the imagination is changed by an angel, not by the impression of a form in no way previously received by the senses, but by local movement of the spirits and humors acting upon and with elementary sense materials present in the mind. The consequent apparitions may or may not be intelligible to the percipient, depending on the perfection of his intellect (*ibid.*, Q. 111, A. 3, pp. 468–469).

[45] Hieronymus Cardanus, or Girolamo Cardano (1501–76), physician, mathematician, and philosopher, taught a doctrine of natural law and natural causes applicable to all finite things but the will of man, and pointed out that "ancient theories of state were constructed with too little reference to the actual, varying conditions of social life" (Benjamin C. Burt, *A History of Modern Philosophy* [Chicago, 1892], I, 73).

division of human faculties into the three classes, memory, reason, and imagination, which was adopted by Francis Bacon." [46]   Telesio [47] has been called "the first of the moderns." He is notable for his open rebellion against the ancients, and for his development of an empirical physiological psychology. To Telesio knowledge begins and ends with sensible data. Observation, then, is the basis of all knowledge; perception is its form.   The soul is corporeal, and operations of the mind are but higher forms of sensation.   The understanding is explained as the action of the soul upon many images coexisting in the mind.   Sensation is the result of motions in the vital spirits in the nerves and the blood stream produced by the joint action of external objects and the interior spirits. Telesio does not, however, regard sensation as a mere physical action; it is rather the recognition by the soul that it is being acted upon, is, in other words, a psychic event which happens when the spirits "go out as it were to meet the incoming shock" of motion from external objects.[48]   A perception is thus a sensation completed by an activity of the mind which "contributes elements not actually contained in the presentation." [49]   Reasoning is a kind of secondary observation through which the mind draws conclusions from a perception of likeness or difference in the images stored in the memory through many perceptions and in the object to be investigated.   This Telesio called "reasoning by similars," which he distinguished from the Aristotelian reason grounded in words.   For such reasoning is related to observation, and its conclusions do not differ in kind from the sensations with which the process be-

---

[46] *Op. cit.*, II, 146.

[47] Bernardino Telesio (1509–88) was born at Cosenza in Calabria in the kingdom of Naples.   His principal work is *De Rerum Natura*, 1546.   Bacon referred to him as "novorum hominum primum," though he took pains to point out his fallacies.   Niel C. Van Deusen has published a study entitled *Telesio: The First of the Moderns* (New York, 1932).   Other accounts may be found in Brett's *A History of Psychology* (London, 1921), Vol. II, and in Léon Blanchet's *Campanella* (Paris, 1920).   [48] Brett, *op. cit.*, II, 147.

[49] *Ibid.* It is of interest to note, in view of later theories such as those of Hobbes, that Telesio believes all sensation to be accompanied by pleasure — the sensation of conservation — or pain — the sensation of corruption and destruction (Van Deusen, *op. cit.*, pp. 58–59).

gan.[50] General concepts are derived from this method of reasoning by analogy: "La notion générale n'est pas autre chose que la superposition des impressions semblables, c'est-à-dire des mouvements produits dans l'esprit vital par l'action d'objets semblables." [51] Such an interpretation of mental processes as natural activities of the individual relates Telesio to the English materialistic psychologists of the seventeenth century, as Brett acutely notes:

. . . By thus interpreting sensation as an activity of the organism not separated by nature from the reason: by practically ignoring the pure reason and throwing emphasis on the complex activity of comparison and discrimination: finally, by presenting the whole as a natural process, tending toward a perceptible good, the preservation of self, Telesius has anticipated the principal parts of the anthropological teaching of Bacon and Hobbes.[52]

Campanella [53] was an ardent follower of Telesio, who differed from his master in his general psychology only in details and in a greater emphasis on the subjective element. He went further than Telesio, however, in developing an aesthetic theory based on this psychology. This is, as one would expect, a generally naturalistic aesthetic. The imagination, as either a reproductive or a creative agency, becomes with Campanella a natural function of the human organism. Memory and imagination, like concepts and discourse, are but continuations of sensation. Sensation itself is an effect of movement, a "passion" rather than a duplication of the object, though, like Telesio, Campanella speaks of perceptions stored in the mind as images. Memory is nothing less than conserved perceptions. Objects are usually recalled by the actual vision of a similar object, at which time associative processes are set up, so that when the past sensation is revived all the connected movements are renewed with it. Thus — and here

[50] Van Deusen, op. cit., p. 60.
[51] Blanchet, op. cit., p. 175.   [52] Op. cit., II, 147–148.
[53] Giovanni Domenica Campanella (1568–1639) was born at Stilo in Calabria. Of his many works it is pertinent to mention here De Sensu Rerum, etc. (1604), Universalis Philosophia seu Metaphysicae (1602–3), and the "Poetica" of his Philosophia Rationalis (1612, 1614, 1617). Léon Blanchet's Campanella contains an excellent summary of his theory.

Campanella is pleased to cite an example used by Telesio —
the thoughts or the image of a voyage on the sea may produce
nausea. If an object is not presented anew the memory takes
the name of imagination. Besides this reproductive act there
is another form of imagination by which the spirit creates new
images more complex, or more simple, than real objects; but
this creative activity implies nothing more than the physical
power of combining or disjoining conserved perceptions, that
is to say it is, like sensation, only a movement of the vital
spirits.[54] The power of passing spontaneously from like to
like, of perceiving similitudes, and of grasping these similitudes in a single apprehension constitutes the unique quality
of human intelligence as manifested in rational and imaginative acts.[55]

Huarte's [56] work preceded Campanella's, and it is much
more important for English aesthetics. A fairly good case
could be made for the influence of Huarte on both Bacon and
Hobbes as well as on various lesser English writers. His
Examen de ingenios para las sciencias was translated in 1594,[57]
and something of its popularity may be suggested in the fact
that by 1616 this translation had been reprinted three times.
It is not strange, then, that ideas from Huarte, or at least parallel to his, should frequently crop up in seventeenth-century
English writings, including those of Hobbes.

The *Examen* is ostensibly an essay in scientific vocational
guidance, founded on the premise that of the many different
wits only one can fall preëminently to any one man, that to
every difference of wit there corresponds only one science, or

[54] Blanchet, *op. cit.*, p. 182.   [55] *Ibid.*, p. 183.
[56] Juan de Dios Huarte was born at Saint-Jean-Pied-de-Port, Basse-Navarre,
between the years 1530 and 1535. According to the estimate of José M. M.
Guardia ("Notice biographique," *Essai sur l'ouvrage de J. Huarte: Examen des aptitudes diverses pour les sciences* [Paris, 1855]), the *Examen* was published in the year
1580; the copy of the first edition in the British Museum is, however, dated 1578.
[57] *Examen de ingenios. The Examination of Men's Wits* . . . , translated out
of the Spanish tongue by M. Camillo Camilli, Englished out of his Italian by
R. C. Esquire. London, printed by Adam Islip for Richard Watkins, 1594.
"R. C." is for Richard Carew. In the British Museum Catalogue the word
"Esquire" is followed in brackets by "and partly by Thomas Carew." Second,
third, and fourth editions appeared in 1596, 1604, and 1616.

art, and that, therefore, success in life is dependent first upon the determination of the particular wit one possesses, secondly upon the intelligent application of that wit to the particular science (practical or theoretic) to which it is fitted. Huarte's conception of wit may be broadly stated as special mental aptitude.[58] His psychology is basically physiological. Following Galen, he believes that predominance in any one of the three powers of mind is relative to certain physical conditions of the body, specifically with respect to heat and cold and to moisture and dryness.

The three faculties of the reasonable soul, the seat of which is the brain,[59] are understanding, memory, and imagination. Huarte presents with unusual clarity, among writers up to his time, the nature and functions of these powers. The memory is a passive faculty which receives and retains impressions; the imagination and the understanding are active, each in its way making use of impressions lodged in the memory, each capable of productive activity in creating things of its own conceiving.[60] The functions of the understanding are three: "the first, to discourse [reason], the second, to distinguish, the third, to Chuse." [61] Of the three faculties the

[58] In the 1591 revision he makes an interesting essay at more specific definition. True wit, Huarte here explains, in terms which in respects suggest some analogy to Coleridge's description of the imagination, has power to body forth well-formed material "Being." It is a generative power, and "becomes pregnant, and brings forth . . . children." Even as a plant or an animal in generation gives to its progeny a real and substantial being, "so Wit has the Power and natural Force to produce and bring forth a son, which the natural philosophers call Notion, or as it has been accounted, the Word of the Spirit." The crucial phrase here is "real . . . being"; for unless such being is given to what is engendered, "as subsisting by it self like as happens to those things which God has made," then there is produced only an accident in the memory, a mere "Idea and Image . . . very far from that, which comes to pass in the ineffable Generation of the Word Divine, where that which is Engender'd, is of *the same Substance with the Father*, as the other things which God has produc'd, represent him from without, by a real and substantial Being, which we now see in them . . ." (*Examen de ingenios: or the Tryal of Wits among Men* . . . . Published Originally in Spanish by Doctor Juan Huartes. And made English from the most Correct Edition by Mr. Bellamy [London, 1698], pp. 4–5).

[59] *Examen de ingenios* (Carew ed.), pp. 54–55.
[60] *Ibid.*, pp. 78–79.
[61] *Ibid.*, p. 65. Later on he expands these to five: "to distinguish, conclude, discourse, judge, and make Choice" (*ibid.*, pp. 105–106), by which, however, since

imagination is by far the most complex in its operations.   It
has both intermediary and creative functions.   As an intermediary it acts between the senses and the memory, and in
both directions between the memory and the understanding.
Its inventive powers are far-reaching, including not only the
combinations of impressions into such complex phantasms as
"mountaines of gold, and calues that flie," [62] the delusions of
men in frenzies and fevers, and the compositions of painting,
poetry, oratory, and music, but the constructions of statesmen
and generals in foreseeing and planning and executing projects
of statecraft and war, and the insight of physicians and other
men of action in knowing immediately, as if by intuition, what
is to be done.[63]

---

to discourse includes reasoning, judging, and concluding, he adds nothing to his
original statement.
    The relation of the memory to the understanding is clearly set forth:
    ". . . But this is vnderstood of the faculties or reasonable wits, which are
discoursiue and actiue, and not of the passiue, as is the memorie, which depends
as well on the moyst, as the vnderstanding doth on the drie. And wee call memorie
a reasonable power, because without it the vnderstanding and the imaginatiue are
of no valure. It ministreth matter and figures to them all, whereupon they may
syllogise conformably to that which *Aristotle* sayth, It behooves that the vnder-
stander goe beholding the fantasmes; and the office of the memorie is, to preserue
these fantasmes, to the end that the vnderstanding may contemplat them, and if
this be lost, it is impossible that the powers can worke; and that the office of
memorie is none other, than to preserue the figures of things, without that it
appertaines thereto to devise them. *Galen* expresseth in these words, Memorie
(verely) laies vp and preserueth in it selfe the things knowne by the sence, and by
the mind, and is therein as it were their store-house and receiuing place, and not
their inuenter" (*ibid.*, pp. 60–61).
    [62] *Examen de ingenios* (Carew ed.), p. 132.
    [63] Huarte's description of the shorthand process of ratiocination which we
know as intuition is quite worth quoting:
    "To attaine this notice, the imagination possesseth certaine vnutterable
properties, with which the same cleereth matters that cannot bee expressed nor
conceiued, neither is there found anie art to teach them. Where-through wee see
a Physition enter to visit a patient, and by meanes of his sight, his hearing, his
smelling, and his feeling, he knoweth things which seeme impossible. In sort, that
if we demaund of the same Physition, how he could come by so readie a knowledge,
himselfe cannot tell the reason: for it is a grace which springeth from the fruitful-
nesse of the imagination, which by another name is tearmed a readinesse of
capacitie, which by common signes, and by vncertaine coniectures, and of small
importance, in the twinckling of an eye knoweth a hundred differences of things,
wherein the force of curing and prognosticating with certainetie consisteth" (*ibid.*,
p. 180).

Of particular interest in Huarte's thought is his conception of a correspondence between the several faculties and an aptitude for the various pursuits of life. His division recalls Cardanus and suggests the classification of functions later to be made by Bacon. Men who have good memories are fitted for the languages, the facts of law, of divinity, cosmography, and so forth. Those who have a good understanding are most likely to excel in school-divinity, the theory of physics, logic, and philosophy.[64] While those who have a good imagination may hope to succeed in oratory, poetry, and the practical arts of life:

> . . . From a good imagination spring all the Arts and Sciences, which consist in figure, correspondence, harmonie, and proportion: such are Poetrie, Eloquence, Musicke, and the skill of preaching: the practice of Physicke, the Mathematicals, Astrologie, and the gouerning of a Commonwealth: the art of Warfare, Painting, Drawing, Writing, Reading, to be a man gratious, pleasant, neat, wittie in managing, and all the engines and deuices which artificers make.[65]

Huarte's first claim to distinction in such a statement rests upon his implicit attribution of the arts mentioned to the imagination. It is also of importance that he refers to the imagination a capacity for public and practical affairs of life. In this he is anticipating by several years Puttenham's similar ascription to the imagination of good generalship, good statesmanship, and all the other arts of civilization, and by over half a century Hobbes's restatement of this idea in his *Elements of Law* and in his *Answer to Davenant*.

Huarte's tendency is to set imaginative capacity apart from the rational and philosophic. He conceives of two main classes of minds, the rationalistic-theoretic and the imaginative-practical. As men incline to the one or the other of these they will excel in the theory of government or in the practice of statecraft, in basic legal principles or the application of these principles in the courts, in the theoretic knowledge of diseases and their cure or in the practice of medicine, in the theory of strategy or in active generalship on the fields of war. On the whole, he would seem to believe of all the main professions

[64] *Ibid.*, pp. 102 ff.   [65] *Ibid.*, p. 103.

what he says of medicine: "that the art . . . is learned with one power and put in execution with another." [66]

An exception may be made to this last statement in the case of such arts as poetry and oratory. Here all belongs to the imagination — both the knowledge of the art and its execution. What Huarte says of the orator may be applied to the poet. The good orator is copious in language, ready in invention, fertile in the use of figures and examples. These are gifts of the imagination; for "All that may be tearmed good figure, good purpose and prouision, comes from the grace of the imagination, as are merrie ieasts, resemblances, quips, and comparisons." [67] The orator must also know how to assemble and present "good examples and comparisons." Through fit examples men most easily learn. And it is certain that devising fables and comparisons "is performed by the imagination, for it is figure, and denoteth good correspondence and similitude." [68] Invention and imagination are identified as requisites to the orator. For to dilate and confirm any matter,

it behooueth, that he haue a verie swift imagination . . . to hunt and bring the game to his hand, and when he wants what to say, to deuise somewhat as if it were materiall. For this cause we said before, that heat was an instrument with which the imagination worketh, for this qualitie lifteth vp the figures, and maketh them to boile. Heere is discouered all that which in them may be seene, and if there fell out nought else to be considered, this imagination hath force not onely to compound a figure possible with another, but doth ioyne also (after the order of nature) those which are vnpossible, and of them growes to shape mountaines of gold, and calues that flie.[69]

So Huarte presents his case for the supremacy of the imagination in poetry and oratory. There is scarcely a hint that reason or judgment has a place. Memory, it is true, is an indispensable adjunct to the imagination; hence books sometimes are an aid in supplying materials where the imagination fails. But a fertile imagination is above such helps; for whatever may be found in books is bounded and limited, whereas "the proper inuention is a good fountaine which alwaies yeeldeth forth new and fresh water." [70] And here

[66] *Examen de ingenios* (Carew ed.), p. 181.   [67] *Ibid.*, p. 131.
[68] *Ibid.*, pp. 135–136.   [69] *Ibid.*, pp. 131–132.   [70] *Ibid.*

Huarte expresses a most extreme, and, it is to be feared, erroneous, view of the independence of the imagination: ". . . those who borrow their conceits out of their own braine, stand not in need of studie, time, or memorie: for they find all readie at their fingers ends." [71]

Despite his tendency to regard the understanding and the imagination as distinct and opposing faculties, Huarte makes some attempt to bring them together. Indeed, he has a somewhat vague ideal of a man in whom there exists the best possible accommodation between the understanding and the imagination, with enough memory to serve each, and he promises to show, in his last chapter save one, how nature can bring about such a union of these powers. This chapter (XIV) has to do with the wit of a king; when Huarte has finished with it, however, he has still left largely unexplained how this balance may be attained. He does, indeed, show some recognition of the fact that in the well-rounded man judgment should be equal to genius; but he does not, as do Hobbes, Coleridge, and Wordsworth after him, suggest such an application to the poet.

Otto Klemm has spoken of Huarte's attempt to relate mental traits with bodily constitution as "fantastic." [72] Perhaps. The *Examen* is certainly a quaint and sometimes amusing book, but it is nevertheless not to be taken lightly. Fallacious as the groundwork of his psychology may have been, there was a seminal quality to Huarte's ideas. No one before his time, to my knowledge, had so unequivocally assigned poetry and the other fine arts to the imagination; no one had so clearly extended the province of the imagination to the practical pursuits of life. It is quite possible that Bacon was recalling him when he made his famous classification of the fields of knowledge, and that Hobbes had him in mind in a half-dozen different passages. Some one should study his influence on English thought. His method, moreover, was the naturalistic method which had been so definitely advanced by Telesio and his school. Like Telesio and, later, Hobbes, his first criterion

[71] *Ibid.*, p. 133.

[72] Otto Klemm, *A History of Psychology*, tr. by Emil Carl Wilm and Rudolph Pintner (New York, Chicago, and Boston, 1914), p. 57.

was experience and his instrument, observation; like Hobbes and Bacon he generally spurned the authority of the ancients. So long as he stuck to experience and observation he had significant things to report. When, however, he passed into the realm of theory and speculation beyond experience, he became on occasion as bizarre as did Hobbes when he tried to refute the Oxford professor and square the circle; and when he ventured to follow authority, as in his obeisance to Galen, he became immediately archaic. But these things count for less than do his acute and fruitful suggestions about various aspects of the human mind. He was a first-rate observer, a keen student of mankind, sufficiently independent in his thinking to utilize the results of his observation and thought in fresh and provocative theory.

Huarte's services to the imagination may broadly be said to supplement those of the Italian group to which Cardanus, Telesio, and Campanella belonged, which Baldwin has acutely characterized as a tendency to take the imagination out of the realm of the remote or merely emotional and to place it among the organic functions of man's mind: "If the imagination accomplishes in its normal working the results formerly attributed to emotional intuition and ecstasy, then this type of apprehension may be put down as one of the recognized functions of cognition. This means that the psychology of the imagination takes its place among the larger problems of the theory of knowledge." [73] This was the rational, empirical tradition to which Bacon and, after him, Hobbes were to attach themselves, and which Hobbes, in particular, through extensive psychological analysis, was to advance beyond any point previously attained.

V

Attention to aesthetic effects began with the early Sophists, Isocrates and Protagoras, and with Plato and Aristotle. But the Sophists were chiefly concerned with a pleasing style, and Plato's interest in moral issues largely obscured his view of

[73] James Mark Baldwin, *History of Psychology* (New York and London, 1913), I, 123-124.

strictly artistic response. Aristotle, however, gave definite
attention to the matter. Indeed, one of the chief differences
between Aristotle's and Plato's critical theories is the shift in
emphasis from moral to aesthetic effects in art. Aristotle
studied each kind of art for "the pleasure proper to it." In
the *Poetics* he justified tragedy on the basis of its emotional
effects,[74] and in the *Rhetoric* he outlined a theory of pleasure
with important implications for a psychology of imaginative
appeal. I shall have occasion later in this essay to refer in
more detail to some of these views.

Cicero and Quintilian taught that oratory should move
and please as well as inform. In treating the subject of delight
they are more generally concerned with pleasure in apt language and rhythmic movement. Yet in both there are evidences of rather penetrating reflection upon the primary sources
of aesthetic effect. Cicero justifies metaphor for its power,
through showing resemblances, to move the minds of the
hearers, and turn them this way and that way; for, he explains, "the very agitation of thought when operating in quick
succession is a pleasure of itself." [75] Similarly, he commends
"the imitation of things," as contributing to pleasure because
"this is one part of an oration which almost brings the actual
circumstances before our eyes." By clearness "we are made
to understand," but through brilliance in imitation "we actually appear to see." [76] Cicero also recognizes the principle
of novelty as a means to pleasure: "For an oration becomes
agreeable when you say anything unexpected, or unheard of,
or novel." [77] To this point he again remarks, "And those

---

[74] The same subject is, of course, touched upon in the *Politics*, and there are
valuable implications for the nature of aesthetic pleasure in *De Anima*, III, ii, 9–10;
Hicks, p. 117.

[75] *The Orator*, xxxix; Yonge, IV, 420–421. Here Cicero is in substantial
agreement with such later thinkers as Hobbes, Dennis, Addison, and Du Bos, all
of whom held that agitation of mind is a condition to pleasure. Long before any
of these men wrote, however, Aristotle had said, in Hobbes's own translation,
"Pleasure is a sudden and sensible motion of the soul, toward that which is natural"
(*The Whole Art of Rhetoric*, I, xi, in *The English Works of Thomas Hobbes of Malmesbury*, ed. by Sir William Molesworth [London, 1839–45]).

[76] *A Dialogue concerning Oratorical Partitions*, vi; Yonge, IV, 491–492.

[77] *Ibid.*

ornaments [embellishments or inventions] are frequently to be
employed, which are of a marvellous and unexpected character,
and also those which are full of monsters, and prodigies, and
oracles . . . for all the expectation and admiration of the
hearer, and all expected terminations, contribute to the
pleasure which is felt in listening to the orator." [78] Recognizing that the mind is a complex thing, he declares, "And that
oration especially influences the hearer which unites several
affections of the mind." [79]

Altogether Cicero gives considerable attention to the causes
of pleasure. He on occasion addresses himself to the problem
of the differences between the pleasure of oratory and the
pleasure of poetry. He finds that in general poets "pay more
attention to the object of giving pleasure to their readers than
to their subject." [80] To achieve this end the poet uses frequent
and daring metaphors, admits both old and new words more
readily, and adheres of necessity to a strict rhythm. The orator, too, speaks rhythmically, but the rhythm of an oration is
not the same as that of a poem: it is less set and it is of a different kind.[81]

The appeal of sounds and rhythm is to the ear, for there "is
a second sort of judgment of the ears." [82] The poet pays more
attention to appeal to the senses, but the orator, too, "ought to
consult that which gives pleasure to the ears." [83] "If we are
asked, What is the circumstance which causes pleasure? we
reply, that it is the same as in verse; the method of which is de-

---

[78] *A Dialogue concerning Oratorical Partitions*, xxi; Yonge, IV, 506.

[79] *Ibid.*, vi; Yonge, IV, 492. The perfect orator, Cicero explains, is one who
has command of a method of speaking calculated at once to teach, to please, and
to excite. "For he is the best orator who . . . both teaches, and delights, and
moves the minds of his hearers. To teach them is his duty, to delight them is credit-
able to him, to move them is indispensable" (*The Treatise on the Best Style of Orators*, i; Yonge, IV, 527–528).

Cicero appreciates the need for different stylistic qualities for different effects. He writes: "For if teaching, we want shrewd sentences; if aiming at giving
pleasure, we want musical ones; if at exciting the feelings, dignified ones. But
there is a certain arrangement of words which produces both harmony and
smoothness; and different sentiments have different arrangements suitable to
them, and an order naturally calculated to prove their point . . ." (*ibid.*, p. 528).

[80] *The Orator*, xx; Yonge, IV, 401.   [81] *Ibid.*, lx; Yonge, IV, 445.
[82] *Ibid.*, xlix; Yonge, IV, 432.   [83] *Ibid.*, xlviii; Yonge, IV, 430.

termined by art; but the ears themselves define it by their own silent sensations, without any reference to principles of art." [84]

Cicero shows clearly that successful oratory is largely a matter of knowing the different means to move and to excite, as well as to inform. The best speaker knows and uses these different means. Not only will he know how to move by bringing "the matter before people's eyes," [85] and by introducing novelty and wonders, but he will be skilled in what the Greeks "call παθητικὸν, by which men's minds are agitated and excited." [86] By this Cicero appears to mean all sorts of energetic and fiery emotional presentations, particularly those calculated to excite pity. Of his own practice the great orator declares that there is "no means by which the mind of the hearer can be either excited or softened" that he has not used. [87]

Quintilian, even more definitely than Cicero, gave consideration to the problem of aesthetic effect. "For it is in its power over the emotions that the life and soul of oratory is to be found," he said. "Without this all else is bare and meagre, weak and devoid of charm." [88] Few orators can sweep the judge before them, compelling him to think with them, weep with them, or share their anger. "And yet it is this emotional power that dominates the court, it is this form of eloquence that is the queen of all." [89] "There is scope for an appeal to the emotions," writes Quintilian, "in every portion of a speech. Moreover, these emotions present great variety, and demand more than cursory treatment." [90] Quintilian gives them more than a cursory treatment. What he has to say can be barely sketched here. He finds the sources of pleasurable emotional excitation in emphasis, in figures, in variety, in wit, in structure, in narrations that move to pity or horror, and most of all in ornament (embellishment) and in vivid illustration that makes the reader or hearer see persons and events as if before his eyes.

Quintilian was so widely read in the seventeenth and

[84] *Ibid.*, lx; Yonge, IV, 445.   [85] *Ibid.*, xl; Yonge, IV, 422.
[86] *Ibid.*, xxxvii; Yonge, IV, 419.   [87] *Ibid.*, xxxviii; Yonge, IV, 420.
[88] *The Institutio Oratoria*, VI, ii, 7; Butler, II, 421.
[89] *Ibid.*, VI, ii, 4; Butler, II, 419.   [90] *Ibid.*, VI, ii, 3; Butler, II, 417.

eighteenth centuries and exerted so much influence on English
critical thought that it would seem worth while here to quote at
some length passages containing his theory of effects.   Certain
of these show considerable acute psychological observation that
foreshadows later preoccupation in aesthetic speculation with
causes and effects.   Thus in one of his most remarkable passages,
a part of which has already been cited (see p. 28), he writes:

> Accordingly, the first essential is that those feelings should prevail
> with us that we wish to prevail with the judge, and that we should be
> moved ourselves before we attempt to move others.   But how are we to
> generate these emotions in ourselves, since emotion is not in our own
> power?   I will try to explain as best I may.   There are certain experiences
> which the Greeks call φαντασίας, and the Romans *visions*, whereby things
> absent are presented to our imagination with such extreme vividness that
> they seem actually to be before our very eyes.   It is the man who is really
> sensitive to such impressions who will have the greatest power over the
> emotions.   Some writers describe the possessor of this power of vivid
> imagination, whereby things, words and actions are presented in the most
> realistic manner, by the Greek word εὐφαντασίωτος; and it is a power
> which all may readily acquire if they will.   When the mind is unoccupied
> or is absorbed by fantastic hopes or day-dreams, we are haunted by these
> visions of which I am speaking to such an extent that we imagine that we
> are travelling abroad, crossing the sea, fighting, addressing the people, or
> enjoying the use of wealth that we do not actually possess, and seem to
> ourselves not to be dreaming but acting.   Surely, then, it may be possible
> to turn this form of hallucination to some profit.   I am complaining that
> a man has been murdered.   Shall I not bring before my eyes all the cir-
> cumstances which it is reasonable to imagine must have occurred in such
> a connexion?   Shall I not see the assassin burst suddenly from his hiding-
> place, the victim tremble, cry for help, beg for mercy, or turn to run?
> Shall I not see the fatal blow delivered and the stricken body fall?   Will
> not the blood, the deathly pallor, the groan of agony, the death-rattle,
> be indelibly impressed upon my mind?
>
> From such impressions arises that ἐνάργεια which Cicero calls *il-
> lumination* and *actuality*, which makes us seem not so much to narrate as
> to exhibit the actual scene, while our emotions will be no less actively
> stirred than if we were present at the actual occurrence.   Is it not from
> visions such as these that Vergil was inspired to write —
>
>> "Sudden her fingers let the shuttle fall
>> And the thread was spilled,"
>
> Or,
>> "In his smooth breast the gaping wound,"
>
> or the description of the horse at the funeral of Pallas, "his trappings laid

aside"? And how vivid was the image of death conceived by the poet when he wrote —

> "And dying sees his own dear Argive home"? [91]

Here Quintilian has outlined a theory of effects based on imaginative conception and presentation which seems to have been followed by subsequent writers, particularly by Puttenham in England — in a passage I shall presently cite (see p. 65) — who in turn appears to have influenced Hobbes in one of his most notable pronouncements on the imagination. [92]

Again, in a remark on wit, we find an anticipation of later discussions of literary taste as analogous to the physical sense:

> . . . When, therefore, we speak of the salt of wit, we refer to wit about which there is nothing insipid, wit, that is to say, which serves as a simple seasoning of language, a condiment which is silently appreciated by our judgment, as food is appreciated by the palate, with the result that it stimulates our taste and saves a speech from becoming tedious. But just as salt, if sprinkled freely over food, gives a special relish of its own, so long as it is not used to excess, so in the case of those who have the salt of wit there is something about their language which arouses in us a thirst to hear. [93]

On the question of effects Quintilian has most to say of figures and ornament. In discussing these subjects he follows Cicero rather closely, and in general presents Cicero's practice as a model for orators to follow. Where Cicero went to the Greeks, Quintilian found it unnecessary to look beyond his illustrious countryman for a standard of excellence. Speaking of the causes of Cicero's great success in his defense of Cornelius, he declares that it was no ordinary presentation of facts for instruction that made the orator prevail with his hearers:

> . . . No, it was the sublimity and splendour, the brilliance and the weight of his eloquence that evoked such clamorous enthusiasm. Nor, again, would his words have been greeted with such extraordinary approbation if his speech had been like the ordinary speeches of every day. In my opinion the audience did not know what they were doing, their applause sprang neither from their judgment nor their will; they were seized with a kind of frenzy and, unconscious of the place in which they stood, burst forth spontaneously into a perfect ecstasy of delight. [94]

---

[91] *The Institutio Oratoria*, VI, ii, 29–33; Butler, II, 433–437.
[92] See pp. 64–66.
[93] *The Institutio Oratoria*, VI, iii, 19; Butler, II, 447–449.
[94] *Ibid.*, VIII, iii, 4; Butler, III, 213.

Such sublimity and splendor came from Cicero's skilful use of ornament. "This gift," declares Quintilian eloquently, "appeals to the enthusiastic approval of the world at large, and the speaker who possesses it fights not merely with effective but with flashing weapons." [95]

There is no better method of exciting the emotions, Quintilian declares, than "an apt use of figures." Whether one wishes to win favor for his cause, to relieve monotony by variation of language, or to indicate meaning in the most seemly way, nothing will better serve than figures.[96] The simile, says Quintilian, is an "admirable means of illuminating our descriptions." This figure "is an ornament to oratory, and serves to make it sublime, rich, attractive or striking, as the case may be. For the more remote the simile is from the subject to which it is applied, the greater will be the impression of novelty and the unexpected which it produces." [97] The most effective figure of all is what Cicero calls "ocular demonstration," or "vivid illustration." Through this device truth is more than made clear, "it thrusts itself upon our notice," and facts upon which the judge must give a decision are "displayed in their living truth to the mind." [98] Praising Cicero for his supremacy in this field, Quintilian inquires,

> . . . Is there anybody so incapable of forming a mental picture of a scene that, when he reads the following passage from Verrines, he does not seem not merely to see the actors in the scene, the place itself and their

---

[95] *The Institutio Oratoria*, VIII, iii, 4; Butler, III, 213. Vital weapons, he thought: "What pleasure can an orator hope to produce, or what impression even of the most moderate learning, unless he knows how to fix one point in the minds of the audience by repetition, and another by dwelling on it, how to digress from and return to his theme, to divert the blame from himself and transfer it to another, or to decide what points to omit and what to ignore as negligible? It is qualities such as these that give life and vigour to oratory; without them it lies torpid like a body lacking the breath to stir its limbs. But more than the mere possession of these qualities is required; they must be deployed, each in their proper place and with such variety that every sound may bewitch the hearer with all the charm of music. But these qualities are as a rule open and direct, manifesting themselves without disguise. They do, however, as I have said, admit of *figures,* as the instances to which I shall proceed will show" (*ibid.*, IX, ii, 4–6; Butler, III, 377).

[96] *Ibid.*, IX, i, 21; Butler, III, 359.

[97] *Ibid.*, VIII, iii, 74; Butler, III, 253.

[98] *Ibid.*, VIII, iii, 61–62; Butler, II, 245.

very dress, but even to imagine to himself other details that the orator does not describe? . . . For my own part, I seem to see before my eyes his face, his eyes, and the unseemly blandishments of himself and his paramour, the silent loathing and frightened shame of those who viewed the scene.[99]

Quintilian is here directly describing the content and emotional quality of aesthetic effect and is assigning its causes. He is ostensibly talking about oratory, but that he would apply the same criteria to poetry is evident from the fact that here, as in similar passages, he introduces examples from Virgil to illustrate his point. "The same vivid impression may be produced by mention of the *accidents* of the situation," he remarks, and quotes,

> Chill shudderings shake my limbs
> And all my blood is curdled cold with fear.[100]

Also:

> And trembling mothers clasped
> Their children to their breast.[101]

Quintilian not only cites such effects as the highest possible accomplishment in oratory (and, by implication, in poetry) but gives a general rule for their attainment: "Fix your eyes on nature and follow her. All eloquence is concerned with the activities of life, while every man applies to himself what he hears from others, and the mind is always readiest to accept what it recognizes to be true to nature." [102]

Thus we find in Cicero and Quintilian a frank emphasis on emotional effects and their sources. Basically, it must be admitted, much of this emphasis is related to rhetorical considerations; there are, however, in the writings of these men, especially in Quintilian, flashes of psychological insight truly remarkable, which we must believe furnished valuable clues for those who were later to develop the psychological method to a greater height.

The interest of Longinus in aesthetic effects is well known. The rediscovery of his treatise in the late seventeenth century in France and England, coming appositely to a period of in-

[99] *Ibid.*, VIII, iii, 64–66; Butler, III, 247.
[100] *Ibid.*, VIII, iii, 70; Butler, III, 251.
[101] *Ibid.* [102] *Ibid.*, VIII, iii, 71; Butler, III, 251.

tensive effort by the new philosophy to rationalize all mental phenomena, did much to forward interest in the causes of delight in art. Readers of the translations by Boileau and others found a clear statement that the desired effect in poetry was to transport the mind of the reader,[103] that images add greatly to the power of writing and speaking — because they make you think you see what is described — that the specific design of the poetical image is enthralment, that poetry seeks in general to stir the passions and the emotions.[104] They found, further, some attempt at defining aesthetic transport: "For, as if instinctively, our soul is uplifted by the true sublime; it takes a proud flight, and is filled with joy and vaunting, as though it had itself produced what it has heard." [105] There, too, were enumerations of some of the elements that produced effects of the sublime — as grandeur in nature, evidence of greatness of soul in an author, a selection and combination of passions into a single whole, harmonious arrangement in poetry. There, likewise, was some attempt at explaining why certain things please: startling images appeal because, "By a sort of natural law, . . . we always attend to what possesses superior force"; [106] grandeur moves us because "not even the entire universe suffices for the thought and contemplation within the reach of the human mind, but our imaginations often pass beyond the bounds of space"; [107] a harmonious structure of language pleases because it appeals to a harmony implanted by nature in the soul of man, calling forth "manifold shapes of words, thoughts, deeds, beauty, melody, . . . born at our birth and growing with our growth." [108]

These ideas were full of implication, and challenge. They raised questions which demanded answer. The steady insistence by Longinus on the integrity of emotional effect in art, his unquestioned emphasis on the part played by imagery in arousing emotion, and his frequent intimation of relationship between the mind and poetry were to exert a great influence

---

[103] Longinus, *op. cit.*, I, 4; Roberts, p. 43.
[104] *Ibid.*, XV, 4; Roberts, p. 85.   [105] *Ibid.*, VII, 2; Roberts, p. 55.
[106] *Ibid.*, XV, 11; Roberts, p. 91.   [107] *Ibid.*, XXXV, 3; Roberts, p. 135.
[108] *Ibid.*, XXXIX, 3; Roberts, p. 143.

in directing the inquiries of thoughtful critics toward problems of poetic appeal.

Yet Longinus, for all his interest in effects, fails to come to real grips with the subject that was to be of absorbing interest to some of the psychological critics of the eighteenth century and to all the great critics of the Romantic period: namely, the constitution of mind that explains aesthetic experience and the nature of the mental activities that characterize artistic creation and aesthetic response. He suggests and implies and generalizes, but does not explore. He refers continually to the passions, and clearly links them with aesthetic effect; yet he does not attempt to explain or define them, which is to say that, unlike Hobbes, he failed to give direct attention to an analysis of the affective side of our nature in its fundamental relation to pleasure in art and to the contribution made by our minds in the experience of beauty. Emphasis in Longinus is still upon the object in art rather than upon the creating and responsive subject.

St. Augustine (A.D. 354–430) repudiates Sophistic doctrines of display for pleasure, but accepts the Ciceronian idea that art should teach, delight, and move.[109] As a preacher his emphasis is on moving: "it was not, however, when I heard their applause but when I saw their tears, that I thought I had produced an effect."[110] As a student of Aristotle, however, he continually shows himself interested in mental processes related to pleasure and pain. It remained for St. Thomas Aquinas to carry such investigation to its height in medieval times. Indeed, if we except Aristotle and Longinus, Aquinas probably went further into the psychological problems of artistic appeal than any other writer preceding Hobbes. His theory has of late received able interpretation at the hands of such writers as Maritain,[111] Callahan,[112] and Gilby.[113] To St.

[109] De Doctrina Christiana, IV, xvii, 34; tr. by J. F. Shaw, in The Works of Aurelius Augustine, ed. by Marcus Dods (Edinburgh, 1872–78), IX, 145.

[110] Ibid., IV, xxiv, 53; Dods, IX, 163.

[111] Jacques Maritain, Art and Scholasticism, with Other Essays, tr. by J. F. Scanlan (New York, 1935).

[112] Leonard Callahan, A Theory of Aesthetic according to the Principles of St. Thomas Aquinas (Washington, 1927).

[113] Thomas Gilby, Poetic Experience (New York, 1935).

Thomas the experience of beauty is a perception of the inner splendor of an object.[114] It is neither a strictly sensuous nor a strictly rational experience. In it the life of the sense is perfected by being suffused by mind: "sense knowledge is transfigured by the reason without losing its warmth." [115] This is made possible by a sort of rational quality in sense itself: "beauty consists in due proportion; for the senses are satisfied in things duly proportioned, as in what is after their own kind because sense, too, is a kind of reason; and so is every cognoscitive faculty." [116] Through aesthetic perception real substance is known: "the mind seizes and possesses a substance in a moving and intimate experience." [117] This substance is the splendor or radiance of form glittering in the beautiful object, perceived, as Maritain interprets St. Thomas, "by means of the intuition of the senses, itself confronted with a glittering intelligibility" which cannot be detached from the senses in intellectual knowledge in the form of a concept. Thus aesthetic perception is a sort of union of mind and sense, which may be described as "intellectualized sense." It cannot be broken down into its components, for the instant definite concepts appear aesthetic joy vanishes; yet the intellectual element is plainly evident in a feeling of "intellectual fullness through which we seem to be swollen with a superior knowledge of the object contemplated." [118]

Through such experience the mind finds repose in the satisfaction of its longings. "The beautiful is the same as the good, and they differ in aspect only. For since good is what all seek, the notion of good is that which calms the desire; while the notion of the beautiful is that which calms the desire, by being seen or known." [119] The man who voiced such ideas had obviously advanced far in the formulation of a psychology of response to beauty.

[114] Maritain, op. cit., pp. 24–25.
[115] Gilby, op. cit., p. 95.
[116] Sum. Theol. (as cited in note 38), Part I, First Number, Q. 5, A. 4, p. 59.
[117] Gilby, op. cit., p. 106.
[118] Maritain, op. cit., pp. 162–163.
[119] Sum. Theol., Part II (First Part), First Number, Q. 27, A. 1, p. 320.

VI

On the question of poetic effects Italian criticism of the Renaissance had in general little to contribute. The prevailing insistence upon a moral end left other considerations at best a secondary place. Critics of the period taught quite uniformly that poetry should delight and instruct, but, ordinarily, pleasure was advocated as an avenue to more effective instruction. Thus we find Varchi saying that the end of poetry is "to remove men from vices, and to lift them to virtue, in order that they may seek their perfection and blessedness." [120] And Castelvetro finds an "oblique pleasure" in tragedy, which consists of our satisfaction in recognizing the fulfilment of our sense of justice. [121] Such statements rather fairly represent a general conviction that much of our delight in epic and tragedy depends on seeing good rewarded and evil punished.

Somewhat related to this theory was the idea that poetry should create admiration. Minturno, in case, holding that poetry should delight and instruct through moving certain passions, maintained that, specifically, it attains its end of instruction through representing the deeds of great men in such a way as to excite admiration. [122] This is a conception that, in varied form, was to gain wide sway in neoclassic thought. Another idea which, like Minturno's, had something of a psychological cast was that of variety as a means to pleasure. Muzio, for example, held that, since every phase of life and art is presented in a great poem, the pleasurable is attained through variety. [123] And Torquato Tasso defends ro-

---

[120] *Opere di Benedetto Varchi ora per la prima volta raccolte con un discorsi di A. Racheli intorno alla filologia del secolo XVI e alla vita e agli scritti dell'autore* (Trieste, 1858), II, 724–B. The translation is by T. Hart in *The Idea of Poetic Justice*, an unpublished thesis, University of Michigan, 1940.

[121] *Poetica d'Aristotile vulgarizzata et sposta per Lodovico Castelvetro* (Basilea, 1576), p. 29. It should be said in fairness to Castelvetro that, perhaps more definitely than any other critic of his age, he taught that poetry should delight. He even maintained that poetry is written to please not the learned aesthete, but the "uncultivated multitude and the common people" (*ibid.*).

[122] *De Poeta* (1559), p. 102; J. E. Spingarn, *A History of Literary Criticism in the Renaissance* (New York, 1925), p. 52.

[123] *Arte poetica* (1555); Spingarn, *op. cit.*, p. 50.

mantic poems on the ground that they contain delightsome variety: "Variety itself may be pleasing, for even a variety of disagreeable things may possibly please." [124]   Even in such cases, however, there is little genuine analysis of the nature and sources of the effects of art, and less that goes beyond recurrence to earlier ideas.

A nearer approach to psychological method is to be found in Campanella's analysis of the element of *utile* in art.   As we have seen, Campanella is in aesthetics primarily naturalistic and utilitarian.[125]   To define the beautiful he finds it necessary to define the good.   The good is that which contributes to the conservation of man, in himself, in his issue, in the memory of posterity, in God.   The good procures to man pleasure — which is the consciousness of preservation — while pain which is caused by evil is the consciousness of destruction.   The beautiful differs from other sorts of pleasure in that it is the external appearance of good, a sign of the good in the thing perceived.   A thing is beautiful because the external form reveals the strength, the health, the hidden wisdom of vital spirits which animate the body, and is able to employ harmoniously each member to its own proper usage.[126]   A strong and blooming woman is judged beautiful because she presents to a high degree all the signs which promise long life and which reveal her as eminently capable of nourishing and conserving the seed which is entrusted to her and of procuring the joys of love.   But man is more beautiful than woman because he presents more numerous marks of strength and wisdom and is more beloved in that he does not love himself.[127]

Aesthetic pleasure consists chiefly in admiration.   The lover enjoys the good, he admires the beautiful.   This distinguishes the beautiful from other *good*.   If one considers in place of the external signs the immediate and direct use of an object the aesthetic character is lost.   It is now no longer

---

[124] *Discorsi dell'arte poetica* (1587); Spingarn, *op. cit.*, p. 119.   Scaliger also may be mentioned here for his recognition of variety and novelty.   Aeschylus, he charges, had "very little variety of plot, and little, if any, novelty; he showed simply one manner, tenor, and treatment" (*op. cit.*, III, 97; Padelford, p. 62).

[125] See p. 41.

[126] Blanchet, *op. cit.*, p. 256.   [127] *Ibid.*, pp. 256–257.

beautiful, but *good* or *agreeable*. Outside the ear a melody is called beautiful; within the ear it is called sweet ("soft"). One calls that beautiful which is known by the senses, as hearing or sight, which communicate at a distance with their object or remain distinct as the intelligence and the internal sense.

The beautiful in art is identified by Campanella with the beautiful in nature. All the technique of art has for its purpose the imitation of nature, as nature has for its end the imitation of God. Finally, the aesthetic sentiment is relative to the physical constitution of the individual. Men prefer grave or light melodies, rugged or soft ones, according as their vital spirits are gross or tenuous, robust or weak.[128]

A sketch of Renaissance critical thought with reference to poetic effect would be incomplete indeed without mention of the Spanish philosopher and litterateur Baltasar Gracián.[129] The Spanish are an outspoken race. There is a forthright, positive quality about their aesthetics that is refreshment to the spirit. Lope de Vega's sly remark that when he wrote his plays he locked up the men of rules with six keys is a case in point. Huarte's definite ascription of the arts to the imagination is another. Gracián's contribution to the tradition is a specific reference of inventive works to genius (*ingegno*), a frank avowal of the rights of emotional response, and a consistent emphasis on taste as a valid criterion in life and, by implication, art.

Gracián is a lover of sensuous beauty, unashamedly enthusiastic about the wonders of the universe and the perfection of art. In *El Criticon* Andrenio admires the earth, the sea, everything together and everything separately.[130] And he is encouraged to continue to admire, for "if admiration is the child of ignorance, it has its recompense in that it is the mother

---

[128] *Ibid.*, p. 259.

[129] Baltasar Gracián y Morales was born in 1601, or 1604, at Belmonte, near Calatayud, and died in 1658. The probable extent of his influence may be judged from the fact that fully half of his works were published outside Spain, chiefly in the Lowlands, and that he was widely and almost immediately translated into many languages — French, English, Dutch, Italian, and German.

[130] *L'Homme d'etrompé, ou le Criticon de Baltazar Gracián*, traduit de l'Espagnol en François (Paris, 1696), p. 18. This work is hereafter cited as *El Criticon*.

of pleasure." [131]   "In the business of giving joy, and of teaching," writes Gracián, "this is a great rule to observe, to proceed
always by feeding their wonder . . . ." [132]   "One cannot admire too much," [133] says Critile, at the close of a rhapsodic
account of a scene of natural beauty.[134] Anticipating Hobbes
and Addison, Gracián regards novelty as one of the chief
causes of aesthetic pleasure.   "That which raises admiration
is the new, in nature as well as art," [135] he declares; and again,
"The new gives joy, and when of a happy turn it puts a double
halo upon the good." [136]   What Gracián says of emotional
effect and novelty in relation to nature may be applied to art.
For, with him, art is only nature realized and perfected by man:

> Art is the fulfilment of nature and as it were its second Creator; it
> completes it, embellishes it, sometimes even surpasses it . . . it corrects all
> that is defective, and gives it a perfection which it does not in itself pos-
> sess. . . . God gave man the empire of the world, then with the aid of
> art he polished it . . . . Art unites itself with Nature, produces every day
> new miracles.[137]

---

[131] *El Criticon*, p. 28.
[132] *Oráculo Manual y arte de prudencia, sacada de los aforismos* . . . (Madrid, 1653),
tr., under the title *A Truthtelling Manual and the Art of Worldly Wisdom*, by Martin
Fischer (Lancaster, Pennsylvania, 1934), No. 212, p. 195.
[133] *El Criticon*, p. 30.
[134] "I found myself all at once, in this center of different beauties, which had
never struck my senses, nor my imagination; . . . I considered all these things
with joy, all seemed perfect to me, all was new to me; I had the same attention
which I had had on the night before while looking at the sky, and even more, the
sky had engaged only my eyes, but *here* all my senses were busy, and still they did
not suffice; I should have liked to have a hundred eyes and a hundred hands, to
satisfy all at once the curiosity of my soul; my spirit was all transported, to see so
large a number of creatures so different in propriety, in nature, in form, in color,
in effects, and in movement; I picked a rose; and contemplating its beauty, I
smelled its good fragrance, I could not keep myself from looking at it nor from
admiring it, I put forth my other hand to take a fruit, my taste contended for the
pleasure with my eyes, and I found that the fruits carried it on the flowers.   In
short, I was so agreeably embarrassed by all these things, that I had trouble leaving
one of them to take another, so much pleasure they gave me all together" (*ibid.*,
pp. 29–30).
[135] *Ibid.*, p. 28. "But what I admired more was to see such a great number
of things, and such a great difference among them, to see so much *plurality* with
so much *singularity*, so that one can not rest his mind in one single leaf of a tree, in
one single blade of grass, nor in one single feather of a bird . . ." (*ibid.*, p. 30).
[136] *Oráculo Manual*, No. 283, p. 255.   [137] *El Criticon*, pp. 154–155.

Gracián celebrates good taste. "Three things make the superman: a fertile mind, a deep understanding, and a cultivated taste." [138] Basically taste is to Gracián a sort of tact for doing the right thing [139] and for making wise choices and judgments without the intervention of reason. His original application is to the conduct of a courtier, but the extension to nature and art is an easy and natural step, as Borinski has suggested.[140] Taste in such things is not only a matter of immediate judgment; it may also have application to heightened awareness, or sensitivity. Taste may be improved and elevated: "Know how to refresh your spirit through nature and through art," admonishes Gracián; "once in every seven years we are made over. Let it mark an elevation and realization of better taste." [141] Gracián in several places mentions novelty and taste together. The novel is congenial to taste, and appears

---

[138] *Oráculo Manual*, No. 298, p. 265.

[139] As Croce points out, remarking that when this "laconic moralist . . . spoke of a 'man of taste,' [he] meant to describe what we call today 'a man of tact' in the conduct of life" (*Aesthetic as Science of Expression and General Linguistic*, tr. from the Italian by Douglas Ainslie [London, 1929], p. 266).

[140] Karl Borinski, *Baltasar Gracián und die Hoflitteratur in Deutschland* (Halle, 1894), pp. 41 ff. Gracián's interest in literature and the fine arts is greater than Borinski, and especially Croce, would make out, and he habitually relates his criteria for these arts to the demands of taste. Thus he stresses the importance of "manner" in all productions of wit. It is manner, he says, that will often "rescue a piece of literature from neglect and obscurity" and make it acceptable to the "present, prevailing taste"; and he lays it down as a maxim in literature that "the most ingenious piece will not be exquisitely pleasing to the taste, if it be not season'd and dish'd up with an agreeable manner" (*The Compleat Gentleman*, tr. by T. Saldkeld [London, 1730], pp. 209, 211). A champion of Latin authors, Gracián expresses his admiration for "the natural Concatenation and Coherence of their Thoughts and Sentiments, their clear resplendent Reason, their sound and strong Judgment, their fruitful and regular Imagination." All is so ordered as "to touch and affect the heart with such Dispositions and Impressions as the Author intended . . . ." "There you see the solid, the sublime, the beautiful, the bright, and the true fine Genius, the just indisputable taste, the *je ne sçay quoy*, the inexpressible, peculiar Charm in every Kind of Writing, that exact point of Perfection which leaves nothing to be wished for, which imposes Silence upon all the Zoilus's and Aristarchus's, all the carping Censors and Criticks in the World . . ." (*ibid.*, p. 164). Such statements show both Huarte's interest in literature and his extension of the principle of taste beyond its application to the conduct of heroes and gentlemen. For further remarks on the *je ne sais quoi* see *The Heroe of Lorenzo*, tr. by Sir John Skeffington (London, 1652), Chap. XIII, or the same chapter in the translation of this book by "a Gentleman of Oxford" (London, 1726).

[141] *Oráculo Manual*, No. 276, p. 248.

to exert a healthful influence on this faculty. People have "an itch for the unusual," says Gracián, because it is "more pleasing, alike to the taste and to the intelligence." [142] In another place he writes, "The novel stands well everywhere because it is different, and refreshing to the taste." [143]

In all this Gracián is striking a quite different key from the dominant tone of didacticism in Renaissance criticism. Man is supposed to enjoy beauty in nature and art, to respond with full native instinct to that which is lovely and grand and new, without too much regard to instructional value. Art and nature have an ameliorating effect it is true: "Refresh then your spirit with Nature and Art." But it is an effect of elevating and renewing the soul through joy, quite independent of moral teaching. And the instrument of appraising this beauty is not reason nor rule, but taste, in immediate, direct apprehension of what is good. Gracián is not, perhaps, deeply psychological; he does, however, find in novelty one prevailing cause of delight, and in his general approach he clears the way for later more profound psychological investigations in aesthetic effects.

VII

Although English Renaissance critics were largely dependent upon preceding Continental theory, they showed tendencies toward productive reflection upon the imagination and aesthetic effects. Thus Puttenham ascribes a high place to the "phantasticall part of man." Harking back to Quintilian and to medieval psychology, he distinguishes between the disordered phantastical and the healthful and good, which is to be designated as *"euphantasioti."* [144] In the latter, imagination combines with "sound and true judgment" in inventive processes which account not only for great poetry but for all other constructive arts of civilization: all notable statecraft, all law and order and social institutions, all art and architecture and mechanical contrivance whatsoever; indeed all knowledge of

---

[142] *Oráculo Manual*, No. 150, p. 141.   [143] *Ibid.*, No. 269, p. 242.
[144] See G. Gregory Smith, *Elizabethan Critical Essays* (Oxford, 1904), II, 410, for the Quintilian reference. The passage is quoted in full on page 52.

the human spirit, which, it is perhaps not too much to say, includes all philosophy.

The passage in which Puttenham expresses these ideas is of such importance as to merit quotation *in extenso:*

For as the euill and vicious disposition of the braine hinders the sounde iudgement and discourse of man with busie & disordered phantasies, for which cause the Greekes call him φανταστικός, so is that part, being well affected, not onely nothing disorderly or confused with any monstrous imaginations or conceits, but very formall, and in his much multiformitie *vniforme*, that is well proportioned, and so passing cleare, that by it, as by a glasse or mirrour, are represented vnto the soule all maner of bewtifull visions, whereby the inuentiue parte of the mynde is so much holpen as with out it no man could deuise any new or rare thing: and where it is not excellent in his kind, there could be no politique Captaine, nor any witty enginer or cunning artificer, nor yet any law maker or counsellor of deepe discourse, yea, the Prince of Philosophers stickes not to say *animam non intelligere absque phantasmate;* which text to another purpose *Alexander Aphrodis[i]ens[is]* well noteth, as learned men know. And this phantasie may be resembled to a glasse, as hath bene sayd, whereof there be many tempers and manner of makinges, as the *perspectiues* doe acknowledge, for some be false glasses and shew thinges otherwise than they be in deede, and others right as they be in deede, neither fairer nor fouler, nor greater nor smaller. There be againe of these glasses that shew things exceeding faire and comely; others that shew figures very monstrous & illfavored. Euen so is the phantasticall part of man (if it be not disordered) a representer of the best, most comely, and bewtifull images or apparances of things to the soule and according to their very truth. If otherwise, then doth it breede *Chimeres* & monsters in mans imaginations, & not onely in his imaginations, but also in all his ordinarie actions and life which ensues. Wherefore such persons as be illuminated with the brightest irradiations of knowledge and of the veritie and due proportion of things, they are called by the learned men not *phantastici* but *euphantasioti*, and of this sorte of phantasie are all good Poets, notable Captaines strategmatique, all cunning artificers and enginers, all Legislators, Polititiens, & Counsellors of estate, in whose exercises the inuentiue part is most employed, and is to the sound and true judgement of man most needful. This diuersitie in the termes perchance euery man hath not noted, & thus much be said in defence of the Poets honour, to the end no noble and generous minde be discomforted in the studie thereof . . . .[145]

---

[145] *The Arte of English Poesie* (1589), Chap. VIII, in Smith, *op. cit.*, II, 19–20. Though Puttenham's book was not published until 1589, there is evidence that it was begun much earlier, possibly by 1565. See *The Arte of English Poesie*, ed. by Gladys Doidge Willcock and Alice Walker (Cambridge, 1936), pp. xliv–liii.

Dr. C. M. Dowlin has shown a number of parallels between Puttenham's ideas in this passage and subsequent statements by Hobbes; [146] of these none are more important than those which express the fundamental similarity in the views of the two men with respect to the place of the good imagination in poetry and in life, and the proper relationship of the judgment to the imagination. Puttenham here clearly precedes Hobbes in announcing a theory that is to figure large in later aesthetics. His service is important not only for this priority but for the decisive character of his defense of the imaginative process. Except in Huarte and Hobbes, there is in all pre-Romantic criticism no finer justification of the imagination as a constructive faculty nor a more eloquent plea for its dignity and integrity.

Both Sir Philip Sidney and Francis Bacon contributed to the psychology of effect. Sidney's main effort in his *Apology* is to restate the basic theories of current neoclassic criticism, with emphasis on the function of poetry to move, to delight, and to teach. He accepts the prevailing dicta on form, decorum, and so forth, and reiterates and enlarges upon the principle of ideal imitation. In all this he is saying little that is new. In incidental remark, however, he presents suggestions for a type of critical approach quite out of harmony with his traditional, formalistic criteria. Sidney had a haphazard mind. It was a learned mind stored with gleanings from wide study in varied fields, but it was not selective nor methodical; it was eager and receptive, but it was young; it knew little of the processes of synthesis. It was, nevertheless, a very poetical mind, and was a familiar to poetic experiences. It is when Sidney talks half off his guard, and upon matters incidental to his main issue, that he is most original. At such times he is all but prophetic of an order in criticism of which England knew little before the Romantic period, and of which France had only glimpses a century after Sidney in Du Bos and his school.

Sidney shows, in spite of an inclination to formalistic cant,

---

[146] Cornell March Dowlin, *Sir William Davenant's Gondibert, Its Preface, and Hobbes's Answer* (Philadelphia, 1934), pp. 52 ff.

that he knows poetry as an experience. In its simplest form this experience is emotional excitation, as when the old ballad moves his heart "like a trumpet"; but it can also be something more complex, a mode of apprehension. "This," he says, writing of the power of poetry to make us perceive, "doth the Comedy handle so in our private and domestical matters, as with hearing it we get as it were an *experience*, what is to be looked for of a niggardly Demea, of a crafty Davus, of a flattering Gnatho, of a vainglorious Thraso." [147] As to the nature and result of this experience Sidney leaves us quite clear. The poet is superior to the philosopher for the reason that, where the philosopher is abstract, the poet presents a "perfect picture": "A perfect picture I say, for he yieldeth to the powers of the mind an image of that whereof the philosopher bestoweth but a wordish description: which doth neither strike, pierce, nor possess the sight of the soul so much as that other doth."

To strike, pierce, and possess the sight of the soul: this is the peculiar function of poetry. Thus poetry not only moves but in moving it leads to vivid apprehensions. What one has merely known about through history or philosophy he comes to *realize* through poetry. In the presence of objects of art a man straightway grows to a "judicial comprehending of them"; matters presented however well "with infallible grounds of wisdom" are apt to "lie dark before the imaginative and judging power, if they be not illuminated or figured forth by the speaking picture of Poesy." Sidney is talking here of aesthetic as opposed to non-aesthetic perception. And he is assigning to aesthetic perception the supreme quality of illumination. Ordinary perception is a fact; aesthetic perception is an experience of reality: "let but Sophocles bring you Ajax on a stage, killing and whipping sheep and oxen, thinking them the army of Greeks, with their chieftains Agamemnon and Menelaus, and tell me if you have not a more familiar insight into anger than finding in the Schoolman his genus

---

[147] The citations from Sir Philip Sidney are all from *An Apology for Poetry*, in *English Critical Essays (Sixteenth, Seventeenth, and Eighteenth Centuries)*, ed. by Edmund D. Jones (London, 1922).

and difference." This is an advance over Horace and Minturno. There is a distinction between poetry as the pleasant mother of science and philosophy and civilization, between poetry as a means to delightful instruction, and poetry which is all this but in addition illuminates life by striking, piercing, and possessing the soul, leading to the kind of insight possible through an expanded awareness of reality.

To Sidney poetry is a delightful and efficient teacher. By no one before his time or since has that idea been more happily phrased:

> Now therein of all sciences (I speak still of human, and according to the humane conceits) is our poet the monarch. For he doth not only show the way, but giveth so sweet a prospect into the way, as will entice any man to enter into it. Nay, he doth, as if your journey should lie through a fair vineyard, at the first give you a cluster of grapes, that, full of that taste, you may long to pass further. He beginneth not with obscure definitions, which must blur the margent with interpretations, and load the memory with doubtfulness; but he cometh to you with words set in delightful proportion, either accompanied with, or prepared for, the well enchanting skill of music; and with a tale forsooth he cometh unto you, with a tale which holdeth children from play, and old men from the chimney corner.

This was no new conception; if Sidney added anything to it at all it was owing to his own clear insight into the fact that much of the value of poetry as a teacher lies in the fact that it disposes one well toward knowledge; and "to be moved to do that which we know, or to be moved with desire to know, *Hoc opus, hic labor est.*"

But when Sidney passed from the well-trodden ground of what poetry can do in its general method of operation into the realm of more particular phases of the psychology of poetic experience he was getting out of the beaten track of Renaissance criticism, was anticipating later attitudes which were to emphasize both what happens in the mind of the poet when and before he writes and what goes on in the mind of the reader or auditor when he responds to a work of art. Sidney probably had little idea of the importance of what he was saying. In the midst of trying to be a critic in the current neoclassic mode, with the obvious intention of placing before his readers the learned point of view, he simply let himself, caught off guard, sometimes talk as a poet, naïvely confessing his own bona fide experiences in the presence of works of art.

Bacon's contribution is more definite and extensive. He specifically assigns poetry to the imagination, and in so doing restates the theory of ideal imitation in such a way as to make it almost new. His general theory that art works by chance and not by reason and that the imagination, by virtue of which art exists, is tied to no laws, is directly hostile to a criticism by "rules." He defends rhetoric against Plato and all comers on the ground that through its legitimate imaginative appeal it may in decisive moments of life become an effective aid to reason. In general, he offers a valuable exposition of the working of the mind in creating poetry and in responding to it, which was to be of considerable influence in later writers.

In presenting his theory of ideal imitation Bacon is making a clear advance over Scaliger and other neoclassicists, who had described the selective process through which a poet builds ideal creations. Bacon reverses the shield, showing what it is in poetry that pleases the mind of man and why it pleases. By creating an ideal life, not only more perfect than the world of humdrum reality but more strange and varied and thrilling, the poet refreshes the mind and exalts the spirit. Poetry thus supplies a great human need; for man is so constituted, Bacon says in effect, that he finds his greatest pleasure in participating in and contemplating an existence of such completeness and diversity and beautiful order as can be attained only in the imagination. The passage in question can scarcely be too much quoted; it is a philosophy of aesthetics in little. I give here the revised version, too seldom reprinted, as translated from the *De Augmentis* by Joseph Devey:

Poetry is a kind of learning generally confined to the measure of words, but otherwise extremely licentious, and truly belonging to the imagination, which, being unrestrained by laws, may make what unnatural mixtures and separations it pleases. It is taken in two senses, or with respect to words and matter. The first is but a character of style and a certain form of speech not relating to the subject, for a true narration may be delivered in verse and a feigned one in prose; but the second is a capital part of learning, and no other than feigned history. And here, as in our divisions, we endeavour to find and trace the true sources of learning, and this frequently without giving way to custom or the established order, — we shall take no particular notice of satire, elegy, epigram, ode, etc., but turn them over to philosophy and the arts of speech, and under the name of poetry treat nothing more than imaginary history.[148]

The justest division of poetry, except what it shares in common with history (which has its feigned chronicles, feigned lives, and feigned relations), is, — 1. Into narrative; 2. Dramatic; and, 3. Allegorical. Narrative poetry is such an exact imitation of history as to deceive, did it not often carry things beyond probability. Dramatic poetry is a kind of visible history, giving the images of things as if they were present, whilst history represents them as past. But allegorical poetry is history with its type, which represents intellectual things to the senses.

Narrative poetry, otherwise called heroic poetry, seems, with regard to its matter, not the versification, raised upon a noble foundation, as having a principal regard to the dignity of human nature. For as the active world is inferior to the rational soul, so poetry gives that to mankind which history denies, and in some measure satisfies the mind with shadows when it cannot enjoy the substance. For, upon a narrow inspection, poetry strongly shows that a greater grandeur of things, a more perfect order, and a more beautiful variety is pleasing to the mind than can anywhere be found in nature after the fall. So that, as the actions and events, which are the subjects of true history, have not that grandeur which satisfies the mind, poetry steps in and feigns more heroical actions.

---

[148] The almost parallel passage in Book II of the English version of 1705 is too well known to need quotation here. There is, in addition, a third version in the first chapter of *Descriptio Globi Intellectualis*, intended as a part of the *Instauratio Magna*, but later rejected (see *The Works of Francis Bacon*, coll. and ed. by James Spedding, Robert Leslie Ellis, and Douglas Denon Heath [New York, 1869], X, 401 ff.): "I adopt that division of human learning which corresponds to the three faculties of the understanding. Its parts therefore are three; History, Poesy, and Philosophy. History is referred to the Memory; Poesy to the Imagination; Philosophy to the Reason." Two of the most interesting variations from the other accounts have to do with poetry as a play of the mind and with the psychological bases of poetry and reason. "For as all knowledge is the exercise and work of the mind," Bacon writes, "so poesy may be regarded as its sport." He then goes on to present a strictly sensational explanation of the origin of intellectual impressions: images are received by sense and fixed in the memory, after which the mind, through perceptions of likeness and difference, "recalls and reviews them, and . . . compounds and divides the parts, of which they consist." If the division and composition are arbitrary, according to the pleasure of the mind, the result is a work of the imagination; but if it is according to "the evidence of things . . . this is the office of reason." It is possible that one cause for Bacon's rejection of this passage was its expression of a more definite psychology than he was willing to commit himself to. Elsewhere he is less specific. As it stands, his statement of general mental processes contains striking similarities to Hobbes's theory.

And as real history gives us not the success of things according to the deserts of virtue and vice, poetry corrects it, and presents us with the fates and fortunes of persons rewarded or punished according to merit. And as real history disgusts us with a familiar and constant similitude of things, poetry relieves us by unexpected turns and changes, and thus not only delights, but inculcates morality and nobleness of soul. Whence it may be justly esteemed of a Divine nature, as it raises the mind, by accommodating the images of things to our desires, and not, like history and reason, subjecting the mind to things. And by these its charms, and congruity to the mind, with the assistance also of music, which conveys it the sweeter, it makes its own way, so as to have been in high esteem in the most ignorant ages, and among the most barbarous people, whilst other kinds of learning were utterly excluded.[149]

Such an approach to poetry is obviously in fundamental opposition to the spirit of French and English neoclassicism, which tended to seek out qualities in a given work or genre and test its success by its relative conformity to prescribed formulae. Bacon's frame of reference for poetry is the human mind itself: in its shaping, creative powers, in its aspirations and desires, in the means by which it is pleased and ennobled and through which it seeks and finds satisfaction of its loftiest impulses. His interest in the psychological bases for poetry, in its fundamental origins, and in the quality of its effects sets him apart from the whole race of traditionalists.

His theory is, indeed, strongly colored by the current demand for moral teaching in art. This appears particularly in paragraphs on dramatic and allegorical poetry, which follow the passage I have quoted. Dramatic poetry would be of excellent use if it were sound and regulated, Bacon writes. Though corrupted in modern times the action of the theatre was carefully watched by the ancients, "that it might improve mankind in virtue." Allegory, Bacon says explicitly, excels all other kinds of poetry, "and appears a solemn sacred thing, which religion itself generally makes use of, to preserve an intercourse between divine and human things." [150] Even here, however, in discussing the comparative merits of drama and

[149] *On the Dignity and Advancement of Learning*, in *The Physical and Metaphysical Works of Lord Bacon*, ed. by Joseph Devey (Bohn ed., London, 1872), II, xiii, pp. 96 ff.

[150] *Ibid.*, pp. 97–98.

allegory, Bacon makes penetrating comments on the nature
of appeal in poetry. Of drama, as a source of good, anticipating in a single pregnant statement much that has since been
said on crowd psychology, he says: "and indeed many wise
men and great philosophers have thought it to the mind as
the bow to the fiddle; and certain it is, though a great secret in nature, that the minds of men in company are more
open to affections and impressions than when alone." [151] The
unique function of allegory, he points out, has ever been to
soften and make clear through imaginative presentation what
the mind could receive hardly if at all in the form of naked
unadorned propositions: "For when the discoveries and conclusions of reason, though now common, were new, and first
known, the human capacity could scarce admit them in their
subtile state, or till they were brought nearer to sense, by such
kind of imagery and examples; whence ancient times are
full of their fables, their allegories, and their similes." [152] The
fables of the ancients are not to be despised and left only to
children and grammarians. They contain things believed and
received long before they were spoken and "appear like a soft
whisper from the traditions of more ancient nations, conveyed
through the flutes of the Grecians." [153] One must go far to
find another so exquisitely poetic expression of the suggestive
quality and remote beauty of Greek mythology.

It is likewise in its capacity for sensuous imaginative appeal
that rhetoric commends itself to Bacon. Rhetoric may be
abused, as logic may teach sophistry, but it has, nevertheless,
a legitimate function. Its true office is not to flatter and mislead, as Plato suggests, but to "apply and recommend the
dictates of reason to the imagination, in order to excite the
affections and will"; its method is to "fill the imagination with
such observations and images as may assist reason." For
rhetoric, "by plainly painting virtue and goodness, renders
them, as it were, conspicuous; for as they cannot be seen by
the corporeal eye, the next degree is to have them set before
us as lively as possible by the ornament of words and the

151 On the . . . Advancement of Learning (Bohn ed.), II, xiii, p. 97.
152 Ibid., II, xiii, p. 98.   153 Ibid.

strength of imagination." [154]   Rhetoric owes its force to its employment of the concrete, it puts imagery ("emblems") into the service of reason: "emblems bring down intellectual to sensible things; for what is sensible always strikes the memory stronger, and sooner impresses itself than what is intellectual." [155]   Rhetoric thus becomes what De Quincey, two centuries later, was to call "literature of power," with the special function of moving the affections and will through imaginative presentation. "Incident unto this," Bacon remarks, in a discussion of "fascination" and "ceremonies," "is the inquiry how to raise and fortify the imagination: for if the imagination fortified have power, then it is material to know how to fortify and exalt it." [156]   But, fortified or not, the imagination, as Bacon conceives its operations in rhetoric or poetry, has power; this it is which distinguishes fable and eloquence alike from plain-speaking, unadorned literature of reason and fact, and it is this which gives to both allegory and rhetoric their extraordinary potency as servants of truth and reason.

In his more direct definitions of the imagination Bacon is hardly consistent. He sometimes makes it a separate faculty, sometimes only an instrument to the other faculties. In discussing creations of the mind he appears to think of it as an independent faculty. Thus he generally refers the inventive arts, including poetry, to the imagination. The famous oft-quoted division of learning into history, poetry, and philosophy in the *Advancement of Learning* (in both the English and Latin versions, particularly in the rejected passage) places the imagination, the special faculty of poetry, on a par with the two

---

[154] *Ibid.*, VI, iii, pp. 234–235. "Hence we conclude," Bacon continues, "that rhetoric can no more be accused of colouring the worst part, than logic of teaching sophistry. For we know that the doctrines of contraries are the same, though their use be opposite; and logic does not only differ from rhetoric, according to the vulgar notion, as the first is like the hand clenched, and the other like the hand open; but much more in this, that logic considers reason in its natural state, and rhetoric as it stands in vulgar opinion; whence Aristotle prudently places rhetoric between logic and ethics, along with politics, as partaking of them both" (*ibid.*, p. 236).

[155] *Ibid.*, V, v, p. 213.

[156] *Of the Advancement of Learning*, ed. by William Aldis Wright (Oxford, 1920), II, xi, p. 146.

other special faculties of memory and reason delegated respectively to history and philosophy. It is here assigned the
unique function of creating ideality and such embellishments
as will charm and win the reader. In a later section, however,
the imagination is represented chiefly as a "messenger," working on the one hand between sense and the understanding,
on the other between the understanding and reason and the
will and affections. It is also credited with rather vague independent functions. The passage in which these ideas occur
is significant and will bear extended quotation:

> The knowledge which respecteth the faculties of the mind of man is
> of two kinds: the one respecting his understanding and reason, and the
> other his will, appetite, and affection; whereof the former produceth posi-
> tion or decree, the latter action or execution. It is true that the imagi-
> nation is an agent or *nuncius*, in both provinces, both the judicial and the
> ministerial. For sense sendeth over to imagination before reason have
> judged: and reason sendeth over to imagination before the decree can
> be acted. For imagination ever precedeth voluntary motion. Saving
> that this Janus of imagination hath differing faces: for the face towards
> reason hath the print of truth, but the face towards action hath the print
> of good; which nevertheless are faces,
>
> Quales decet esse sororum.
>
> Neither is the imagination simply and only a messenger; but is invested
> with, or at least wise usurpeth no small authority in itself, besides the
> duty of the message. For it was well said by Aristotle, *That the mind hath*
> *over the body that commandment, which the lord hath over a bondman; but that*
> *reason hath over the imagination that commandment which a magistrate hath over a*
> *free citizen;* who may come also to rule in his turn. For we see that, in
> matters of faith and religion, we raise our imagination above our reason;
> which is the cause why religion sought ever access to the mind by simili-
> tudes, types, parables, visions, dreams. And again, in all persuasions that
> are wrought by eloquence, and other impressions of like nature, which do
> paint and disguise the true appearance of things, the chief recommenda-
> tion unto reason is from the imagination. Nevertheless, because I find
> not any science that doth properly or fitly pertain to the imagination, I
> see no cause to alter the former division. For as for poesy, it is rather a
> pleasure or play of imagination, than a work or duty thereof. And if it
> be a work, we speak not now of such parts of learning as the imagina-
> tion produceth, but of such sciences as handle and consider of the imagi-
> nation. No more than we shall speak now of such knowledges as reason
> produceth (for that extendeth to all philosophy), but of such knowledges as
> do handle and inquire of the faculty of reason: so as poesy had his true

place. As for the power of the imagination in nature, and the manner of fortifying the same, we have mentioned it in the doctrine *De Anima*, whereunto most fitly it belongeth. And lastly, for imaginative or insinuative reason, which is the subject of rhetoric, we think it best to refer it to the arts of reason. So therefore we content ourselves with the former division, that human philosophy, which respecteth the faculties of the mind of man, hath two parts, rational and moral.[157]

Bacon's argument in this passage is ambiguous. We are told that imagination lies between sense and reason, that its office is to transmit impulses and impressions from sense to reason and to receive back from the reason ideas and impulses to be interpreted in action. As such it cannot be regarded as a separate faculty with functions of its own in the broad economy of learning, at least in those fields worthy the name of science. Rhetoric is to be assigned to "the arts of reason"; poetry, it is true, is by implication to be referred to the imagination, but only as a play, not a work. Even so, Bacon is constrained to make large concessions to the imagination, allowing it, in spite of his main thesis of its subservience, almost the dignity of unabridged autonomy. Though in most regions of learning it is but the handmaiden of reason and the will, it serves as a free citizen rather than as a bondman, and on occasion it takes over authority, and rules in its own right. Such is the case in matters of faith and religion, as well as in processes of persuasion in all forms of eloquence. Moreover, it appears to exercise no small power in the execution of voluntary motion, for Bacon's language permits the interpretation that, having received messages from the reason, the imagination assumes authority in directing action. Little as he may have intended to do so, Bacon seems to be implicitly admitting that imagination, in usurping a place of equal rank with reason, is a separate faculty.

The psychology of the passage is equivocal, and leaves Bacon in difficulties, hardly relieved by his explanation, in a remark which anticipates Kant's later famous dictum[158] that poetry is rather "a pleasure or play of the imagination than a

---

[157] *Of the Advancement of Learning* (Wright ed.), II, xi, pp. 147–148.
[158] *Kant's Critique of Judgment*, I, i, 21; tr. by J. H. Bernard (London, 1914), pp. 207–208.

work or duty thereof." For this at once plunges our philosopher into a further inconsistency: if allegorical poetry is a means of teaching truth pleasantly and effectively, as Bacon quite generally insists that it is, then it is truly a work, and not a play of the mind. The best way to account for this latter contradiction, perhaps, is to assume that in his thinking on the matter Bacon made a distinction between imaginative products that serve truth — as allegory, some drama, the inventive parts of rhetoric — and those which are created merely for the pleasure of the mind, in which the poet with no primary concern for teaching merely feigns events and characters rather than illustrates history and philosophy. That he at least entertained this idea appears from remarks on the relation of the fable to its moral — remarks which one regrets Le Bossu did not see and heed. These occur in the discussion of allegory following the definition of poetry and its kinds:

> Nevertheless, in many like encounters, I do rather think that the fable was first, and the exposition devised, than that the moral was first, and thereupon the fable framed. For I find it was an ancient vanity in Chrysippus, that troubled himself with great contention to fasten the assertions of the Stoics upon the fictions of the ancient poets; but yet that all the fables and fictions of the poets were but pleasure and not figure, I interpose no opinion. Surely of those poets which are now extant, even Homer himself (notwithstanding he was made a kind of scripture by the later schools of the Grecians), yet I should without any difficulty pronounce that his fables had no such inwardness in his own meaning. But what they might have upon a more original tradition, is not easy to affirm; for he was not the inventor of many of them.[159]

---

[159] *Of the Advancement of Learning* (Wright ed.), II, iv, p. 104. In another notable pronouncement Bacon shows recognition of the wider function of art to preserve in enduring form the life and truth of past ages — preserving it, too, not as an imitation but as an original creation to fill and stir the minds of men of succeeding ages. It is a noble utterance, worthy in respects to be placed beside Wordsworth's and Keats's words on the same subject:

"We see then how far the monuments of wit and learning are more durable than the monuments of power or of the hands. For have not the verses of Homer continued twenty-five hundred years, or more, without the loss of a syllable or letter; during which time infinite palaces, temples, castles, cities, have been decayed and demolished? It is not possible to have the true pictures or statues of Cyrus, Alexander, Caesar, no nor of the kings or great personages of much later years; for the originals cannot last, and the copies cannot but leese of the life and

But, however ambiguous Bacon's statements on the subject may sometimes be, he leaves no doubt of his conception of the imagination as an agency of vast powers. It is specifically the active agent in poetry, as in all other inventive arts. It may create for its own satisfaction, or for purposes of moral instruction. It builds in effect another nature which augments and supplements the empirical world of fact. Its appeal is to the affections and the will. The source of this appeal is concrete representation. Freed from the laws of matter, it may in poetry delight the mind with shadows of an ideal world better than reality, and, while it raises the soul to divine views, it charms with the variety and novelty of its inventions.

Bacon does not give us a complete aesthetic. It is also true that considerable parts of his theory are of a neoclassic trend, his emphasis on allegory in case; yet as Spingarn has said, "he was an Elizabethan, and touched by the romantic longings of his time." [160] His idea that art becomes more delightful when strangeness is added to beauty foreshadows Pater's definition of Romanticism, and his assertion that art works by chance, not by rule, places him in opposition to the main tendency of criticism in the century that was to follow. His writings are filled with fortunate intimations of the dignity of the imagination and of a psychology of aesthetic response. Bacon thus becomes an important predecessor of Hobbes, Addison, and other critics who turned their attention to the imagination and who sought to establish a basis for judging art through a study of the mind in its natural reactions. His bare outline proved to be powerful in suggestion. Professor

---

truth. But the images of men's wits and knowledges remain in books, exempted from the wrong of time and capable of perpetual renovation. Neither are they fitly to be called images, because they generate still, and cast their seeds in the minds of others, provoking and causing infinite actions and opinions in succeeding ages. So that if the invention of the ship was thought so noble, which carrieth riches and commodities from place to place, and consociateth the most remote regions in participation of their fruits, how much more are letters to be magnified, which as ships pass through the vast seas of time, and make ages so distant to participate of the wisdom, illuminations, and inventions, the one of the other?" (*ibid.*, I, viii, pp. 72–73).

[160] J. E. Spingarn, "Jacobean and Caroline Criticism," in *The Cambridge History of English Literature* (Cambridge, 1911), VII, 260.

Spingarn is thoroughly right when he declares that "Bacon helped transform the theory of literature." [161]

Even so, Bacon left much to be more thoroughly defined. His statements, ascribing both artistic creation and aesthetic effects to the idealizing functions of the imagination, valuable as they are, usually end in generalities. He failed in practical criticism to come to particular instances in showing how poetry charms; he fell short, moreover, in investigating with clarity and thoroughness the mental activities and the relation of these activities to one another, leaving us with a psychology which, particularly as it relates to the imagination, is ambiguous and obscure. It remained for Hobbes to explore more specifically the processes which Bacon, like his predecessors, had neglected to explain. We shall see that Hobbes was to make definite and important advances toward clearer views.

[161] *Op. cit.*, p. 258.

CHAPTER III

Hobbes's Theory of Imagination

I

HOBBES'S conception of fancy and imagination is incidental to his attempt to relate all human phenomena to natural law, and is in accord with the physiological psychology which he evolved in process of his speculations. Repudiating the current teachings of the schools, which, "not knowing what Imagination, or the Senses are," pass on many false doctrines to the effect that imaginations rise of themselves, and have no cause, or that they come from God, or from the Devil, and thus "with many words making nothing understood," repeat the jargon of medieval faculty psychology,[1] Hobbes sets out anew to describe the operations of the mental faculties as they can be known from a strictly rational and empirical point of view. Man's mind owes its genius and growth to experience: "There is no other act of mans mind . . . naturally planted in him . . . but to be born a man, and live with the use of his five Senses." [2] Hobbes's first query is, What causes sensation? That answered, he is ready to proceed to define "fancy," "imagination," "wit," and allied terms.

[1] *Leviathan*, ed. by Ernest Rhys (London, Toronto, and New York, 1914), I, ii. Hobbes does not refer directly to medieval psychology. His words, however, leave little room for doubt that he is striking at the scholastic doctrines still honored in seventeenth-century schools: "Some say the Senses receive the Species of things, and deliver them to the Common-sense; and the Common Sense delivers them over to the Fancy and the Fancy to the Memory, and the Memory to the Judgement, like handing of things one to another, with many words making nothing understood."

[2] *Ibid.*, I, iii. Elsewhere he writes: "Man's nature is the sum of his natural faculties and Powers" (*The Elements of Law*, ed. by Ferdinand Tönnies [Cambridge, 1928], I, i, 4).

79

It should be remarked before we proceed further that, though his intentions of beginning all over were sincere, Hobbes derived much from both classical and medieval psychology. He inherited also some of their confusions. His use of terms is far from consistent, even within the same work; the variation in different works is still more marked. This is especially true of the important word "fancy." With Hobbes, fancy is sometimes merely an image-forming faculty as in original perception,[3] sometimes no more than an image-retaining faculty, as in memory;[4] again it is a beautifying and adorning agency,[5] and still again a constructive faculty, with power to divide, unite, and create into shapely form.[6] In the latter function it is at one time purely a creative-perceptive power independent of judgment, with special aptitude in discerning similitudes,[7] at another, it includes judgment, or the power of perceiving dissimilitudes;[8] in both cases it seems to be identified with "wit." Hobbes ordinarily makes no clear distinction between fancy and imagination, though, as we shall see, he does have in mind, especially in matters relating to aesthetics, a rather specialized field for the operation of the fancy. And, altogether, even if we cannot claim for Hobbes the virtue of absolute consistency, it is a tribute to the integrity of his thought that a careful examination of all he has to say reveals a fairly unified view.

In *Leviathan* (1651) Hobbes defines sense and proceeds to a discussion of the terms "fancy," "memory," and "imagination," all too frequently without clear distinction. Here he builds upon his philosophic theory that motion is the cause of

---

[3] *Leviathan*, I, i; also "Physics, or the Phenomena of Nature," in *The Elements of Philosophy*, IV, xxv, 2–3, in *The English Works of Thomas Hobbes of Malmesbury*, ed. by Sir William Molesworth (London, 1839–45).

[4] *Leviathan*, I, ii; *The Elements of Philosophy*, IV, xxv, 3.

[5] *The Answer to Davenant*, in *Critical Essays of the Seventeenth Century*, ed. by J. E. Spingarn (Oxford, 1908), II, 59–60.   [6] *Ibid*.

[7] *Leviathan*, I, viii; also *The Virtues of an Heroic Poem*, Spingarn, II, 70, and *The Elements of Law*, I, x, 4.

[8] *Leviathan*, I, viii, and *The Elements of Law*, I, x, 4; also *The Answer to Davenant*, Spingarn, II, 60. Some of these discrepancies may no doubt be attributed to progress in thought; others seem traceable to the inherent difficulty in adapting to a new system of ideas a terminology already badly muddled — one which to this day, incidentally, is rarely used with any precision.

knowledge. All conceptions begin with sense impression, motion from external objects striking upon the nervous mechanism, causing "a resistance, or counter-pressure, which . . . because *Outward*, seemeth to be some matter without." This "seeming" or "fancy" is what men call "sense." Hence the impressions of light, color, heat, cold, hardness, and so forth. All in reality are but motion; [9] "for motion produceth nothing but motion. But their apparance to us is Fancy, the same waking that dreaming." Fancy, then, as here used is merely the elementary stage in perception, the mental *inner* resulting from the impingement of the physical *outer*. "And though at some certain distance the reall, and very object seem invested with the fancy it begets in us; Yet still the object is one thing, the image or fancy is another. So that Sense in all cases, is nothing els but original fancy . . . ." [10]

In the very next chapter Hobbes is to use "fancy" in the Greek sense, as signifying "appearance," to serve as an equivalent to what the Latins called "imagination," in describing that which remains in the mind after the original object is removed: the "image" of the thing seen. The Latins used "imagination" to refer to all sense images, as well as to those of sight — improperly, Hobbes asserts; yet he at once adopts the Latin extension of the term, thus identifying fancy and imagination. "IMAGINATION, therefore, is nothing but *decaying sense*." With intrusion of other external stimuli, earlier images become obscured, so that "after great distance of time our imagination

[9] It should be recalled that this ascription of sensation and imagination to motion was no new thing in philosophy, since similar explanations are to be found in Empedocles, Plato, and Aristotle, to say nothing of numerous later writers, including the Stoics, Telesio, and Campanella. Aristotle defines imagination, the phantasm of sense impression, as "a motion generated by actual perception" (*De Anima*, III, iii, 13; tr. by Robert Drew Hicks [Cambridge, 1907], p. 129). Hicks has noticed the relationship between Aristotle's and Hobbes's ideas. Aristotle, says Hicks, defines the imagination as "a motion made by actual perception, a motion distinct from, yet similar to, the motion which constituted the original perception, or, as Hobbes translates, 'All fancies are motions within us, reliques of those made by sense' " (Intro. to *De Anima*, p. liii). Aristotle had said: "and imagination is thought to be a species of motion, and not to rise apart from sensation, but only in sentient beings and with the objects of sense for objects" (*De Anima*, III, iii, 11; Hicks, p. 127).

[10] *Leviathan*, I, i.

of the Past is weak"; voices once heard grow dim; particular streets in cities fade, and leave only *memory*.

> . . . This *decaying sense*, when wee would express the thing it self (I mean *fancy* it selfe [but even this is not the "original fancy" of the first chapter]), we call *Imagination*, as I said before: [11] But when we would express the *decay*, and signifie that the Sense is fading, old, and past, it is called *Memory*. So that *Imagination* and *Memory* are but one thing, which for divers considerations hath divers names. [12]

Up to this point, the word "fancy" has been used to describe two things: the original image of sense perception and the image which remains after perception. "Fancy" in the second sense has been identified with "imagination," which, in turn, has been defined merely as "memory." There is so far no implication of the relation of either to aesthetics. In the next paragraph, however, in his definition of simple and compound imagination, Hobbes evidently has an eye to artistic processes:

> Much memory, or memory of many things, is called *Experience*. Againe, Imagination being only of those things, which have been formerly perceived by Sense, either all at once, or by parts at severall times; The former (which is the imagining of the whole object, as it was presented to the sense) is *simple Imagination;* as when one imagineth a man, or horse, which he hath seen before. The other is *Compounded;* as when from the sight of a man at one time, and of a horse at another, we conceive in our mind a Centaure. So when a man compoundeth the image of his own person with the image of the actions of an other man; as when a man

---

[11] In both the earlier *Elements of Law* (1640) and the later *Elements of Philosophy* (1655) a similar identification of fancy and imagination occurs. "And this obscure conception [the image remaining after the sense is past] is that we call PHANTASY or IMAGINATION: imagination being (to define it) conception remaining, and by little and little decaying from and after the act of sense" (*The Elements of Law*, I, iii, 1). In *The Elements of Philosophy*, Hobbes is plainly uneasy in calling fancy and imagination one thing, but, after making a slight, though significant, qualification, he proceeds to his former identification: "But the motion of the organ, by which a phantasm is made, is not commonly called sense, except the object be present. And the phantasm remaining after the object is removed or past by, is called fancy, and in Latin *imaginatio;* which word, because all phantasms are not images, doth not fully answer the signification of the word fancy in its general acceptation. Nevertheless, I may use it safely enough, by understanding it for the Greek φαντασία.

"IMAGINATION therefore is nothing else but *sense decaying*, or *weakened*, by the absence of the object" (IV, xxv, 7).

[12] *Leviathan*, I, ii.

imagins himself a *Hercules* or an *Alexander* (which happeneth often to them that are much taken with reading of Romants) it is a compound imagination, and properly but a Fiction of the mind.[13]

This idea is reiterated in *The Elements of Philosophy*, where Hobbes explains that "in the silence of sense, there is no new motion from the objects, and therefore no new phantasm, unless we call that new, which is compounded of old ones, as a chimera, a golden mountain, and the like." [14]

The "compounded" imagination cannot perforce be a purely mechanical act. Some faculty of mind must be at work to bring together images not formerly connected. In the back of his mind Hobbes was evidently from the first troubled by the common-sense recognition that in the processes he is describing there must be, in translating motion into ideas, and in combining with each other ideas already present, a part played by the mind itself. His conception of "outward pressure," in response to sense impression, indicates an indispensable reciprocal activity of mind in the formation of images of "original fancy"; this, however, might still be merely

---

[13] *Ibid.*

[14] Hobbes is repeating almost verbatim a passage from the 1640 *Elements of Law* (see I, iii, 4). The illustration of a "golden mountain" recalls St. Thomas Aquinas: "Avicenna, however, assigns . . . a fifth power, which combines and divides imaginary forms: as when from the imaginary form of gold, and the imaginary form of a mountain, we compose the one form of a golden mountain, which we have never seen" (*Summa Theologica*, tr. by Fathers of the English Dominican Province [London, 1911–25], Part I, Third Number, Q. 78, A. 4, p. 86). The idea of the power of fancy, or imagination, to combine its phantasms at will was, indeed, quite common before Hobbes, as Donald F. Bond ("The Neo-Classical Psychology of the Imagination," *A Journal of English Literary History*, IV [1937], 247–248) has noted. The Stoics had presented this idea through Chrysippus (see p. 27); Albertus Magnus was one of several Scholastics who discussed the power of imagination to conceive of such things as a man with two heads "or a being with a human body, the head of a lion, or the tail of a horse" (see Murray Wright Bundy, *The Theory of Imagination in Classical and Mediaeval Thought* [Urbana, Illinois, 1927], p. 190). Huarte likewise had ascribed to the imagination the power to compound images at will: "This imagination hath force not onely to compound a figure possible with another, but doth ioyne also (after the order of nature) those which are vnpossible, and of them growes to shape mountaines of gold, and calues that flie" (*Examen de ingenios. The Examination of Men's Wits*, tr. by R. C. [Richard Carew] [London, 1594], p. 132). And Bacon had, of course, allowed to the poet the capacity and right to "join that which nature had severed."

mechanical. But the production of such mental combinations as chimeras and golden mountains and fictions of oneself in the rôle of another implies some constructive principle or principles belonging to the mind itself, with power to bring together elements from past experience. This, as well as other more extended powers, such as the capacity to create poems and the arts of civilization, Hobbes ascribes to the imagination, or fancy, aided by judgment, working, under the laws of association or independently of them, in its own private, internal world of the memory.

Before we consider this aspect of Hobbes's thought in more detail, however, let us examine further his ideas of perception and the problems of memory, fancy, and judgment. Perception itself may be, indeed it often is, according to Hobbes, a kind of compounded imagination. This idea occurs in Part I ("Computation or Logic") and Part IV ("Physics") of *The Elements of Philosophy*.[15]

Hobbes proposes for himself in the "Physics" the problem of "finding out by the appearances or effects of nature, which we know by sense, some ways and means by which they may be, I do not say they are, generated." [16]   By appearances or effects Hobbes means phantasms, perceptions, or conceptions produced by motion from objects in nature. To arrive at a solution it is necessary, he explains, to inquire into "the causes of our perception, that is, the causes of those ideas and phantasms which are perpetually generated within us whilst we make use of our senses . . . and in what manner their generation proceeds." [17]   Hobbes's explanation is frankly based upon introspection and observation and is professedly — charmingly — tentative:

[15] Since this work, though it had been in progress for some years, was not published until 1655–58, its pronouncements may be thought to contain Hobbes's more mature theory on questions he had discussed in *The Elements of Law* and in *Leviathan*. Some of the ideas contained in this book which most closely approximate theory expressed in the earlier works have been cited in previous pages. These ideas, however, are embedded in a matrix of illuminating exposition which contains evidence of insight into psychological phenomena beyond that shown in his previous books, beyond, indeed, what is ordinarily attributed to Hobbes or to any other philosopher of the mechanical school.

[16] *The Elements of Philosophy*, IV, xxv, 1.   [17] *Ibid.*

. . . The principles, therefore, upon which the following discourse depends, are not such as we ourselves make and pronounce in general terms, as definitions; but such, as being placed in the things themselves by the Author of Nature, are by us observed in them; and we make use of them in single and particular, not universal propositions.[18]

In the ensuing discussion, although the ideas of motion inward and of "outward pressure" are reiterated, there is indicated a much more definite and complicated mental activity, as concomitant and essential to perception. What, it may be inquired, accounts for the translation of motion into mind-stuff? If perception is merely motion in reaction to motion, why does not motion upon any body result in perception? Hobbes's reply is instructive as an evidence of his close scrutiny of his problem and of the observable facts of mind which throw light upon its solution. Sense perception is made by reaction, but "it is not necessary that everything that reacteth should have sense." [19] It is true that inanimate bodies might so react that a phantasm would be created, but unless these bodies were furnished with organs, such as living creatures have, fit for the retaining of motion made in them, such impressions would be lost. Perception, then, and other mental acts consequent upon perception depend on such special organs as the brain, the nerves, the arteries, and the heart, in their specific capacity to perform functions indispensable to mental processes. How these organs act and what functions they perform in the acquisition and use of ideas become, then, inevitable subjects of inquiry.

In defining "sense" Hobbes now definitely adds to his previous descriptions of perception as a mechanical process by stating, first that there can be no sense without sense and secondly that this sense which causes sense is memory and judgment:

. . . And as for the causes of sense, we cannot begin our search of them from any other phenomenon than that of sense itself. But you will say, by what sense shall we take notice of sense? I answer, by sense itself, namely, by the memory which for some time remains in us of things sensible,

[18] *Ibid.* The empirical trend in Hobbes is here prominent.
[19] *Ibid.*, IV, xxv, 5.

though they themselves pass away. For he that perceives that he hath perceived, remembers.[20]

Here the element necessary to perception is memory plus a somewhat indefinite act of self-conscious recognition on the part of the sentient. From this passage alone it might appear that memory concerns only the single phantasm caused by motion from the exciting object. In following Hobbes's argument, however, we find that perception involves memory not only of the new phantasm but of previous phantasms, with the addition of a specific activity of judgment through comparison and contrast:

> For by sense, we commonly understand the judgment we make of objects by their phantasms; namely, by comparing and distinguishing those phantasms; which we could never do, if that motion in the organ, by which the phantasm is made, did not remain there for some time, and make the same phantasm return. Wherefore sense, as I here understand it, and which is commonly so called, hath necessarily some memory adhering to it, by which former and later phantasms may be compared together and distinguished from one another.[21]

This is immediately followed by the clarifying statement that sense, therefore, "must necessarily have in it a perpetual variety of phantasms, that they may be discerned one from another." For, though motion from a single unvaried object might strike continually upon the sensory organ, unless there were other phantasms with which to compare the phantasm thus made there could be no perception ("sense"), "it being almost all one for a man to be always sensible of one and the same thing, and not to be sensible at all of any thing." [22]

Perception thus becomes a much more complicated affair than mere mechanical motion setting up a reacting motion in a sentient object. It requires not one but many phantasms (images or motions) and involves the activities of an organ

---

[20] *The Elements of Philosophy*, IV, xxv, 1.

[21] *Ibid.*, IV, xxv, 5. This explanation has an added interest in its relation to Locke's later conception of ideas of reflection as the product of "internal sense" (*Of Human Understanding*, II, i, 4, in Vol. I of *The Works of John Locke* [London, 1867]). Unfortunately Hobbes neglects to show how the original phantasms, necessary to sense perception, got into the mind, and therefore leaves his case seriously incomplete. [22] *Ibid.*

capable of memory and judgment. Such a description has much significance as an indication of a step in Hobbes's thinking toward a conception to be developed in later psychology: namely, that every act of perception is in reality a creative act in which materials from relevant past experience coalesce with incoming stimuli to form the inner reality of the thing perceived. This, of course, is a not distant equivalent to Kant's idea of perception and to Coleridge's theory of primary imagination.[23] It would be idle to maintain that Hobbes meant exactly the same thing that Kant and Coleridge had in mind; yet he was dealing with the same mental phenomenon, and it is not too remote a possibility to infer that introspection had led him to essentially the same conclusions — though his age had learned neither to recognize nor to express them with clearness.

Another striking statement which has a bearing on Hobbes's notion of perception occurs in the "Computation or Logic," in a description of the process whereby a man, seeing an object that can at a distance be discerned only as "body," becomes aware upon a nearer view that this object is a "man." This process Hobbes labels "ratiocination," which, in turn, he calls

[23] As set forth in *Biographia Literaria* (ed. by J. Shawcross [Oxford, 1907]), particularly Chaps. VII, XII, and XIII. In perception, the initial act of knowledge, Coleridge conceives of two infinite, indestructible forces which "counteract each other by their essential nature," but which in the act of cancelling each other, give birth through their interpenetration to a *tertium quid* which is self-consciousness (*ibid.*, I, 198). These two forces are mind and matter, the subjective self, or intelligence, and objective reality, or nature, conceived in its limited passive and material sense, "as comprising all the phenomena by which its existence is made known to us" (*ibid.*, I, 174). In the act of knowledge a reciprocal concurrence is required in which "the objective and subjective are instantly united." It is obvious that if the resultant perception is to be anything but blind force meeting blind force — which could scarcely be an improvement over Hartley's ideas of mechanical response — there must be some regulatory principle at work to determine the nature and form of this process. Coleridge conceives of the imagination as this principle. This is the Primary Imagination of his definition (*ibid.*, I, 202), the esemplastic faculty through which the external world about us becomes transformed into inner reality. The Secondary Imagination is identical in the kind of its agency, but differs in degree and mode of its operation, and it applies specifically to secondary mental processes of thought and invention, in which materials from experience, melted down into their elements — dissolved and diffused — become the object of the mind's conscious activity, and are brought together under laws of organic being into new complex organizations, such as those of poetry, drama, and music.

"computation," or the addition "in our silent thoughts" of the qualities which, through previous experience, we know to belong to the animal man. Thus our recognition of "man" is made up of a combination of previous conceptions each modifying the other and all merged into unity in a single final percept. Hobbes's conclusion to this exposition will set the matter in a clearer light:

> Lastly, when by looking fully and distinctly upon it, he conceives all that he has seen as one thing, the idea he has now is compounded of his former ideas, which are put together in the mind in the same order in which these three single names, *body — animated — rational*, are in speech compounded into this one name, *body-animated-rational*, or *man*.[24]

Hobbes goes on to make application of his principle to other objects: "In like manner, of the several conceptions of *four sides, equality of sides*, and *right angles*, is compounded the conception of a square." Here, as before, various different conceptions gained through experience or demonstration are represented as merging in a process of memory, addition, and recognition into a single percept. It is true that Hobbes uses the term "conception" to describe this phenomenon, which he is treating under the head of rational processes, but the act is in reality one of perception, involving the elements of judgment and memory, which he is later in the book to include in complete sense perception. The difference is one in terms only, as is apparent from a careful reading of the passage in context. Effects and appearances of things to sense, he goes on to say, "are faculties or powers of bodies, which make us distinguish them from one another." [25] When we perceive a certain body in motion we know (perceive) it is a man and not a tree, for previous experience has taught us that men have the property of motion but trees have not. This actual (if not fully stated) recognition of the fact that every perception is a fusion of the immediate sense impression with previous perceptions, a bundle of apperceptions, again indicates the importance of Hobbes for subsequent Romantic psychology.

All this constitutes a considerable modification of the idea of "compounded imagination" as applied to a combination

---

[24] *The Elements of Philosophy*, I, i, 3.   [25] *Ibid.*, I, i, 4.

of images received previously from unlike objects, "as when, from the sight of a man at one time, and of a horse at another, we conceive in our mind a Centaure." Hobbes's recognition of the fact that perception itself involves an act of compounding images carries him beyond this elementary principle of fanciful combination, and is in accord with more fundamental explanations which he searches out in both the earlier and the later works for the more complex operations of thought and fancy.

Failure to appreciate the full significance of Hobbes's ideas of perception tentatively developed in *The Elements of Philosophy* has led to strictures on his theory not fully warranted by the facts. Hazlitt, for instance, who was in general quite favorably disposed toward Hobbes, found error in him, in common with other mechanical philosophers, on the ground that his theory exaggerates the importance of the senses, while it allows no place for the understanding. He also objected to what he felt was Hobbes's impossible theory that the mind could have only one idea at a time.[26] In all our ideas, says Hazlitt, there is another act or faculty of mind for which sensation cannot account. A sensation is "the perception produced by the impression of the several parts of an outward object, each by itself, on the correspondent parts of an organized sentient being: by an idea I mean the conception produced by a number of these together on the same conscious principle." [27] This principle is the "understanding," "the superintending faculty, which alone perceives the relations of things, and enables us to comprehend their connexions, forms, and masses." [28] The operation of this faculty presupposes more than one idea in the mind at a time; indeed, "if the mind cannot have two ideas at the same time, it can never have any, since all the ideas we know of consist of more than one." [29] Our idea of "table," for instance, is made up of a variety of ingredients furnished by the senses: hardness, color, shape, use, and so forth. But

---

[26] *Literary Remains of the Late William Hazlitt*, ed. by E. L. Bulwer and Sergeant Talfourd (London, 1836), I, 163–164.

[27] *Ibid.*, p. 241.   [28] *Ibid.*

[29] *Ibid.*, pp. 252–253. Hazlitt is here writing on Locke's essay, but he has Hobbes in mind also.

without the surrounding and forming power of intellect we could never have a unified idea of a single object.[30] The mind itself, which "alone is formative," must act upon its materials, to give shape and cohesion to related elements and form them into a whole. Otherwise all would be disjointed, unrelated in the mind. A statue broken and mutilated, its parts scattered, would be harmony itself beside any idea that could result from mere sensible impression of the parts; without the understanding reacting on the senses, and informing the eye with judgment and knowledge, there would be no possibility of comparing the different impressions received: no one part could have the slightest reference to any other part or to the whole — all would be one mass of unmeaning, unconscious confusion.[31] Such confusion, he maintained, was the only possible logical end according to the mechanical philosophy.

The interesting fact is, however, that Hobbes himself seems to have anticipated these objections. He did not, to be sure, use the same terms as Hazlitt, but when he showed that there could be no sense without previous sense, that there could be no perception without the intervention of memory and the comparing power of judgment, that, moreover, our perception of a man or a square as a unique identifiable object is a compound of several previous perceptions and concepts, he was unquestionably implying both the existence of more than one idea in the mind at once and an essential act of mind upon its materials.

II

Beyond perception, by what law do separate ideas already in the mind become united? Hobbes's reply, which may be found variously worded in *Leviathan*, *The Elements of Law*, and *The Elements of Philosophy*, is to present a rather elementary theory of association, modified by the idea that desire, or appetite, acts as a directive power impelling the mind to some specific end, and by a theory of fancy and judgment as determinative, selective agencies in combining elements of experience.

[30] Hazlitt, *Literary Remains*, I, 243.   [31] *Ibid.*, pp. 245–246.

Ideas may follow each other through mere contiguity: "For in the motion of any continued body, one part follows another by cohesion," [32] or they may follow in cause and effect relationships,[33] or in succession according to the original order in which they appeared in the mind.[34] Such a "Trayne of Imaginations" — Hobbes does not use the word "association" — may be casual and incoherent, as is usual in dreams, or orderly, as in directed thought. The first of these is characterized in *Leviathan* as "*Unguided, without Designe*," in which "there is no Passionate Thought to govern and direct" its course to some designed end. The second is "*regulated* by some desire, and designe." [35] Midway between the completely casual and the well-directed train of imagination is what Hobbes calls a "RANGING" of thought [36] — "wild ranging" is his phrase in the *Leviathan* [37] — in which a certain coherence appears, in that one idea logically belongs to another. Thus in a discourse on the Civil War a malicious questioner inquired what was the value of a Roman penny, having in mind in one instant of thought, "for Thought is quick," a whole chain of connections between Judas' betrayal of Christ for thirty pence and the present treason against Charles.[38] So Hobbes comments upon that almost instantaneous coalescence of stimulus and memory, of new and old percepts, of concept and judgment, which, however we may explain it or whatever we may call it, must ever remain one of the greatest marvels of mental phenomena.[39]

Transcending such chance association of images, or ranging of thought, however fortunate may be the outcome in particu-

[32] *The Elements of Philosophy*, I, xxv, 8.
[33] *Leviathan*, I, iii.
[34] *Ibid.* "But as wee have no Imagination, whereof we have not formerly had Sense, in whole, or in parts; so we have no Transition from one Imagination to another, whereof we never had the like before in our Senses . . . . But because in sense, to one and the same thing perceived, sometimes one thing, sometimes another succeedeth, it comes to passe in time, that in the Imagining of any thing, there is no certainty what we shall Imagine next; Onely this is certain, it shall be something that succeeded the same before, at one time or another" (*ibid.*).
[35] *Ibid.*   [36] *The Elements of Law*, I, iv, 3.
[37] *Leviathan*, I, iii.   [38] *Ibid.*
[39] Coleridge called it "imagination"; William James, "unconscious cerebration."

lar cases, are those voluntary processes of mind which are
regulated by the passion of desire. For desire furnishes a
guidance to approved ends, and through it the mind may
summon whatever thoughts it will to go with any other thought
to achieve its proposed design. Desire thus becomes the impelling motive to that "discourse of mind" which distinguishes
the effective active intellect from its opposite, where there is
no guidance and the mind wanders from point to point without reason. For when we have fixed our thoughts on a desired
attainment, "the End, by the greatnesse of the impression,
comes often to mind, in case our thoughts begin to wander." [40]
Hobbes names two kinds of trains of regulated thought. In
the first, having imagined an effect we seek the causes or the
means which produced it.[41] Or, to use the more picturesque
description of *The Elements of Law*, appetite leads men to discover (imagine) a way to attainment, as of honor, by what we
may call "hunting or tracing, as dogs trace the beast by the
smell, and men hunt them by their footsteps; or as men hunt
after riches, place or knowledge." [42] In the second, having

[40] *Leviathan*, I, iii.   [41] *Ibid.*

[42] I, iv, 4. Hobbes's use of "appetite" and "desire" should be distinguished
from the meaning given to "*appetitus*" or "*inclinatio*" by St. Thomas Aquinas. To
Hobbes appetite is the result of experience. Some experiences give pleasure and
so present a promise of good in repetition or extension; some give pain and so
present a promise of evil in repetition or extension. From considerable experience
a man learns to weigh, in deliberation, the relative desirability of this act or that.
Then appetite becomes will (*Leviathan*, I, vi, vii, xi). To Aquinas, however, appetite is native to man, as to all other being. As Professor Leo Ward, using materials
from *Sum. Theol.*, Part I, Second Number, Q. 93, A. 6, and Q. 94, A. 2, and *Contra Gen-
tiles*, Book IV, Chap. XXII (in "Natural Tendency in the Thought of St. Thomas,"
an unpublished paper delivered before the Michigan Academy, 1938), has admirably summed up the matter, "the *appetitus* or native desire of a thing" is "an
inclination, a tendency native to it because arising from its nature or form."
Man "has in common with all being a tendency to preserve his being, and in
common with animals a tendency to sex life and the training of his offspring, and
also a properly human tendency to life in line with reason: e.g. a tendency to
know the truth about God, a tendency to live with other people," and so forth.
In other words, man's "inner native bent is towards good and all good," and "there
always remains in man," however his will may be corrupted, a tendency, which
seems to derive from God and is directed to attainment of something like His
absolute perfection, "to do all good." Like Aquinas, Hobbes conceives of man's
appetite as an inclination toward the good. But he would take strong exception
to certain points in the theory of the great Scholastic. Regarding appetite as a
resultant of physiopsychological response to phenomenal experience, and repudi-

imagined a given thing we seek out all the possible effects that can be produced by it; that is to say we imagine what we can do with it when we have it.[43]

Both of these types of regulated "discourse of mind" may be summarized as "nothing but *seeking*, or the faculty of Invention, which the Latines call *Sagacitas*, and *Solertia*," which is to say, "a hunting out of the causes, of some effect, present or past; or of the effects, of some present or past cause." When a man seeks something he has lost, "his mind runs back, from place to place, and time to time, to find where, and when he had it." Or "his thoughts run over the same places and times, to find what action, or other occasion might make him lose it." Again a man knows of a certain place within the range of his seeking, "and then his thoughts run over all the parts thereof, in the same manner, as one would sweep a room, to find a jewell; or as a Spaniel ranges the field, till he find a sent; or as a man should run over the Alphabet, to start a rime."[44] These are forms of "*Remembrance*, or Calling to mind." But it is memory working through the links of association under the direction of desire, or what we now call will. The process of inferential reasoning next described by Hobbes is still within the range of associative memory.

Sometimes a man desires to know the event of an action; and then he thinketh of some like action past, and the events thereof one after another; supposing like events will follow like actions. As he that foresees what wil become of a Criminal, re-cons what he has seen follow on the like Crime before; having this order of thoughts, The Crime, the Officer, the Prison, the Judge, and the Gallowes. Which kind of thoughts is called *Foresight*, and *Prudence*, or *Providence;* and sometimes *Wisdome;* though such conjecture, through the difficulty of observing all circumstances, be very fallacious. But this is certain; by how much one man has more experience of things past, than another; by so much also he is more Prudent, and his expectations the seldomer faile him. The *Present* onely has a being in Nature; things *Past* have a being in the Memory onely, but things *to come* have no being at all; the *Future* being but a fiction of the

ating innate principle or influence from noumenal being, he would stoutly deny that this desire is implanted at birth or that it owes its existence to deity; he would also maintain that, so far from being a native impulse to attain to godlike perfection, man's inclination to good has its origin in an urge for self-preservation and well-being.   [43] *Leviathan*, I, iii.   [44] *Ibid.*

mind, applying the sequels of actions Past, to the actions that are Present; which with most certainty is done by him that has most Experience . . . .[45]

So Hobbes describes voluntary acts of mind in processes of association through the command of desire, and indicates something of the importance of remembered experience to the validity of these acts.

In *The Elements of Philosophy* he goes a step further, suggesting mental acts in which desire, or appetite, cuts through the channels of association to bring together ideas which may have had no previous association in the mind. Venturing again to clarify the troublesome problem of how ideas ("motions," "phantasms," "images") already in the mind enter into varied combinations, he points out that, however much the whole may seem a matter of chance, it is not in reality as casual a thing as many may think, "that phantasms in . . . great variety proceed from one another; and that the same phantasms sometimes bring into the mind other phantasms like themselves, and at other times extremely unlike." [46] As in *Leviathan* and *The Elements of Law*, Hobbes is resorting to an explanation based upon the principles of association and of appetite and of the determinative agencies of fancy and judgment. The difference is that he here passes quickly over the idea of association, going little further than to remark that "in the motion of any continued body, one part follows another by cohesion," and that after successive motions from a number of objects the "phantasms [which remain after the objects are removed] are renewed as often as any one of these motions becomes predominant above the rest," and "in the same order in which . . . they were generated by sense." [47] His appeal to appetite, involving in part a contradiction of what he has said about association, is, however, more definite and more extended. He also adds the element of judgment.

Association hardly explains the more difficult phenomenon of combinations of elements that have been long in the mind and have come together without relation to original contiguity. For (Hobbes uses, with apparent illogicality, the conjunctive "so") "when by length of time very many phantasms have

[45] *Leviathan*, I, iii.   [46] *The Elements of Philosophy*, IV, xxv, 8.   [47] *Ibid.*

been generated within us by sense, then almost any thought
may arise from any other thought; insomuch that it may
seem a thing indifferent and casual which thought shall follow
which." [48]   It is here that appetite and judgment operate to
reduce to order what might otherwise be mental chaos.
Through appetite and judgment the mind is led first to imagine for itself a desired end, then to seek out and select the
necessary phantasms to achieve that end: "For the thought
or phantasm of the desired end brings in all the phantasms,
that are means conducing to the end . . . . But this supposes
both appetite, and judgment to discern what means conduce
to the end, which is gotten by experience; and experience is
store of phantasms, arising from the sense of very many
things." [49]   In sleep, phantasms occur without order, since,
though they are aroused by motion or appetite proceeding
from the heart to the brain, there is neither thought of a desired
end, nor judgment, to give order and coherence.   The order
and coherence of waking thought proceed only "from frequent
looking back to the desired end, that is, from consultation." [50]

In this discussion Hobbes once more uses, as in *Leviathan*
and in *The Elements of Law*, the phrase "discourse of mind";
the emphasis is now, however, not upon a mechanical association of ideas but upon perceptions of likeness and difference
in phantasms that may have entered the mind from varied
sources at varied times.   The arising of ideas in sense is mentioned, it is true, but the weight of Hobbes's remark is upon
ideas originating in imagination.   "The perpetual arising of
phantasms, both in sense and imagination, is that which we
commonly call discourse of the mind, and is common to men
with other living creatures.   For he that thinketh, compareth
the phantasms that pass, that is, taketh notice of their likeness
or unlikeness to one another."   It is in just such comparison
and contrast that fancy and judgment consist: "And as he
that observes readily the likenesses of things of different nature,
or that are very remote from one another, is said to have a
good fancy; so he is said to have a good judgement, that finds
out the unlikenesses or differences of things that are like one

[48] *Ibid.*   [49] *Ibid.*   [50] *Ibid.*, IV, xxv, 9.

another." [51] Such activity, Hobbes explains, is to be attributed
not to "a common organ of sense, distinct from sense of perception properly so called, but is memory of the differences of
phantasms remaining for some time; as the distinction between hot and lucid is nothing else but the memory both of a
heating, and of an enlightening object." [52]

Hobbes has in this passage, it seems to me, drawn together
his ideas of perception and of that secondary act, which is like
perception, whereby the memory re-presents to the mind images of past perceptual experience. In each case the fancy
and judgment act as discerning powers to link those phantasms
which are alike and to set apart those which are unlike. The
union by the fancy of materials which, though they are remote
from each other or appear unlike, have a natural, logical kinship represents those combinations that escape the ordinary
mind; while judgment sits by to sift out such deceiving appearances as to the casual eye would pass for likenesses. The "good
fancy" and the "good judgment," operating within the field of
memory, thus become the active principles through which the
mind deals with its materials. The method through which they
work may be associative, but it may also transcend ordinary association in conformity with a law of inherent similitude, perceiving and bringing together items of experience not previously
related in the mind.

III

With this brief survey of his psychology before us, we are
now ready to make application and extension of some of
Hobbes's basic principles to artistic processes. In order to do
this it will be necessary to examine, with more specific reference
to aesthetic ends than has yet been done, Hobbes's use of such
terms as "appetite," "wit," "memory," "fancy," and "judgment." The concept of imagination will inevitably enter such
a discussion, but it must be noted that in his direct exposition
of aesthetic matters Hobbes almost never uses the word, em-
ploying instead, in his references to creative acts, the ancient
and medieval term "fancy." Hobbes's definition of wit is of

[51] *The Elements of Philosophy*, IV, xxv, 8.   [52] *Ibid.*

paramount importance in such an examination. It cannot be considered, however, without relation to its chief components, appetite, fancy, and judgment.

Of the factors that distinguish the active from the sluggish or dull intellect Hobbes regards none as of more importance than appetite. Thus he constantly and unequivocally emphasizes appetite as essential to a vigorous, lively, and orderly mind. We have seen that in *Leviathan*, *The Elements of Law*, and *The Elements of Philosophy* alike Hobbes looks upon appetite as a force even more potent than association in directing man's thoughts to a given end. Equally important is appetite in giving impulse to thought. In *The Elements of Philosophy* appetite is shown to have power to arouse phantasms in the absence of sense objects; and in *Leviathan* and *The Elements of Law* it is made the inalienable condition to what, if Hobbes had used the word, he must have called genius — wherein a good fancy unites with a good judgment in a bright, quick-ranging mind. In *Leviathan* he writes:

> And therefore, a man who has no great Passion for any of these things; but is, as men terme it indifferent; though he may be so farre a good man as to be free from giving offence; yet he cannot possibly have either a great Fancy or much Judgement, For the Thoughts are to the Desires, as Scouts, and Spies, to range abroad, and find the way to the things Desired: All Stedinesse of the minds motion, and all quicknesse of the same, proceeding from thence. For as to have no Desire, is to be Dead: so to have weak Passions, is Dulnesse . . . .[53]

The contrary of dulness, says Hobbes, in *The Elements of Law*, is a "quick ranging of mind . . . joined with curiosity of comparing the things that come into his mind one with another." [54] If in comparisons a man delights in finding "unexpected similitudes" he is said to have a good fancy: "from thence proceed those grateful similes, metaphors, and other tropes, by which both poets and orators have it in their power to make things please or displease, and shew well or ill to others, as they like themselves." [55] If, however, in making comparisons, a man

---

[53] *Leviathan*, I, viii.   [54] *The Elements of Law*, I, x, 4.
[55] *Ibid.* When Locke (*Of Human Understanding*, II, xi, 2) defines "fancy" ("wit") as the power to perceive and put together quickly ideas that resemble each

is apt in "discerning suddenly dissimilitude in things," he is said to have good judgment, by which virtue of mind "men attain to exact and perfect knowledge . . . : for to judge is nothing else than to distinguish and discern."

This last passage will at once recall the statements in *The Elements of Philosophy* about a "good fancy" and a "good judgment" quoted a few pages back. Hobbes is now making a more specific application, however. He has in mind, among other things, the signs of artistic genius, which he finds to consist first in eagerness and delight in making comparisons, secondly in a special aptitude through the fancy for discovering unusual likenesses which may become the material for pleasing image-bearing language. He also has in mind a definition of wit, which immediately follows: "and both fancy and judgment are commonly comprehended under the name of WIT, which seemeth a tenuity and agility of spirits, contrary to that restiveness of the spirits supposed in those that are dull." [56]

It appears from this that wit, like fancy and judgment, is inseparably related to the faculty of making comparisons. Wit is the more comprehensive term, since it includes both fancy and judgment. Hobbes's statement about judgment leaves doubt as to whether this faculty has any relation to literary ends; we must look elsewhere for evidence on this point. Fancy, however, definitely appears to have such a relation — in the perception of such likenesses as find expression in metaphor and simile. Wordsworth, describing the structure of the imaginative mind, writes

> Of that interminable building rear'd
> By observation of affinities
> In objects where no brotherhood exists
> To common minds.[57]

---

other, and "judgement" as the power to discern unlikeness, he probably has this and similar passages in mind, and regards himself as in agreement with Hobbes. Hobbes displays his superior acuteness in reasoning on aesthetic matters by specifying, as Locke does not, (1) that the similitudes shall be "unexpected" and (2) that the similitudes or dissimilitudes shall be such as are but rarely observed by others. Addison (*The Spectator*, No. 62), quoting Locke, corrects him on this point, insisting upon the elements of unexpectedness and difficulty.

[56] *The Elements of Law*, I, x, 4.

[57] *The Prelude*, ed. by Ernest de Selincourt (London, 1933), (A), II, 401–405.

Hobbes's poet (and orator, too) is likewise one who differs from
other men by virtue of such refined perceptive powers.

In a near parallel passage in *Leviathan* this quality of sharp-
ened perceptiveness is made even more emphatic when Hobbes
says that the similitudes noted by a good fancy are "such as
are but rarely observed by others." Hobbes has here re-
turned to a consideration of the subject of fancy, judgment,
and wit, enlarging the scope of his inquiry through further
exposition and clarifying it through more precise definition.
He here appears to identify a "good fancy" with a "good wit,"
distinguishing both from judgment:

> And whereas in this succession of mens thoughts there is nothing to
> observe in the thing they think on, but either in what they be *like one an-*
> *other,* or in what they be *unlike,* or *what they serve for,* or *how they serve to such*
> *a purpose;* Those that observe their similitudes, in case they be such as
> are but rarely observed by others, are sayd to have a *Good Wit;* by which,
> in this occasion, is meant a *Good Fancy.* But they that observe their dif-
> ferences and dissimilitudes; which is called *Distinguishing* and *Discerning*
> and *Judging* between thing and thing; in case, such discerning be not
> easie, are said to have a good Judgement . . . .[58]

This is incorporated in a discussion of natural virtue, or wit,
which Hobbes defines as "that *Wit,* which is gotten by Use
onely and Experience; without Method, Culture, or Instruction." [59] This natural wit "consisteth principally in two things:
Celerity of Imagining (that is, swift succession of one thought to
another;) and steddy direction to some approved end." [60]

Hobbes distinguishes "natural" from "acquired" wit. Natural wit is derived from experience, and depends for excellence
upon right appetites, quickness of memory, a lively imagination, and a good judgment. Its synonym is "prudence." [61]
The synonyms for acquired wit are "reason" and "science."
This wit is derived by "method and instruction"; it is "grounded
on the right use of Speech; and produceth the Sciences."
In another place Hobbes defines Reason and Science more
definitely:

> By this it appears that Reason is not as Sense, and Memory, borne
> with us; nor gotten by Experience onely, as Prudence is; but attayned

---

[58] *Leviathan,* I, viii.   [59] *Ibid.*   [60] *Ibid.*   [61] *Ibid.*

by Industry; first in apt imposing of Names; and secondly by getting a good and orderly Method in proceeding from the Elements, which are Names, to Assertions made by Connexion of one of them to another; and so to Syllogismes, which are the Connexions of one Assertion to another, till we come to a knowledge of all the Consequences of names appertaining to the subject in hand; and that is it, men call SCIENCE. And whereas Sense and Memory are but knowledge of Fact, which is a thing past, and irrevocable; *Science* is the knowledge of Consequences, and dependance of one fact upon another: by which, out of that we can presently do, we know how to do something else when we will, or the like, another time: Because, when we see how any thing comes about, upon what causes, and by what manner; when the like causes come into our power, we see how to make it produce the like effects.[62]

It is apparent that Hobbes classes poets among men of natural rather than acquired wit. The poet is a man of prudence rather than of science. Not all men of prudence are poets, but all poets are men of prudence. This is not to say that poets are inferior — indeed, as we shall see in examining *The Answer to Davenant* and further passages in *Leviathan*, they may at times be superior — but it is to say they are different. We shall also see, and this is a thing of great importance in arriving at Hobbes's final view of poetry, that the good poet must not be devoid of judgment, however great may be his endowment of fancy. Men of prudence are described by Hobbes in highly respectful terms:

When the thoughts of a man, that has a designe in hand, running over a multitude of things, observes how they conduce to that designe; or what designe they may conduce unto; if his observations be such as are not easie, or usuall, This wit of his is called PRUDENCE: and dependeth on much Experience, and Memory of the like things, and their consequences heretofore. In which there is not so much difference of Men, as there is in their Fancies and Judgements . . . .[63]

Yet, it must be admitted that when Hobbes is preoccupied with the problem of rational or scientific truth he is likely to depreciate poetry and its handmaiden fancy. Thus in his discussion of science in the fifth chapter of *Leviathan* he quite throws out poetic language as a means to science, reckoning it as one of the seven "absurdities" which proceed from the wrong use of language in processes of ratiocination:

[62] *Leviathan*, I, v.   [63] *Ibid.*, I, viii.

The sixth, to the use of Metaphors, Tropes, and other Rhetoricall figures, in stead of words proper. For though it be lawfull to say, (for example) in common speech, *the way goeth, or leadeth hither, or thither, The Proverb sayes this or that* (whereas wayes cannot go, nor Proverbs speak;) yet in reckoning, and seeking of truth, such speeches are not to be admitted.

Here, as is occasionally the case elsewhere, Hobbes is under the influence of the rhetorical tradition and fails to distinguish between oratory and poetry. But, as we shall see, the method of similitudes and tropes is the method of poetry as well as of eloquence; it is also the method of fancy. The method of "acquired wit," or science, on the other hand, is predominantly the method of logical relationships through the exercise of reason and judgment.

In the eighth chapter of *Leviathan* Hobbes makes this distinction the basis of assigning varying degrees and proportions of fancy and judgment to the several types of discourse. In history, "Judgement must be eminent. . . . Fancy has no place, but onely in adorning the stile"; likewise in "Demonstration, in Councell, and all rigorous search of Truth [in logic and science] Judgement does all." Fancy has a use here only so far as the "understanding have need to be opened by some apt similitude." The part of fancy in "Orations of Prayse and in Invectives" and in "Hortatives and Pleadings" is an even lower one. In the latter, fancy is required where "Disguise [rather than truth] serveth best to the Designe in hand"; in the former fancy is predominant, "because the designe is not truth, but to Honour or Dishonour." Hobbes will allow no place whatever to fancy in discourses having to do with the esoterics of anatomy and physics. Likewise, in sermons or in other public discourses before persons unknown or before those whom we ought to reverence, there must be no fanciful "play with sounds" and "Gingling of words," such as might be permitted in low or familiar company.[64] With particular application to this last instance, Hobbes remarks that "the difference is onely the want of Discretion. So that where Wit is wanting, it is not Fancy that is wanting, but Discretion," and is led to

[64] *Ibid.*

declare, "Judgement therefore without Fancy is Wit, but Fancy without Judgement not." [65]

Here we arrive at the complete reverse of Hobbes's previous statement — quoted some pages back — identifying a "good wit" with a "good fancy." Neither of these statements, however, can be taken as Hobbes's final view of the matter. Each represents a moment of particular emphasis, in which, first with his attention centered on effect-seeking poetry, and secondly with the ends and methods of truth-seeking science in mind, he misstates his case as a whole. To understand this case we must examine further passages having to do with fancy and judgment, especially in relation to poetry, and must then seek to reconcile various conflicting utterances in final definitions of wit and fancy.

A careful reading in context of the passage in *Leviathan* in which Hobbes makes a "good fancy" equivalent to a "good wit" shows that the exclusion of judgment here is apparent rather than real. "Fancy, without the help of Judgement," Hobbes goes on to say, "is not commended as a Vertue"; and in further explication he writes:

> Besides the Discretion of times, places, and persons, necessary to a good Fancy, there is required also an often application of his thoughts to their End; that is to say, to some use to be made of them. This done; he that hath this Vertue, will be easily fitted with similitudes, that will please, not onely by illustration of his discourse, and adorning it with new and apt metaphors; but also, by the rarity of their invention. But without Steddinesse, and Direction to some End, a great Fancy is one kind of Madnesse; such as they have, that entring into any discourse, are snatched from their purpose, by every thing that comes in their thought, into so many, and so long digressions, and Parentheses, that they utterly lose themselves: Which kind of folly, I know no particular name for: but the cause of it is, sometimes want of experience; whereby that seemeth to a man new and rare, which doth not so to others: sometimes Pusillanimity; by which that seems great to him, which other men think a trifle: and whatsoever is new, or great, and therefore fit to be told, withdrawes a man by degrees from the intended way of his discourse. [66]

Such qualification shows that, in his thinking, however strongly some of his wording may suggest the contrary, Hobbes does

[65] *Leviathan*, I, viii.   [66] *Ibid.*

not conceive of a good fancy, hence of a good wit, as separate from judgment. The key word here is no doubt "good."

Quintilian, and after him, Puttenham, had sharply distinguished between a lawless, capricious fancy and a well-regulated, or a good, one. Puttenham's word for those who possess the first, from which comes only disorder and confusion, is "*phantastici*," but he calls those who possess the second "*euphantasioti*," among whom are "all good Poets, notable Captaines . . . all cunning artificers and enginers," all, in short, who have contributed to the arts of civilization. This good fancy, he says, "is to the sound and true judgement of man most needful." [67] Such a distinction is clearly implied by Hobbes. His discussion as a whole, in spite of certain partially contradictory assertions, leaves no uncertainty as to his position on this point. There is a fancy which is merely wild invention and there is a fancy which is well regulated and well directed.[68] The first leads to madness, the second to some of the most commendable works of prudence, poetry in case, and, as we shall see later, to other highly desirable arts of civilization.

Even in the instances I have cited where fancy has been assigned a secondary position — except in the last two cases where it is ruled out completely [69] — Hobbes is speaking of the good fancy. Its place in history, philosophy, and other forms of discourse where plain truth is the main intent is subordinate, yet legitimate. It is admitted in accordance with the dictates of reason and discretion. A good fancy, then,

[67] See pp. 64–65 of this book.

[68] The fancy of dreams is of the lawless sort. Dreams are unlike the orderly "discourse of thought" not only in that their ideas occur with neither rhyme nor reason, but in that they are made up of partly fictitious phantasms, which, because they are aroused freshly from internal motion from the heart, are "clear as in sense itself" (*The Elements of Philosophy*, IV, xxv, 9). With relation to these phantasms, moreover, since there is no memory, there can be neither "fancy" nor "judgment" in the sense of taking notice of likenesses and differences: "To conclude, when we dream, we do not wonder at strange places and the appearance of things unknown to us, because admiration requires that the things appearing be new and unusual, which can happen to none but those that remember former appearances; whereas in sleep, all things appear as present" (*ibid.*).

[69] In fact, he presents this extreme view only in reaction to a type of discourse that he elsewhere labels "levity," to which he denies any relation to true wit and which he would refuse to acknowledge as a product of a "good fancy." See p. 106 and note of this book.

may be assumed as an ingredient in the wit of such writers. When we come to poetry, not only is the fancy essential, but it is explicitly predominant, the judgment, we may infer, serving merely to furnish ballast and to give direction: "In a good Poem, whether it be Epique, or Dramatique; as also in Sonnets, Epigrams, and other Pieces, both Judgement and Fancy are required: But the Fancy must be more eminent; because they [poems] please for the Extravagancy; but ought not to displease by Indiscretion." [70]   Judgment is here made subordinate; it is, however, requisite — that is, if the poem is good.   If judgment is absent then the fancy is bad and true wit wanting.   Hobbes is clear on the point: "And in any Discourse, whatsoever, if the defect of Discretion be apparent, how extravagant soever the Fancy be, the whole discourse will be taken for a signe of want of wit; and so will it never when the Discretion is manifest, though the Fancy be never so ordinary." [71]

When we recall that Hobbes would completely rule out fancy in discourses on scientific subjects and in sermons and certain addresses to strangers and dignified personages, the last statement appears comprehensible as applying to works of judgment only.   For the rest, that is in all discourse in which fancy is admissible or required, there must be sufficient judgment to relieve the work of evidence of indiscretion; poetry would certainly fall in this class.   It is thus that Hobbes provides for that union of imagination and judgment in poetry which was later to receive much emphasis in English criticism.

[70] *Leviathan*, I, viii.
[71] *Ibid.* It is difficult to see, in view of Hobbes's frequent and explicit assertions to the contrary, how a modern critic like Mr. Mark Van Doren could believe that Hobbes ruled out the judgment in works of fancy. "When Hobbes and Davenant separated Fancy from Judgment," writes Mr. Van Doren, "and sent it off to play alone, they condemned it to dull company. Their æsthetics, in setting reason over against imagination, did reason no great service and did imagination real harm. Dryden belonged on the side of so-called reason. He was not a child of fancy; he never lived what is often too glibly termed the life of the imagination. His true home was the house of Judgment; and his true game was the adult game of common sense" (*The Poetry of John Dryden* [New York, 1920], p. 41). Such misinterpretations come, surely, from accepting traditional cant rather than from a close reading of one's author. One of the main achievements of Hobbes was to find a place in poetry for both fancy and judgment, united in coöperative effort.

In those sections of *The Answer to Davenant* (1650) and *The Virtues of an Heroic Poem* (1675) where Hobbes addresses himself to a discussion of the subject, he definitely maintains the supremacy of the fancy, insisting at the same time on the exercise of judgment. The passage in the *Answer* will be examined later. That in the *Virtues* will serve our immediate purpose:

> A fourth [virtue of an heroic poem] is in the Elevation of Fancie, which is generally taken for the greatest praise of Heroique Poetry; and is so, when governed by discretion. For men more generally affect and admire Fancie than they do either Judgment or Reason, or Memory, or any other intellectual Vertue; and for the pleasantness of it, give to it alone the name of Wit, accounting Reason and Judgment but for a dull entertainment. For in Fancie consisteth the Sublimity of a Poet, which is that poetical Fury which the Readers for the most part call for. It flies abroad swiftly to fetch in both Matter and Words; but if there be not Discretion at home to distinguish which are fit to be used and which not, which decent and which undecent for Persons, Times, and Places, their delight and grace is lost. But if they be discreetly used, they are greater ornaments of a Poem by much than any other.[72]

Here Fancy is again specifically made the active principle of poetry, an instrument of invention, flying abroad to search out materials, bringing in both matter and words which, through the aid of a selective judgment, are to be built into structures of beauty and delight. Fancy and wit are again named as equivalents, but only momentarily and tentatively. Men give to fancy "alone the name of Wit," says Hobbes. His own qualification follows closely, however: "but if there be not Discretion at home . . . their delight and grace is lost." He is once more saying, in effect, that in a "good wit" there will be found a due proportion of fancy and judgment.

From what has preceded we may deduce with fair accuracy Hobbes's definition of wit. By wit Hobbes seems to have reference to that capacity for ready "discourse of mind" which is marked by quickness of perception, unusual aptness in discerning likenesses and differences, and general agility in the pursuit of ideas and the use of them to some definite end. Judgment, as well as fancy, is requisite, and seems native to natural

---

[72] Spingarn, II, 70.

wit. The proportion of fancy to judgment will vary in different kinds of wit. In acquired wit judgment will be the more prominent; in natural wit, fancy. The historian and the scientist, for example, will have much judgment but little fancy; the poet, on the contrary, requires a preëminence of fancy, with less, though sufficient, judgment. All fancy, or all judgment, despite certain isolated statements to the contrary, is not sufficient for a good wit. Such statements are not true to Hobbes's meaning as a whole. All judgment and no fancy, he would assuredly say, must end in dulness; and, however important the place of fancy in constructive processes, it can be of no avail without a due measure of judgment. "Fancy without Judgement is not commended a Vertue." For, "without Steddinesse, and Direction to some End, a great Fancy is one kind of Madnesse." It should be noted, as indeed it has been by Professors Ustick and Hudson,[73] that Hobbes is careful to differentiate the wit he is talking about from that cheaper sort which he calls levity, a defect "which betrayeth also mobility in the spirits, but in excess, An example whereof is in them that in the midst of any serious discourse, have their minds diverted to every little jest or witty observation." [74] Hobbes's "wit" is neither superficial nor cheap. It is rather a thing of the efficient intellect; it has to do with the enabling faculties of mind; it implies active passions to give impulse and direction, wealth of experience, and amplitude of the mental powers of fancy and judgment, duly proportioned and balanced according to specific ends in those higher functions of perception, rationalization, and creation which distinguish men from brutes.

IV

The man of wit who is a poetic genius will be distinguished from other men in that he will be superlatively endowed with fancy. He will have exact judgment, much experience, and

[73] W. Lee Ustick and Hoyt H. Hudson, "Wit, 'Mixt Wit,' and the Bee in Amber," *The Huntington Library Bulletin*, No. 8 (1935), p. 108. This article is invaluable for a presentation of ideas of seventeenth-century wit.

[74] *The Elements of Law*, I, x, 5.

a full memory. Lively appetites will direct the formative activities of his mind to definite ends. But these things will be subordinate to an operative fancy which perceives similarities not easily observed and ranges over the wide field of memory, selecting and collecting materials for poetic creations to be put into constructions of language that will please with their concreteness and the range and variety of their invention. However much Hobbes may depreciate fancy in other forms of discourse, he grants to it unequivocal supremacy in the field of poetry.

It should be observed, however, that in this application Hobbes assigns to fancy a quite particularized function. He refers it now not to original images nor to retained phantasms, but to a power of mind to select and combine. Fancy, as the faculty of poetic perception and invention, definitely parts company with imagination, the faculty of receiving and retaining images. This conception of fancy Hobbes quite consistently maintains in his more specific critical treatises. It is, as we have seen in the extract quoted a few pages back, succinctly expressed in *The Virtues of an Heroic Poem;* and it occurs in amplified form in a remarkable passage in *The Answer to Davenant.*

This passage is notable for many things, but not the least, in connection with the point I have just made and with ideas considered earlier in this chapter, for an important dichotomy. The word "imagination" has disappeared, but not the idea. That part of it which has to do merely with retaining images and was previously identified with "memory" — simple imagination — is now made the exclusive property of memory; while that part which has to do with combining images, that is the "compounded imagination," is made over to fancy. Fancy and memory are no longer synonymous; for memory, important as it is, now becomes but the storehouse within which fancy, the explorer and architect, guided by the judgment, operates to find out, select, and construct into artful unities the materials needed for its purposes.

Time and Education begets experience; Experience begets memory; Memory begets Judgement and Fancy; Judgement begets the strength and structure, and Fancy begets the Ornaments of a Poem. The Ancients therefore fabled not absurdly in making memory the Mother of the Muses. For memory is the World (though not really, yet so as in a looking glass) in which the Judgment, the severer Sister, busieth her self in a grave and rigid examination of all the parts of Nature, and in registring by Letters their order, causes, uses, differences, and resemblances; Whereby the Fancy, when any work of Art is to be performed findes her materials at hand and prepared for use, and needs no more then a swift motion over them, that what she wants, and is there to be had, may not lie too long unespied. So that when she seemeth to fly from one *Indies* to the other, and from Heaven to Earth, and to penetrate into the hardest matter and obscurest places, into the future and into her self, and all this in a point of time, the voyage is not very great, her self being all she seeks; and her wonderful celerity consisteth not so much in motion as in copious Imagery discreetly ordered & perfectly registred in the memory, which most men under the name of Philosophy have a glimpse of, and is pretended to by many that, grosly mistaking her, embrace contention in her place. But so far forth as the Fancy of man has traced the ways of true Philosophy, so far it hath produced very marvellous effects to the benefit of mankinde. All that is beautiful or defensible in building, or marvellous in Engines and Instruments of motion, whatsoever commodity men receive from the observations of the Heavens, from the description of the Earth, from the account of Time, from walking on the Seas, and whatsoever distinguisheth the civility of *Europe* from the Barbarity of the *American* savages, is the workmanship of Fancy but guided by the Precepts of true Philosophy. But where these precepts fail, as they have hitherto failed in the doctrine of Moral vertue, there the Architect, *Fancy*, must take the Philosophers part upon her self. He therefore that undertakes an Heroick Poem, which is to exhibit a venerable & amiable Image of Heroick vertue, must not only be the Poet to place & connect, but also the Philosopher, to furnish and square his matter, that is, to make both Body and Soul, colour and shadow of his Poem out of his own Store: Which how well you have performed I am now considering.[75]

Hobbes has presented in this passage one of the finest justifications of the constructive imagination to be found in literature — even Shelley did not write more eloquently or convincingly of its powers. It contains in germ the best thought in aesthetics of the eighteenth and early nineteenth centuries: the ideas of Gerard on imagination and genius, of Hume on imagination and philosophy, of Coleridge on the relationship between imagination and other faculties in poetry — the conception that a good poet shall be first a philosopher,

[75] *The Answer to Davenant*, Spingarn, II, 59–60.

and that there must be an essential equilibrium between the judgment and the spontaneous creative powers.

The old negative connotations of Plato's phantasy have disappeared. The fancy here, as an architect able to create, is responsible for all those achievements of civilization which have depended upon the inventive, constructive powers of the mind. She it is who, seeing what is required and what is to be had, is able to choose from the storehouse of experience and construct new forms better fitted to meet men's greatest needs.[76]

This part of Hobbes's idea is clearly not a mere repetition of Sidney's notion, and Horace's before him, that the poet is responsible for the growth of civilization. Neither Horace nor Sidney had gone so far into the idea of this constructive function of the imagination. To them the poet was a seer who knew and taught and refined — and of course inculcated the best moral ideas through example, an idea which Hobbes does not forget — but they did not venture behind the seerlike function to an examination of the mental processes. Nor did

[76] Here, as elsewhere, Hobbes's general attitude toward fancy is in sharp contrast to Locke's. Locke's comments on the imagination and fancy are usually derogatory. Granting full powers to the constructive faculties of the mind in forming complex ideas, he nevertheless makes a distinction between complex ideas that are real and ideas that are imaginary, or, to use another term, fantastical. "Fantastical or chimerical, I call such ideas as have no foundation in nature," he explains (*Of Human Understanding*, II, xxx, 1, 3). Dreams and fancies, imaginations of centaurs, harpies, and other extravagancies, are thus constantly set off, at least by implication, from the realities of things. "All the art of rhetoric — all the artificial and figurative application of words" to be found in eloquence "are for nothing else but to insinuate wrong ideas, move the passions, and thereby mislead the judgment, and so indeed are perfect cheats" (*ibid.*, III, x, 34). The attractions of works of fancy are so great, however, that only the most prudent escape: "There are so many ways of fallacy, such arts of giving colours, appearances, and resemblances by their court-dresser, the fancy, that he who is not wary to admit nothing but truth itself . . . cannot but be caught" (*Of the Conduct of the Understanding*, in Vol. I of *The Works of John Locke* [London, 1867], 33). Locke can only observe with regret that the universal fondness for such arts of fallacy shows "how little the preservation and improvement of truth and knowledge is the care and concern of mankind." With the general preference against him, he quite realizes the futility of resistance, however, and admits as much. "I doubt not but it will be thought great boldness if not brutality in me, to have said this much against it," he writes. "Eloquence, like the fair sex, has too prevailing beauties in it to suffer itself ever to be spoken against; and it is vain to find fault with those arts of deceiving, wherein men find pleasure to be deceived" (*ibid.*).

they think, as does Hobbes, of extending the dynamic principle of poetic activity, namely, the imagination, to other spheres of creative achievement.[77]   To Hobbes men of genius, whether astronomers, architects or inventors, discoverers or geographers, mathematicians or statesmen, are to be accounted for by the fortunate union of a quick fancy and philosophic judgment. No one, except the Hobbes-inspired Charleton, so far as I can recall, was to say anything like this again for a full hundred years, when Gerard wrote his book on genius.

Moreover, Hobbes comes nearer here to a conception of the mind as a unity, rather than a collection of separate faculties, than anyone else, I believe, until Addison.[78]   Memory begets fancy and judgment, it is true, and fancy flits about among the materials of memory for her materials; but there is, Hobbes suggests, a oneness in these powers.   For even in a voyage to the Indies the distance is not great; it is herself fancy seeks.

And in this connection, Hobbes presents a fascinating idea of man's mind as the manufactory of poetic products.   All the materials of poetry, he asserts plainly, as they are affected both by the shaping agency of the fancy and by the judicial services of the judgment, "to make both Body, and Soul, colour and shadow of his poem," must come out of the mind's own store. Moreover, as we know, if we go back to all Hobbes has said, the activity of the fancy to be effective for poetry must be shot through with the warming fires of the passions to raise it from the plane of the commonplace and dull.   A quick fancy is, furthermore, the informing power which makes delightful, as well as possible, all extraordinary intellectual activity.   This is a marked advance over neoclassic theories of imitation to be found among Hobbes's predecessors, Vida in case, and among

[77] Only Huarte and Puttenham, to my knowledge, had done this. It is possible that both Puttenham and Hobbes, in ascribing the practical arts of civilization to the imagination, were encouraged by the example of Huarte. Neither of these predecessors had, of course, given the idea so secure a psychological setting as does Hobbes, and Huarte, especially, fails to see, unlike Hobbes, that the imagination without judgment avails little in achieving the ends described.

[78] Addison, it will be recalled, in one place takes exception to the faculty psychology: "there is no such division in the soul itself, since it is the whole soul that remembers, understands, wills, or imagines" (*The Spectator*, No. 600).

many who came after him in both England and France, including Boileau and Pope.

Mr. Dowlin believes that Davenant, in his Preface to *Gondibert*, was largely influenced in his theories by Hobbes, with whom he had discussed such matters and whose works he had certainly read.[79] There is much to support Mr. Dowlin's view, though it is quite possible that Davenant exerted a reciprocal influence, aiding Hobbes to a fuller and bolder expression of ideas that, though implicit, had been only partially enunciated in his earlier works. It would seem fair, then, to examine Davenant's own description of the creative agency in poetry (which Hobbes calls fancy) for further evidence of Hobbes's meaning. Davenant calls this agency "wit," a term to which he applies, indeed, three separate meanings. One of these, that which finds expression in such vain dexterity of language as results in conceits and other false coinages, is accounted as wit only by the injudicious. The other two may, however, be properly applied to poetry, as well as, it becomes clear, to other forms of constructive activity. True wit is, first, the substance of poetry. As such, it is "the laborious and lucky resultances of thought," having both happiness and care. "It is a Webb consisting of the subt'lest threds; and like that of the *Spider* is considerately woven out of our selves." Woven, that is, not by chance but by design. All things are done either by chance or on consideration, but the "works of Chance are accomplishments of an instant, having commonly a dissimilitude, but hers [the works of wit] are the works of time and have their contextures alike." [80] Thus "wit" is the accomplishment itself, the completed fabric, of poetic composition, in which like has been woven into like to form a unified well-created whole.

But to Davenant "wit" is more than the substance of poetry; it is also the agency and process through which the substance is created. Here Davenant is nearest Hobbes: "*Wit* is not only the luck and labour, but also the dexterity

---

[79] Cornell March Dowlin, *Sir William Davenant's Gondibert, Its Preface, and Hobbes's Answer* (Philadelphia, 1934).

[80] "Preface to *Gondibert*," Spingarn, II, 20.

of thought, rounding the world, like the Sun, with unimaginable motion, and bringing swiftly home to the memory universall surveys." [81] Wit, Davenant goes on to say picturesquely, is the "Soul's *Powder*," which, if suppressed, blows up and ascends easily toward heaven, though by nature it can make little progress to the cell of the devil. Wit, he further explains, "breaks through all about it as farr as the utmost it can reach, removes, uncovers, makes way for Light where darkness was inclos'd, till great bodies are more examinable by being scatter'd into parcels, and till all that find its strength . . . worship it for the effects as deriv'd from the Deity." [82] These effects are to be discovered in the distinctive virtues we most prize in great divines, statesmen, and military leaders. In poets it is "a full comprehension of all recited in all these, and an ability to bring those comprehensions into action." [83]

Davenant's definition of wit is on the whole quite inferior to Hobbes's description of fancy — the two are plainly talking of the same thing; yet, in many respects, it illuminates Hobbes's meaning. A careful reading of the two passages suggests that Hobbes in the *Answer* is assuming the rôle of a teacher, saying over in explicit language a lesson which his pupil has only imperfectly recited. In doing this he enlarges upon what he has previously written and, discarding the equivocal term "wit," fixes definitely upon the word "fancy" to describe the assembling, constructive faculty through which the mind makes use of the materials of experience for poetry and the other arts of civilization. He also reiterates, apparently with deliberate emphasis, a part of his theory that Davenant had slurred over, at best had only implied: the importance of the judgment in works of fancy.

Addressing a poet strictly on aesthetic matters, Hobbes lets himself out, as it were, and writes of fancy and its workings with more freedom and warmth than he might otherwise have shown. He has, too, no doubt, been stimulated by some of Davenant's remarks to clearer thought and more specific utterance on the processes of poetic composition; so that, though

---

[81] "Preface to *Gondibert*," Spingarn, II, 20.
[82] *Ibid.*, II, 21.   [83] *Ibid.*

most of the ideas that occur here are to be found elsewhere in his writing, they are expressed with a certainty and directness and fulness that are new.

V

The preceding examination has been carried on under the assumption that in order to understand Hobbes's theory of the imagination, or, more broadly, the creative process, it is necessary to know the psychology upon which this theory rests: in other words that we must first find Hobbes's ideas of the make-up of the poet's mind before we can understand how that mind can and does work in poetic creation. Two major problems present themselves in such a procedure: first, that of arriving at some sort of resolution of the paradox of belief in a mechanical basis for perception and other mental process with their origin in external stimulation, and a conception of a self-originating activity carried on within the mind; second, that of discovering the meaning Hobbes attaches to his terms, the nature and scope of the functions he assigns to each faculty described by these terms, and the relations of these functions to each other in both poetic and non-poetic processes.

These two questions are so nearly related that they can hardly be considered separately, and they have, consequently, been treated together in the preceding pages. The problem of volitional versus mechanical activity appears less difficult as we study closely all that Hobbes has to say on the matter. For, in spite of his consistently maintained theory that all the materials of knowledge originate in sense perception, motion from without impinging on the peculiar structure which is man's nervous system, it turns out that he is far from conceiving of the mind as a merely passive and helpless mechanism acting in response to external stimulus. In sum, considering all his qualifications and the implications of these qualifications, Hobbes's whole theory is less mechanical than it first appears. Thus, as we have seen, there is always in the perceiving act an "outward pressure" from the mind to meet the motion from without. Moreover, even elementary perception is impossible without memory of some previous sense impression with which to compare the incoming impression; and all ideas of objects in more complex perception, as of a man or of a square, are made up of a composite of ideas held in the memory and re-presented on the occasion of the fresh external stimulus to form a synthetic whole. It is true that Hobbes fails to show how the first perception would be produced; but he is tacitly admitting powers of mind which function in perception to aid in the conversion of motion into idea. In other words, perception is not a mere imprint of image upon the nervous system as of a seal on wax, but, as is the case in the theory of the Stoics and of Telesio and Campanella, it is an *effect* to which the mind itself contributes something. This conception appears in its most significant form, for the study we are making, in the attribution to the fancy and the judgment of special capacities to link together, at the moment of perception, ideas that are like and to discriminate between those that are unlike.

Hobbes's theory of association, which in its first form appears mechanical, and of desire or appetite, allows of even more extended powers of mind to deal with its materials independently of immediate external stimulus. Desire is here the saving factor. When desire enters in, first to control the direction of associative activity, but further to guide the fancy to new combinations and the judgment to new distinctions, the mind may be said to be working independently without benefit of any external impulsion. If it is insisted that this operation is still mechanical, let it at least be said that, whatever the original source of its impulses and materials, here is a machine operating on its own power and with its own resources, and in its own way at its own volition.

Granting the capacity of mind so to operate, it is not difficult to pass to a conception of the various faculties performing in special ways to invent and create the various instruments and arts which we observe to be the chief distinction of civilized man. Throughout his writings Hobbes admits man's ability to imagine things which are not true or present: fictions of the future, fictions of his own importance, of his own and others' acts. When he comes to poetry he assigns this power to form fictions almost exclusively to the fancy. In poetry — in other arts, too, for that matter — Hobbes brings the theatre of mental activity entirely within doors. Now memory is the world, and fancy and judgment operate exclusively within this world. Working in an enlarged capacity, with freer scope than in perception or even in the other secondary acts of mind, fancy ranges over the whole field of accumulated experience to discover like materials for her structures, with judgment watchfully at hand to discriminate and restrain.

Among the distinctive things in Hobbes's theory of imaginative creation is his tendency to get away from traditional neoclassic ideas of imitation. There is no place in his theory for divine inspiration, no place for the imitation of authors, nor a study of authors for materials or for ideas of beauty — unless such materials have been put to the test of examination through experience — no suggestion of studying specific objects in nature for the sake of selecting those more perfect qualities that may be combined into ideal form. Hobbes's works of fancy are, indeed, ideal, in that they belong to the mind and are created by acts of the mind: that is, though the materials with which the mind works were originally received through sense, at the time fancy and judgment coöperate to re-form these materials, they exist wholly in the secondary world of mental experience to be re-presented to the mind through memory and imagination. Hobbes's theory may be said, then, to neighbor more closely on Aristotle's theory of universals — abstractions — than on the Ciceronian and Renaissance notions of ideal imitation; it is still closer to Coleridge's doctrine of the secondary imagination.

Huarte and Bacon had both ascribed large powers to the imagination in relation to poetry, but Hobbes is far in advance of either in developing a consistent theory of imaginative creation. Beside Hobbes Huarte is a child in psychological speculation. He talks in broad terms about certain perceptive and creative acts which he assigns to the imagination, and he makes valuable suggestions about specific operations of the imaginative faculty; but his explanations are naïve, founded on chimerical notions of temperature and humidity as the bases of mental aptitudes. Bacon goes a step further than Huarte, especially in implications for an experiential basis for imaginative acts, but he is still under the spell of current theories of ideal imitation, to a less extent of divine inspiration; he thinks of imaginative construction as a play of mind, or even as a lucky chance; he neglects to show the relation of the imagination to the other faculties, and in general fails to develop a definite psychological background. Hobbes, like Huarte and Bacon, would separate poetry as a work of imagination from works of fact like history — for poetry is "manners feigned," not a record of actual men and events. But at its best, poetry is to Hobbes the highest kind of truth, even performing the philosopher's part where philosophy fails. It is one of the natural and legitimate activities of the human mind. It is a thing of judgment as well as of fancy, and its basis is the reality of a wide experience through which the mind is loaded with rich memories and wide and deep knowledge. And in this, again, Hobbes advances beyond his predecessors in giving dignity and worth to imaginative creations.

Hobbes's ideas on the imagination are valuable and forward-looking. In giving him due credit we must not, however, ignore defects and gaps in his theory. It is a theory that, in expression at least, lacks somewhat in consistency and completeness. Looking backward to ancient and medieval psychologies it inherits some of their confusions; pointing forward to newer ways of thought, it foreshadows without bringing into full definition later conceptions of the creative imagination as the active principle in perception and artistic composition.

Hobbes's use of terms is often tantalizing. Thus he makes fancy, in passages dealing with poetic construction, a creative agency similar in respects to the imagination of Romantic and present-day thought; but he elsewhere ascribes to this faculty quite other functions. When we read in *The Answer to Davenant* that very splendid description of the mind's power to construct poetry out of its own inner reality through the guiding agency of judgment, we must not forget that in other places we have been told that fancy is original perception, that fancy is the faculty of retaining images, like memory and imagination, and again, that to have a "good fancy" is to have a "good wit" and "good judgment." It is true that when we examine Hobbes's statements closely we find that he is using his terms in different applications, often with purposeful distinction. This does not, however, prevent a certain amount of difficulty in the mind of the reader. Even in the notable passage in *The Answer to Davenant*, the statement "Judgement begets the strength and structure, and Fancy begets the Ornaments of a Poem" seems unfortunate, as overemphasizing one aspect of the function of fancy, and understating another. For as one reads through the paragraph, it is apparent that fancy does much more than merely beget what we ordinarily mean by ornaments: she gathers the materials, and builds with them. It helps in getting Hobbes's meaning, however, to know that to him the "ornaments" of a poem include the fable or fiction, the amplitude and variety of incident, the images and descriptions and similitudes — all evidences of fulness of experience and fertility of invention; and that judgment is in reality not a begetting but a ruling power. In a previous passage Hobbes had made one of the indispensables of a "good fancy" ("natural wit") a steady direction to some approved end. When he here declares "her wonderful celerity" to consist "in copious Imagery discreetly ordered & perfectly registred in the memory," he evidently means much the same thing, since he is praising the "workmanship of Fancy . . . guided by the Precepts of true Philosophy."

The inner consistency of meaning here as elsewhere is, however, somewhat obscured by a phraseology that needs a particular interpretation. The varied use of terms in general suggests what must be a quite common experience among explorers in a new field — a searching for a way to express ideas still vague, a groping toward truth rather than realized possession of a clear conception. To quote any single statement without reference to the whole is likely to lead to grave error.

CHAPTER IV

Hobbes's Doctrine of Effects

I

ONE of the distinctive things about Hobbes is his tolerant attitude toward works of the imagination. Unlike Locke, who distrusted the fancy and its works as extravagant and inimical to truth, Hobbes found a way, by conceiving of a blend for artistic purposes of fancy and judgment in which fancy was chief but judgment indispensable, to give fancy and its products both dignity and importance. Hobbes is, in general, inclined to judge a work by its effects rather than by its conformity to traditional standards. He is willing to concede much to the principle of delight: "I know that variety of story, true or feigned, is the thing wherewith the reader is entertained most delightfully."[1] In quite the same vein he writes: "What, though you out-go the limits of certain history? Do painters, when they paint the face of the earth, leave a blank beyond what they know? Do not they fill up the space with strange rocks, monsters, and other gallantry, to fix their work in the memory of men by the delight of fancy?"[2] This is Hobbes the lover of romance and strange histories speaking, from convictions formed by his own experience. As a philosopher, he found ways to explain and justify the pleasure he took in works of fancy.

Hobbes's doctrine of effects is quite as important for modern aesthetics as is his theory of imagination. Although his approach is indirect and his findings incidental — for he did not

[1] Letter to Edward Howard, 1668, in *The English Works of Thomas Hobbes of Malmesbury*, ed. by Sir William Molesworth (London, 1839–45), IV, 459.
[2] *Ibid.*

deliberately set out to analyze artistic processes — his ultimate achievement was to lay a firm foundation for a psychology of aesthetic response. The pertinent theory here lies embedded in empirical inquiries into the nature and workings of the passions.

To Hobbes the passions are the mainspring of human actions. But the passions in turn take their character from, and exist in integral relationship to, the phenomena of pleasure and pain. Pleasure and pain, except such as arise directly from sense, are resultants of vital internal motion. Just as conception is the product of motion to and within the head, pleasure and pain have their origin in motions to the heart. Pleasure or pain results from a quickening or a slackening of vital motion induced by motion from sense. If vital motion is helped, the effect is pleasure and appetite; if vital motion is hindered, the effect is pain and aversion or fear.[3] Put into other words:

> This motion, in which consisteth pleasure or pain, is also a solicitation or provocation either to draw near to the thing that pleaseth, or to retire from the thing that displeaseth. And this solicitation is the endeavour or internal beginning of animal motion, which when the object delighteth, is called APPETITE; when it displeaseth, it is called AVERSION, in respect of the displeasure present, but in respect of the displeasure expected FEAR.[4]

All the passions, then, "called passions of the mind" consist of appetite and aversion. And "all Appetite, Desire and Love, is accompanied with some Delight more or less; and all Hatred, and Aversion, with more or less Displeasure and Offence." [5]

Hobbes very early establishes the principle that the explanation of pleasure and pain is to be sought within ourselves and not in the object. "As colour is not inherent in the object, but an affect thereof upon us, caused by . . . motion in the object . . . so neither is sound in the thing we hear, but in ourselves." [6] Similarly, the heat we feel from fire is in ourselves. "For our heat is pleasure or pain, according as

---

[3] *The Elements of Philosophy*, IV, xxv, 12, in *The English Works of Thomas Hobbes of Malmesbury.*
[4] *The Elements of Law*, ed. by Ferdinand Tönnies (Cambridge, 1928), I, vii, 2.
[5] *The Elements of Philosophy*, IV, xxv, 13.
[6] *The Elements of Law*, I, ii, 9.

it is extreme or moderate; but in the coal there is no such thing." [7]   As it is in the conceptions (including pleasures) that arise by vision, so it is in all conceptions from the other senses, "the subject of their inherence is not the object, but the sentient." [8]   From this Hobbes further deduces "that whatsoever accidents or qualities our senses make us think there be in the world, they are not there, but are seemings and apparitions only.   The things that really are in the world without us, are those motions by which these seemings are caused." [9]   Hobbes has here anticipated all later aestheticians who were to conceive of beauty as subjective.

A significant instance of what may be read into such passages as these we have been considering is to be found in Hazlitt's essay on Hobbes.[10]   Hazlitt's analysis, it may be said, is discriminating, often acute.   He is in general taking exception to the basic assumptions of Hobbes's philosophy, as being merely mechanical and, consequently, inadequate in explaining the operations of the mind.   Hobbes fails, Hazlitt maintains, because he ignores the important principle of the "understanding," and the way it works in transforming sense experience into ordered conception and reason.[11]   He gives Hobbes credit, however, for originating most of the important concepts to be found in Locke, Hartley, and other later mechanical philosophers, and in general dignifies his place in the history of thought: he "was indeed," says Hazlitt, "the father of the modern philosophy." [12]   He also ascribes to Hobbes the fundamental ideas of Berkeley's idealism, using as evidence not only the passage from *The Elements of Law* from which I have just quoted — which he reproduces *in extenso* — but much of the first chapter from *Leviathan*.   "It is evident [writes Hazlitt] that in this account he has laid the foundation of Berkeley's ideal system, though he does not seem anywhere to have gone the whole length of that doctrine." [13]

This is an interesting statement coming from Hazlitt,

[7] *The Elements of Law*, I, ii, 9.   [8] *Ibid.*   [9] *Ibid.*, I, ii, 10.
[10] *Literary Remains of the Late William Hazlitt*, ed. by E. L. Bulwer and Sergeant Talfourd (London, 1836), I, 115 ff.
[11] *Ibid.*, I, 163.   [12] *Ibid.*, I, 123.   [13] *Ibid.*, I, 131.

himself an idealist — though, because of his empiricism and
dualism, he can be classified neither with Berkeley nor with
Kant and Coleridge — who in general charges to Hobbes the
predominant bias toward materialism and mechanical reasoning in modern metaphysics.   It is, however, a tribute to a certain honesty in Hazlitt and to the closeness with which he had
read Hobbes that he should acknowledge in him foundations
for the ideal point of view.   For Hobbes's psychological investigations led him at times to observations that point inevitably to the conclusion that, so far as the mind of man is
concerned, there can be no reality but inner reality — that
is, the reality of perceptions, conceptions, and emotions, with
all their possible interpenetrations and structures, whatever
their source, however they are produced.   As we have seen,
according to Hobbes's theory in *The Elements of Philosophy*,
even perception is impossible without the agency of a power
of mind which he calls "memory," and the activity of judging
through comparison or contrast.   Furthermore, such conception is made possible only through the invention of names
arbitrarily assigned to ideas, through which they may be recalled and used by the mind in orderly processes of thought.[14]
Through names ideas are abstracted from their external
sources and become the exclusive property of mind for reasoning or imaginative processes.   Thus every mind, after accumulating a store of experiences, that is, ideas to which it has
attached names, becomes a world of its own, able at will to
order these ideas into new combinations for science or poetry,
independently of immediate contact with the external world.

This is a species of idealism, though, in spite of what Hazlitt says, it is not Berkeleyan idealism.   There is certainly no
trace in Hobbes of the Berkeleyan notion of divine intervention
in either the reception or the use of ideas, and Hobbes could
have had no sympathy with Berkeley's denial of the integrity
of matter.   Hobbes does, however, furnish a basis for a conception of intellectual ideas which have passed beyond the
stage of representations of externality to the imagination, and
which through the instrumentality of names have been given

[14] See pp. 11–12 of this book.

over with a certain measure of completeness to the dominion of the mind. He even shows — and here we return to the point from which we began this digression — that the ideas derived from original sense impressions are not mere images, but are transformations of motion into subjective effects and that in all conceptions that arise from sense "the subject of their inherence is not the object, but the sentient."

That delight, or the sense of beauty, should be regarded as not only subjective but relative, depending on individual reactions which in turn are governed by individual experiences, is inherent in Hobbes's philosophical conceptions. Since mind is caused by motion from material bodies, the unique structure of any mind at any moment represents the sum of its unique experiences. Not only is the individual mind itself in constant flux (so long as its experiences with the external world continue), but its mode of reactions will differ from those of other minds. Individual reactions, then, cannot be referred to any set standards. The idea of subjective, and, incidentally, relative, standards in taste and morals is clearly expressed in *Leviathan:*

> But whatsoever is the object of any mans Appetite or Desire; that is it which he for his part calleth *Good:* and the object of his Hate and Aversion, *Evill;* And of his Contempt, *Vile* and *Inconsiderable.* For these words of Good, Evill, and Contemptible, are ever used with relation to the person that useth them: There being nothing simply and absolutely so; nor any common Rule of Good and Evill, to be taken from the nature of the objects themselves; but from the Person of the man . . . .[15]

This forthright statement is closely followed by exposition which relates the term "good" to either beauty or morals, and affirms the natural tendency of man to move toward the good (the beautiful, the delightful, or the profitable).

In defining "good" Hobbes resorts to the Latin word *"pulchrum,"* which, according to the object or idea to which it applies, is to be variously interpreted as *"Fayre," "Beautifull," "Handsome," "Gallant," "Honourable," "Comely,"* or *"Amiable."* All these words signify a "Mine, or Countenance" which promises good. The "good," then, Hobbes summarizes, rather

---

[15] *Leviathan*, ed. by Ernest Rhys (London, Toronto, and New York, 1914), I, vi.

illogically, is to be classified under three heads: good in the promise, which is *"Pulchrum"*; good in effect, as the end desired, which is called *"Jucundum,"* or delightful; and good as the means, which is called *"Utile,"* or profitable.[16] Now when the motion from a given object strikes the sensory organs setting up motions which proceed to the mind and to the heart, it creates an appearance which promises good or evil, according to whether pleasure or pain follows. If the effect is pleasurable, it is accompanied by a promise of good, in which a sense of well-being is mingled with delight. The real internal effect Hobbes describes as "nothing but motion or endeavour which consisteth in appetite . . . to . . . the object moving." And further, "This motion, which is called appetite . . . seemeth to be a corroboration of vital motion, and a help thereunto." [17] Objects that give pleasure, therefore, may be regarded as life-giving as opposed to those that give pain, which may be assumed to be life-destroying. It follows, then, that works of art, scenes in nature, as well as all else that gives men pleasure, with a consequent desire, or appetite, to continue, or repeat, or extend experience with them are to be accounted as vitalizing and life-giving, hence good. Such a view helps explain Hobbes's fundamental tolerance for literature and other products of the imagination.

Let us remember, however, that such words as "good," and "beautiful" (*"pulchrum"*) "are ever used with relation to the person that useth them," [18] and we recognize that Hobbes, for all his attempt to reduce the phenomena of man's mind to law, must admit that men pass judgments on objects of beauty according to individual taste. Thus we find Hobbes's influence leading in two directions. In his rationalistic outlook and mechanistic attitude he may be regarded as giving comfort to the neoclassic tradition, especially to that branch of it which emphasizes the importance of good sense, judgment, and stylistic precision; but his emphasis on the variability of mental reactions to the same stimuli lends support to the Romantic school of taste in asserting the integrity of personal likes and dislikes, whatever the traditionalists may hold to the

[16] *Ibid.*   [17] *Ibid.*   [18] *Ibid.*

contrary. When Hobbes wrote his critiques of specific poems like *Gondibert* and Homer's epics he judged them, not according to set formulae, but from the point of view of content and qualities of style suitable to please a cultivated taste. His method is still objective, to be sure, but he is in a sense setting up his own standards of taste. To read these essays beside Le Bossu's treatise is to perceive how far Hobbes leans toward the liberal, unconventional side of the question.

Hobbes at one point ascribes the perception of pleasure and pain to a sort of sixth sense, the product of mechanical action of blood, nerves, and muscles upon the heart. Discussing sense and animal motion in a consideration of the five external senses, he remarks: "But there is another kind of sense, of which I will say something in this place, namely, the sense of pleasure and pain, proceeding not from the reaction of the heart outwards, but from continual action from the outermost part of the organ towards the heart." [19] Such a statement forecasts the later notion of an internal sense of beauty in Shaftesbury, Hutcheson, and others. Locke was to apply the phrase "internal sensations" to pleasurable and painful responses, [20] thus furnishing a link between Hobbes

[19] *The Elements of Philosophy*, IV, xxv, 12. Elsewhere Hobbes used "sixth sense" and with it "internal" sensation in a quite different application: "For when the conception of the same thing cometh again, we take notice that it is again; that is to say, that we have had the same conception before; which is as much as to imagine a thing past; which is impossible to sense, which is only of things present. This therefore may be accounted a sixth sense, but internal . . . and is commonly called REMEMBRANCE" (*The Elements of Law*, I, iii, 6).

[20] *Of Human Understanding*, II, xx, 3, in Vol. I of *The Works of John Locke* (London, 1867). See my article "Addison and Hutcheson on the Imagination," *A Journal of English Literary History*, II (1935), 215–234, for a fuller treatment of this subject. It is of interest that Edward Reynolds had used the phrase "inward senses" with a different application: "Now for these inward senses . . . I take . . . Memory and Fancie or Imagination, to have a more excellent degree of perfection in man; as being indeed the principall Store-houses and Treasuries of the operations of the Soule" (*A Treatise of the Passions and Faculties of the Soul of Man* [London, 1650], p. 13). Huarte (1578) also had applied the term "inward" to the senses in a manner similar to that of Reynolds: "By this so plaine and manifest a matter, which passeth through the outward senses, we may gather what that is in the inward. With this selfe power of the soule, we understand, imagine, and remember. But if it be true, that every worke requires a particular instrument, it behooveth of necessitie, that within the braine there be one instrument for the understanding; one for the imagination, and

and those critics of the school of taste who were to adapt the
idea more definitely to aesthetic discussion.

II

It will help in understanding Hobbes's ideas of aesthetic
response to examine briefly the distinction he makes between
the different types of pleasures. In *Leviathan* he classifies
pleasures under "pleasures of sense" and "pleasures of the
mind." Pleasures of sense are such as arise from objects present, and include "all Onerations and Exonerations of the
body, as also all that is pleasant in the *Sight, Hearing, Smell,
Tast,* or *Touch*." Pleasures of the mind are such as arise from
"the Expectation, that proceeds from foresight of the End,
or Consequence of things; whether those things in the Sense
Please or Displease." [21] They are generally called "JOY."
The word "sensual" is introduced, but is dismissed with the
rather unenlightening remark that its use in a derogatory
sense "has no place until there be Lawes." The earlier *Elements of Law* contains a clearer distinction between sensual
and non-sensual response. Hobbes here defines sensual pleasures as those which definitely belong to some particular corporeal organ of sense, naming specifically the acts by which
"man is invited to meat" and by which we give "continuance

---

another different from them for the memorie . . ." (*Examen de ingenios. The
Examination of Men's Wits*, tr. by R. C. [London, 1594], p. 52). Burton (1621)
had made a similar application of the term "inner senses" to the *common sense*, the
phantasie, and the *memory*. Thus "*Phantasie* or imagination," he says, "is an inner
sense which doth more fully examine the species perceived by *common sense*, of
things present or absent, and keeps them longer, recalling them to mind again,
or making new of his own" (*The Anatomy of Melancholy* [London, 1838], I, 1, ii, 7).
Before any of these writers St. Thomas Aquinas had, of course, held a theory of
"interior powers of sensitive apprehension" and of inward response to contrast or
external sense. Thus, he says, "Pleasure and pain can arise from a twofold apprehension, namely, from the apprehension of an exterior sense; and from the
interior apprehension of the intellect or of the imagination. Now the interior
apprehension extends to more objects than the exterior apprehension: because
whatever things come under the exterior apprehension, come under the interior,
but not conversely" (*Summa Theologica*, tr. by Fathers of the English Dominican
Province [London, 1911–25], Part II [First Part], First Number, Q. 25, A. 2,
p. 407).

[21] *Leviathan*, I, vi.

to our species." [22]   Non-sensual pleasure, on the other hand, is not "particular to any part of the body," and is called "delight of the mind" — or "joy."   In the following chapter, discussing the things that please and displease, Hobbes makes a further distinction.   There are, he says, three kinds of conceptions:

> . . . one is of that which is present, which is sense; another of that which is past, which is remembrance; and the third, of that which is future, which we call expectation . . . .   And every of these conceptions is pleasure present.   And first for the pleasures of the body which affect the sense of touch and taste, as far as they be organical, their conception is sense; so also is the pleasure of all exonerations of nature; all which passions I have before named sensual pleasures; and all their contraries, sensual pains.[23]

Such are Hobbes's general statements about the three types: sensual pleasures, pleasures of sense, and pleasures of the mind ("joy," "delight of the mind").   It is necessary to examine more specifically his meaning for each of these terms and the distinction he makes among them in practical application.

What, for example, is the precise difference between sensual pleasure and pleasure of the mind?   The preceding definitions show that the word "sensual" is applied to "pleasures particular to any part of the body," and to all "Onerations and Exonerations of the body," that is, organic sensations that have to do with eating, drinking, coition, and so forth (in general, we may assume, those pertaining to touch and taste).   Pleasures of the mind are, in contrast, those in which, through an act of the imagination, response to a given stimulus is raised from the physical to the mental plane.   This occurs when expectation or promise of good contributes to an experience which transcends the mere corporeal titillation.   The difference between a sensual and a mental pleasure does not necessarily, then, reside in the nature of the act or stimulus which gives occasion to it, but in the type of response made by the recipient.   Thus coition may be a purely sensual act; but it may be much more, depending upon what takes place in the

---

[22] *The Elements of Law*, I, vii, 9.   [23] *Ibid.*, I, viii, 2.

individual concerned; it is sensual, Hobbes explains, "but there is in it also a delight of the mind; for it consisteth of two appetites together, to please, and to be pleased; and the delight men take in delighting is not sensual, but a pleasure or joy of the mind, consisting in the imagination [let us say *realization*] of the power they have so much to please." [24] Little, I think, need be added to this illustration of the elementary distinction Hobbes wishes to draw between the two pleasures in question.

There remains, however, to distinguish between pleasures of sense and pleasures of the mind. Pleasures of sense, we have learned from definitions already presented, are such as to include all those sensations which may be labeled sensual; but we have also seen that sense impressions may ascend to the level of pleasures of mind, particularly when these impressions have become transmuted into images concerned with remembrance or expectation. The test seems to be whether the mind itself, through the imagination, adds anything to original sensation in the way of a promise or a realization of good. A nice distinction made by Hobbes, with regard to odors, will help at this point. Odors, he explains, may, if they are organical — that is, I judge, if they merely affect the organ of smell — give sensual pleasure or displeasure. But this pleasure or displeasure may be, indeed usually is, of the mind. Thus a certain odor coming, or thought to come, from ourselves, gives no offense, but coming from another displeases us. The displeasure arises not from the intrinsic nature of the odor, nor from its organic effect, but from a conception (imagination) of a hurt or an evil to come.[25] This odor becomes, then, the occasion for a passion — in this case an aversion — the passion arising from an imagined evil. Conversely, we may assume that the odor of a rose, since it causes a conception of a good to arise, is also the occasion for a passion — in this case an appetite — hence, for a "pleasure of the mind." That is, it is a perception accompanied by a sense of well-being in which the mind has added to the original image something relative to the future which contains in it a promise of good.

[24] *Ibid.*, I, ix, 15.   [25] *Ibid.*

In summary, then, sensual pleasure has to do with the gratification of physical appetite, and is referable to some specific part of the body. It fails to penetrate the periphery of the mind; and relates itself in no way to the larger issues of present or future well-being. Pleasure of the mind, on the other hand, is internal, that is, it is a response of the mind either to an image of an object present to the sense or to one called up from within, which creates, is accompanied by, or is modified by some appetite or passion. It is characterized by an extension of experience in which the mind adds something of its own to the original or recalled impression, and it may be described as a delightful motion of mind in reaction to the presentation of imagery, which contains a recognition or a promise of good beyond the immediate sensation. Pleasure of sense may eventuate either in sensual delight or in pleasure of the mind, depending upon the extent to which the response remains merely physical or becomes intellectualized through memory or imagination.

III

Conceptions of the past and conceptions of the future, as well as conceptions of sense, Hobbes asserts, are each "pleasure present." This is true because through the imagination the image of an expected good or a remembered good is brought before the mind as if it were actually present to the sense. Hence it would seem logical to refer such pleasures to the imagination. And in *Leviathan* Hobbes himself makes precisely this reference. Commenting upon the desire for fame after death, Hobbes explains that even though the pleasure of present fame is denied, yet such a desire is not vain, "because men have a present delight therein, from the foresight of it, and of the benefit that may redound thereby to their posterity, which, though they now see not, yet they imagine, and anything that is pleasure to the sense, the same also is pleasure in the imagination." [26] The pleasure of the mind which had been described as "foresight" thus becomes purely a pleasure of an imagined state of things which, for the mo-

[26] *Leviathan*, I, xi.

ment, stands before the vision as if the reality were present. Hobbes's remark that "anything that is pleasure to the sense" is also "pleasure in the imagination" again indicates that he makes no such distinction between the pleasures of sense and those of the mind as between sensual delight and delight of mind.

This phrase "pleasure in the imagination" has an importance that has never to my knowledge been noticed. It recalls Aristotle and anticipates Addison, who was to write a series of papers on the "Pleasures of the Imagination" to the end of explaining aesthetic response, in the presence of beautiful objects or in the experience of art, as fundamentally a delight in the presentation or re-presentation to the mind of pictures through the imagination.

Certain phases of Aristotle's thought permit an entertaining comparison. To Aristotle the imagination is concerned with the reception, the retention, and the recall of sensible images. These images are the forms of things received by motion transmitted through the senses. More specifically, imagination "is the faculty in virtue of which we say that an image presents itself to us." [27] Now, though Aristotle states specifically that imagination is "generated by actual perception," [28] he also holds that the imagination is called into play in recall and in expectation. [29]

Aristotle does not appear to relate the pleasure experienced in the actual presence of objects to the imagination as Addison does later, but he does clearly connect with the imagination the pleasure we take in recalled objects in memory and in constructed objects in hope. Many passages might be cited to show that this is Aristotle's view:

. . . And since to be pleased is to experience a certain feeling, and imagination is a kind of weak perception, the man who remembers or hopes must be haunted by a certain image of that which he remembers or hopes. [30]

---

[27] *De Anima*, III, iii, 6; tr. by Robert Drew Hicks (Cambridge, 1907), p. 125.
[28] *Ibid.*, III, iii, 13; Hicks, p. 129.
[29] *The Rhetoric*, I, xi, 6; tr. by Sir Richard Claverhouse Jebb (Cambridge, 1909), p. 47.   [30] *Ibid.*

. . . And, generally, all things which, when present, give joy, also supply, as a rule, pleasures of memory or hope.[31]

Hobbes's use of the phrase "Pleasure in the imagination" in referring to the satisfaction we take in future honor and glory is of peculiar interest in this connection. For Aristotle's pleasures of memory and hope might be accurately called "pleasures in the imagination," in that the pleasure accompanies the formation of an image, or of images, of that which, if actually occurring at the time, would give pleasure: "there is a pleasure in remembering the lost, and, in a manner, seeing him as he lived and moved."[32] Even in such more abstract matters as honor the pleasure lies in contemplation of an image of oneself as in the desired state of being: "Honour, again, and reputation are among the pleasantest things; since each man comes to imagine that he is such, as the estimable man should be . . . ."[33] The joys of friendship are to be similarly explained: "Again, a friend is among pleasant things; since to love is pleasant, (no one loving wine who does not find joy in it), and to be loved is pleasant; for here too one has the imagination of possessing a goodness, which all, who perceive it, desire."[34] Aristotle even finds that a certain pleasure that we take in anger is dependent upon the picture-making faculty: "A certain pleasure attends on it [anger], not only for this reason, but also because men dwell in thought on the act of the revenge. So the image, which then arises, excites pleasure, like the imagery of dreams."[35] Fear and its contrary boldness owe their pain and pleasure, respectively, to images in the mind: "Fear may be defined as a pain or trouble arising from an image of coming evil."[36] In boldness, "hope is attended by an image of salutary things as near, and of terrible things as non-existent or far off."[37]

The cases cited here from Aristotle have to do with pleasure in the practical rather than in the aesthetic sphere. There is justification, however, for a quite general application to aes-

[31] The Rhetoric, I, xi, 9; Jebb, p. 47.
[32] Ibid., I, xi, 12; Jebb, p. 48.
[33] Ibid., I, xi, 16; Jebb, p. 48.
[34] Ibid., I, xi, 17; Jebb, p. 49.
[35] Ibid., II, ii, 2; Jebb, p. 70.
[36] Ibid., II, v, 1; Jebb, p. 81.
[37] Ibid., II, v, 16; Jebb, p. 83.

thetics. The definition and discussion of pity in the *Rhetoric* — which occurs, incidentally, in the same section as the passages I have quoted — make this clear. "Pity," says Aristotle, "may be defined as a pain for apparent evil . . . befalling a person who does not deserve it, when we might expect such evil to befall ourselves or some of our friends. . . . Plainly the man who is to pity must be such as to think himself or his friends liable to suffer some ill, and ill of such a sort as has been defined, or of a like or comparable sort." [38] Later, in application of his theory, he adds that men pity "those like them in age, in character, in moral state, in rank, in birth; for all these examples make it more probable that the case may become their own." [39] Making the danger appear near to the observer adds to the effect. Hence, "it follows that those who aid the effect with gesture, voice, dress — in a word, who dramatise — are more piteous; for they cause the evil to seem near by setting it before the eyes as future or past." [40] Through implication and direct reference Aristotle has here brought his theory of representative images as a means to pleasure or pain into the region of art. There can be little doubt that in this whole discussion he has in mind the pity and fear of tragedy. From the preceding examples we know that such pity and fear, and any pleasure accompanying it, would be attended by pictures in the mind of the spectator's self, or of his friends, in a similarly dangerous plight. Dramatic representation is a patent aid to such vicarious experience, Aristotle shows, and so brings his reasoning to focus in a speculation upon the cause and nature of the aesthetic experience to be had in the theatre.

It is a logical step to apply Aristotle's theory to the wider field of narrative poetry. Wherever, indeed, pleasure in art depends upon self-identification with the characters in poetry, fiction, or drama, we may assume that this pleasure is to a large degree dependent upon the pictures furnished through the imagination; for aesthetic pleasure centers about the concrete presentation, through recall or construction, of pictures

[38] *Ibid.*, II, viii, 2; Jebb, p. 89.   [39] *Ibid.*, II, viii, 13; Jebb, p. 89.
[40] *Ibid.*, II, viii, 14; Jebb, p. 91.

in the mind. Aristotle attaches great importance to metaphor as a means to please and to excite the affections, and he shows specifically that the peculiar virtue of metaphoric language is to produce a sense of actuality by setting things "before the eyes" of the hearer or reader.[41] It does not appear that Aristotle thought of the imagination as a faculty of the mind with a special function of taking pleasure; it was rather that he regarded the imagination as able to furnish the mind with that in which it takes delight: definite images. The mind is so constituted that it finds pleasure in the presentations of the imagination. At one point in *De Anima* he says in effect that even in mathematics a man can actually think only with an image before him.[42] He would evidently say that images are a condition to pleasure, in that a man experiences mental pleasure only when there is an image before him (physical pleasure, of course, cannot be included in this). We may then say with some assurance that to Aristotle most of the pleasures of the mind are basically pleasures in (or *of*) the imagination.

A brief examination of further passages in Hobbes descriptive of the passions and their associated pleasures will make the analogy I am drawing more striking.

"Glorying," writes Hobbes, "is that exultation of the mind" which arises "from imagination of a mans own power and ability."[43] "REVENGEFULNESS is that passion which ariseth from an expectation or imagination of making him that hath hurt us, to find his own action hurtful to himself, and to acknowledge the same."[44] "Pity is imagination or fiction of future calamity to ourselves, proceeding from the sense of another man's present calamity. . . . The contrary of pity is HARDNESS of heart, proceeding either from slowness of imagination, or from extreme great opinion of their own great

---

[41] *The Rhetoric*, III, x, 6; Jebb, p. 168.
[42] "And for this reason, as without sensation a man would not learn or understand anything, so at the very time when he is actually thinking he must have an image before him. For mental images are like present sensations except that they are immaterial. . . . I reply that neither these nor the rest of our notions are images, but that they cannot dispense with images" (*De Anima*, III, viii, 3; Hicks, p. 145).
[43] *Leviathan*, I, vi.   [44] *The Elements of Law*, I, ix, 6.

exemption of the like calamity." [45] Love of persons for pleasing the sense only is "lust," but love of persons "acquired from Rumination, that is, Imagination of Pleasure past," is "LUXURY." [46] "Lust," we have seen, may be either sensual or otherwise; when it is not sensual but a delight of mind, it becomes so through an imaginative act: "the delight men take in delighting is not sensual, but a pleasure or joy of the mind, consisting in the imagination of the power they have so much to please." [47]

Briefly, then, the passions described by Hobbes — pleasures or their opposites — are, like the pleasures of Aristotle, to be traced to the imagination. This becomes even clearer when we recall that with Hobbes all conceptions or apparitions of the mind proceed from image-making motions, which, either when made from objects that are present or when raised from past experience, are accompanied with impressions of good (appetite) or of evil (aversion); [48] and it is still more evident when we consider the implications of his doctrine that we can conceive of nothing for the future except through remembrance — imagination of the past, since "all conception of future [pleasure] is conception of power able to produce something" and that therefore whoever expects "pleasure to come must conceive [imagine] withal some power in himself by which the same may be attained." [49] That the imagination should become the special reference for pleasures, other than the merely sensual, is inalienable to Hobbes's system of thought. This is a fact of unusual significance for his relation to the growth of emphasis on imagination in aesthetic theory in subsequent English aesthetics.

IV

We need not, however, limit ourselves to the implications of Hobbes's general theory for the place of imagination in aesthetic response. For he himself, on occasion, makes the

---

[45] *Ibid.*, I, ix, 10.   [46] *Leviathan*, I, vi.
[47] *The Elements of Law*, I, ix, 15.   [48] *Ibid.*, I, vii, 1, 2, and 4.
[49] *Ibid.*, I, viii, 3.

application to artistic processes. Thus he quite definitely attributes to the imagination the power of literature to arouse the passions. In persuasion, he explains, we "aim at getting opinion from passion"; but in literature "the end is to raise passion from opinion," and in doing this "it is no matter whether the opinion be true or false, or the narration historical or fabulous . . . . For not truth, but image, maketh passion; and a tragedy affecteth no less than a murder well acted." [50]

Again, in a passage in *The Whole Art of Rhetoric* Hobbes makes clear his conception of the nature of the aesthetic experience which may eventuate from vivid imagery:

> Forasmuch as there is nothing more delightful to a man, than to find that he apprehends and learns easily; it necessarily follows that those *words* are most *grateful* to the ear, that make a man seem to see before his eyes things signified.
>
> And therefore *foreign* words are unpleasant, because *obscure;* and *plain* words, because *too manifest*, making us learn nothing new. But *metaphors* please; for they beget in us, by the *genus*, or by some *common* thing to that with another, a kind of *science*. As when an *old man* is called *stubble;* a man suddenly learns that he grows up, flourisheth, and withers like grass, being put in mind of it by the qualities common to *stubble* and to *old men*.
>
> That which a *metaphor* does, a *similitude* does the same; but with less *grace*, because with more *prolixity*.[51]

This, to be sure, is based on Aristotle's description of metaphor in the first paragraph of Chapter X, Book III, of the *Rhetoric*, but it is a very free paraphrase and contains an amplification that amounts to an important gloss on Aristotle's meaning. For where Aristotle says that metaphor pleases because it gives us "a *new* perception," Hobbes specifies the type of information that is given: a sort of heightened awareness, or illumination, that flashes suddenly on the mind in an instant perception of integral relationship. This effect is akin to Pater's "sense of fact" and to the "species of revelation" of Coleridge. It is what Aristotle partially suggests, but does not

---

[50] *The Elements of Law*, I, xiii, 7.

[51] *The Whole Art of Rhetoric*, III, ix, in *The English Works of Thomas Hobbes of Malmesbury*. In a later paragraph Hobbes writes: "*Animation* is that expression which makes us seem to see the thing before our eyes. As he that said, *The Athenians poured out their city into Sicily;* meaning, they sent thither the greatest army they could make. And this is the greatest grace of an oration" (*ibid.*).

fully express. Metaphors "beget in us . . . a kind of *science*," Hobbes declares: that is, we get all at once the result that might have been attained through the slower reasoning process. Nowadays we call this "intuition" — which may be defined as a kind of shorthand ratiocination. Such passages reveal the genuine insight of Hobbes and help establish his right to a high place in the development of modern aesthetics, especially with that phase of it which is concerned with a psychological analysis of the effects produced by works of art.

We have seen that the association of imagination with pleasure is integral to Hobbes's system. Equally integral is his theory that strong passions and desires are essential to the good life. And the two are intrinsically related. For, since pleasure and desire are engendered by an imagination of a good to come, imaginative response is a way both to the passion of pleasure and to the passion of appetite for new or continued activity. But imaginative response is itself both motion and the result of motion engendered by the same sort of pleasure and appetite which it promotes. Now Hobbes clearly regards man's happiness as dependent upon a continuation of this sort of circular, reciprocal process, motion and pleasure and appetite ever producing more motion and pleasure and appetite.

The theory that agitation is the beginning of delight, hence of happiness, is explicit in Hobbes's teaching. For, "Seeing all delight, and appetite presupposeth a farther end, there can be no contentment but in proceeding," [52] he asserts. Not

---

[52] *The Elements of Law*, I, vii, 7. It is interesting to note that with Aristotle, also, desire is the beginning of motion, and that motion is one of the conditions to pleasure. "Hence it is invariably the object of appetency which causes motion . . ." (*De Anima*, III, x, 4; Hicks, p. 15). Pleasure is defined by Aristotle as "a kind of motion of the soul, and a settling, sudden and sensible, into our proper nature; and pain the contrary" (*The Rhetoric*, I, xi, 1; Jebb, p. 46). Desire for what men regard as good and as contributing to life most commonly moves them to action, and normally such motion is attended by pleasure. In *De Anima* Aristotle remarks that "when the sensible thing is pleasant or painful, the pursuit or avoidance of it by the soul is a sort of affirmation or negation" (III, vii, 2; Hicks, p. 141). "In fact," says Aristotle, "to feel pleasure or pain is precisely to function with the sensitive mean, acting upon good or evil as such" (*ibid.*). "The words of the text," remarks Hicks, "recall *Eth. Nic.* 1174b 14 sqq., the well known passage . . . in which A[ristotle], who consistently maintained that

attainment, but the struggle to attain brings happiness: "Felicity . . . consisteth not in having prospered, but in prospering." [53] To lack desire and passion is to Hobbes virtually synonymous with non-existence: "For as to have no Desire, is to be Dead: so to have weak Passions, is Dulnesse. . . ." [54]

It should be borne in mind that Hobbes excludes from the factors contributing to man's good the pleasures and appetites of sensuality. For indulgence in the sensual takes away inclination to such worthy pursuits as honor and knowledge. "And this is it which men call DULNESS; and proceedeth from the appetite of sensual or bodily delight. And it may well be conjectured, that such passion hath its beginnings from a grossness and difficulty of the motion of the spirits about the heart." [55] Sensuality then — and let us recall that Hobbes is probably limiting his application to feasting and to excess in sexual matters — is to be condemned as having its origin in grossness and its culmination in lethargy. Opposed to the wasted life of dulness and dead desire is the happy state of lively appetite and eager motion to be observed in men of animated passions. Herein is illustrated the contrary of dulness: "that quick ranging of mind . . . which is joined with curiosity of comparing one thing that comes into his mind one with another." [56] And to possess this quality of ranging and curiosity is to be called blessed; for this is not only pleasure, but the beginning of knowledge and imagination, hence of philosophy and art. The pleasure Hobbes is here describing is, then, "pleasure of mind," characterized by emotional excitation, heightened awareness, mental alertness, and accompanied by an appetite to learn and to do. As such it is the indispensable condition to the good life.

Hobbes's theory of specific pleasures of the mind rests upon

----

pleasure was akin to ἐνέργεια as distinct from κίνησις, expounds his theory that pleasure is the concomitant of normal activities and attends upon the functions of every faculty of sense or thought, though the highest pleasure is only experienced when the faculty, being perfect, works upon a perfect object . . ." (ibid., p. 528). For a translation of this passage, X, iii, see The Nicomachean Ethics of Aristotle, tr. by J. E. C. Welldon (London, 1897), p. 325.

[53] The Elements of Law, I, vii, 7.
[55] The Elements of Law, I, x, 3.
[54] Leviathan, I, viii.
[56] Ibid., I, x, 4.

his general doctrine of desire, and of motion to satisfy desire: "Felicity is a continuall progresse of the desire from one object to another." [57] Progress presupposes power, or a sense of power, however; so that we must add to appetite, as a condition to pleasure, such a consciousness of power as will promise reward of desire, or, to use Hobbes's own term, a "fruition of good." [58]

Chief among the sources of man's pleasure, according to Hobbes, is his desire for novelty. Novelty, or a sense of new experience, is closely linked with curiosity and a desire for knowledge. "Because curiosity is delight, therefore, all novelty is so." [59] This is not only one of the most universal of human traits, Hobbes holds, but is, along with reason, clearly unique to man: "*Desire* to know why, and how, [is] CURIOSITY; such as is in no living creature but *Man*": so that man is distinguished from other "animals" "not onely by his reason but also by this singular passion." [60] Curiosity, as contrasted with sensual pleasures, is a "lust of the mind" with a perseverance in the continual search for knowledge that exceeds any brief vehemence of carnal pleasure.[61]

As there is no pleasure known to man more universal, there is none higher or more rewarding:

Forasmuch as all knowledge beginneth from experience, therefore also new experience is the beginning of new knowledge and the increase of experience the beginning of the increase of knowledge; whatsoever there-

---

[57] *Leviathan*, I, xi.

[58] *The Elements of Law*, I, viii, 3.

[59] *Ibid.*, I, ix, 18. Aristotle, who found that among natural motions of the soul that cause pleasure are novelty and variety and surprise, may be cited in comparison: "To change is pleasant; for to change is to follow nature; since what is always the same creates an excess of the established state: whence the saying,

'Change of all things is sweet.'

For this reason, too, occasional visitors or things are pleasant; for it is a change from the present, and besides, the occasional has variety" (*The Rhetoric*, I, xi, 20–21; Jebb, p. 49). From the *Poetics* we learn that elements of pleasure in tragedy are surprises and sudden reversals in fortune. In a passage in the *Rhetoric* Aristotle rationalizes this pleasure: "Sudden reverses and narrow escapes are pleasant, being all in the nature of marvels" (I, xi, 24; Jebb, p. 50).

[60] *Leviathan*, I, vi.   [61] *Ibid.*

fore happeneth new to a man, giveth him hope and matter of knowing somewhat that he knew not before. And this hope and expectation of future knowledge from anything that happeneth new and strange, is that passion which we commonly call ADMIRATION; and the same considered as appetite, is called CURIOSITY, which is appetite of knowledge. As in the discerning faculties, man leaveth all community with beasts at the faculty of imposing names; so also doth he surmount their nature at this passion of curiosity. . . . And from this passion of admiration and curiosity, have arisen not only the invention of names, but also the supposition of such causes of all things as they thought might produce them. And from this beginning is derived all philosophy: as astronomy from the admiration of the course of heaven; natural philosophy from the strange effects of the elements and other bodies. And from the degrees of curiosity proceed also the degrees of knowledge among men . . . .[62]

These ideas may be associated with Hobbes's general theory of pleasure in agitation as opposed to lethargy, the satisfaction to be had in quickened pulses, heightened awareness. They are corollary to his conviction that a stirring of the animal spirits through appetite is a condition not only to immediate delight but to the good life in general, and that only those things which contribute to this end are worthy of our attention: "As for those objects, if there be any such, which

---

[62] *The Elements of Law*, I, ix, 18. I venture again to cite Aristotle, who regarded the satisfaction of our desire to learn as one of the chief sources of pleasure. To learn and to admire are pleasant, he explains, for admiring implies a desire to learn, "and learning implies coming into the track of nature." Hence arises much of our delight in art: "Again, since learning and admiring are pleasant, it follows that pleasure is given by acts of imitation, such as painting, sculpture, poetry, and by every skilful copy, even though the original be unpleasant: for one's joy is not in the thing itself; rather there is a syllogism — 'This is that'; and so it comes that one learns something" (*The Rhetoric*, I, xi, 21–23; Jebb, p. 49).

It also seems pertinent to quote St. Thomas Aquinas on the subject of wonder and the desire to learn. Aristotle, Aquinas points out, says that wonder is the cause of pleasure. This is to be explained by the fact that "wonder is a kind of desire for knowledge; a desire which comes to a man when he sees an effect of which the cause either is unknown to him, or surpasses his knowledge or faculty of understanding. Consequently wonder is a cause of pleasure, in so far as it includes a hope of getting the knowledge which one desires to have. For this reason whatever is wonderful is pleasing, for instance things that are scarce" (*Sum. Theol.*, Part II (First Part), First Number, Q. 32, A. 8, pp. 385–386). In further explanation Aquinas remarks: "Wonder gives pleasure, not because it implies ignorance, but in so far as it includes the desire of learning the cause, in so far as the wonderer learns something new" (*ibid.*, p. 386).

do not at all stir the mind, we are said to contemn them." [63]
The idea of pleasure in novelty and in the learning of the
new is as old as Aristotle and had been transmitted to the
modern world through such an effective agency as the medieval Aristotelian St. Thomas Aquinas; it ran through much
eighteenth-century thought and has persisted to the present —
undoubtedly because it is firmly based on psychological fact.
Aquinas perhaps offered as sound an interpretation of the
basis of this pleasure as has yet been ventured:

> It is pleasant to do what we are wont to do, inasmuch as this is con-
> natural to us, as it were. And yet things that are of rare occurrence can
> be pleasant, either as regards knowledge, from the fact that we desire to
> know something about them, in so far as they are wonderful; or as re-
> gards action, from the fact that the *mind is more inclined by desire to act
> intensely in things that are new*, as stated in *Ethics x*, since more perfect opera-
> tion causes more perfect pleasure.[64]

Descartes fully recognized the pleasure to be derived from
novelty,[65] as did Hobbes's English contemporary, Edward
Reynolds.[66] Bacon, it will be recalled, explicitly indicates novelty as one of the elements contributing to the delectation
that is in literature: "Because true history representeth actions

[63] *The Elements of Philosophy*, II, xxv, 13.
[64] *Sum. Theol.*, Part II (First Part), First Number, Q. 32, A. 8, p. 386. In
the passage in *The Nicomachean Ethics* to which Aquinas refers Aristotle offers a
rationale of the pleasure in the new. Proceeding from the premise that, given a
normal object of thought or sensation and a normal contemplative subject, there
will always be a pleasure in sense or other mental activity, Aristotle inquires why
it is that "nobody feels pleasure continuously." "It is probably because we grow
weary," he replies. "Human beings are incapable of continuous activity, and as
the activity comes to an end, so does the pleasure; for it is a concomitant of the
activity. It is for the same reason that some things give pleasure when they are
new, but give less pleasure afterwards; for the intelligence is called into play at
first, and applies itself to its object with intense activity . . . but afterwards the
activity ceases to be so intense and . . . consequently the pleasure fades away"
(X, iv; Welldon, p. 326).
[65] Particularly in *The Passions of the Soul* (1649), Articles LXXII–LXXVIII, in
The Philosophical Works of Descartes, tr. by Elizabeth S. Haldane and G. R. T. Ross
(Cambridge, 1911–12), II, 363–366.
[66] For Reynolds's views see *op. cit.*, pp. 173, 175–176, 211–214. A more complete treatment of the idea of novelty in the seventeenth century may be found in
my article "Addison and Some of His Predecessors on 'Novelty,'" *PMLA*, LII
(1937), 1114–1129.

and events more ordinary and lesse interchanged, therefore Poesy endueth them with more rarenesse and more unexpected and alternative variations." [67] Huarte, also, had stated the general principle of novelty, without, however, reference to aesthetic matters, other than making the general assertion that novelty is a property of the imagination.[68] It is not necessary to believe that Hobbes owed his ideas to any one of these; it is instructive, however, to note that, working in a tradition which goes back to Aristotle, he finds no difficulty in accommodating it to his own mechanical system.

Hobbes's application of the principle of novelty to aesthetic processes and effects, though sometimes indirect, is unequivocal. He habitually associates fancy with the novel and the wonderful, and he shows that metaphor, freshness of expression, and apt invention in poetry owe their appeal largely to novelty. A writer who possesses the virtue of a good fancy, says Hobbes, "will be easily fitted with similitudes, that will please, not onely by illustration of his discourse, and adorning it with new and apt metaphors; but also by the rarity of their invention." [69] Two essentials in the production of poetry, he remarks further, are to know well and to know much: "A signe of the latter is novelty of expression, and pleaseth by excitation of the minde; for novelty causeth admiration, and admiration curiosity, which is a delightful appetite of knowledge." [70] Again he declares, "From Knowing Much proceedeth the admirable variety and novelty of Metaphors and Similitudes, which are not possible to be lighted on in the compass of a narrow

---

[67] *Of the Advancement of Learning*, ed. by William Aldis Wright (Oxford, 1920), II, iv, 2, p. 102.

[68] "And this is the propertie not onely of the imagination, but also of all the other powers which gouerne man: for which cause we see, that the stomacke when it hath twice fed vpon one kind of meat, straight-waies loatheth the same: so doth the sight one selfe shape and colour; the hearing one concordance, how good soever; and the vnderstanding one selfe contemplation" (*op. cit.*, p. 82).

[69] *Leviathan*, I, viii.

[70] *The Answer to Davenant*, in *Critical Essays of the Seventeenth Century*, ed. by J. E. Spingarn (Oxford, 1908), II, 63. Davenant himself professed that his endeavor "in bringing Truth . . . home to mens bosoms" in *Gondibert* had been "to lead her through unfrequented and new ways, and from the most remote Shades, by representing Nature, though not in an affected, yet in an unusual dress" (Spingarn, II, 23).

knowledge."[71]   Still commenting upon the value of an impression of newness in figure and diction, he writes,

. . . As the sense we have of bodies consisteth in change and variety of impression, so also does the sense of language in the variety and changeable use of words. I mean not in the affectation of words newly brought home from travail, but in new and with all significant translation to our purposes of those that be already received, and in far fetch't but withal apt, instructive, and comly similitudes.[72]

When Hobbes writes in *The Answer to Davenant* that fancy begets the ornaments of a poem he has reference not only to graceful similitudes but to the inventions which give a work its amplitude and variety.   Hence it follows that "Elevation of Fancie" is one of the greatest virtues of epic poetry: "for men generally affect and admire Fancie more than they do either Judgment, Reason, or Memory . . . .   For in Fancy consisteth the Sublimity of a Poet."[73]   The end of an heroic poem, Hobbes tells us, is to excite admiration, and fancy has achieved certain marvelous effects both here and in the practical affairs of life.[74]   What Hobbes has in mind by these marvelous effects, in part at least, he makes clear in his praise of Homer for the "Amplitude of his Subject," which, he says, is "nothing but variety, and a thing without which a whole poem would be no pleasanter than an epigram, or one good verse."[75]   In this Homer vastly exceeds Virgil.   Homer's work abounds in "Images of Shipwracks, Battles, Single Combats, Beauty, Passions of the mind, Sacrifices, Entertainments, and other things, whereof Virgil . . . has scarce the twentieth part."[76]   Such,

[71] *Ibid.*, p. 65.   W. Lee Ustick and Hoyt H. Hudson, "Wit, 'Mixt Wit,' and the Bee in Amber" (*The Huntington Library Bulletin*, No. 8 [1935], p. 110), have noticed that in adapting Aristotle's eleventh chapter of Book III, where it is said that "metaphors should be drawn from objects which are proper to the object, but not too obvious," Hobbes shifts the emphasis to the last element, transmuting it in effect into a statement for novelty: "Such *Metaphors* as these [i.e. attributing life to inanimate things, as in saying that the sword 'devours'] come into a Mans minde by the observation of things that have similitude and proportion one to another.   And the more unlike, and unproportionable the things be otherwise, the more grace hath the Metaphor."
[72] *The Answer to Davenant*, Spingarn, II, 65.
[73] *The Virtues of an Heroic Poem*, Spingarn, II, 75.
[74] *The Answer to Davenant*, Spingarn, II, 60.
[75] *The Virtues of an Heroic Poem*, Spingarn, II, 71.   [76] *Ibid.*, p. 75.

we may assume, are the elements which Hobbes had in mind when in *Leviathan* he declared that fancy must be more prominent than judgment in a poem, because poems "please for the Extravagancy." [77]

It must be recalled, however, that he steadily insists that the judgment should exercise control over fancy. Undirected fancy, he points out, may lead the poet to introduce the "new and rare" to his disadvantage; for without steadiness and direction to some great end a great fancy is one form of madness. Similarly, in *The Answer to Davenant*, referring to overwrought attempts to produce effects of the marvelous, he takes issue with those who insist on exorbitancy of the fiction, and sternly reiterates the doctrine of probability. "Beyond the actual marks of nature a poet may now go," he grants; "but beyond the conceived possibility of nature never," for "the Resemblance of truth is the utmost limit of poetical Liberty." [78] It is interesting to see, however, and it is indicative of the general tolerance he shows toward the fanciful and novel, that Hobbes admits as legitimate material for poetry what Dryden and Addison both approved after him, the popular beliefs of a people, even though they seem far-fetched and extravagant: "In old time amongst the Heathen such strange fictions and Metamorphoses were not so remote from the Articles of their Faith as they are now from ours, and therefore were not so unpleasant." [79] For non-epic poems he also, quite surprisingly, admits certain novelties that Addison was later roundly to condemn as "false wit," that is, the contriving of "verses into the formes of an Organ, a Hatchet, an Egg, an Altar, and a paire of Wings." [80]

Hobbes's doctrine of novelty, and its concomitant fancy, is therefore all nicely qualified in a manner quite familiar to one acquainted with later English aesthetics; yet Hobbes leaves no room to doubt that a good poem is essentially a product of the imagination (fancy), however well regulated by judgment it may be, and that the basis of its power to give pleasure lies in marvelous and surprising fictions.

[77] *Leviathan*, I, viii.
[79] *Ibid.*

[78] Spingarn, II, 62.
[80] *Ibid.*, p. 57.

The importance Hobbes attaches to novelty as a source of pleasure is to be observed in the place it takes in his quite incidental aesthetics. For example, he makes it one of the elements that account for pleasure in the tragic or painful. How can we explain the fact, inquires Hobbes, that men take pleasure in beholding from the shore the danger of them that are at sea in a tempest, or in watching from a safe castle two armies charge each other in the field? Certainly there is more joy than grief in so doing, or men would never flock to see such spectacles, he remarks. "Nevertheless there is in it both joy and grief. For as there is novelty and remembrance of our own security present, which is delight; so is there also pity, which is grief. But the delight is so far predominant, that men usually are content in such a case to be spectators of the misery of their friends." [81]

This explanation shows how far mechanistic philosophy had carried a certain portion of the seventeenth century from Aristotle with regard to the effects of pity and fear in tragic representation. For pity, fear, and grief are with Hobbes passions of aversion, the opposite of pleasure. "Pity is imagination or fiction of future calamity to ourselves, proceeding from the sense of another man's present calamity." [82] Men pity those they love, or others who are regarded as innocent. There is, however, no suggestion in Hobbes of purification or purgation through the arousal of pity, or of fear, each of which is with him equally negative to pleasure; and he shows no appreciation of the effects of tranquility induced by great tragedy. "Felicity consisteth not in the repose of a mind satisfied." Such a doctrine applies better to romances and to epic poetry than to the tragedy of Sophocles and Shakespeare.

[81] *The Elements of Law*, I, ix, 19. As I have pointed out in a previous publication ("Addison and Some of His Predecessors on 'Novelty,'" *PMLA*, LII [1937], 1117 ff.), Hobbes here appears to be recalling Lucretius: "It is sweet, when on the great sea the winds trouble its waters, to behold from land another's deep distress; not that it is a pleasure and delight that any should be afflicted, but because it is sweet to see from what evils you are yourself exempt. It is sweet also to look upon the mighty struggles of war arrayed along the plains without sharing yourself in danger" (*De Rerum Natura. On the Nature of Things*, II, 1–6; tr. by H. A. J. Munro [Bohn ed., London, 1914], p. 41).
[82] *The Elements of Law*, I, ix, 10.

The pleasure he finds in witnessing tragic events, either in life or in artistic representation, must then lie in a counterbalancing element: the joy of mind arising from agitation caused by novelty and the imagination (remembrance) of our own relative security.[83]

It is worth noticing that in consistently denying pleasure in repose Hobbes differs not only from Aristotle, who seems to have regarded a return to the calm of equilibrium after intensity of passion a condition to aesthetic pleasure, but from nearly all other thinkers who have given the matter consideration.[84] St. Thomas Aquinas, who in certain respects links Aristotle with Hobbes in having made the most thoroughgoing and significant inquiries into psychological problems relating to aesthetics to be found in the intervening centuries, and whose ideas sometimes closely parallel those of both Aristotle and Hobbes, believed thoroughly that appetite and motion are a means of pleasure; and he also believed in the efficacy of the new and wonderful as stimulants to a delightful search for knowledge; but, even more than Aristotle, he considered repose the ultimate in aesthetic and moral experience. Thus we find Aquinas saying that "the notion of the beautiful is that which calms the desire," [85] and that the appetite of love and the movement caused by the appetite are followed by a "rest which is *joy*." [86] Likewise he writes that "pleasure is a kind of repose of the appetite in a suitable good," [87] and, again, "All things seek pleasure in the same way as they seek good: since pleasure is the repose of the appetite in good." [88]

In another place Aquinas takes exception, somewhat equivocally indeed, to Plato's argument that pleasure is to be had from "movement and becoming":

[83] Hobbes does not himself make the transference to tragedy, but what he says elsewhere justifies application: "For to be pleased in the fiction of that which would please if it were reall is a Passion so adhaerent to the Nature, . . . of man . . . as to make it a Sinne, were to make Sinne of being Man" (*Leviathan*, II, xxvii).

[84] The Abbé du Bos is a notable exception, and lesser ones are minor writers and critics of the eighteenth century who agree with Du Bos that violent emotion is a sufficient end in itself.

[85] *Sum. Theol.*, Part II (First Part), First Number, Q. 27, A. 1, p. 320.

[86] *Ibid.*, Q. 26, A. 2, p. 314.

[87] *Ibid.*, Q. 38, A. 1, p. 441.

[88] *Ibid.*, Q. 34, A. 2, p. 399.

. . . But, judging from his [Plato's] arguments, he fails in two points. First, because, from observing that sensible and bodily pleasure consist in a certain movement and *becoming*, as is evident in satiety from eating and the like; he concluded that all pleasure arises from some *becoming* and movement: and from this, since *becoming* and movement are the acts of something imperfect, it would follow that pleasure is not of the nature of ultimate perfection.— But this is seen to be evidently false as regards intellectual pleasures: because one takes pleasure, not only in the *becoming* of knowledge, for instance, when one learns or wonders . . . ; but also in the act of contemplation, by making use of knowledge already acquired.[89]

Hobbes seems to have found little place in his theory for repose or contemplation as a means to pleasure — a noteworthy fact in a philosopher.[90] His emphasis on agitation was no doubt to exercise a considerable influence toward giving the emotions a place of respectability in literature, but it is also likely that it had something to do with the vitiating tendency in certain quarters in eighteenth-century thought to make violent emotions their own end.

Another of the pleasure-giving passions to which Hobbes pays considerable attention is the tendency to laughter. This passion "hath no name," says Hobbes, but "it is always joy." [91] Hobbes feels himself to be a pioneer in venturing an analysis of laughter: "but what joy, what we think, and wherein we triumph when we laugh, hath not hitherto been declared by any." [92] As so frequently happens, when philosophers or freshmen attempt to reduce a term to the confines of formal definition, Hobbes does only scant justice to his subject and his own views thereon when he tries to set laughter to neatly precise formulae: "*Sudden Glory*, is the passion which maketh those *Grimaces* called LAUGHTER; and is caused either by some sudden act of their own, that pleaseth them; or by the appre-

---

[89] *Ibid.*, Q. 34, A. 3, pp. 400–401.

[90] It is true that Hobbes says, in *Leviathan*, I, xi, that "the voluntary actions, and inclinations of all men, tend, not onely to the procuring, but also the assuring of a contented life." But he immediately points out the prevalence of a "restlesse desire of Power after power," because no man can be assured of the power and means to live well which he has "without the acquisition of more." The goal of reposeful possession of what one has striven for appears to be, therefore, but a pleasant dream which has small relation to reality.

[91] *The Elements of Law*, I, ix, 13.   [92] *Ibid.*

hension of some deformed thing in another, in comparison whereof they suddenly applaud themselves." [93] This is in *Leviathan*. The summary in *The Elements of Law* is similar:

> I may therefore conclude, that the passion of laughter is nothing else but a sudden glory arising from sudden conception of some eminency in ourselves, by comparison with the infirmities of others, or with our own formerly: for men laugh at the follies of themselves past, when they come suddenly to remembrance, except they bring with them any present dishonour. It is no wonder therefore that men take it heinously to be laughed at or derided, that is, triumphed over. [94]

Such is the definition which later, when Addison had apparently approved it,[95] set Hutcheson's teeth on edge and drew from him the vigorous attack in his "Essay on Laughter," in the *Dublin Magazine*, in 1725.

In further probings into his subject, however, Hobbes qualifies the "sudden glory" idea with the suggestion that "men laugh at jests, the wit whereof always consisteth in the elegant discovering and conveying to our minds some absurdity or another." [96] These jests, moreover, must be new [97] — again we meet the familiar demand for novelty — "forasmuch as the same thing is no more ridiculous when it groweth stale or usual, whatsoever it be that moveth laughter, it must be new and unexpected." Even here, it is "a sudden imagination of our own odds and eminence" that creates the laughter. But the satirical element should be subordinated to the incongruous; for

> . . . Laughter without offence, must be at absurdities and infirmities abstracted from persons, and where all the company may laugh together. For laughing to one's self putteth all the rest to a jealousy and examination of themselves; besides it is vain glory, and an argument of little worth, to think the infirmities of another sufficient matter for his triumph. [98]

---

[93] *Leviathan*, I, vi.
[94] *The Elements of Law*, I, ix, 13.
[95] *The Spectator*, ed. by G. Gregory Smith (London, 1897), No. 47.
[96] *The Elements of Law*, I, ix, 13.
[97] Cf. Huarte (*op. cit.*, p. 82): "Hereto may be added, that merriments (besides that they must haue a good proportion, and be vttered to the purpose) must be new, and not tofore heard or seene."
[98] *The Elements of Law*, I, ix, 13.

Laughter that rises from incongruity, not from a sense of superiority, is, then, really the only legitimate kind. The other is a mark of vainglory; is, moreover, as Hobbes says at the close of his definition in *Leviathan*, if much indulged in, a "sign of Pusillanimity. For great minds one of the proper workes is, to help and free others from scorn, and compare themselves onely with the most able." [99]

This dignified attitude of reserve is carried into Hobbes's practical criticism, when, in *The Answer to Davenant*, he disapproves, for tragedy or epic, of mirth and scurrility or "any action or language that moveth much laughter."

> . . . The delight of an *Epique* Poem consisteth not in mirth, but admiration. Mirth and Laughter is proper to *Comedy* and *Satyre*. Great persons that have their mindes employed on great designes have not leasure enough to laugh, and are pleased with the contemplation of their own power and vertues, so as they need not the infirmities and vices of other men to recommend themselves to their own favour by comparison, as all men do when they laugh.[100]

Read alone, this sounds like a refrain from the familiar neoclassic song of decorum; but, considered as a part of Hobbes's whole theory, it is at once seen to be something different from a repetition of doctrinal cant: it is founded in a philosophical conception of the causes and effects of laughter, which denies to men of dignity and worth anything like free indulgence in this passion.

Hobbes makes a clear distinction between glory and vainglory. Glory is a reasonable ground for pleasure; "Vaine-Glory," like supercilious laughter, is held suspect:

> . . . Joy, arising from imagination of a mans own power and ability is that exultation of the mind which is called GLORYING: which if grounded upon the experience of his own former actions, is the same with *Confidence:* but if grounded on the flattery of others, or onely supposed by himself, for delight in the consequence of it, is called Vaine-Glory.[101]

Glory, then, is valid self-esteem in one who is accustomed to build an inner reality upon actual and potential performance, but vainglory is a falsely romantic estimate founded upon fancied worth and derived achievement. The fiction of actions by

[99] *Leviathan*, I, vi. [100] Spingarn, II, 64. [101] *Leviathan*, I, vi.

ourselves, which were never done but only imagined, Hobbes
tells us in *The Elements of Law*, is glorying:

> . . . but because it begetteth no appetite nor endeavour to any further
> attempt, it is merely vain and unprofitable; as when a man imagineth
> himself to do the actions whereof he readeth in some romant, or to be
> like unto some other man whose acts he admireth. And this is called Vain
> Glory: and is exemplified in the fable by the fly sitting on the axletree,
> and saying to himself, What a dust do I raise! [102]

One would expect such a quality to elicit disapprobation from
Hobbes, who had a native antipathy for the false and superficial.
Vainglory in irrational imaginings, like laughter at the expense
of weaker men, is a mark of pusillanimity: "The gallant madness of Don Quixote is nothing else but an expression of such
height of vain glory as readings of romants may produce in
pusillanimous men," he declares.[103]

Hobbes names other pleasures of the mind. He speaks in
various places of the delight in skill and good craftsmanship
and of the pleasure to be had in imitation. He writes of the
natural pleasure man takes in the fictions of those things which
would please if they were real.[104] In his essay on heroic poetry
he furnishes an impressive list of "all those things — which
concur to make the reading of an Heroique Poem pleasant." [105]
In general, "the work of an Heroique Poem is to raise Admiration." This is brought about by the right choice of words;
by the structure or style of these words; by the contrivance
of the story; by the "Elevation of Fancie"; by the justice and
impartiality of the poet; by the clearness of descriptions; and,
finally, by the "Amplitude and Variety" of the subject, which
by definition have, like the "Elevation of Fancie," to do with
the new and the surprising.[106]

Hobbes, in one place, addresses himself to the problem of
the nature and cause of pleasure in sounds and colors. Simple
sounds like those from the bell or the lute please because an
equality continued is pleasure. Many sounds agreeing (harmony) please for the same reason as unison. "Sounds that differ

---

[102] *The Elements of Law*, I, ix, 1.   [103] *Ibid.*, I, x, 9.
[104] *Leviathan*, II, xxvii.
[105] *The Virtues of an Heroic Poem*, Spingarn, II, 68.   [106] *Ibid.*

in any height please by inequality and equality alternate," as Galileo has shown in his dialogue, the higher note striking twice for one stroke of the other, so that they strike together the second time. The phenomenon of pleasure in "air," which consists "of one note after another, diversified both by accent and measure," puzzles Hobbes, but he has an explanation: "I conjecture the reason to be, for that some of them may imitate and revive some passion which otherwise we take no notice of." This, it may be remarked, makes "air," through its appeal to the imagination, a pleasure of the mind rather than of sense. Hobbes's account of our pleasure in colors goes little further than to indicate that we take pleasure in both equality and a certain inequality in light: "And therefore colours, the more equality is in them, the more resplendent they are. And as harmony is a pleasure to the ear . . . ; so perhaps may some mixture of divers colours be harmony to the eye, more than another mixture." [107]

These may seem very naïve explanations; yet much of their significance lies in the fact that they are serious *attempts* at explanation, and indicate the trend in Hobbes toward an aesthetic of psychological emphasis. By turning his attention to the problem of emotional response he was setting an example which was to be widely followed. He not only encouraged a tolerant attitude toward the emotions, but demonstrated a method of analysis. Without this powerful precedent, one may say with little hesitation that the criticism of Dryden, Dennis, Addison, and others who made notable contributions to a psychology of effect would have been different. Formalism might, indeed, have gained something of the sway in England that without a Hobbes it had attained in France.

[107] *The Elements of Law*, I, viii, 2.

CHAPTER V

Hobbes's Critical Essays

I

THE volume of Hobbes's direct literary criticism is small, and it is largely theoretical rather than practical. Some of the important passages in these essays have been cited and discussed in previous sections of this study. There remain, however, a number of ideas that will bear examination in their relation to Hobbes's theory as a whole and to his particular theories of epic and history, and of imitation, style, and so forth.

Hobbes's two chief pieces of criticism, *The Answer to Davenant* (1650) and *The Virtues of an Heroic Poem* (1675), reveal to a considerable degree the effects of his psychological approach and much of the independence of accepted authority to be expected in one who took conscious pride in charting new courses in thought. There are, to be sure, evidences of lingering influences of conventional criticism, manifesting themselves in a certain deference to the authority of the classics and a disposition to emphasize style, which savor of the rhetorical tradition. The weight of such evidence is overbalanced, however, by the prevailingly fresh point of view and by the fact that, on the whole, the traditional elements are given a new turn, or are even absorbed in the general current of Hobbes's psychological analysis.

Even the brief Introduction to the translation of Thucydides' *History*, written about 1628, before Hobbes had formulated his major theory, shows evidence of independence and something of interest in the psychological approach. It contains, moreover, ideas of style that were to be more fully developed in later writings. The statement about independence of attitude in this Introduction must, however, in consideration of the fact that Hobbes shows more deference to some of the ancient writers than is his wont in later years, be somewhat qualified. For, in his prefatory words "To the Readers," he remarks, in a tone quite conventional for the age, "It hath been noted by divers, that Homer in poesy, Aristotle in philosophy, Demosthenes in eloquence, and others of the ancients, in other knowledge, do still maintain their primacy: none of them exceeded, some not approached, by any in these later ages." [1] And further on, in the Introduction proper, he quotes with approval passages from such ancient critics — whom he seems to have studied thoroughly — as Plutarch, Cicero, Marcellinus, and Lucian. Of more modern writers he cites most frequently the Belgian scholar Justus Lipsius (1547–1606). A like deference is shown to tradition in his division of his treatment of "elocution" into "disposition or method, and style." [2] In later criticism he quotes nobody, and we know that, much as he obviously derived from Aristotle, he was in his maturity to take open exception to his philosophical views.

On the other hand, though he in one place quotes Dionysius of Halicarnassus with respect,[3] he in general makes vigorous denial of this rhetorician's views on Thucydides.[4] A third of the Introduction, indeed, is devoted to an analysis and refutation of the judgments of Dionysius. The spirit of this refutation may be best judged from Hobbes's comment on the first "two criminations" on Thucydides advanced by the Greek critic: "I think there was never written so much absurdity in so few lines." [5] Hobbes considers the objections of Dionysius in order, and proceeds to show their absurdity.

One of his strictures on Dionysius turns upon a point that was to become important in Hobbes's theory: namely, truth to experience. Hobbes is here, indeed, writing of the requirements of good history, but, as we have seen, his demand for

---

[1] *The History of the Grecian War written by Thucydides. Translated by Thomas Hobbes of Malmesbury*, in *The English Works of Thomas Hobbes of Malmesbury*, ed. by Sir William Molesworth (London, 1839–45), VIII, vii.

[2] *Ibid.*, pp. xxii, xxix–xxxii.   [3] *Ibid.*, p. xxiii.
[4] *Ibid.*, pp. xxiv–xxx.   [5] *Ibid.*, p. xxvi.

essential truth was to be carried over into his general aesthetic doctrine. Dionysius had argued for the superiority of Herodotus over Thucydides in that the one wrote of pleasant and glorious things grateful to the Grecian reader, whereas the other took an "evil argument in hand," writing of such calamities of war, such desolation and destruction of cities as his readers must abhor to read. Hobbes replies in a paragraph that is a philosophy of history in little:

> Now let any man consider whether it be not more reasonable to say: That the principal and most necessary office of him that will write a history, is to take such an argument as is both within his power well to handle, and profitable to posterity that shall read it, which Thucydides, in the opinion of all men, hath done better than Herodotus: for Herodotus undertook to write of those things, of which it was impossible for him to know the truth; and which delight more the ear with fabulous narrations, than satisfy the mind with truth: but Thucydides writeth one war; which, how it was carried from the beginning to the end, he was able certainly to inform himself: and by propounding in his proeme the miseries that happened in the same, he sheweth that it was a great war, and worthy to be known; and not to be concealed from posterity, for the calamities that then fell upon the Grecians; but the rather to be truly delivered unto them, for that men profit more by looking on adverse events, than on prosperity: therefore by how much men's miseries do better instruct, than their good success; by so much was Thucydides more happy in taking his argument, than Herodotus was wise in choosing his.[6]

Hobbes here displays his characteristic balance. History, like poetry, he believed, should instruct; even history, his full discussion shows, must delight if it is to succeed, but delight must not be purchased at the expense of truth. In an earlier paragraph he had written: "For in *truth* consisteth the *soul*, and in *elocution* the *body* of history. The latter without the former is but a picture of history, and the former without the latter unapt to instruct."[7]

Hobbes continually applauds Thucydides' adherence to the true and natural. Dionysius aims at "the delight of the present hearer," says Hobbes, "but Thucydides intended his work for a perpetual possession for posterity." Whoever reads him will approve his way of handling his subject above an alternate treatment suggested by Dionysius:

6 *The History of the Grecian War*, p. xxiv.   7 *Ibid.*, p. xx.

. . . the method is more natural; forasmuch as his purpose being to write of one Peloponnesian war, this way he has incorporated all the parts thereof into one body; so that there is unity in the whole, and the several narrations are conceived only as parts of that. Whereas the other way, he had sewed together many little histories, and left the Peloponnesian war, which he took for his subject, in a manner unwritten: for neither any part nor the whole could justly have carried such a title.[8]

This is not particularly original doctrine, but it is sound common sense, a quality notable in Hobbes throughout his aesthetic speculations. The judgment it contains is based not on fine-spun theory squared with a set of preconceived notions of what history should be, such as Dionysius brought into play in his critique of Thucydides, but on the ability of a given piece of historical writing to do its work as measured by sustained appeal to readers of its own and succeeding generations. This is the spirit which is to characterize Hobbes's later excursions into critical theory and practice.

Evidence of Hobbes's interest in emotional effects is shown in his commendation of Thucydides for his power to make the reader see and feel. Actions and persons are so placed before the reader that he sees them as with his own eyes and responds emotionally to their significance. On this point Hobbes quotes Plutarch with full acceptance of his views:

Thucydides aimeth always at this: to make his auditor a spectator, and to cast his reader into the same passions that they were in that were beholders. The manner how Demosthenes arranged the Athenians on the rugged shore before Pylus; how Brasidas urged the steersman to run his galley aground; how he went to the ladder or place in the galley for descent; how he was hurt, and swooned, and fell down on the ledges of the galley; how the Spartans fought after the manner of a land-fight upon the sea, and the Athenians of a sea-fight upon land: again, in the Sicilian war, how a battle was fought by sea and land with equal fortune: these things, I say, are so described and so evidently set before our eyes, that the mind of the reader is no less affected therewith than if he had been present in the actions.[9]

In further comment on his author's ability to move and please Hobbes cites Cicero:

[8] *Ibid.*, p. xxvii.
[9] *Ibid.*, p. xxii. Hobbes is quoting from Plutarch's *De Gloria Atheniensium.*

Cicero in his book entitled *Orator*, speaking of the affection of divers Greek rhetoricians, saith thus: "And therefore Herodotus and Thucydides are the more admirable. For though they lived in the same age with those I have before named," (meaning Thrasymachus, Gorgias, and Theodorus), "yet were they far from this kind of delicacy, or rather indeed foolery. For the one without rub, gently glideth like a still river; and the other" (meaning Thucydides) "runs stronglier, and in matter of war, as it were, bloweth a trumpet of war. And in these two (as saith Theophrastus) history hath roused herself, and adventured to speak, but more copiously, and with more ornament than in those that were before them." [10]

This, says Hobbes, commends the gravity and dignity of Thucydides' language. But it also commends his graces of style and his skill in invention and the use of figures, qualities aimed to afford delight, all of which Hobbes warmly approved.

Hobbes was deeply interested in style when he translated Thucydides, so much concerned, indeed, that he evidently submitted his manuscript to the judgments of the severest critics he knew.[11] He was no doubt drawn to Thucydides as much by the simplicity and force of his language as by the weight of his subject. In his Introduction he praises Thucydides for his perspicuity, for the gravity and dignity, the pithiness and strength, and the purity and propriety of his style.[12] It is true that he concedes something to Dionysius's charge that Thucydides is "obscure and licentious." The licentiousness is observable in a very few sentences, somewhat long. Even these, however, are not difficult for the attentive reader. The other charge is quite as easily answered:

. . . For the rest, the obscurity that is, proceedeth from the profoundness of the sentences; containing contemplations of those human passions, which either dissembled or not commonly discoursed of, do yet carry the greatest sway with men in their public conversation. If then one cannot

---

[10] *The History of the Grecian War*, p. xxii.

[11] Sir Robert Ayton, poet, critic, and scholar, and Ben Jonson. See Aubrey, who writes ('*Brief Lives*,' *Chiefly of Contemporaries*, ed. by Andrew Clark [Oxford, 1898], I, 365), "And he desired Ben: Johnson, and this gentleman [Ayton], to give their judgment on his style of his translation of Thucydides." When in his "To the Readers," prefatory to his Thucydides, Hobbes writes, "Though this translation have already past the censure of some, whose judgments I very much esteem . . ." (*The History of the Grecian War*, p. vii), he is no doubt referring to Ayton and Jonson.   [12] *The History of the Grecian War*, pp. xxi–xxiii.

penetrate into them without much meditation, we are not to expect a man should understand them at the first speaking.[13]

Not only is profound thought, with whatever clarity it may be expressed, difficult to grasp at a first reading, but at best only the few will be able to understand it: "for a wise man should so write, (though in words understood by all men), that wise men only should be able to commend him." [14] Thus Thucydides may be excused for a certain difficulty for common readers in those passages where he is philosophically minded. Hobbes would not, however, condone such obscurity in "narrations of things done, nor in the descriptions of places or of battles." [15] But in these respects "Thucydides is most perspicuous"; he is, in fact, to be commended for his rare power so to present these things as to make the reader see them as before his own eyes.

Altogether, Hobbes finds that Thucydides writes in a style of unusual perfection; that he writes with judgment, both in his larger designs and in the selection and expression of details; that he possesses qualities almost divine, which make for the perennial attraction of judicious readers. In the end he is able to sum up his conclusions in the words of Justus Lipsius in the notes to his *De Doctrina Civili:*

. . . Thucydides, who hath written not many nor very great matters, hath perhaps yet won the garland from all that have written of matters both many and great. Everywhere for elocution grave; short, and thick with sense; sound in his judgments; everywhere secretly instructing and directing a man's life and actions. In his orations and excursions, almost divine. Whom the oftener you read, the more you shall carry away; yet never be dismissed without appetite.[16]

---

[13] *Ibid.*, p. xxix.   [14] *Ibid.*

[15] Though he does make certain interesting observations on Thucydides which remind one of Coleridge's later suggestion that a certain amount of obscurity is necessary to the continued appeal of a work (*Anima Poetæ*, ed. by E. H. Coleridge [Boston and New York, 1895], p. 4), and of present-day suspicion of writing that is too easy to understand. Thucydides' eloquence was not "fit for the bar," observes Hobbes, "but proper for history, and rather to be read than heard. For words that pass away (as in public orations . . .) without pause, ought to be understood with ease, and are lost else; though words that remain in writing for the reader to meditate on, ought rather to be pithy and full" (*The History of the Grecian War*, p. xxxi).

[16] *The History of the Grecian War*, pp. xxxi–xxxii.

This last contains also the idea of the value of Thucydides for instruction, which carries us back to the "Epistle Dedicatory to Sir William Cavendish," where this book is commended to him as "having profitable instruction for noblemen, and such as may come to have the management of great and weighty actions." [17]

Throughout the criticism of Thucydides one detects the sturdy reliance on his own judgments that is to characterize Hobbes's later thought. His ideas are not always original; indeed they are sometimes couched in the very language of tradition, as in the case of his remarks upon instruction as the end of literature. But the spirit in which he writes is independent, and is anticipatory of his later more complete divergence from authority.

His vigorous general rebuttal of Dionysius, whom he only once quotes with approval, is indicative of his impatience with systemized dogma in aesthetic discussion. One by one he batters down not only the judgments of the Greek rhetorician but the neatly designed system for historical writing upon which they are founded.

II

In *The Answer to Davenant* and in *The Virtues of an Heroic Poem*, though he does not attack any writer or any system, Hobbes quietly ignores set codes, building his critiques on the psychological principles he has now advanced. It is true that some of these principles run a broad parallel to seventeenth-century neoclassic theory. He evolves again theories of unity of action, verisimilitude, and decorum. He is in accord with the current dictum that poetry is for the delight and instruction of mankind; in spite of his strong tendency toward realism, he admits a species of ideal imitation. His emphasis upon the epic as the noblest form of poetry and on great personages as the proper characters for the epic is again in harmony with the majority opinion of contemporary neoclassic writers. He also places emphasis on a great style,

[17] *The History of the Grecian War*, p. v.

either in dialogue or in narrative, as the only fitting medium for heroic poetry,[18] and even yields to the conservative view with respect to the superiority for literary purposes of the ancient languages over the modern, on the ground that Greek and Latin have become "immutable, which none of the modern tongues are like to be." [19]

Thus far Hobbes sounds conventional enough. It turns out, however, when we examine his expression of these views, that in virtually every case he is basing his dictum not on received opinion but on logical deduction from observation and from premises in his own system of thought. His authority is neither Aristotle nor Horace nor their neoclassic interpreters, but nature and the postulates that may be derived from a study of nature. Where he goes beyond nature to literature his appeal is not to the dogma of the critics, but to the great writers themselves as they reveal adherence to nature and to the principles of psychological effect.

It is significant that, though Hobbes knew Aristotle well, both in *The Answer to Davenant* and in *The Virtues of an Heroic Poem* he quite ignores the sixfold criteria of the *Poetics*. Like Aristotle, he searches for definite bases for judgment, but the standards he names are his own. Thus, in the *Virtues*, he gives, in lieu of the elements named by Aristotle — plot, character, diction, thought, spectacle, and song — his own list of seven "virtues": choice of words, construction, contrivance of the story or fiction, elevation of fancy, the justice and impartiality of the poet, clearness of descriptions, and amplitude of the subject.[20] The substitution, one is bound to feel in reading this piece of rather mediocre criticism, is not wholly fortunate, and merits, to some extent at least, Dryden's severe censure to the effect that Hobbes, in attending first to diction, before considering design, disposition, manners, and thoughts, began his praise of Homer where he should have ended it.[21] Hobbes's classification of virtues gives him, nonetheless, as we

[18] *The Answer to Davenant*, in *Critical Essays of the Seventeenth Century*, ed. by J. E. Spingarn (Oxford, 1908), II, 64. [19] *Ibid.*, p. 65.
[20] *The Virtues of an Heroic Poem*, Spingarn, II, 68 ff.
[21] "Preface to the *Fables*," in *Essays of John Dryden*, ed. by W. P. Ker (Oxford, 1926), II, 252.

shall see later, opportunity to place the emphasis he desired on certain points peculiar to his manner of thought.

In the *Answer*, a much more successful essay in criticism, Hobbes's approach is even more individual. He gives attention to characters, plot, expression, and sentiments, to the general problem of imitation, and to matters of effect, but all quite in his own way. The subject of poetry is the "manners of men, not natural causes; manners presented, not dictated; and manners feigned . . . not found in men." [22] The poets, whose work it is to imitate "humane life . . . to avert men from vice and incline them to virtuous and honourable actions," have taken as their field "three regions of mankinde, Court, City, and Country." From thence have proceeded three kinds of poetry: "Heroique, Scommatique, and Pastorall." Each of these is again divided, according to the manner of representation, into two kinds: narrative and dramatic. The narrative form of the heroic poem is the epic, the dramatic is the tragedy; satire is the narrative, comedy, the dramatic form of the scommatic type; while the pastoral may be either a bucolic or a comedy. Hobbes denies a place in his scheme to sonnets, eclogues, and epigrams on the ground that they are but essays and parts of a poem, and to historical and philosophic pieces in that they are concerned with natural causes rather than the manners of men or with actual rather than feigned events. Lucretius, Empedocles, and Lucan are thus denied a place among poets. Verse alone does not make poetry.[23]

Hobbes's direct, and obviously his chief, concern is with heroic poetry, and with the epic form of it. The epic deals with men of the court, princes and heroes, men of high degree. It should portray these great persons as models of virtue, yet as true examples of human nature. The idea of representing epic characters as models of their kind seems to place Hobbes on the side of all those critics from Minturno to Dryden who applied the doctrine of ideal imitation to heroic poetry; but, as I shall presently show, his theory has a turn to it which distinguishes it from the generality. It may be said here that

[22] *The Answer to Davenant*, Spingarn, II, 55.   [23] *Ibid.*, pp. 55–56.

the prescription for model characters is conditioned throughout in Hobbes by his demand for an empirical knowledge of the mind and the ways of mankind.

The word "natural" occurs frequently in his brief critical essays. In the one representative example of excellence in *Gondibert* singled out in the *Answer*, the "Description of Love in the person of Birtha," Hobbes finds such "true, perfect, and natural a Love to the Life," as he would challenge any other "painter" to draw.[24] Hobbes's theory of verisimilitude has its basis in a demand for the true and natural rather than in a fancied need for deluding spectators and readers into a sense of witnessing actual life. The reader of an epic knows well enough that he is dealing with feigned actions, not history, and will consequently accept a certain overstepping of actuality. There is a limit, however, beyond which the poet may never go without offense to discriminating readers. There are those who are pleased with nothing less than "exorbitancy" of fiction and see no beauty in a poem unless it is so bold as to exceed not only the *work*, but also the *possibility* of nature: "they would have impenetrable Armours, Enchanted Castles, invulnerable bodies, Iron Men, flying Horses, and a thousand other such things, which are easily feigned by them that dare." [25] From all such Hobbes warmly dissents:

> . . . For as truth is the bound of Historical, so the Resemblance of truth is the utmost limit of Poeticall Liberty. In old time amongst the Heathen such strange fictions and Metamorphoses were not so remote from the Articles of their Faith as they are now from ours, and therefore were not so unpleasant. Beyond the actual works of nature a poet may now go; but beyond the conceived possibility of Nature, never.[26]

---

[24] *Ibid.*, p. 61. "Poets are Painters," says Hobbes here; and again in the *Virtues* he writes, "For a Poet is a Painter, and should paint Actions to the understanding with the most decent words, as Painters do Persons and Bodies with the choicest colours to the eye" (Spingarn, II, 71). He is, however, adopting only the language of the *ut pictura poesis* tradition rather than the fallacy itself. There is no suggestion in either passage of emphasis on descriptive poetry; presenting actions through words to the understanding with all the clarity and force with which a painter sets figures and color before the eye is something quite different from confusing the functions of the two mediums.

[25] *The Answer to Davenant*, Spingarn, II, 61.

[26] *Ibid.*, p. 62.

Such is Hobbes's case for verisimilitude. It is instructive to note that, according to his theory, poetic probability is relative, varying from age to age according to the received opinion of the time. Virgil and Homer are not then to be censured for their gods and other supernatural machinery nor Ovid for his strange tales of transformations, for the articles of faith of their respective ages permitted such matter as "conceived possibilities." Hobbes is here in an unobtrusive fashion setting Davenant to rights for his rather inflexible attitude toward the supernatural in ancient poetry; [27] at the same time he is setting an example in liberality and balance for some of his distinguished successors. Both Dryden and Addison — Dryden evidently under the influence of Hobbes, Addison with Dryden in mind — were to state views similar to Hobbes's. Dryden, defending the "enthusiastic parts" of poetry, declares that the "heroic poet is not tied to a bare representation of what is true, or exceeding probable"; for

> . . . 'Tis enough that, in all ages and religions, the greatest part of mankind have believed the power of magic, and that there are spirits or spectres which have appeared. . . . Some men think they have raised a great argument against the use of spectres and magic in heroic poetry, by saying they are unnatural; but whether they or I believe there are such things, is not material; 'tis enough that, for aught we know, they may be in Nature; and whatever is, or may be, is not properly unnatural.[28]

Elsewhere he writes, "And poets may be allowed the like liberty for describing things which really exist not, if they are founded on popular belief. Of this nature are fairies, pigmies, and the extraordinary effects of magic." [29] Addison, it will be recalled, defending the "Fairy Way of Writing," in *The Spectator*, No. 419, refers directly to Dryden and offers an even more liberal argument for the poetic probability of ghosts and fairies, of "Witchcraft, Prodigies, Charms, and Enchantments," where there is popular belief in them, or even when popular belief is lacking — if the imaginative reader cares temporarily to suspend disbelief.

[27] "Preface to *Gondibert*," Spingarn, II, 4.
[28] *An Essay of Heroic Plays* (1672), Ker, I, 153–154.
[29] *The Author's Apology for Heroic Poetry and Poetic License* (1677), Ker, I, 187. See p. 203 of this book.

Hobbes's theory of verisimilitude presents a nicely balanced position between an extreme of realism and unrestrained fancy. Fidelity to nature is requisite, but the "conceived possibilities" for being and action in men's minds is also a part of nature, and therefore a legitimate subject for the poet's imitation. Few today would seriously challenge this general view. It is perhaps not far from Aristotle's meaning when he preferred a "probable impossibility" to an "improbable possibility." Hobbes is again insisting on a due balance between fancy or wit and judgment.

A strong sense for the proprieties leads Hobbes to a view virtually parallel with the prevailing neoclassic theory of decorum. One of the chief "Indecencies" of an heroic poem is a disproportion between persons and their actions illustrated in "representing in great persons the inhumane vice of Cruelty or the sordid vice of Lust and Drunkenness." [30] The ancients rightly reserved such actions for monsters and giants. Similarly, Hobbes regards it as indecorous to "represent scurrility or any action or language that moveth much laughter." For,

> Great persons that have their mindes employed on great designes have not leasure enough to laugh, and are pleased with the contemplation of their own power and vertues, so as they need not the infirmities and vices of other men to recommend themselves to their own favour by comparison, as all men do when they laugh.[31]

Hobbes's appeal is to verisimilitude and truth, not to convention. He does, indeed, cite the example of the ancients on the matter of the indecorum of vice in great persons; but in his remarks on laughter he returns to his usual criterion of truth to human nature.

The theory of structure revealed by Hobbes is again related to his dictum that a poem be true and natural. He makes no ado over the principle of unity, but the few things he does say show how completely he disregards the conventional approach. The virtues of an heroic poem, he says, are all comprehended under the one word "Discretion": "And Discretion consisteth in this, That every part of the Poem be conducing, and in good order placed, to the End and Designe of the

[30] *The Answer to Davenant*, Spingarn, II, 64.   [31] *Ibid.*

Poet." [32]   A comprehensive view, surely, and one that accords very well with Hobbes's general emphasis on effects. Writing more specifically on structure, in terms that are first geographical, then physiological, finally moral, he praises Davenant for his skill in so conducting his poem that all the actions conjoin in two main streams:

> Observing how few the Persons be you introduce in the beginning, and how in the course of the actions of these (the number increasing) after several confluences they run all at last into the two principal streams of your Poem, *Gondibert* and *Oswald*, methinks the Fable is not much unlike the Theater. For so, from several and far distant Sources, do the lesser Brooks of *Lombardy*, flowing into one another, fall all at last into the two main Rivers, the *Po* and the *Adice*. It hath the same resemblance also with a mans veins, which, proceeding from different parts, after the like concourse insert themselves at last into the two principal veins of the Body. But when I considered that also the actions of men, which singly are inconsiderable, after many conjunctures grow at last either into one great protecting power or into two destroying factions, I could not but approve the structure of your Poem, which ought to be no other then such as an imitation of humane life requireth.[33]

This picturesque description amounts to a statement of organic unity, according to which, through growth into oneness rather than in arbitrary collocation, the elements of a poem merge into a structure, or into related structures, similar to life itself. The argument is based wholly on empirical and logical principle, with no trace of deference to classical or neoclassical doctrines. In further exposition Hobbes shows that consistency in characterization is necessary, and that the style should be in keeping with the characters and with the specific design of the poem. Speaking to the first point, Hobbes commends "that clearness of memory by which a Poet, when he hath once introduced any person whatsoever speaking in his Poem, maintaineth in him to the end the same character he gave him in the beginning." [34] Speaking to the second, he names as a capital example of indecency in the heroic poem the disproportion which occurs when the poet uses a dialect of the "Inferior sort of People," foreign to the characters proper to

---

[32] *The Virtues of an Heroic Poem*, Spingarn, II, 67.
[33] *The Answer to Davenant*, Spingarn, II, 60.   [34] *Ibid.*, pp. 63-64.

an epic. "Another is to derive the Illustration of any thing from such Metaphors or Comparisons as cannot come into mens thoughts but by mean conversation and experience of humble or evil Arts, which the Person of an *Epique* Poem cannot be thought acquainted with." [35] In general, the language of a poem is acceptable when it fits, "with all significant translation to our purposes." So we find Hobbes holding for unity of structure and unity of tone and treatment, but on grounds of what is natural and effective, rather than of what authorities have said.

Dryden's complaint that Hobbes begins his criticism of the epic where he should end, that is with style, is only partially justified, and has less force, moreover, when we consider the fact that Hobbes makes expression virtually inseparable from substance. In his own thought, Hobbes obviously began where he should have begun — with the materials for poetry and the processes of mind by which these materials are reconstructed into poetry.

It is a fact of first importance that Hobbes unequivocally assigns poetic creation to the imagination (fancy). Huarte, Puttenham, and Bacon had done that also, and perhaps Hobbes is only elaborating on what he had learned from Bacon and others who had written on the subject. But the method and the extent of his elaboration give to his theory a significance which can hardly be too much emphasized. The course of his thought, as has been indicated in a preceding section, follows the unique psychological system he has devised. The poetic activity is strictly subjective. Fancy chooses her details, not from external objects, as did Zeuxis when he painted the ideal face and figure of Helen, with the five most beautiful maidens of Crotona before him, but from the broad field of remembered experience. These details are joined, not according to an idea of beauty mysteriously implanted in the mind from above [36] or evolved from the sight of many fine artistic models,[37] but according to the dictates of the judging faculty

---

[35] *Ibid.*, p. 64.
[36] As in Cicero's explanation; see p. 35 n. of this book.
[37] As in Du Fresnoy, for instance.

of a mind working in harmony with the principles of true philosophy: that is, principles derived from a study of nature and the habit of proceeding from causes to their effects.[38]

Hobbes's theory allowed for more of individuality of manner than did that of his more traditionally minded contemporaries. So far as the neoclassic idea of imitation provided for individual treatment of a subject by an artist, the explanation lay in one of two methods or a combination of the two: (1) a unique conception of ideal beauty gained through a grasp of the divine idea [39] or through a study of models of the most perfect art, usually of the ancients,[40] and an accommodation of examples from nature to this conception; (2) a special skill and correctness and perfection in execution of the kind that Boileau and Pope at times emphasized. In both cases the successful artist must employ to a high degree the principle of selectivity. Hobbes acknowledges, at least implicitly, this very important principle. The notion of an idea of perfect beauty was, however, repugnant to his whole system of thought, and, though he shows, particularly in *The Virtues of an Heroic Poem*, considerable deference to Homer and Virgil, he nowhere urges the poet to study models for an image of excellence. His appeal is rather to the nimbleness of fancy, truth to nature, and the restraints of judgment. And, since quickness of fancy and accuracy of judgment are, on the whole, relative matters, dependent on the degree to which these faculties are developed in any individual, the standard for their products must, by implication, also be somewhat relative. Nature, we may assume, remains constant. But the degree of truth and perfection to be found in artistic imitations of nature will naturally be conditioned both by the extent of a given poet's experience, consequently by the volume and richness of his stored memories, and by the particular operations of fancy and judgment upon these materials.

It is true that Hobbes made much of style. His stress,

---

[38] See pp. 12–16 of this book.
[39] For example, Cicero's theory; see p. 35 n. of this book.
[40] An instance of this view in its maturity is to be found in Du Fresnoy's *Art of Painting*.

however, is not upon polish, grace, and correctness, but upon perspicuity and adequacy to the purpose in hand. The majesty of the epic style of the Greeks and the grace of their hexameters is, indeed, unmistakably commended,[41] and Homer is praised for his images, with a somewhat grudging admission of Virgil's borrowed excellence in this department.[42] This praise is, however, not for a given style per se, but for a manner fitted to the particular high inventions of these poets. Hobbes's first interest is in a style most perfectly adapted to its subject and to the ends sought by the poet. This is to be attained by a close adherence to nature. Addressing himself directly to the problem of "expression," he condemns those writers who imitate books rather than nature. Hobbes's discussion here reveals an inextricable blend in his thinking of matter and manner; his censure is equally of those who borrow matter with those who borrow style:

> There remains now no more to be considered but the Expression, in which consisteth the countenance and colour of a beautiful Muse, and is given her by the Poet out of his own provision, or is borrowed from others. That which he hath of his own is nothing but experience and knowledge of Nature, and specially humane nature, and is the true and natural Colour. But that which is taken out of Books (the ordinary boxes of Counterfeit Complexion) shews well or ill, as it hath more or less resemblance with the natural, and are not to be used without examination unadvisedly. For in him that professes the imitation of Nature, as all Poets do, what greater fault can there be then to bewray an ignorance of nature in his Poem,— especially having a liberty allowed him, if he meet with any thing he cannot master, to leave it out? [43]

Here Hobbes makes his famous declaration that it is to know well and to know much that gives to a poem true and natural color. The first means to have distinct and clear images in the mind, eventuating in "perspicuity, property, and decency." The second permits novelty of expression with consequent excitation of the mind to pleased admiration.

Walter Charleton has probably best suggested Hobbes's thought in his specification of much knowledge as a means to

---

[41] *The Answer to Davenant*, Spingarn, II, 56–57.
[42] *The Virtues of an Heroic Poem*, Spingarn, II, 73–74.
[43] *The Answer to Davenant*, Spingarn, II, 62.

novelty, when, analyzing the error of a "rambling wit," he writes, "The Reason of which Errour seems to be grounded upon defect of Experience, which makes them imagine that to be new and remarkable, which to more knowing heads is really stale and trivial; and that to be great and considerable, which to others of some observation is not so." [44] Charleton does not mention Hobbes in this passage, and is applying the dictum "to know much" to a different immediate purpose. He has, nevertheless, given a clear reason for much experience if one is to achieve novelty, and one which, no doubt, was in the mind of Hobbes. The uninformed man will be forever venturing ideas and expressions which seem to him new and striking, but will be to others flat and stale. Only the well-experienced wit possesses and recognizes what is new in idea and language, and so he only can be expected to achieve novelty.

As opposed to such clear, natural, but withal fresh expression Hobbes singles out, for special disapprobation, unmeaning pedantic bombast and ambitious obscurity:

> There be so many words in use at this day in the English Tongue, that though of magnifique sound, yet (like the windy blisters of a troubled water) have no sense at all, and so many others that lose their meaning by being ill coupled, that it is a hard matter to avoid them; for having been obtruded upon youth in the Schools by such as make it, I think, their business there (as 'tis exprest by the best Poet)
>
> *With terms to charm the weak and pose the wise,*
>
> they grow up with them, and, gaining reputation with the ignorant, are not easily shaken off.
>
> To this palpable darkness I may also add the ambitious obscurity of expressing more than is perfectly conceived, or perfect conception in fewer words than it requires. Which Expressions, though they have had the honor to be called strong lines, are indeed no better than Riddles, and, not onely to the Reader but also after a little time to the Writer himself, dark and troublesome. [45]

Thus picturesquely and vigorously Hobbes registers his distaste for language that is pretentious, or artificial, or borrowed,

---

[44] *Two Discourses. I. Concerning the Different Wits of Men: II. Of the Mysterie of Vintners* (London, 1669), p. 29.

[45] *The Answer to Davenant,* Spingarn, II, 63.

or inadequate, that in general is superimposed upon, does not grow out of, clear ideas. Hobbes's antipathy to canting word and phrase is quite as genuine as was Wordsworth's in a later age, and was based on similar grounds.

True originality, even decency, of expression lies in sincere individual language, in the closest possible correspondence of word with thought. The effectiveness of a good poetical style depends upon the ease with which it can be read and the sense of variety and freshness it conveys. Foreign words, except such as have been in so long use as to become vulgar, are to be avoided, as are technical and other school words — in part for the benefit of the more linguistically unskilled women readers [46] — and the order is to be such as to afford the least possible difficulty. For a distinct virtue of the heroic poem consists in a "natural contexture of the words," which reveals not the labor but the natural ability of the poet:

. . . For the order of words, when placed as they ought to be, carries a light before it, whereby a man may foresee the length of his period, as a torch in the night shews a man the stops and unevenness in the way. But when plac'd unnaturally, the Reader will often find unexpected checks, and be forced to go back and hunt for the sense, and suffer such unease, as in a coach a man unexpectedly finds in passing over a furrow.[47]

Hobbes admits that the conventions of verse may put some constraints upon the poet in achieving this so natural and easy style. Individuality may here again assert itself, however; for the poet has "liberty to depart from what is obstinate and to chuse somewhat else that is more obedient to such Laws, and no less fit for his purpose." [48]

As we have seen, Hobbes attributes novelty of expression, and consequent ability to arouse the feelings, to a full background of experience. After digression he returns to this point in a notable paragraph which contains in little a rather complete theory of style:

From *Knowing much*, proceedeth the admirable variety and novelty of Metaphors and Similitudes, which are not possible to be lighted on in the compass of a narrow knowledge. And the want whereof compelleth

---

[46] *The Virtues of an Heroic Poem*, Spingarn, II, 68.
[47] *Ibid.*, p. 69.   [48] *Ibid.*

a Writer to expressions that are either defac'd by time or sullied with vulgar or long use. For the Phrases of Poesy, as the airs of musick, with often hearing become insipide, the Reader having no more sense of their force than our Flesh is sensible of the bones that sustain it. As the sense we have of bodies consisteth in change and variety of impression, so also does the sense of language in the variety and changeable use of words. I mean not in the affectation of words newly brought home from travail, but in new and with all significant translation to our purposes of those that be already received, and in far fetch't but withal apt, instructive, and comly similitudes.[49]

When Wordsworth struck out in his Preface and the Appendix to the Preface at the tired phrases and furbished diction of eighteenth-century poetry and spoke for a natural organic language that accurately expressed individual thought and feeling he was scarcely saying more than Hobbes has put into this brief paragraph. Hobbes is allowing far more for poetic figure than is to be found in Wordsworth's statements — not, however, than is exemplified in his verse — and his emphasis on novelty would have put Wordsworth on his guard; but, fundamentally, may we not say that Hobbes is speaking for very much what Wordsworth demanded: namely, the commonly received language of men so applied to poetic purposes as faithfully to translate the truths of nature, through the medium of the writer's own experience, to the end of arousing the emotions of the reader and of creating in him an impression of newness, a sense of fresh delight, in apprehensions of that to which he might otherwise have remained insensible? Hobbes's last sentence readily recalls Wordsworth's description of poetic effect as a "perception perpetually renewed of language closely resembling that of real life, and, yet, in the circumstances of metre differing from it so widely"; [50] and his remarks about the effects of novelty remind us of Coleridge's account of his own and Wordsworth's purposes in writing the *Lyrical Ballads:* an ambition to excite "the sympathy of the reader by a faithful adherence to the truth of nature," to give "the interest of novelty by the modifying colors of imagina-

    [49] *The Answer to Davenant*, Spingarn, II, 65.
    [50] William Wordsworth, "Preface to *Lyrical Ballads*" (1800), in *Wordsworth's Literary Criticism*, ed. by Nowell C. Smith (London, 1905), p. 35.

tion," and in so doing to awaken the mind "from the lethargy of custom." [51] There are marked differences between Hobbes and Wordsworth, but their agreement on the basic principles of true originality is striking. Each proclaimed in his own way the necessity of knowing and following nature and of relying on stores of experience for poetic materials; each declared the necessity of a language appropriate to express the exact truth of nature, simple and inartificial, yet invested with enough strangeness to awaken the sleeping attention and to excite delight.

[51] S. T. Coleridge, *Biographia Literaria*, ed. by J. Shawcross (Oxford, 1907), II, 5, 6. Coleridge's description of these purposes suggests at once the likeness and the difference between Hobbes and the great Romanticists. To Hobbes nature applied to men only, and for the most part to men in courts and cities. He did, indeed, admit a place to pastoral poetry (*The Answer to Davenant*, Spingarn, II, 55), and spoke of "a plainness, and though dull, yet a nutritive faculty in rurall people, that endures a comparison with the Earth they labour"; but of the inclusive Romantic theory he had only a faint conception, and he would have completely balked at Coleridge's remarks, in succeeding sentences of the passage I have quoted, about the supernatural and the desirability of awakening in the reader "feelings analogous to the supernatural."

CHAPTER VI

Two Disciples of Hobbes: Davenant and Charleton

I. DAVENANT

OF LITERARY men who were influenced by Hobbes Sir William Davenant appears to be the earliest, and he is in some respects the most thoroughgoing in his allegiance. He shows this allegiance in rather ostentatious professions of independence of authority and tradition, in a theory of poetry drawn from nature, in an emphasis on effects rather than on formal quality, and a corollary interest in the psychological processes of creation as manifested in wit and fancy. Davenant's ideas of wit and fancy have been briefly examined in a previous chapter. The other points I have named remain to be considered.

Davenant begins his Preface on a note of skepticism, as if he would at once show his friend and teacher that he desired himself to be classed among the *mathematici*, who speak from experience and knowledge, rather than the *dogmatici*, whose words are but the echo of unproved opinion. He is for original genius and new ways of writing rather than for imitation of the masters. He respects Homer, but is against following him with blind devotion. Homer, he admits, is to be justly reverenced as one standing on a hill among poets, like an ancient "Sea-mark" by which others may steer a safe course; but, he hastens to explain, "Sea-marks are chiefly useful to Coasters, and serve not those who have the ambition of Discoverers, that love to sail in untry'd seas." Hence it comes about that the example of Homer does very well for those "whose satisfy'd

Wit will not venture beyond the track of others"; though it serves but ill for those more adventurous ones "who affect a new and remote way of thinking, who esteem it a deficiency and meanness of minde to stay and depend upon the authority of example." [1] This is a boldly independent utterance, and it is written in the very spirit of Hobbes.

Davenant goes on to find shortcomings in not only Homer but Virgil, Lucan, Statius, Tasso, and Spenser. Of these, Virgil, Statius, and Tasso are particularly reprehensible for their tendency to imitate their predecessors: Virgil copying Homer; Statius imitating Virgil; Tasso owing most of his faults to the ancients. "And 'tis with Originall Poems as with the Originall Pieces of Painters, whose Copies abate the excessive price of the first Hand." [2] "Such limits to the progress of every thing, even of worthiness as well as defect, doth Imitation give; for whilst we imitate others, we can no more excel them, then he that sailes by others Mapps can make a new discovery . . . ." [3] Such sentiments are a fit prologue to the main arguments of the Preface. In devising his poem Davenant tells us — not without a trace of prideful triumph — he has turned from the traditions of books to Nature in all her hidden walks.[4] He has gone to men for his patterns of human life and has written in "cheerful obedience to the just authority of experience." He has relied not on inspiration and vision, but on labor and judgment and maturity, and, as we have seen, on the disciplined power of fancy and wit engendering out of empirical knowledge.[5]

. . . For that grave Mistris of the World, *Experience*, (in whose profitable School those before the Flood stay'd long, but we like wanton children come thither late . . .) hath taught me that the engendrings of unripe age become abortive and deform'd, and that after obtaining more years, those must needs prophesy with ill success who make use of their Visions in Wine; That when the ancient Poets were vallew'd as Prophets, they were long and painful in watching the correspondence of Causes ere they presum'd to foretell effects, and that 'tis a high presumption to en-

---

[1] "Preface to *Gondibert*," in *Critical Essays of the Seventeenth Century*, ed. by J. E. Spingarn (Oxford, 1908), II, 1–2.
[2] *Ibid.*, p. 5.   [3] *Ibid.*, p. 7.   [4] *Ibid.*, p. 26.
[5] See pp. 111–112 of this book.

tertain a Nation . . . with hasty provisions; as if a Poet might imitate the familiar dispatch of Faulkoners, mount his *Pegasus*, unhood his *Muse*, and with a few flights boast he provided a feast for a Prince. Such posting upon *Pegasus* I have long since forborne, and during my Journey in this worke have mov'd with a slow pace, that I might make my survays as one that travaild not to bring home the names, but the proportion and nature, of things . . . .[6]

This is doctrine that Davenant well knew would appeal to Hobbes; for he is but freely adapting ideas that had appeared in *The Elements of Law* descriptive of the true teacher, who, having gone on slowly, from humble beginnings, to learn the nature of things, knows what he teaches, and so begets belief and understanding in those who hear him.[7] It is, so far as it goes, a new poetic creed.

Davenant shows less reliance on Hobbes, but is still in his spirit, when he praises the English drama as unrivaled in presenting heroic actions in a "pleasant and instructive" manner;[8] in his confessed resolution to write an epic after the plan of drama — "proportioning five Books to five Acts, Cantos to Scenes";[9] and in his theory of love and ambition (or honor) as motivating forces in poetry,[10] an idea which is to become the theme song for heroic tragedy. All this is evidence of a willingness, even eagerness, to venture out beyond the established "Sea-marks" in literary theory and practice.

Davenant reveals in many ways his sympathy with Hobbes's ideas of effects in literature. The end of his poem is to please and to bring truth "home to mens bosoms."[11] His means has been to lead "through unfrequented and new ways, and from the most remote Shades, by representing Nature, though not in an affected, yet in an unusual dress." A work must give satisfaction for its probability, but variety and expectation and surprise are indispensable. Therefore, following the "Meanders of the English stage," he has cut the walks

[6] "Preface to *Gondibert*," Spingarn, II, 23–24.
[7] *The Elements of Law*, I, xiii, 3; see also p. 112 of this book.
[8] "Preface to *Gondibert*," Spingarn, II, 17.   [9] *Ibid.*
[10] *Ibid.*, pp. 14–15. This idea had, it is true, appeared in French criticism, but there is little doubt that Davenant was emboldened to extend the legitimate passions proper to heroic poetry by Hobbes's example in giving a new dignity to the emotions in general.   [11] *Ibid.*, p. 23.

of his poem with counterturns and interwindings which will appear to men, he hopes, "as pleasant as a summer passage on a crooked River, where going about and turning back is as delightful as the delayes of parting Lovers." [12]   He has sought, he explains, to convey "all the *shadowings, happy strokes, secret graces,* and even the *drapery*," which constitute one of the chief beauties of the English drama.   So Davenant echoes Hobbes's theory of truth made acceptable through novelty and variety and such other ornaments as fancy and judgment may dictate.

Without using the word, Davenant adopts the principle of "admiration" as a valid end in epic or dramatic poetry. Images of action in the songs of poets, "recording the praises of Conduct and Valour," have ever prevailed upon men's minds.[13]   In pursuing this idea Davenant falls easily into the vein of Sidney's *Apology.*   Poetry is an effective aid to morality and good government, he argues, "for as Poesy is adorn'd and sublim'd by Musick, which makes it more pleasant and acceptable, so Morality is sweetned and made more amiable by Poesy." [14]   The minds of the people must be won to good ends by persuasion, but persuasion can be best effected not by sermons, laws, philosophy, and so forth, but by the poets, "whose art is more then any enabled with a voluntary and chearfull assistance of Nature, and whose operations are as resistlesse, secret, easy, and subtle as is the influence of Planets." [15]

This idea of utility, the theory of poetry as a pleasant teacher, is no new thing in criticism, but there is in Davenant a consistent emphasis on effects and a scientific turn to his reasoning that, one suspects, would not have been present except for Hobbes's influence.   Thus Davenant's "and of the Minde Poesy is the most natural and delightful Interpreter" would not have been at home in Sidney's *Apology.*   Nor should we expect in writings before Hobbes the following approach to the "sweet teaching" argument:

. . . Because the subject on which they should work is the Minde, and the Minde can never be constrain'd, though it may be gain'd by per-

---

[12] *Ibid.,* p. 18.   [13] *Ibid.,* pp. 36–37.   [14] *Ibid.,* p. 49.   [15] *Ibid.,* p. 45.

swasion: And since Perswasion is the principal instrument which can bring to fashion the brittle and mishapen mettal of the Minde, none are so fit aids to this important work as Poets.[16]

Davenant has his eye on psychological processes, and reduces the efficacy of poetry for teaching to something like a phenomenon of natural law: the art of poetry, aided by nature, operates on the mind of man in ways as secret, subtle, and resistless as is the influence of the planets. Thus we see Davenant not only deriving new ideas from Hobbes but learning from him how to throw over old ones the coloring of the new ways of thought about poetry in its relation to the mind.

However much in Davenant may have been traditional, he was himself firmly convinced that his theory and method in poetry were new. Twice in his Preface he speaks of his "new building," and he writes firmly, somewhat audaciously, of his right to follow untrodden paths:

. . . If I be accus'd of Innovation, or to have transgressed against the method of the Ancients, I shall think my self secure in beleeving that a Poet, who hath wrought with his own instruments at a new design, is no more answerable for disobedience to Predecessors, then *Law-makers* are liable to those old Laws which themselves have repealed.[17]

"Davenant," declares Mr. Dowlin, "cares not one iota for authority. . . . We may notice that not once does he use the word authority or cite an authority." [18]   It is more accurate to say that he cares not one iota for traditional neoclassic authority. The authority of Hobbes he eagerly proclaims, expressly acknowledging him as his guide and teacher. Publicly thanking him for his critical services in examining *Gondibert* before publication, Davenant even goes to the somewhat extravagant length of implying that no one could succeed in the new way of writing without enlisting Hobbes's aid; for who is "so learn'd," he inquires, "that can hope, when through the several ways of Science he seeks Nature in her hidden walks, to make his Journey short, unless he calls you to be

<hr>

16 "Preface to *Gondibert*," Spingarn, II, p. 45.
17 *Ibid.*, p. 20.
18 Cornell March Dowlin, *Sir William Davenant's Gondibert, Its Preface, and Hobbes's Answer* (Philadelphia, 1934), p. 32.

his Guide?" [19] Whoever is so guided is safe from the ambush of enemies lying in wait for those who travel new ways; for "from such, you, and those you lead, are secure, because you move not by common Mapps, but have painfully made your own Prospect, and travail now like the Sun, not to inform your self, but to enlighten the world." [20] We must make allowance in all this for seventeenth-century convention of dedicatory compliment. When, however, we consider that these eulogistic sentences quite adequately reflect the spirit and theme of the Preface as a whole we recognize in them something more than convention: they represent the disciple paying due tribute to the master, whose approbation he eagerly craves.

Davenant's *Gondibert* is not much of a poem perhaps, but the Preface is a significant piece of criticism. In spite of certain vagaries it contains implications for a sounder doctrine of poetic invention than, except for those announced by Hobbes himself, can be found again in criticism until Edward Young's letter on "Original Composition," Samuel Johnson's Preface to his Shakespeare and some of his essays in the *Rambler*, and Lessing's *Laokoon*.[21] And this doctrine bears all the earmarks of derivation from Hobbes's insistence that the good poet writes from the mind, from stores of experience gathered in the memory through actual observation of men (nature), out of which the fancy, guided by judgment, selects and brings together materials for the poetic structure.

[19] "Preface to *Gondibert*," Spingarn, II, 28.   [20] *Ibid.*
[21] One of Lessing's most cogent strokes at the fallacy of hunting for the sources of poetry in the plastic arts and vice versa is made in a passage where he attributes to the true poet original observation and experience rather than a febrile copying of another's representations. Refuting the suggestion of Spence (*Polymetis*, Dial. viii) that Tibullus had borrowed his conception of Apollo from an old painting, he writes eloquently, "The 'nova nupta verecundia notabilis' of Echion may have been in Rome, may have copied a thousand and a thousand times; but does that prove that bridal modesty itself had vanished from the world? Because the painter had seen it, was no poet ever to see it more, save in the painter's imitation? Or when another poet describes Vulcan as wearied, and his face, scorched by the furnace, as red and burning, must he have first learnt from the work of a painter, that toil wearies and heat reddens? Or when Lucretius describes the changes of the seasons, and in natural succession conducts them past us . . . are we to suppose that he was an ephemeral who had never lived through a whole year, had never experienced these changes in his own person?" (Gotthold Ephraim Lessing, *Laokoon*, tr. by E. C. Beasley [Bohn ed., London, 1914], pp. 56–57).

II. Walter Charleton

In Walter Charleton's discourse on wit [22] the evidences of Hobbes are so patent that one is tempted to discard the word "influence" for the less polite term which would probably be used in our own day were a similar case of such obvious borrowing to occur. Perhaps, however, Charleton saves himself from a charge of too flagrant plagiarism by mentioning Hobbes in three or four passages as the source of his ideas, always with open respect. In one instance he calls him "our incomparable Mr. Hobbs"; in another place he cites a passage from *The Elements of Law*, with the parenthesis, "as Mr. Hobbes excellently observes." Usually, however, he merely gives Hobbes's thought, often his words, as his own, with some show, through reference to ancient authors and use of the classical terms, of going behind Hobbes to more remote sources.

In Charleton we find the same impulse to research in psychological modes that marked Hobbes's investigations. Like Hobbes, he is not primarily interested in aesthetic problems, though his applications to poetry and, on occasion, to oratory, are sometimes more direct. His chief concern is with the question of how and why men differ in wit, that is to say, in intellectual power and efficiency. He begins his inquiry with definitions of wit, taking his point of departure from the Latin *"ingenium."* This word has two uses. It denotes first, "The power of *Understanding* proper to mankind; as may be instanced in that memorable sentence of *Sallust*, (*in initio Belli Catilinarii*): *Mihi rectius esse videtur, ingenii, quam virium opibus gloriam quærere.*" [23] *"Ingenium"* is used more commonly, however, "to denote a man's natural Inclination or Propension to some things or actions more than to others." [24] Wit is sometimes understood, also, as

Aptness to Discipline or Promptitude to learn: which the ancient Græcians, both Philosophers and Orators, called 'Ευμαθία; the *Latines*, *Docilitas*, *bona indoles*, to which our Language hath no word answerable, but *Toward-*

---

[22] *Two Discourses. I. Concerning the Different Wits of Men: II. Of the Mysterie of Vintners* (London, 1669). Hereafter cited as *Concerning the Different Wits of Men*.
[23] *Ibid.*, p. 10.   [24] *Ibid.*, p. 11.

liness, now almost obsolete. If you enquire wherein this happy Faculty doth consist, they tell you that it is not simple, but composed of three others.[25]

The first of these is *"Acumen"* or *"celeritas discendi,"* that is, "a quick or nimble apprehension of what is taught." [26] This idea is presently amplified in terms largely borrowed from Hobbes. A good imagination is related to a quick-working mind. An easy succession of one thought upon another, the author explains, makes for "quickness or celerity"; the opposite is dulness, or "in extreme measure, *stupor* or *sottishness.*" Celerity gives rise to a "twofold difference of Wit," that of the *"Ranging"* mind and that of the mind that fixes and narrowly examines. The former sort has "a Genius disposed to Poësy and Invention" (when it does not run to the extremity of *"Folly"* or *"Extravagancy"*); the latter, to philosophy, civil law, and controversy.[27] The second characteristic of wit is a "Faculty whereby a man, from what he hath learned, hunts after what he hath not learned: the same with that the *Romans* term *Sagacitas*, and our incomparable Mr. *Hobbs* renders *Ranging.*" [28] The third is memory, or "Retention of what is learned." [29]

Proceeding more specifically to a consideration of the nature of wit, Charleton finds, like Hobbes, that there are a natural wit and an acquired wit. Natural wit is that which grows up with us, accruing from "Use and Experience, without the help of Method, culture, or Doctrine"; [30] acquired wit, on the other hand, is derived through "study of Learning and polite Education," and is "no other but *Reason*, which arising from the right use of speech, produces Arts and Sciences; and seems to be only an Effect or Product of the former cultivated

---

[25] *Ibid.*   [26] *Ibid.*, p. 12.

[27] *Ibid.*, pp. 22–24. The sources in Hobbes are *Leviathan*, I, iii and viii, and *The Elements of Law*, I, x, 4. Cf. "This Naturall Wit, consisteth principally of two things; *Celerity of Imagining*, (that is, swift succession of one thought to another;) and *steddy direction* to some approved end. On the Contrary a slow Imagination maketh that Defect, or fault of the mind, which is commonly called Dulnesse, *stupidity* and sometimes by other names . . ." (*Leviathan*, I, viii).

[28] Charleton, *op. cit.*, p. 12. The reference is to *Leviathan*, I, iii, or to *The Elements of Law*, I, iv, 3.

[29] Charleton, *op. cit.*, p. 13.   [30] *Ibid.*, pp. 33–34.

by *industry*." [31]   Most of this is too close to the words of Hobbes to be called paraphrase.

Following Hobbes still further, Charleton finds that the two chief elements in wit are judgment and imagination:

> . . . By *Judgement*, we distinguish subtilty in objects neerly resembling each other, and discerning the real dissimilitude betwixt them, prevent delusion by their apparent similitude.   This *Act* of the Mind the Grecians term Διάγνωσις, the Latins, *Judicium* and *Dignotio;* and we *Discretion*. The *Faculty* it self, Aristotle (*Ethic.* 6. c.7) names Ἐυσυνεσία, the Latins, *subtilitas ingenii;* from them the Italians, *sottigliezza*, and *sottilitá;* the French, *subtilitè;* and we, *subtilty*, which is no other but a certain perspicacity of the Mind, whereby it is able to compare things one with another, and discern the difference betwixt them, notwithstanding they appear very much alike. [32]

> . . . By *Imagination* . . . we conceive some certain similitude in objects really unlike, and pleasantly confound them in discourse: which by its unexpected *Fineness* and allusion, surprising the Hearer, renders him less curious of the truth of what is said.   This is very evident in the use of *Simile's*, *Metaphors*, *Allegories*, and other *Tropes* and *Figures* of *Rhetorick;* . . . serving rather for plausibility, than for demonstration. [33]

The power of these over the "affections" of most people is so great "that the whole Art of *Oratory* is grounded thereupon . . . ."

In spite of the introduction of learned allusions not used by Hobbes Charleton is here little more than paraphrasing the definitions of judgment and fancy in *Leviathan* (I, viii) and in *The Elements of Law* (I, x, 4).   He has, indeed, used "imagination" where Hobbes used "fancy," but the purport is the same.

Elsewhere, Charleton employs "fancy" in a sense exactly equivalent to Hobbes's use of the word.   In a passage in which he again virtually copies Hobbes he writes:

> . . . Phansie without moderation of Judgement, seldom attains to commendation: but judgement or Discretion though unassisted by Phansie,

---

[31] Charleton, *op. cit.*, p. 34.   For the convenience of the reader I quote Charleton's source for this in Hobbes: "By Naturall . . . I mean that *Wit*, which is gotten by Use onely and Experience; without Method, Culture, or Instruction" (*Leviathan*, I, viii); and: "As for *acquired Wit*, (I mean acquired by method and instruction) there is none but Reason; which is grounded on the right use of Speech; and produceth the Sciences" (*ibid.*).

[32] Charleton, *op. cit.*, pp. 19–20.   [33] *Ibid.*, pp. 20–21.

always deserves praise. In Poets, both Phansie and Judgement are required; but Phansie ought to have the upper hand, because all Poems, of what sort soever, please chiefly by Novelty.

In *Historians*, Judgement ought to have the chair; because the Virtue of History consisteth in Method, Truth, and Election of things worthy narration: nor is there need of more Phansie, than what may serve to adorn the stile with elegant language.

In *Panegyries*, and *Invectives*, Phansie ought to take place; because they have for their end not truth, but praise or dispraise, which are effected by comparisons illustrious, or vile or ridiculous: and Judgement doth only suggest Circumstances, by which the action is rendered laudable or blameable.[34]

The place of judgment in discourse and in the affairs of life is to restrain fancy from excesses in her otherwise lawless activities. A good natural wit, where the fancy is curbed by judgment, manifests itself in a steady prosecution to some definite end. But where there is no exercise of discretion the uncurbed fancy runs to the extravagancy of madness. Once more Charleton is giving us Hobbes's ideas, often his very words:

But in all, besides that discretion of times, places, and persons, which renders Phansie commendable, and wherein Civil prudence and the good Menage of affairs doth principally consist; there is required also *Constant Prosecution* of the Scope or *End* proposed, that is frequent application of our thoughts to the subject about which we are conversant. For, so there will occur to us apt similitudes, such as will not only illustrate, but also adorn our discourse, and excite pleasure in the hearers by the rarity of their invention. Whereas if there be not a constant regulation of thoughts to some certain End; the more we are conducted by heat of Phansie, the

---

[34] *Ibid.*, pp. 24–26. Charleton's agreement with Hobbes in these sentences is unmistakable. Hobbes had written: "The former, that is, Fancy, without the help of Judgement, is not commended as a Vertue: but the later which is Judgement, and Discretion, is commended for it selfe, without the help of Fancy . . . . In a good Poem . . . both Judgement and Fancy are required: But the Fancy must be more eminent; because they please for the Extravagancy . . . .

"In a good History, the Judgement must be eminent; because the goodnesse consisteth, in the Method, in the Truth, and in the Choyse of the actions that are most profitable to be known. Fancy has no place, but onely in adorning the stile.

"In Orations of Prayse and in Invectives, the Fancy is præmominant; because the designe is not truth, but to Honour or Dishonour; which is done by noble, or by vile comparisons. The Judgement does but suggest what circumstances make an action laudable or culpable" (*Leviathan*, I, viii). It would be interesting to know whether Charleton was deliberately copying, with a slight verbal disguise, or whether he merely had a very retentive memory.

nearer we come to *Extravagancy*, which is a degree of *Madness*, such as is observed in those *Rambling* Wits, who (as we said even now) having entred into discourse of one thing, are by every new hint, however remote and impertinent, transported from their subject into so many digressions and Parentheses, that not recovering what at first they intended to speak, they lose themselves, as in a Labyrinth. The Reason of which Errour seems to be grounded upon defect of Experience, which makes them imagine that to be new and remarkable, which to more knowing heads is really stale and trivial; and that to be great and considerable, which to others of some observation is not so. For, whatever is new, great and memorable, if it occurr to the Mind of one speaking of another subject, is wont to seduce him from his purpose.[35]

Charleton's application of his theory to discourse, poetry in case, is obvious. It is, moreover, the application indicated by Hobbes. Fancy is the inventive and adorning, judgment the discretionary, faculty. Fancy furnishes the similitudes and the rare incidents which give pleasure through vivid imagery and novelty; judgment, resting its decisions on the authority of experience, selects and rejects the offerings of fancy in terms of the end proposed.

It is indicative of the fidelity of Charleton to Hobbes that, though in this passage, inconsistently with his final view, he appears to make experience the test of a good wit, as Hobbes had done in the third paragraph of Chapter VIII of *Leviathan*, he almost immediately, again in the wake of Hobbes, corrects this impression by pointing out that the difference of wit in men — natural wit, or prudence, at any rate — depends not only upon the wealth of experience but upon the degree of fancy and judgment with which they are endowed:

When a man, therefore, haveing proposed to himself some certain End, and in his thoughts running over a multitude of things, as means conducible therunto, doth quickly perceive which of them is most probable, and how it may be brought to effect his design: this man is said to have a *good Wit*, and the *Habit* hereof is called Φρόνησις and 'Ευβουλία *Prudence*. Which depends upon Experience and Remembrance of many the like Antecedents, with the like Consequents. But herein men differ not one from another so much as in Judgement and Phansy; because men of equal age, may not be very unequal in Experience, as to the quantity,

---

[35] Charleton, *op. cit.*, pp. 27–29. The undoubted source is again *Leviathan*, I, viii. Cf. also *The Elements of Law*, I, x, 4 and 5.

though one hath more of experience in some things, and another in others; since every one hath his particular affairs, concernments and wayes of managing them: and a Husband-man, though rude and illiterate, is yet wiser in his own business, than a Philosopher in another mans. Whence that rule, *Cuiq; in sua arte credendum.*[36]

In this difference of fancy and judgment in men, particularly as it relates to a due proportion of the two for the immediate purpose in hand, Charleton seems to find his most satisfactory explanation of the tantalizing phenomenon of the different wits of men. And it is not too much to say, that, except for details, particularly in application, he derived the whole from Hobbes.

Five years after the appearance of *Concerning the Different Wits of Men* Charleton offered to the public his second essay into the field of psychological analysis, the *Natural History of the Passions.*[37] Here, though he was probably first inspired to his undertaking by Hobbes's analysis of the passions, he is more eclectic in his sources. He quite evidently has been re-reading his Aristotle as well as delving into Descartes, Gassendi, Kenelm Digby, and, with particular enthusiasm, the recent work of Dr. Willis, *De Anima Brutorum.* There is also evidence that he had been reading the Scholastics and the Cambridge Platonists. The work as a whole is a strange potpourri of divergent theory, illustrative of the muddle of psychological thought in which the late seventeenth century found itself. Charleton recurs here to a problem that had been the chief concern of Thomas Wright and Edward Reynolds, which, indeed, had engaged the attention of many previous thinkers from Plato and Aristotle through St. Augustine, St. Thomas Aquinas, and others too numerous to mention: the war between reason and the emotions — between the "rational soul" and the "sensitive soul" — and the best means of curbing those violent passions which militate against the attainment

[36] Charleton, *op. cit.*, pp. 30–31. For the original of this in Hobbes see *Leviathan*, I, viii, the paragraph beginning: "When the thoughts of a man, that has a designe in hand, running over a multitude of things, observes how they conduce to that designe," etc.

[37] Charleton, *Natural History of the Passions.* Printed by T. N. for James Magnes in Russell Street, near the Piazza in Convent Garden (London, 1674).

of tranquility and repose of mind. Charleton himself professes his effort as "research after the most powerfull Remedies against . . . Excesses" of the passions.[38] In this general aim Charleton was parting from Hobbes, who, though he spoke against false emotions and appetites and urged a just balance of fancy by judgment, yet gave the passions an assured dignity as the source of happiness and achievement in the good life. With Charleton's interest in tranquility of mind Hobbes therefore would have had small sympathy, and he would have had even less with the peculiar religious bases of some of Charleton's reasonings.

Even so, there is a good deal of Hobbes in Charleton's essay, and, though this is more likely to appear in dilute form than was the case in the treatise on wit, it must have aided in passing certain Hobbian ideas on to those who, like Dryden, read Charleton with respect. The nuances in Charleton's theory, wherein he inclines to Descartes, wherein to Gassendi, wherein to Hobbes, wherein he is influenced by new anatomical theory and discovery, would require a more extended treatment than is within the scope of the present study. It may be said in general, however, that, though he rejects the Cartesian notion of the "*glandula pinealis*" as the lodging place of the rational soul — a belief which revealed the philosopher's ignorance of anatomy [39] — he is, in his ideas on the passions, nearer to Descartes than to Hobbes. Although he accepts the principle of the animal spirits and of the participation of the heart in the generation of the passions, and goes far in describing the physical expansions and contractions that characterize passionate responses, he is rather less physiological in his explanations than is Hobbes. He finds that, though many passions are physical, some are metaphysical, and some are moral.[40] These vary in proportion to the dominion of the rational over the sensitive (or corporal) soul.[41]

[38] *Natural History of the Passions*, p. 6.
[39] *Ibid.*, pp. 16–18.   [40] *Ibid.*, pp. 74–75.
[41] In his treatment of the passions in his chief medical work (*Enquiries into Human Nature*, in VI. Anatomic Prælections . . . [London, 1680]) his emphasis is, however, entirely physiological. Here he insists that a study of anatomy is essential to a knowledge of the passions. "For the passions seem to be in general, only

Whereas Hobbes identifies the will with appetite, Charleton recognizes the will as an attribute of the rational soul operative on the passions; he likewise conceives of the rational soul as concerned in all acts of apprehension. The imagination is, as in Descartes, intermediate between sense and intellect, presenting images received from sense for the operations of the higher faculty, but it is also — and herein lies a mystery which Charleton does not attempt to solve — the seat, indeed "the imperial palace," of the intellect. A series of brief passages will present his view:

> Her *Acts* also equaly declare her transcendent Powers. That act of simple apprehension, which in Brutes is Imagination, is in Man *Intellection;* and the intellect presides over imagination, discerning the Errors of it occasion'd by the senses, and correcting them; yea subliming the notions thereof into true and usefull ones.[42]

> But as for all *vehement* affections, or *perturbations* of the *Mind*, by which it is . . . inclined to this or that side, for prosecution of good, or avoidance of evil: *these* certainly ought all to be ascribed to the *Corporeal* Soul; and seem to have their original in the seat of th' *Imagination*, probably the middle of the brain. Nevertheless, for that the Intellect, as it reviews all Phantasms formed by imagination, and at pleasure regulates and disposes them; so it not only perceives all concupiscences . . . but also . . . moderates, governs, and gives law to them.[43]

> For the *Second*, viz. the *Rational* Souls chief *seat* or Mansion in the body, tho I cannot conceive how, or in what manner an *immaterial* can reside in a *material* because I can have no representation or idea in my mind of any such thing: yet nevertheless when I consider that all impressions of sensible objects, whereof we are any way conscious, are carried immediately to the *Imagination;* and that there likewise all Appetites, or spontaneous conceptions and intentions of actions are excited; I am very apt to judge the *Imagination* to be the *Escurial*, or imperial palace of the Rational Soul . . . . I think therefore, I may affirm it to be probable, that this *Queen* of the Isle of Man hath her *Court*, and *Tribunal* in the noblest part of the *Sensitive* Soul, the *Imagination*, made up of a select assembly of the most subtil Spirits Animal, and placed in the middle of the Brain.

certain commotions of the spirits and blood, begun in the seat of the Imagination, propagated through the Pathetick nerves to the heart, and thence transmitted up again to the brain: and therefore whosoever would duly enquire into their nature . . . will soon find himself under a necessity to begin at Anatomy . . ." (p. 493).

[42] *Natural History of the Passions*, pp. 48–49.
[43] *Ibid.*, pp. 56–57.

As for the *Conarion*, or *Glandula pinealis* seated near the center of the brain, wherein *Monsieur Des Cartes* took such pains to lodge this Celestial ghest; all our most curious Anatomists will demonstrate that Glandule to be ordained for another, and that a far less noble use, which here I need not mention.[44]

This is plainly not the doctrine of *Leviathan* or *The Elements of Law*. It represents, however, an interesting progress in speculation upon problems of the imagination, deriving impetus from the investigations of Hobbes, Descartes, and others, and pointing to later theories in which the imagination is to be given a place of ever-increasing importance. Charleton's chief divergence from Hobbes in this psychological excursion lies in a sharper differentiation of the imagination from the intellect — growing out of his primary assumption of two souls, a sensitive corporal soul and a rational soul — and a more definite attempt to locate the seats of the respective faculties than Hobbes ever made.

Though these larger psychological postulates necessarily lead him somewhat away from Hobbes, Charleton shows, in his description of the passions and appetites and of the origin of pleasure and pain, obvious reliance upon the accounts in *Leviathan* and *The Elements of Law*. He here reveals the influence of his closer studies in physiology, but his basic conception is derived from Hobbes:

. . . when the Imagination conceives anything to be embraced as good, or avoided as evil; presently by the spirits residing in the brain, and ranged as it were into order, the Appetite is formed; and then the impression being transmitted to the Heart, according as that is contracted or dilated, the blood is impelled and forced to various fluctuations and irregular motions: and thence the appetite being by instinct transmitted to the nerves ordained for that use, they cause motions of the solid parts respective thereunto. And this we may conjecture to be the *order of motions* excited successively in the phantasy, spirits, blood and solid parts, in every Passion of the mind of what sort soever.[45]

And again he writes:

. . . all *Affects* which external objects can possibly excite in us . . . may be commodiously referred to two general heads, namely *Pleasure*, and *Pain*. For, whatever is perceived by the Senses, appears to the Soul to

---

[44] *Natural History of the Passions*, pp. 62–67.   [45] *Ibid.*, p. 71.

be *Good,* or *Evil,* gratefull, or offensive; and whatever is offered to her under the apparence of *Good,* or Gratefull, instantly causeth some certain *Pleasure* in her: as on the contrary, whatever is represented to her as *Evil,* or offensive, as quickly raiseth in her some kind of *Pain,* or trouble: provided . . . she apprehend herself to be anyway concerned in such good, or evil.[46]

One need only reread Chapter VI of *Leviathan* and Chapter VII of *The Elements of Law* to find the inspiration for these passages.

In proceeding to specific passions in this later treatise, Charleton now and again falls into his old habit of the discourse on wit of appropriating Hobbes's words as well as his ideas. It is true that he recurs on occasion to Descartes, as when he cites the French philosopher in his description of "love" [47] and gives his definition of "commiseration," impartially, along with that of Hobbes:

Manifest it is therefore, that in *some, Commiseration* is nothing but imagination of future calamity to ourselves, proceeding from the sense of another mans calamity; as it is defined by Mr. Hobbs: in *others,* a species of *Grief,* mixt with *Love* or *Benevolence* toward those whom we observe to suffer under some evil, which we think they have not deserved; as it is defined by *Monsieur des Cartes.*[48]

Elsewhere, however, he draws on Hobbes alone. Describing the passion of curiosity and its relation to delight and novelty and new learning, he writes:

When the image of any *new* and *strange* object is presented to the Soul, and gives her hope of knowing somewhat that she knew not before; instantly she *admireth* it, as different from all things she hath already known; and in the same instant entertains an appetite to know it better, which is called *Curiosity* or desire of Knowledge.

In words that, though rearranged, are quite as near Hobbes, he continues:

And because this *Admiration* may [be] and most commonly is excited in the Soul before she understands, or considers whether the object be in itself convenient to her or not: therefore it seems to be the *first* of all passions, next after Pleasure and Pain; and to have no *Contrary* . . . . Common it is doubtless to Man with *Beasts;* but with this *difference,* that in *Man* it is always conjoyned with *Curiosity;* in Beasts, not.

---

[46] *Ibid.,* p. 82.   [47] *Ibid.,* pp. 103 ff.   [48] *Ibid.,* p. 131.

Beasts consider only how far the new thing may serve them, but men look for origins and causes. Hence arise natural philosophy and astronomy, admiration being the mother of knowledge. So also arises delight.

> Now this Passion [curiosity] is reducible to *delight*, because *Curiosity* is delight: and so by consequence is *Novelty* too, but especially that novelty from which a Man conceiveth an opinion of *bettering* his own estate, whether that opinion be true or false: for in such case, he stands affected with the hope that all Gamesters have while the cards are shuffling; as *Mr. Hobbs* hath judiciously observed.[49]

Quite as faithfully, though he also includes more detailed physiological explanations,[50] Charleton follows Hobbes in his initial account of laughter:

> . . . whatsoever it [the occasion] be, there must concur therein these three *Conditions* following. (1.) it must be *new* and *surprising;* because whatsoever is ridiculous at first, ceaseth to be so when grown stale. (2.) it must be such a novelty as may suggest to us a conception of some *eminency* or advantage in our selves above another whom the occasion chiefly concerns: for, why are we naturally prone to laugh at either a *jest* . . . or at the mischances and infirmities of others; unless from hence, that thereby our own *abilities* are the more set off and illustrated, and recommended

---

[49] *Natural History of the Passions*, pp. 87–88. The source is *The Elements of Law*, I, ix, 18. The extent of Charleton's debt may be seen by comparing the last sentence quoted with its prototype in Hobbes: "Because curiosity is delight, therefore also all novelty is so, but especially that novelty from which a man conceiveth an opinion true or false of bettering his own estate. For in such case they stand affected with the hope that all gamesters have while the cards are shuffling."

[50] *Natural History of the Passions*, pp. 144 ff. A sample of Charleton's physiological ventures here may be of interest: "For (as the same most curious Dr. Willis reasoneth . . .) when the Imagination is affected with some pleasant and new conceipt, instantly there is caused a brisk and placid motion of the heart, as if it sprung up with joy to be alleviated . . . of its burden. Wherefore that the blood may be the more speedily discharged . . . into the Lungs . . . the *Diaphragm* . . . briskly agitated is by nimble contraction drawn upwards; and so making many vibrations, doth at once raise up the *Lungs* and force them to expell the blood out of their vessels . . . and to explode the aire out of their pipes into the windpipe, and this by frequent contractions of their lax and spongy substance, answerable in time and quickness to the vibrations of the *Midriff*. And then because the same *Intercostal* nerve, which communicateth with the nerve of the *Diaphragm* below, is conjoyned above also with the nerves of the jaws and muscles of the face; thence it is, that the motions of Laughter being once begun in the brest, the *face* also is distorted into gestures or grimaces pathetically correspondent thereunto (*ibid.*, pp. 149–150).

to us by way of comparison? (3.) It must not touch our own, or our friends *honour;* for, in that point we are too tender to tolerate, much less to laugh at a jest broken upon our selves, or friends, of whose dishonour we participate. These requisites in a ridiculous cause considered, we may venture to conclude, that *Laughter is an effect of sudden, but light Joy arising from the unexpected discovery of some* infirmity *in another not our* friend, *and from* imagination *of our own* eminency, and exemption *from the like.* Here then . . . is something of *Admiration* from the *Novelty,* something of *Aversion* from the *Infirmity,* & something of *Joy* or *triumph* from our opinion of some *eminency* in ourselves.[51]

In these sentences Charleton has virtually repeated Hobbes's presentation in *The Elements of Law,*[52] with some little rearrangement of the phrases but no additions. He had previously, this time citing Hobbes, spoken against the folly of laughing at one's own jests, declaring that

such laughter is (1) a mark of slowness of conception, (2) an evidence of self-love, (3) an injury to the jest by robbing it of surprise, (4) a source of jealousy and self-examination for the whole group. Besides all this (as *Mr. Hobbes* excellently observes, in his Book of *Humane Nature*) it is Vain-glory, and an argument of little worth, to think the infirmity of another sufficient matter for his Triumph.[53]

It would be possible to adduce further parallels and near parallels to Hobbes in Charleton's two essays. To do so would be purely gratuitous, however. Enough has been given to show how strongly Charleton was under the spell of the physio-psychological theories of *Leviathan* and *The Elements of Law.* It is true that his psychology, particularly in the later discourse on the passions, varies from Hobbes's, and that in this essay also he differs from Hobbes on the question of tranquility as a way to happiness,[54] hence on the desirability of moderating the

---

[51] *Ibid.,* pp. 145–146.
[52] *The Elements of Law,* I, ix, 13.
[53] *Concerning the Different Wits of Men,* p. 135.
[54] Hobbes leaves no doubt as to his position on this point: "*Continuall successe* in obtaining those things which a man from time to time desireth, that is to say, continuall prospering, is that men call FELICITY; I mean the Felicity of this life. For there is no such thing as perpetuall Tranquility of mind, while we live here; because Life it selfe is but Motion, and can never be without Desire, nor without Feare, no more than without Sense. What kind of Felicity God hath ordained to them that devoutly honour him, a man shall no sooner know, than enjoy; being joyes, that now are as incomprehensible, as the word of Schoolemen *Beatificall Vision* is unintelligible" (*Leviathan,* I, vi).

passions. But in the main outlines and in many specific details of the part of his theory that bears upon aesthetic matters
he is almost slavish in adherence to his great contemporary.
It appears reasonable to assume, then, that he became an
instrument for transmitting to those who read him — among
whom may be numbered with little question Dryden and
Addison — Hobbes's notions of wit, fancy, and judgment, as
well as his emphasis on novelty as a way to pleasure and new
knowledge.

Charleton cannot, perhaps, be regarded as an original
thinker.[55] He was a wide reader, willing on occasion to make
some parade of his learning, one who quickly caught up any
new thing and enthusiastically passed it on in indifferent synthesis with other items from his reading. Yet the influence
of such men is often great; further study is needed to show the
full effects of Charleton's writings upon his contemporaries
and successors,[56] but in the meantime we may assume that he
played a considerable part in linking the conceptions of the
new philosophy, as found in Hobbes especially, with a gradually
emerging psychological aesthetics.[57]

[55] I have reference to his ideas in aesthetics only. Of his considerable writings in the field of medicine, his chosen profession, I am not competent to judge.
His eminence as an anatomist and physician may be attested to, however, by the
evidence of recognition by the Royal College of Physicians and by the fact that
he was for some time court physician to Charles II.

[56] The British Museum copy of the first edition of the treatise *Concerning the
Different Wits of Men* bears a penned note containing the sentence: "This work
is said to have been much consulted by Locke." I do not know who wrote the
statement, but I could easily believe it true. It is even possible that certain evidences of Hobbes in Locke may have come through Charleton as intermediary.

[57] Frederic Manning, who recognizes the influence of Hobbes upon Charleton
but regards him chiefly as falling between Gassendi and Descartes in philosophy,
has this to say of his main function in the history of thought: "To us the ideas and
principles of Descartes and Harvey have an extension and significance which they
did not have for their own contemporaries, and the historical value to us of such
men as Charleton consists in the fact that he presents these principles and ideas to
us in direct relation to the age surrounding them, and bare of the additional
significance and extension which they have acquired in the course of three centuries" (Charleton, *Epicurus's Morals: Collected, and Faithfully Englished*, with an
Introductory Essay by Frederic Manning [London, 1926], p. x).

CHAPTER VII

The Psychological Approach in Dryden

I. WIT AND IMAGINATION

OF THE professional poets and critics between Hobbes and Addison none offered more fruitful suggestions toward a psychological approach than did Dryden. Dryden's basic aesthetic tenet, that in poetry the public must be pleased at any price, "religion and good manners only excepted," [1] seems to have led him to more than a usual study of what pleased. His remarks pointing to a psychology of effect are frequent and illuminating. He was, moreover, deeply interested in the creative processes involved in poetic composition, and altogether he presents a valuable theory of these processes. In his speculations on such matters Dryden no doubt drew from many sources, but he is obviously much indebted to Hobbes.

How conscious Dryden was of the problems of artistic creation and how wisely attentive he was to them may be seen from remarks in his earliest essays. Thus his conception of the formative process is admirably suggested in the "Epistle Dedicatory of *The Rival Ladies*," where he speaks of his work, "before it was a play; when it was only a confused mass of thoughts, tumbling over one another in the dark; when the fancy was yet in its first work, moving the sleeping images of things towards the light, there to be distinguished, and then either chosen or rejected by the judgment . . . ." [2] Composition is a delicate task, and success in achieving the desired results difficult indeed. Even the best plays, Dryden points out,

---

[1] "Dedication of *Examen Poeticum*," in *Essays of John Dryden*, ed. by W. P. Ker (Oxford, 1926), II, 1.   [2] Ker, I, 1.

can scarcely be considered perfect: "For the stage being the representation of the world, and the actions in it, how can it be imagined, that the picture of human life can be more exact than life itself is?" [3]   Dryden sees the problem of so managing imaginary persons and actions that "the spectators may rest satisfied that every cause was powerful enough to produce the effect it had" as a most strenuous one, which requires the working at their fullest stretch of the faculties concerned:

> . . . Plotting and writing in this kind are certainly more troublesome employments than many which signify more, and are of greater moment in the world: the fancy, memory, and judgment, are then extended (like so many limbs) upon the rack; all of them reaching with their utmost stress at Nature; a thing so almost infinite and boundless, as can never fully be comprehended, but where the images of all things are always present.[4]

Dryden's terms for the creative process here are precisely those of Hobbes and Charleton: fancy, judgment, and memory. The sum of these, as we shall see, again as in Hobbes and Charleton, is wit. Like them, too, Dryden sometimes uses the word "imagination" for fancy, on at least one notable occasion to indicate a separate function. Also, like Hobbes and Charleton, Dryden often fails to distinguish clearly between these terms. Hobbes, it will be recalled, tended to ascribe the inventive function, particularly in the more complex structures of poetry, to the fancy, more generally reserving for the imagination the simpler duties of putting together (or compounding) images in smaller units — such as a centaur or a golden mountain — or of picturing one's own possible fortunes or acts or the consequences of acts. In general, Dryden seems to follow Hobbes in this.

Briefly stated, Dryden's theory is that the inventive process consists in the coöperative action of fancy and judgment working with the materials of experience. Even more definitely than Hobbes — perhaps, however, only because he expresses himself more clearly — Dryden emphasizes for good poetry the necessity of an equipoise of fancy and judgment. Fancy

---

[3] "Epistle Dedicatory of *The Rival Ladies*," Ker, I, 2.   [4] *Ibid.*, I, 3.

collects and retains, but, in herself, has no power of discrimination.

The necessity for a right balance in this coöperative enterprise of fancy and judgment is unequivocally stated: "Fancy and Reason go hand in hand; the first cannot leave the last behind: and though Fancy, when it sees the wide gulf, would venture over, as the nimbler, yet it is withheld by Reason, which will refuse to take the leap, when the distance over it appears too large." [5] An overbalance of fancy leads, as Hobbes had said, to madness:

> Men that are given over to fancy only, are little better than madmen. What people say of fire, *viz.* that it is a good servant, but an ill master may not unaptly be applied to fancy; which, when it is too active, rages, but when cooled and allayed by the judgment produces admirable effects. . . .
> Fanciful poetry and music, used with moderation are good; but men who are wholly given over to either of them, are commonly as full of whimsies as diseased and splenetic men can be. Their heads are continually hot, and they have the same elevation of fancy sober which men of sense have when they drink.[6]

The remedy for too much fancy is judgment, without which no man has a right to set himself up for a poet: "No man should pretend to write, who cannot temper his fancy with his judgment: nothing is more dangerous to a raw horseman, than a hot-mouthed jade without a curb." [7] Judgment is likewise essential to the permanency of poetry:

> For this reason, a well-weighed judicious poem, which at its first appearance gains no more upon the world than to be just received, and rather not blamed than much applauded, insinuates itself by insensible degrees into the liking of the reader: the more he studies it, the more it grows upon him; every time he takes it up, he discovers some new graces in it. And whereas poems which are produced by the vigour of imagination only have a gloss upon them at the first which time wears off, the

---

[5] *A Defence of an Essay of Dramatic Poesy* (1668), Ker, I, 128.

[6] "Preface to *Notes and Observations on the* EMPRESS OF MOROCCO" (1674), in *The Works of John Dryden*, ed. by Sir Walter Scott and George Saintsbury (Edinburgh and London, 1882–93), XV, 405–406. Dryden collaborated with Shadwell and John Crowne in writing this preface.

[7] *The Grounds of Criticism in Tragedy* (1679), Ker, I, 222.

works of judgment are like the diamond; the more they are polished, the more lustre they receive.[8]

On the other hand, an overplus of judgment with a failing in the warmth of fancy tends to destroy poetic quality:

> . . . There is required a continuance of warmth, to ripen the best and noblest fruits. Thus Horace, in his First and Second Book of Odes, was still rising, but came not to his meridian till the Third; after which, his judgment was an overpoise to his imagination: he grew too cautious to be bold enough; for he descended in his Fourth by slow degrees, and, in his Satires and Epistles, was more a philosopher and a critic than a poet.[9]

Such statements leave room for no doubt as to Dryden's true position on the necessity of both imagination and judgment, and the right relationship of one to the other, in good poetry.[10]

We are now ready for a consideration of Dryden's more specific expositions of such terms as "wit," "fancy," "imagination," and "judgment." The best passages for such a purpose are to be found in three separate essays written over a period of twenty years, each one coming at the subject from a different approach, yet all, in spite of certain variations in terminology and emphasis, reaching conclusions which are in fundamental agreement.

---

[8] "Dedication of the *Aeneis*" (1697), Ker, II, 225.

[9] "Dedication of the Translation of the *Georgics*," Scott and Saintsbury, XIV, 3.

[10] It is of interest that Dryden maintains that one of the principal virtues of rhyme is that it is an aid in securing a proper balance between fancy and judgment. The best presentation of this idea occurs in the "Epistle Dedicatory of *The Rival Ladies*," where, among other arguments for rhyme, he says: "But that benefit which I consider most in it, because I have not seldom found it, is, that it bounds and circumscribes the fancy. For imagination in a poet is a faculty so wild and lawless, that like an high-ranging spaniel, it must have clogs tied to it, lest it outrun the judgment. The great easiness of blank verse renders the poet too luxuriant; he is tempted to say many things, which might better be omitted, or at least shut up in fewer words; but when the difficulty of artful rhyming is interposed . . . the fancy then gives leisure to the judgment to come in, which, seeing so heavy a tax imposed, is ready to cut off all unnecessary expenses. This last consideration has already answered an objection which some have made, that rhyme is only an embroidery of sense, to make that which is ordinary in itself pass for excellent with less examination. But certainly, that which most regulates the fancy, and gives the judgment its busiest employment, is like to bring forth the richest and clearest thoughts" (Ker, I, 8).

The first of these is the notable exposition of wit in the Preface to the early *Annus Mirabilis* (1667). Professor Ker has observed that this is the most systematic treatment of its subject in all Dryden. This statement needs some qualification. For, though the treatment is consciously systematic and though it may be truthfully said to contain in germ virtually all that Dryden had to say in his later works on wit, fancy, imagination, and judgment, it is, nevertheless, somewhat immature and does not by any means say Dryden's last word on the subject.

Dryden here begins with the generalization, "The composition of all poems is, or ought to be, of wit," and then proceeds to explain his meaning. Distinguishing between "Wit writing," the faculty, and "Wit written," the product, he defines the first as "no other than the faculty of imagination in the writer, which, like a nimble spaniel, beats over and ranges through the field of memory, till it springs the quarry it hunted after; or, without metaphor, which searches over all the memory for the species or ideas of those things which it designs to represent." [11]

"*Wit written*," Dryden continues, "is that which is well defined, the happy result of thought, or product of imagination." [12] This is wit in its general notion, Dryden explains. He will proceed to the "proper wit of an Heroic or Historical Poem." This consists chiefly in "the delightful imagining of persons, actions, passions, or things." It lies neither in the sting of an epigram, nor in a poor antithesis, nor in a fine jingle, nor in a grave moral sentence,

. . . but it is some lively and apt description, dressed in such colours of speech, that it sets before your eyes the absent object, as perfectly, and more delightfully than nature. So then the first happiness of the poet's imagination is properly invention, or finding of the thought; the second is fancy, or the variation, deriving, or moulding of that thought, as the judgment represents it proper to the subject. The third is elocution, or the art of clothing and adorning that thought, so found and varied, in apt, significant, and sounding words: the quickness of the imagination is seen in the invention, the fertility in the fancy, and the accuracy in the expression. [13]

[11] "Preface to the *Annus Mirabilis*," Ker, I, 14.
[12] *Ibid.*   [13] *Ibid.*, I, 15.

From some of his phrasing as well as from his basic conception it would appear that Dryden is here working under the influence of Hobbes,[14] with perhaps Davenant and Charleton in the offing; and, like these predecessors, he employs his terms with some overlapping of meaning. He is using "wit" in an inclusive sense embracing imagination, fancy, judgment, and elocution, even as Hobbes had made it equivalent to fancy and judgment. Unlike Hobbes, Dryden distinguishes between imagination and fancy, giving two names, as Hobbes did not, to the two functions of searching over the fields of memory for desired materials and of varying and shaping and embellishing these materials to given ends. Imagination has the special function of invention, or finding the thought. But fancy is also a phase of invention, in that, one assumes, it searches out more particular and varied details, alters those it wishes to alter, and fashions all, under the dictates of judgment, into ideal form. Elocution is the objective expression of this ideal structure, again under the direction of judgment, in accurate and artistic language.

I have used the phrase "ideal form" to describe the product of imagination and fancy in the preceding somewhat at

[14] Dryden's figure of imagination as a nimble spaniel ranging through the field of memory recalls Hobbes's picturesque phrase, "ranging spaniel" (*The Elements of Law*, ed. by Ferdinand Tönnies [Cambridge, 1928], I, iv, 4), in his characterization of an activity of mind which he elsewhere calls "celerity of imagining" (*Leviathan*, ed. by Ernest Rhys [London, Toronto, and New York, 1914], I, viii), and his description of fancy, when any work of art is to be performed, as making a swift motion over the materials of memory, "that what she wants, and is there to be had, may not lie too long unespied" (*The Answer to Davenant* in *Critical Essays of the Seventeenth Century*, ed. by J. E. Spingarn [Oxford, 1908], Vol. II). Professor Ker (*op. cit.*, I, 287) compares Dryden's passage with Davenant's description of wit. There is undeniable likeness. The "nimble spaniel," however, particularly points to Hobbes. So also does Dryden's description of imagination as a searching over the memory for its quarry. Davenant has wit "bringing home to the memory" its surveys. Not only is Dryden nearer to Hobbes than to Davenant in his wording, but he is truer to Hobbes and his psychology than is Davenant. Moreover, Davenant does not make the distinction between fancy and judgment that we find in Hobbes. With him wit is used to cover the finding of thought, the embellishments, and the expression. Dryden follows Hobbes in trying to make finer distinctions than Davenant attempts. It is quite possible that Dryden had the passages from both Hobbes and Davenant in mind, but there would seem little question that he derived much more from Hobbes than from Davenant.

a venture, yet, I believe, with full warrant. The idea is not explicit in Dryden's description, but it is implicit, especially when we recall his general adherence to the principle of ideal imitation. The quarry for which imagination beats over the field of memory is not specific images of remembered men and events; it is rather "the species or ideas of those things which it designs to represent," or, may we hazard, the *universal* in the Aristotelian sense of the term. Dryden narrows his discussion to the heroic poem. In such a poem, the *Aeneid* for instance, the imagination finds (invents) the general idea of the whole — a Trojan hero, who after many vicissitudes founds the new Latin nation — and it may proceed from there to the general framework of the piece. The fancy varies the original sketch, fills in details, derives (invents) characters and incidents, molds its materials into a whole. Neither it nor the imagination is giving a copy of actual people or events stored in the memory; both are creating ideal form, though with materials from the memory.

Now this, admittedly, is not all Hobbes, though, as I have shown, Hobbes, too, accepted a kind of ideal imitation. It is partly Aristotelian, partly Latin, Medieval, and Renaissance; but it is also partly Hobbian. The whole argument is an instructive example of using a new method — in this case, the Hobbian method of psychological analysis — to bring together into one pattern new and old ideas. It is a signal instance of the subtle manner in which the scientific, psychological approach, given its chief impetus in England by Hobbes, is to permeate, as time goes on, the main body of English critical thought.

The second of the loci for valuable hints on Dryden's ideas of wit and its allied terms occurs in the Preface to *The Mock Astrologer* (1671). In this essay Dryden considers, in a somewhat casual running commentary, characteristics of the various poetic forms with specific reference to wit, fancy, and judgment. It should be remarked that throughout this discussion Dryden uses the word "fancy" to the exclusion of "imagination." It is possible that he had decided that the distinction he had previously made was but wiredrawing, or too difficult to keep.

Or perhaps the clue is to be found in his remark regarding the work of the poets and the graces of a poem that "the story is the least part of either: I mean the foundation of it" — and, as we have seen, this foundation is the work of imagination. But if the term imagination is dropped, fancy is made even more important.

In remarks on the various forms Dryden ranks farce, comedy, and serious poetry (tragedy or epic) in an ascending order of worth. Each in turn shows a varying proportion of fancy to judgment. Farce, which is lowest in the scale, is nearly all fancy; it is, moreover, an undesirable sort of fancy, which has in it neither the ideal quality necessary to great poetry nor a sufficient admixture of judgment to assure truth to life. Serious poetry, at the other extreme, is also predominantly fancy, but it is fancy working in the ideal realm rather than with the surfaces of life (as in farce), and it also has, we may assume, sufficient judgment for the requisite "propriety of thoughts and words" which belong to wit. But let us examine Dryden's own words:

> . . . Comedy consists, though of low persons, yet of natural actions and characters; I mean such humours, adventures, and designs, as are to be found and met with in the world. Farce, on the other hand, consists of forced humours, and unnatural events. Comedy presents us with the imperfections of human nature: Farce entertains us with what is monstrous and chimerical. The one causes laughter in those who can judge of men and manners, by the lively representation of their folly or corruption: the other produces the same effect in those who can judge of neither, and that only by its extravagances. The first works on the judgment and fancy; the latter on the fancy only: there is more of satisfaction in the former kind of laughter, and in the latter more of scorn . . . . In short, there is the same difference betwixt Farce and Comedy, as betwixt an empiric and a true physician: both of them may attain their ends; but what the one performs by hazard, the other does by skill. And as the artist is often unsuccessful, while the mountebank succeeds; so farces more commonly take the people than comedies. For to write unnatural things is the most probable way of pleasing them, who understand not Nature. And a true poet often misses of applause, because he cannot debase himself to write so ill as to please his audience.[15]

---

[15] "Preface to *An Evening's Love or the Mock Astrologer*," Ker, I, 135–136.

Thus decisively Dryden assigns to comedy and farce the specific quality of each and gives to each its relative rank. Few critics have more effectively disposed of the claims of farce to a place as true art. Comedy is better, for it represents the exercise of both judgment and fancy; even so, as we shall see, it is likely to be judgment in excess of fancy, and fancy working in a different mode from its wont in tragedy and epic.

Dryden's description of the creative activity involved in serious plays reveals at once the relative importance which he attached to tragedy and epic and the high esteem in which he held true fancy, which is essential to wit in the proper sense. It is here that, defending Shakespeare and others against the charge of borrowing their plots, he asserts that the story is the least part of a poem — that is, story regarded as "the foundation of it before it is modelled by the art of him who writes it." For,

... On this foundation ... the characters are raised: and since no story can afford characters enough for the variety of the English stage, it follows, that it is to be altered and enlarged with new persons, accidents, and designs, which will almost make it new. When this is done, the forming it into acts and scenes, disposing of actions and passions into their proper places, and beautifying both with descriptions, similitudes, and propriety of language, is the principal employment of the poet; as being the largest field of fancy, which is the principal quality required in him: for so much the word ποιητής implies. Judgment, indeed, is necessary in him; but 'tis fancy that gives the life-touches, and the secret graces to it; especially in serious plays, which depend not much on observation. For, to write humour in comedy (which is the theft of poets from mankind), little of fancy is required; the poet observes only what is ridiculous and pleasant folly, and by judging exactly what is so, he pleases in the representation of it.[16]

The distinction Dryden would make between the highest kind of wit, which displays itself in "a propriety of thoughts and words elegantly adapted to their subject," and those lower kinds of acumen where judgment predominates over fancy (as in comedy) or where fancy reigns without judgment (as in farce) is made more emphatic in a remark on Jonson, whom he much admired but to whom he refused to grant true wit:

16 *Ibid.*, I, 146–147.

. . . To make men appear pleasantly ridiculous on the stage, was, as I have said, his talent; and in this he needed not the acumen of wit but that of judgment. For the characters and representations of folly are only the effects of observation; and observation is an effect of judgment. Some ingenious men, for whom I have a particular esteem, have thought I have much injured Ben Johnson, when I have not allowed his wit to be extraordinary: but they confound the notion of what is witty, with what is pleasant. That Ben Johnson's plays were pleasant, he must want reason who denies: but that pleasantness was not properly wit, or the sharpness of conceit, but the natural imitation of folly; which I confess to be excellent in its kind, but not to be of that kind which they pretend.[17]

In these last passages, in which the balanced wit of serious poetry is distinguished from the lopsided judgment of comedy and the unmitigated fancy of farce, Dryden has suggested a special function for judgment that is different from ordinary connotations of the word, even as he himself at times uses it. The judgment exercised by Jonson in writing comedy is not mere discretion in selecting and ordering from the materials offered by fancy, and restraint in expression, as Dryden depicts it in the Preface to *Annus Mirabilis*. It is rather a way of perceiving, an acumen in discerning the incongruities of life, the false and ridiculous in men about us. Elsewhere, in noting that Horace, in his old age, had developed an overbalance of judgment, Dryden remarks that judgment is "the effect of observation." But there he is apparently thinking of judgment as restraint, for he notes that Horace grew "too cautious to be bold enough." [18] Now, however, he is obviously speaking of Jonson's judgment as the result of observation in the Hobbian sense of aptness in discerning dissimilitudes. This, conjoined with accuracy in presenting what is seen in actual life, is Jonson's forte; but it is art operating, as is always the case with comedy, on a relatively low plane. Farce is an even less worthy form of art, for fancy here works in the same lower regions of actuality in which judgment operates in comedy, but without the virtue of naturalness and truth. The fancy exercised in serious plays, in contrast, is creative of a new reality, an ideal world of heightened passion and elevated

[17] "Preface to *An Evening's Love or the Mock Astrologer*," Ker, I, 138.
[18] "Dedication of the Translation of the *Georgics*," Scott and Saintsbury, XIV, 3.

thought and action; it is inventive of both character, incident, and expressional form and is discriminatively selective in all these fields. Here, again, we see Dryden's strong leaning toward a species of ideal imitation. In the best art nature always appears as better than it is in reality. Such idealization is integral to true wit, hence to great poetry. In all this Dryden has not only reiterated the claims made for fancy in the Preface to *Annus Mirabilis*, but he has given to fancy the functions there assigned to elocution; for he names as the "largest field for fancy" in a play "the forming of it into acts and scenes, disposing of actions and passions into their proper places, and beautifying both with descriptions, similitudes, and propriety of language." He has also made fancy, as before, the chief agency for ideal creation. The invention of the plot or story in its larger outlines — previously assigned to the imagination, if my analysis is correct — is made of relatively small importance, is, indeed, almost taken for granted. And even judgment appears in reduced perspective; it is essential, but is subordinate to fancy.

In spite of the fact that the theory of the two presentations is fundamentally the same, Dryden is generally nearer to Hobbes in this discussion than in the earlier Preface to the *Annus*. He limits his terms to "wit," "fancy," and "judgment" — as does Hobbes when he is discussing poetry. His emphasis on fancy in serious plays recalls Hobbes's dictum that in poetry, though judgment is present, "fancy is chief." Similarly his assignment of expressional functions to fancy remind us that Hobbes had made fancy the begetter of those metaphors and similitudes which lend delight to poetry and give it power, through imagery, to raise the passions. And, as we have seen, his special idea of judgment as an effect of observation — a discernment of dissimilitudes — also has its prototype in Hobbes.

The third locus for a study of Dryden's ideas of the faculties of artistic processes is the passage containing his famous definition of wit as "a propriety of thoughts and words . . . elegantly adapted to the subject." [19] This was written twenty

[19] *The Author's Apology for Heroic Poetry and Poetic Licence* (1677), Ker, I, 190.

years later than the Preface to *Annus Mirabilis*, sixteen years
after the essay affixed to *The Mock Astrologer*. It may therefore be regarded as possessing some added significance as an
expression of Dryden's maturity. This is, indeed, an important
definition, with far broader implications than has sometimes
been supposed. It is much more than a statement for neoclassic correctness. Actually — and this appears when we study it
in context and when we compare it with related passages —
it contains the idea of the proper relationship between fancy
and judgment in the finding and selecting of materials for a
poem and in clothing these materials in suitable language.
More specifically, Dryden is here submitting a brief for the full
play of fancy in poetic creation under such restrictions as may
be dictated by taste and good sense.

The question of context is important, for the definition
comes at the end of a discussion in which Dryden is examining
the best means of securing proper effects in poetry. The
poet's way, he has pointed out, is to sound and probe the passions of men and so to image these passions as to arouse the
minds of his readers to a high pitch of emotional delight:

> Imaging is, in itself, the very height and life of Poetry. It is, as Lon-
> ginus describes it, a discourse, which, by a kind of enthusiasm, or extraor-
> dinary emotion of the soul, makes it seem to us that we behold those
> things which the poet paints, so as to be pleased with them, and to admire
> them.
> If poetry be imitation, that part of it must needs be best which describes
> most lively our actions and passions; our virtues and our vices; our follies
> and our humours . . . .[20]

So Dryden goes on, extolling as a means to effect not only the
imaging of things known but the imaging of fictional beings
such as chimeras and angels, and in so doing he takes occasion
to defend a considerable degree of poetic license in both the
fictions (thoughts) and the expression of a poem.

To make such images is not only the liberty but the obligation of a poet, if he is to write what is pleasing and memorable.
Dryden defines "Poetic Licence" as "the liberty which poets
have assumed to themselves, in all ages, of speaking things in

[20] *The Author's Apology for Heroic Poetry and Poetic Licence*, Ker, I, 186.

verse, which are beyond the severity of prose." [21]   It is this which marks the boundary between oratory and poetry. Dryden has specific reference to "the thought or imagination of a poet" which "consists in fiction," apart from language.   He would set no limit to the poet's liberties in inventing beings which are not in nature, except that he keep within the range of popular belief.   Poetic license applies equally to language, however; for "those thoughts must be expressed."   And here, in telescoped statement, Dryden defends the use of tropes and figures — which he has shortly before told us were "invented because it was observed they had such and such effect upon the audience." [22]   Some sober critics may ridicule a high-pitched figurative expression, but such laughter is folly, for "an image, which is strongly and beautifully set before the eyes of the reader, will still be poetry when the merry fit is over, and last when the other is forgotten." [23]   Justification for license in fiction and language may be found in our predecessors: "This is that birthright which is derived to us from our great forefathers, even from Homer down to Ben; and they who would deny it to us, have, in plain terms, the fox's quarrel to the grapes — they cannot reach it." [24]

The extent to which these liberties may be carried Dryden will not attempt to determine, since Horace himself did not. "But it is certain that they are to be varied, according to the language and age in which an author writes." [25]   Certainly, too, we may follow Horace in his demand that a poem be all a piece and that unlike thoughts shall not be joined together. But Horace found no fault with either Homer or Virgil for the extravagance of their fiction when they introduced "gods in the wars of Troy and Italy," nor would he have "taxed Milton, as our false critics have presumed to do, for his choice of a supernatural argument," though he would blame a Christian author for mingling heathen deities in a Christian poem, as Tasso has done. [26]

At this point Dryden deduces his definition of wit as "a propriety of thoughts and words, or . . . thoughts and words

[21] *Ibid.*, I, 188.   [22] *Ibid.*, I, 184.   [23] *Ibid.*, I, 188.
[24] *Ibid.*, I, 189.   [25] *Ibid.*   [26] *Ibid.*, I, 189–190

elegantly adapted to the subject," by which he means plainly
— in view of the preceding argument — that wit is such a due
balance of judgment and fancy in the invention and expression
of poetic fictions as is best fitted to stir the passions and to
produce, without offense to the judicious, the pleasures proper
to poetry. Dryden's definition, which has sometimes been
regarded as a reactionary and inadequate statement for formalism, quite out of harmony with his previous fruitful expressions
on wit, thus becomes a climax to one of the finest pieces of
critical research in all his essays: a firm restatement of the
principle that good poetry is founded in the liberty of a spacious
imagination, working, in both the selection and expression
of its materials, under the restraints of a good judgment.

Throughout this discussion Dryden is on the liberal side
of the question. He is defending himself and others against
the doctrines of strait-laced formalists. And in this defense he
mingles ideas that he has learned from many sources, among
them Longinus and Hobbes. The Longinian theory of enthusiasm produced by vivid images is restated, and Hobbes's
principle of wit as a just proportion of fancy and judgment is
again the basis of the argument — though now Dryden adopts
the term "imagination" just as in the Preface to *The Mock
Astrologer* he used "fancy." The method is again the Hobbian
method of psychological analysis, and some of the conclusions
are close to Hobbes's. "But . . . how are hippocentaurs and
chimeras, or how are angels and immaterial substances to be
imaged?" Dryden now inquires. By the "conjunction of two
natures, which have a real separate being," he replies;[27] and
by "giving angels the likeness of beautiful young men. Thus,
after the pagan divinity, has Homer drawn his gods with human
faces: and thus we have notions of things above us, by describing them like other beings more within our knowledge."[28]

This is an exemplification not only of the Hobbian mode
of inquiry, but of the Hobbian theory of fancy working with

---

[27] *The Author's Apology for Heroic Poetry and Poetic Licence*, Ker, I, 187. Dryden
mentions and quotes Lucretius as his authority; but the idea had also been stated
by Hobbes in his exposition of "compounded imagination." Just here, however,
it is the method of Hobbes which is in question.   [28] *Ibid.*

the materials of experience. Such also is the case in the treatment of the question raised with regard to the license that
may be allowed a poet in imaginative, or ideal, creations.
Hobbes had said that the poet may go beyond the actual
works but not beyond the "conceived possibility" of nature.[29]
Dryden grants the poet liberty to invent things which do not
exist "if they are founded on popular belief." Here, as elsewhere in Dryden, evidence of debt to Hobbes is inferential
rather than certain; yet one cannot read this passage, with
Hobbes in mind, without feeling assurance that without the
influence of Hobbes it would not have been the same.

Even after making full deduction for differences in language
and in specific detail there is a fundamental consistency in the
ideas presented in the three expositions we have examined.
In each there is expressed the conception of a free activity of
fancy (or imagination) in inventing fictions with richness and
variety of character added to the broad foundation of the
story; in each there is expressed the further creative activity of
deriving images and expressing them in appropriate language:
a language which must be within the bounds of judgment,
but which is to be allowed such liberties as are sanctioned by
poetic custom and dictated by the demands of poetic effect.
In all three passages judgment is made essential, but, as in
Hobbes, the fancy is given chief place (in spite of the rather
misleading term "propriety" in the last); in all three serious
poetry is given first recognition; and in all three a heightened
language colored by apt figures of speech is indicated, for "all
reasonable men will conclude it necessary, that sublime subjects ought to be adorned with the sublimest, and consequently
often with the most figurative expressions." [30] This is Dryden's
own gloss on his phrase "a propriety of thoughts and words."

Dryden's essays at describing the imaginative process bulk
much larger than even the total of the passages I have quoted
would indicate. It is apparent that his mind is much occupied
with the problem. As I have shown, there is considerable
evidence of the influence of Hobbes. This appears in both

[29] *The Answer to Davenant*, Spingarn, II, 62.
[30] *The Author's Apology for Heroic Poetry and Poetic Licence*, Ker, I, 190.

Dryden's terms and conclusions and in the spirit and method
of his inquiry. There are often striking similarities in idea and
language, as in the definitions in the Preface to *Annus Mirabilis;*
but even where the language is different the basic conceptions
remain. Thus the important definition of wit in *The Author's
Apology for Heroic Poetry and Poetic Licence* is still in the spirit
of Hobbes, though the terms are different. The passage in
which this definition occurs plainly shows other influences, but
this only gives it added interest as showing Dryden's accommodation of ideas from varied sources, especially from his new
enthusiasm, Longinus, to his previously evolved theory of wit
as a happily proportioned endowment of fancy and judgment.
This is a fact illustrative of the complexity of the influences
playing upon the mind of Dryden, who, heir to a vast body
of critical thought of various ages and literatures from Aristotle down to his own day, seized now upon this theory, now
upon that, in an eagerly inquiring eclecticism in which, since
few matters were ever settled, a persistent endeavor at ad-
justment and readjustment went on to the end. Some of this
same complexity is to be observed in Dryden's ideas of the
proper effects of poetry, which is the subject of the ensuing
discussion.

II. Psychology of Effects

Dryden's ideas of aesthetic effects are closely related to
his theory that "delight is the chief, if not the only, end of
poesy." [31] Following Hobbes, who was himself preceded by
Minturno, Corneille, and other Renaissance critics, he definitely states that the end of an heroic poem is to excite "admiration." [32] Both tragedy and epic, he insists, in order to be
successful must create "concernment." [33] A tragedy should
delight and instruct. But before it can either give delight or
instruct effectively, it must arouse the passions and warm and
elevate the imagination; for, important as poetry may be as a

[31] *A Defence of an Essay of Dramatic Poesy,* Ker, I, 113.
[32] "Such descriptions or images, well wrought . . . are . . . the adequate
delight of Heroic Poesy; for they beget admiration, which is its proper object"
("Preface to *Annus Mirabilis*" [1667], Ker, I, 18).
[33] *An Essay of Dramatic Poesy,* Ker, I, 53, 58.

means of teaching, "instruction can be admitted but in the second place, for poesy only instructs as it delights. 'Tis true, that to imitate well is a poet's work; but to affect the soul, and excite the passions, and, above all, to move admiration (which is the delight of serious plays), a bare imitation will not serve." [34]

Like the Englishman he was, Dryden set effect before correctness. "Let the French and Italians value themselves on their regularity; strength and elevation are our standard," [35] he once explained. More than once he showed himself in sympathy with the Longinus ideal of transport. "Imaging is, in itself, the very height and life of Poetry," he declares. "It is, as Longinus describes it, a discourse, which, by a kind of enthusiasm, or extraordinary emotion of the soul, makes it seem to us that we behold those things which the poet paints, so as to be pleased with them, and to admire them." [36]

In his great *Essay of Dramatic Poesy* Dryden rests his argument for the modern and English, as opposed to the Greek and French, drama decisively on the principle that a play should in the last analysis be judged not on its conformity to rule, but on its power to interest and move an audience. The ancients, asserts Eugenius, swerving from the rules of their own art by misrepresenting nature to us, have failed "in the one intention of a play, which was to delight." Among the Romans Ovid, indeed, showed a genius proper for the stage: "he had a way of writing so fit to stir up a pleasing admiration and concernment, which are the objects of a tragedy, and to show the various movements of a soul combating betwixt two different passions, that, had he lived in our age, or in his own could have writ with our advantages, no man but must have yielded to him." [37] Comparing Ovid's characters with Virgil's

[34] *A Defence of an Essay of Dramatic Poesy*, Ker, I, 113. Dryden's definition of admiration shows quite clearly the emotional quality of this delight. Admiration is "that noble passion to which poets raise their audience in highest subjects, and they have then gained over them the greatest victory, when they are ravished into a pleasure which is not to be expressed by words" ("Dedication to *Amboyna*," Scott and Saintsbury, V, 5).

[35] "Dedication of the *Aeneis*," Ker, II, 229.

[36] *The Author's Apology for Heroic Poetry and Poetic Licence*, Ker, I, 186. See also Ker, I, 180, 220, etc. [37] *An Essay of Dramatic Poesy*, Ker, I, 53.

Dido, he remarks: "I have a greater concernment for them: and that convinces me that Ovid has touched those tender strokes more delicately than Virgil could." [38]   The *Medea*, Dryden thinks, cannot be attributed to Ovid, for "it moves not my soul enough to judge that he, who in the epic way wrote things so near the drama as the story of Myrrha, of Caunus and Biblis, and the rest, should stir up no more concernment where he most endeavoured it." [39]   Seneca, too, had some high moments. They occurred, however, not when he was most regular, but when he showed most power to move the passions:

> . . . The master-piece of Seneca I hold to be that scene in the *Troades*, where Ulysses is seeking for Astyanax to kill him; there you see the tenderness of a mother so represented in Andromache, that it raises compassion to a high degree in the reader, and bears the nearest resemblance of any thing in their tragedies [the ancients'] to the excellent scenes of passion in Shakespeare, or in Fletcher. [40]

The chief sin of a tragedy with Dryden was to leave one cold.   In judging the French, Neander points continually to their inability to achieve effects.   The French fail to give us a "lively imitation of Nature."   Their beauties are "the beauties of a statue, not of a man": they are "not animated with the soul of poesy." [41]   The French heroes, Dryden says, "are the most civil people breathing; but their good breeding seldom extends to a word of sense; all their wit is in their ceremony; they want the genius which animates our stage; and therefore 'tis but necessary, when they cannot please, that they should take care not to offend." [42]   The French plots are barren, lacking in the complexity of design and the "variety and copiousness" which so much please in our English plays; their verses are cold, their speeches lacking in passion. [43]   In contrast, when Shakespeare describes anything, "you more than see it,

---

[38] "Preface to *Annus Mirabilis*," Ker, I, 16.
[39] *An Essay of Dramatic Poesy*, Ker, I, 53.
[40] *Ibid.*, I, 53–54.   [41] *Ibid.*, I, 68.
[42] "Preface to *All for Love*," Ker, I, 193–194.
[43] *An Essay of Dramatic Poesy*, Ker, I, 70, 72. The French, Neander maintains, have achieved only dulness: "by their servile observations of the Unities of Time and Place, and integrity of scenes, they have brought on themselves that dearth of plot, and narrowness of imagination, which may be observed in all their plays" (*ibid.*, I, 76).

you feel it too." [44] All this is making the issue squarely one of effect, not of formal perfection.

In *The Grounds of Criticism in Tragedy* (1679), where Dryden came, perhaps, to his best balanced expression on Shakespeare, the premise upon which he works is that an author is to be judged by the effect he creates. "To invent therefore a probability, and to make it wonderful, is the most difficult undertaking in the art of Poetry; for that which is not wonderful is not great." [45] The object of tragedy is to work upon the passions of pity and fear. To be sure, Dryden is here avowedly following Rapin and Le Bossu, but his emphasis and applications are his own, for he justifies Shakespeare, and Fletcher, too, rules or no rules. Shakespeare, for all his failings, chiefly in expression, was one who "understood the nature of the passions." [46] And "To describe these naturally, and to move them artfully, is one of the greatest commendations which can be given to a poet: to write pathetically, says Longinus, cannot proceed but from a lofty genius." [47]

Dryden's discussion of Fletcher's *King and No King* practically eventuates in a contention that that theory of drama is good which works in practice. Whatever its faults, this play *takes* with its audience, a fact which cannot be wholly ascribed to "the excellency of the action; for I find it moving when it is read." [48] Since the plot is obviously faulty, its strength must lie in its touches of passion, or we may conclude that "even in imperfect plots there are less degrees of Nature, by which some faint emotions of pity and terror are raised in us: . . . for nothing can move our nature but by some natural reason, which works upon passions. And, since we acknowledge the effect, there must be something in the cause." [49] This is a notable pronouncement. Accept it in its implications, and you have rejected that part of the neoclassic assumption which maintained that there could be no legitimate pleasure in a work of art not conforming to the prescribed formulae. The burden now placed on the critic is to analyze the effect, and to dis-

[44] *Ibid.*, I, 80.
[45] *The Grounds of Criticism in Tragedy*, Ker, I, 209.   [46] *Ibid.*, I, 224.
[47] *Ibid.*, I, 220.   [48] *Ibid.*, I, 212.   [49] *Ibid.*

cover and understand what has produced that effect. The cause is not to be questioned, but to be explained. Here is definite foreshadowing of the Coleridgean and the modern approach to criticism.

Dryden cannot accept all of Fletcher and Shakespeare: his neoclassic taste for refinement and correctness in language leads him quite consistently to object to much of their expression as overornamental, or swelling, or even bombastic; [50] he is often moved to find fault with their mingling of comedy with tragedy, [51] and to cavil at their double actions and loosely knit scenes and at their lapses in decorum and judgment. When all possible has been said on this side of the question, however, the fact remains that Fletcher's and Shakespeare's plays produce the effects that great plays are supposed to produce. [52]

The trend of Dryden's thinking on the importance of effects is further revealed in his answer to Rymer. [53] The value of this document lies not in a logically developed theory, but in suggestions embedded in tentative, unpremeditated thoughts as they come to the acute mind of an honest, discerning student of literature, who has learned not only to think independently of received dogma, but to be skeptical of such dogma wherever it conflicts with experience. The challenge to the Aristotelian dicta, necessarily based on incomplete evidence — since "Aristotle knew not our modern plays"; [54] the mild, but firm insistence throughout on a wider basis of appeal than pity and terror; the emphasis on effect as of more importance than adherence to convention: all are indications of a new kind of criticism. Dryden's challenge to Rymer is in part a patriotic defense of English drama; but its foundation is deeper than that: it is basically a challenge to any criticism that denies the fact of success through giving delight as the right criterion in judging literature.

The English have undeniably succeeded. It is true, their

[50] *The Grounds of Criticism in Tragedy*, Ker, I, 224, 226-227.
[51] Ker, I, 50, 60, 208. Though see his defense of tragicomedy, *infra*, p. 213.
[52] *The Grounds of Criticism in Tragedy*, Ker, I, 220, 227-228.
[53] *Heads of an Answer to Rymer's Remarks on the Tragedies of the Last Age*, Scott and Saintsbury, XV, 381 ff.   [54] *Ibid.*, XV, 383.

tragedies have not always been limited in appeal to the Aristotelian pity and fear; but if we grant as a true definition that tragedy exists "to reform manners by a delightful represen- tation of life in great persons by way of dialogue," we must grant also that "not only pity and terror are to be moved — but generally love of virtue, and hatred of vice." Since this is true, "in tragedy pity and terror, though good means are not the only. For all the passions in their turns, are to be set in a ferment; as joy, anger, love, fear, are to be used as the poet's commonplaces, and a general concernment for the principal actors is to be raised . . . ." [55] Such an extension of the number of passions it is legitimate to raise in tragedy may, no doubt, be traced in part to the influence of Hobbes, who dignified the passions in general, by making agitation of soul a condition to pleasure; it would seem to be in part the result of Dryden's own observation which led him to accept the passion of love particularly as a proper motivation in many successful modern plays. In a later note he cites Rapin's confession that French tragedies now run all on the *tendre*, with the observation that "love is the passion which most predominates in our souls." [56] This recalls Dryden's in- sistence on the importance of love in the heroic play,[57] and the lines in his *Conquest of Granada:*

and
> Had life no love, none would for business live,

> Praise is the pay of heaven for doing good;
> But love's the best return for flesh and blood.

As love is particularly suited to excite the passion of pity, for no suffering touches more than that of lovers, so the execution of poetic justice is designed to arouse emotions of pity. In both of these particulars the English excel; in both, the Greeks were deficient: "they neither administered poetical justice, of which Mr. Rymer boasts, so well as we; neither knew they the common-place of pity, which is love." [58]

[55] *Ibid.*   [56] *Ibid.*, XV, 388.
[57] *An Essay of Heroic Plays,* Ker, I, 150.
[58] *Heads of an Answer to Rymer's Remarks on the Tragedies of the Last Age,* Scott and Saintsbury, XV, 390.

It is on the power of Elizabethan drama to move the passions, to create intense and pleasing effects, when they are either acted or read, that Dryden rests his case against Rymer. Rymer had maintained that if Fletcher's and Shakespeare's plays had pleased, it was due to the acting and the spectacle only. To which Dryden counters vigorously with the argument that whoever acts them, the event is the same: "the same passions have always been moved," which proves, he asserts, in words that recall a similar passage in *The Grounds of Criticism*, "that there is something of force and merit in the plays themselves, conducing to the design of raising these two passions." It is not even necessary to see them acted to feel their force. "I dare appeal to those who have never seen them acted," he asserts confidently, "if they have not found these two passions moved within them . . . ." [59]   This is in effect a declaration for the integrity of pleasures of the imagination. Dryden has previously gone so far as to assert the superiority of the book to the stage in capacity to give pleasure: "The words of a good writer . . . will make a deeper impression of belief in us than all the actor can persuade us to . . . as a poet in the description of a beautiful garden, or a meadow, will please our imagination more than the place itself can please our sight." [60]   This is a statement to which Lamb, holding for the greater truth and effectiveness of mental reaction over theatrical presentation, would have heartily subscribed. The idea of pleasing the imagination foreshadows Addison's explanation of aesthetic response as a pleasure of the imagination.

Dryden was not only convinced of the preëminent importance of emotional effects in poetry; he was, like Hobbes, also interested in their nature and causes. Thus he was much concerned to find the source of Shakespeare's power to move the passions. He found it, in general, in that great dramatist's range and fertility of imagination, his knowledge of the passions, his mastery in character drawing. Shakespeare had of all poets the "largest and most comprehensive soul"; he had

---

[59] *Heads of an Answer to Rymer's Remarks on the Tragedies of the Last Age*, Scott and Saintsbury, XV, 385.
[60] *An Essay of Dramatic Poesy*, Ker, I, 63.

great wit and almost unbounded inventive power.[61] He drew
his characters with universal quality, but made them distinct,
with natural individual passions, true to their age and condition;[62] and at his best portrayed these characters and their passions in such language as to set them as it were before our eyes.[63]

Throughout his essays, though he seldom attempts systematic analysis, Dryden is actively probing into the mystery of
aesthetic pleasure, and more than once he probes deep and
true. Indeed, Dryden shows at times a unique aptitude for
psychological investigation. Thus we find him listing "pointed
wit and sentences affected out of reason" among the obstacles
to moving the passions, with the acute remark: "No man is
at leisure to make sentences and similes, when his soul is in
an agony."[64] Such an argument for the simple language of
passion would alone set Dryden apart from the whole race of
merely formalistic critics. Again, his complete case for wit as
a "propriety of thoughts and words," discussed in a preceding
section of this book (pp. 199–202), is, as we have seen, a treatise
in little on what enables poetry to fulfil the Longinian demand
for "enthusiasm." The value of his general conclusion that
such an effect is achieved through the apt expression of the
rich inventions of fancy working under the guidance of judgment, just within the bounds of license, has already been
pointed out.[65]

Dryden's own gloss on this definition, written fourteen years
later in the Preface to *Albion and Albanius*, no doubt conveys
the implication he originally intended: "Propriety of thought
is that fancy which arises naturally from the subject, or which
the poet adapts to it. Propriety of words is the clothing of
those thoughts with such expressions as are naturally proper to
them; and from both these, if they are judiciously performed,
the delight of poetry results."[66]

Prosaic as this may sound, we need only recall that Dryden's

[61] *Ibid.*, I, 79–80.
[62] *The Grounds of Criticism in Tragedy*, Ker, I, 218, 219, 224.
[63] *An Essay of Dramatic Poesy*, Ker, I, 80.
[64] *The Grounds of Criticism in Tragedy*, Ker, I, 223.
[65] See p. 202 of this book.
[66] "Preface to *Albion and Albanius*," Ker, I, 271.

phrase "judiciously performed" permits both inventions of fancy up to the limits of popular acceptance (even to chimeras and angels, and devils, and the multifarious characters of English drama) and the inclusion in "expression" of all sorts of ornament in the form of tropes and figures [67] to see the comprehensiveness of his view. Probabilities which are wonderful,[68] clearly defined characters [69] so presented as to arouse concernment,[70] naturally and artfully aroused passions,[71] sublime thoughts and sublime words [72] are some of the sources of pleasure named by Dryden. Solid sense and elegant expression, the true sublime rather than fustian and ostentation, harmony of numbers, in general a well-weighed, judicious, polished performance marked by clearness, purity, easiness and magnificence of style, are other elements which please the reader of judgment.[73] Freedom of imagination and variety Dryden finds chief sources of pleasurable effect, and he praises the English in contrast with the French for superiority in these qualities.[74] Shakespeare's Caliban is cited as an admirable example of copiousness of imagination,[75] and his practice of mixing tragedy and comedy, sometimes condemned, is excused as a means, through variety, of pleasing an audience.[76] Dryden justifies himself for breaking "a rule for the sake of variety." [77]

Defending tragicomedy, Dryden (in the person of Neander) makes an excursion into the psychology of effect which shows, as well as anything in all his essays, how fruitfully he had pondered the nature and sources of pleasure in dramatic representation:

[67] *The Author's Apology for Heroic Poetry and Poetic Licence*, Ker, I, 184.
[68] *The Grounds of Criticism in Tragedy*, Ker, I, 209.
[69] *Ibid.*, I, 224, 229.
[70] *Ibid.*, I, 211: "and that it is from our concernment we receive pleasure is undoubted."   [71] *Ibid.*, I, 220.
[72] "Dedication of the *Aeneis*," Ker, II, 233: "how shall I imitate his noble flights where his thoughts and words are equally sublime?"
[73] *Ibid.*, II, 223, 224, 225, 228.
[74] *An Essay of Dramatic Poesy*, Ker, I, 76–78.
[75] *The Grounds of Criticism in Tragedy*, Ker, I, 219.
[76] *An Essay of Dramatic Poesy*, Ker, I, 69–70.
[77] "Dedication of *The Spanish Friar*," Ker, I, 249. Cf. Lope de Vega's "for often that which breaks the rules is thereby pleasant to the taste," Ker, II, 292.

. . . As for their new way of mingling mirth with serious plot, I do not, with Lisideius, condemn the thing, though I cannot approve their manner of doing it. He tells us, we cannot so speedily recollect ourselves after a scene of great passion and concernment, as to pass to another of mirth and humour, and to enjoy it with any relish: but why should he imagine the soul of man more heavy than his senses? Does not the eye pass from an unpleasant object to a pleasant in a much shorter time than is required to this? and does not the unpleasantness of the first commend the beauty of the latter? The old rule of logic might have convinced him, that contraries, when placed near, set off each other. A continued gravity keeps the spirit too much bent; we must refresh it sometimes, as we bait in a journey that we may go on with greater ease. A scene of mirth, mixed with tragedy, has the same effect upon us which our music has betwixt the acts; and that we find a relief to us from the best plots and language of the stage, if the discourses have been long.[78]

If anyone before Dryden attempted to apply the theory of contrast and relief to the aesthetics of tragedy I am unaware of it. Dryden's lively interest in psychology and his persistent empiricism, leading him in his criticism to keep his eye close to the object and observe effects at first hand, bore fruit in penetrating reflection and independent conclusions of a sort we usually associate with the utterances of Coleridge and De Quincey over a century later. Dryden's explicit faith in observation and experience as opposed to convention and dogmatism stands clearly revealed in this whole passage. His conclusion is firmly confident:

. . . I must therefore have stronger arguments, ere I am convinced that compassion and mirth in the same subject destroy each other; and in the mean time cannot but conclude, to the honour of our nation, that we have invented, increased, and perfected a more pleasant way of writing for the stage, than was ever known to the ancients or moderns of any nation, which is tragi-comedy.[79]

Elsewhere Dryden defends the frequent use of drums and the representation of battles in his *Conquest of Granada*, on the ground that such devices are necessary

to produce the effects of an heroic play; that is, to raise the imagination of the audience, and to persuade them, for the time, that what they behold on the theatre is really performed. The poet is then to endeavour

---

[78] *An Essay of Dramatic Poesy*, Ker, I, 69–70.   [79] *Ibid.*, I, 70.

an absolute dominion over the minds of the spectators; for though our fancy will contribute to its own deceit, yet a writer ought to help its operation.[80]

Here is the whole doctrine, in little, of stage illusion, with a recognition of the necessity of a suspension of disbelief. The idea of the willingness of the audience to believe is not expressed, but is clearly implied. In an earlier essay, in dealing with the same subject, Dryden's implication of willingness is stronger: "and Reason," he states picturesquely, "suffers itself to be so hoodwinked, that it may better enjoy the pleasures of the fiction." [81]

Voluntary or otherwise, however, the surrender is not to be to an illusion of absolute reality. Dryden quite consistently holds: first, that probability alone, not actuality, is necessary; [82] secondly, that the reality represented should be heightened by selection and art. "The converse, therefore, which a poet is to imitate," he writes, "must be heightened with all the arts and ornaments of poetry; and must be such as, strictly considered, could never be spoken by any without premeditation." [83] The best painters know, Dryden points out, "that there may be too near a resemblance in a picture: to take every lineament and feature is not to make an excellent piece, but to take so much only as will make a beautiful resemblance of the whole: and with an ingenious flattery of nature, to heighten the beauties of some parts, and hide the deformities of the rest." [84] This follows closely on the heels of Dryden's assertion that "delight is the chief, if not the only, end of poesy." It is, we may assume, the happiness of wit — fancy aided by judgment — as described in preceding paragraphs of this chapter, to search out and mold into new forms those elements in nature, stored in memory, or taken from the life as the case may be, that will contribute to such a beautiful resemblance as is here prescribed.[85]

---

[80] *An Essay of Heroic Plays*, Ker, I, 154–155.
[81] *A Defence of an Essay of Dramatic Poesy*, Ker, I, 128.
[82] *Ibid.* and *An Essay of Heroic Plays*, Ker, I, 153.
[83] *A Defence of an Essay of Dramatic Poesy*, Ker, I, 113–114.
[84] *Ibid.*, I, 114.
[85] It will be recalled that Dryden allows comedy a nearer approach to realism than he sanctions for serious poetry (*supra*, pp. 196 ff.). Even in comedy, however,

A further resultful excursion into the psychology of effect occurs in *A Parallel of Poetry and Painting*, in a passage dealing with imitation. Dryden had previously defined a play as a "lively imitation of nature." [86] This imitation must be truthful, "For the spirit of man cannot be satisfied but with truth, or at least verisimility." [87] This ideal occurs frequently in Dryden: "Shakespeare looked inwards and found nature there"; [88] Chaucer was to be judged "a man of a most wonderful comprehensive nature," because of his great knowledge of humanity, and his power to portray life convincingly.[89] This is clearly a concession to realism, though Dryden's realism is habitually, even with reference to comedy, tinged with enough idealism to require the heightening necessary to please.[90] In the passage from *A Parallel* which we are now considering Dryden reiterates this principle of truth in imitating nature as requisite to pleasure: "The imitation of nature is therefore justly constituted as the general, and indeed the only, rule of pleasing, both in Poetry and Painting." [91] What comes nearest to a resemblance of nature, he continues, is the best, though this is not to be understood as all of nature, but that which can be most profitably imitated; for "it follows not, that what pleases most in either kind is therefore good, but what ought to please." [92] Hence the poet and painter alike should know what is most beautiful in nature to imitate. The most noble subject is most beautiful: tragedy is therefore more beautiful than comedy, having greater persons and a more noble sub-

---

the judgment works with highly selected materials. In *A Parallel of Poetry and Painting*, where he emphasizes the principle of ideal imitation, accepting Bellori's statement that "the artful painter and the sculptor, imitating the Divine Maker, form to themselves . . . a model of the superior beauties; and . . . endeavor to correct and amend the common nature, and to represent it . . . without fault, either in colour, or in lineament" (Ker, II, 118), he draws a further distinction, to the effect that the highest idealization of all is to be found in epic poetry, since epic heroes only are perfect (*ibid.*, II, 127).

[86] *An Essay of Dramatic Poesy*, Ker, I, 36.
[87] *Ibid.*, I, 59.   [88] *Ibid.*, I, 79, 80.
[89] "Preface to the *Fables*" (1700), Ker, II, 262–263.
[90] See P. H. Frye, *Dryden and the Critical Canons of the Eighteenth Century*, University of Nebraska Studies, Vol. VII (Lincoln, 1907).
[91] *A Parallel of Poetry and Painting*, Ker, II, 137.   [92] *Ibid.*, II, 136.

ject, "and thence is derived the greater and more noble pleasure." [93]

Dryden proceeds to cite Aristotle on the cause of pleasure in imitation, offers a comment in which he quite plainly shows that he misinterprets Aristotle's meaning,[94] and proposes what appears to him a better explanation:

> . . . As truth is the end of all our speculations, so the discovery of it is the pleasure of them; and since a true knowledge of Nature gives us pleasure, a lively imitation of it, either in Poetry or Painting, must of necessity produce a much greater: for both these arts, as I said before, are not only true imitations of Nature, but of the best Nature, of that which is wrought up to a nobler pitch. They present us with images more perfect than the life in any individual; and we have the pleasure to see all the scattered beauties of Nature united by a happy chemistry, without its deformities or faults. They are imitations of the passions, which always move, and therefore consequently please; for without motion there can be no delight, which cannot be considered but as an active passion. When we view these elevated ideas of nature, the result of that view is admiration, which is always the cause of pleasure.[95]

This passage is a curious mixture of traditional with forward-looking psychological criticism. Such remarks as that about being pleased with only what ought to please are pure neo-classic cant, and the general attitude toward ideal imitation is obviously traditional. The discussion as a whole takes a turn, however, that shows the influence of the new interest in psychological analysis. Dryden is going further than a mere statement for ideal imitation and its corollaries: he is examining the causes for pleasure in the process. His explanation is at bottom a version of Hobbes's theory that the discovery of knowledge is pleasure, and that without agitation of the passions there can be no pleasure. His assertion that "without motion there can be no delight" is precisely in accord with the Hobbian doctrine that all pleasure has its beginnings in internal motion and that all delight is appetite. Such pronouncements make Dryden an important link in the chain which runs from

---

93 *A Parallel of Poetry and Painting*, Ker, II, 136.
94 As Thomas Twining shows in his edition of Aristotle's *Poetics*. See Scott and Saintsbury, XIX, 314.
95 *A Parallel of Poetry and Paintiug*, Ker, II, 137–138.

Hobbes, through Addison, Du Bos, and others, to the great Romanticists, in the doctrine that there is in the mere excitation of the emotions a certain pleasure, and that without such excitation there can be no aesthetic experience.

This emphasis on the fundamental importance of moving the passions in poetry is in accord with Dryden's other ideas on the subject that we have been considering. It led him quite consistently away from subservience to the rules, to a study of what pleases and why it pleases. Once a critic has accepted the principle that "since we acknowledge the effect there must be something in the cause," and then, in his investigation of causes, finds his clue not in the external object but in the natural workings of men's minds, he is well on the way from formalistic to psychological criticism.

Speculations upon the integrity of effects and on the universality of the passions in application to poetry inevitably drove Dryden to recognitions of the principle of taste — that irreconcilable foe of the formalistic approach. Thus it is only a logical sequence to his reasoning elsewhere that he writes in the Preface to the Translation of Ovid's *Epistles:*

> . . . for, all passions being inborn with us, we are almost equally judges when we are concerned in the representation of them. Now I will appeal to any man, who has read this poet [Ovid], whether he finds not the natural emotion of the same passion in himself, which the poet describes in his feigned persons? His thoughts, which are the pictures and results of those passions, are generally such as naturally arise from those disorderly motions of our spirits.[96]

Such an appeal to individual experience and such assumptions of a common instrument for perceiving value in art lie at the root of all theories of taste. With Dryden it is a natural corollary to his criterion that delight is the first end of poetry and that moving the passions is the chief means of producing delight.

The phases of Dryden's critical theory having to do with artistic creation and response have been examined in the foregoing sections as an aspect of the influence of Hobbes. It must not be assumed, however, that Dryden owed everything

[96] Ker, I, 233.

in this theory to Hobbes. That would be greatly to over-
simplify the problem. Dryden was an eclectic, and he drew
into his speculations matter from many and varied sources.
He had read extensively in aesthetic theory, from Aristotle to
the last French formalist. He was also widely acquainted
with the non-critical literature of many nations, particularly of
France, and he knew the Cartesian philosophy and the new
science. Professor Bredvold has convincingly shown how Dryden's skepticism was related to a complexity of philosophical
currents of thought of the age, and was derived from many
sources — Montaigne, Charron, Sextus Empiricus, Descartes.[97]

Reading his Italian and French critics Dryden could have
found mentions of wit and distinctions between fancy and
judgment.[98] He could have found similar distinctions in Bacon.
In Le Bossu and Rapin he would have encountered a certain

[97] Louis I. Bredvold, *The Milieu of John Dryden*, University of Michigan
Publications (Ann Arbor, 1934).

[98] Rapin, for example, writes definitely of the relation of judgment to wit.
He even recognized that genius might rise above the rules. Thus he declares of
Lope de Vega: "But he had a Wit too vast to be confin'd to Rules, or admit of
any Bounds; 'twas this oblig'd him to abandon himself to the Swing of his *Genius*,
because he might alway rely on it" (René Rapin, *Reflections on Aristotle's Treatise
of Poesie*, in *The Whole Critical Works of Monsieur Rapin*, tr. by "Several Hands"
[London, 1706], II, 224).
Again we find him declaring that Homer had the "vastest, sublimest, pro-
foundest, and most universal Wit that ever was" (*ibid.*, II, 138). We find him,
too, talking of the "celestial Fire" of the true genius, and citing Horace on the
necessity for recognizing the difference between such genius and mediocre talent:
"For (saith he) there must be a greatness of Soul, and something Divine in the Spirit [of the
true genius]. There must be lofty Expressions, and noble Thoughts, and an Air of Majesty
to bear that name" (*ibid.*, II, 137). In another place: "This Genius is that celestial
Fire intended by the Fable, which enlarges and heightens the Soul, and makes it
express things wth a lofty Air" (*ibid.*, II, 139). The ultimate end of poetry is
public good, says Rapin, but its immediate goal is delight. To this end it "labours
to move the Passions, all whose motions are delightful, because nothing is more
sweet to the Soul than Agitation" (*ibid.*, II, 141); it "never speaks but with
Figures, to give a greater lustre to the Discourse; and is noble in its Idea's, sublime
in the Expressions, bold in the Words . . ." (*ibid.*, II, 141–142). To achieve its
aim poetry must be admirable — that is, it must create wonder, and it must be so
managed as to work the greatest effect on the soul of the spectator. This is to be
accomplished by "exact *Distinction* of the different Degrees of *Passion* . . . . For
this gives the *Draught of Nature*, and is the most *infallible Spring* for moving the soul."
Judgment and art must be used; "for by a *Passion* that is Imperfect and abortive,
the Soul of the *Spectator* may be *shaken;* but this is not enough, it must be *Ravish'd*"
(*ibid.*, II, 175).

emphasis on the passions, and even elementary essays in analysis of effects. For, in spite of their formalism, the French critics also were touched by the new philosophy and were not oblivious of the facts of experience. The influence of Descartes and his followers made itself continually felt in late seventeenth-century criticism. Longinus, too, appeared on the scene to contribute to Dryden's psychology of effect. It must be pointed out, however, that, like Le Bossu and Rapin, he came under Dryden's notice after his main ideas, at least in tentative form, had been advanced. Even so, the case for the French critics and for Longinus in shaping Dryden's final theory cannot be ignored.

There is another source for qualification in the fact that Dryden at times shows disapproval of Hobbes, as when he calls Hobbes's translation of Homer "bald," and declares that the old philosopher, "studying poetry as he did mathematics too late," began his criticism of Homer where he should have left off — that is, with his diction.[99] Professor Bredvold, pointing to this passage and to a second in the Preface to *Sylvæ* (1685), in which Dryden plainly expresses doubts of Hobbes's full sincerity and shows signs of irritation at his aggressive self-assurance,[100] correctly remarks that "Dryden's attitude towards Hobbes must from the beginning have involved reservations." [101]

It is clear, however, that Dryden had read Hobbes with care and that in various ways he made considerable use of his ideas. Professor Merritt Y. Hughes has shown Dryden's indebtedness to Hobbes in the political ideas of characters in his plays,[102] and Professor Bredvold has pointed out what seem conclusive references in Dryden "to the dilemma of free-will and necessity — the great ethical problem raised in a new form by Hobbism." [103] A direct testimony to Dryden's attitude toward Hobbes is contained in Aubrey's, possibly biased, remark in his *Lives:* "Mr. John Dreyden, Poet Laureat, is his great admirer, and oftentimes makes use of his doctrines in

[99] "Preface to the *Fables*," Ker, II, 252.
[100] "Preface to *Sylvæ*" (1685), Ker, I, 259.
[101] *Op. cit.*, pp. 68–69.
[102] "Dryden as a Statist," *Philological Quarterly*, VI (1927), 335–350.
[103] *Op. cit.*, pp. 66–68.

his playes." Then he adds the note, presumably showing the source of his information: "from Mr. Dreyden himselfe." [104] Let us recall, too, that Dryden spoke, evidently with pride, of "our Hobbes" and called him "our poet and philosopher of Malmesbury." [105]

In the present study Dryden's use of Hobbes's psychology in its bearing on aesthetic problems and of those passages in his writings having direct reference to poetry is alone in question. The evidence for such use, even admitting continual interweaving with ideas from other sources, seems decisive. It is not only the use and the unique application of Hobbes's terms "wit," "imagination," "fancy," and "judgment" and the rather frequent echoes in his writing of Hobbes's actual phrasing that is in point here; it is even more the general cast of Dryden's speculations: his scientific method, his willingness to examine and to test out, his eager interest in psychological processes, his concern with causes and effects, his preoccupation with the passions, his acceptance of the Hobbian principle of motion as essential to pleasure, and his adoption of such more particular aspects of Hobbes's theory as the idea that variety or novelty is one of the chief sources of delight and that the discovery of truth (such as is revealed in artistic imitations of nature) is a fundamental cause of pleasure. The fact that many of these elements had at different times previously appeared in other writers, some in one some in another, is a basis for argument against attributing too much influence to Hobbes. But they had not appeared in any *one* other writer, nor in quite the same form, and the inference for Dryden's substantial debt to Hobbes stands. Dryden is, in certain important aspects of his work, clearly in the Hobbian tradition of the psychological approach to aesthetic problems.

[104] John Aubrey, 'Brief Lives,' Chiefly of Contemporaries, ed. by Andrew Clark (Oxford, 1898), I, 372. The note appears to have been written 1679–80.
[105] "Preface to Sylvæ," Ker, I, 259. We may also recall his remark in the "Preface to the Fables": "In the mean time to follow the thrid of my discourse (as thoughts, according to Hobbes, have always some connexion.) so from Chaucer I was led to think on Boccace, who was not only his contemporary, but also pursued the same studies . . ." (Ker, II, 248).

CHAPTER VIII

The Psychological Approach in Dennis

I

IN JOHN DENNIS the shift in emphasis from object to subject in critical speculation was to make further progress.
Dennis is a more important figure in criticism than has been
usually acknowledged. His reputation suffered at the hands
of Pope, who made unmerciful fun at his expense,[1] and of
Warburton, who, in the Preface to his edition of Shakespeare,
classed him with the critics *terrible*, Rymer, Gildon, and Oldmixon.[2] After that he was generally neglected.

Mr. H. G. Paul has made some amends for the comparative neglect into which Dennis had fallen; [3] and Professor J. G.
Robertson has taken up arms on his behalf. Robertson goes so
far as to say that "John Dennis has good claims to be Addison's
predecessor." Dennis, he points out, did his best to save what
was to be saved of the philosophy of Hobbes for the literary
theory of the new century. "He showed that just Hobbes'
sensualistic psychology provided a basis for defining the function of imagination in poetry, and its relation to the better
understood processes of reason." Dennis, Robertson admits,

---

[1] *The Dunciad*, I, 106; III, 173–184. The facts as to Pope's part in the devas-
tating attack upon Dennis in *The Narrative of Doctor Robert Morris, concerning the
strange and deplorable Frenzy of Mr. John Dennis, an officer at the Customs House* (London,
1734) are not fully known. He seems at least to have inspired it. See Paul's
account, pp. 68–70 of work cited in note 3.

[2] D. Nichol Smith, *Eighteenth Century Essays on Shakespeare* (Glasgow, 1903),
p. 105. A true criticism, says Warburton, is not to be raised "mechanically on the
Rules which *Dacier*, *Rapin*, and *Bossu* have collected from Antiquity; and of which
such kind of Writers as *Rymer*, *Gildon*, *Dennis*, and *Oldmixon* have only gathered
and chewed the Husks."

[3] Harry Gilbert Paul, *John Dennis, His Life and Criticism* (New York, 1911).

was "unfortunately, content as a rule to compromise. He was inadequate, and in late years he retrogressed," yet "without him, the literary theory of the *Spectator* would certainly have been less distinguishable from that of Dryden." [4]

One of the probable reasons that Dennis was discredited, aside from the effects of his inflammable temper, was that the body of his criticism seems a tissue of inconsistencies. He not only compromises, but apparently contradicts himself. He was an ardent follower of the French formalistic critics, Le Bossu in particular; but he at the same time eagerly embraced the liberalizing doctrines of Longinus, and he early fell under the influence of the new philosophy with a specific leaning to the psychological implications in the teachings of Hobbes. Dennis illustrates, almost better than anyone else of his age, the results of the confluence of these elements — which likewise show themselves in various of his contemporaries, notably Dryden and Addison — in a mind which is receptive and philosophically inclined, but not strong enough nor systematic enough to bring them into reconciliation. Dennis's criticism in consequence is likely to appear a curious potpourri of conflicting theories and judgments.

The dual effects in criticism of Hobbian and Cartesian philosophy and the new science merit notice at this point. On one side was a rationalism which, in its ambition to reduce all things in the world to logic and order, justified and fortified the "rules" and the neat schematizations of such a critic as Le Bossu. This influence seems to have extended to virtually every alert mind of the period. A. F. B. Clark has fairly stated the case in a comment on Le Bossu's influence:

> . . . We too often forget how much the age which witnessed the founding of the Royal Society and the spread of the Cartesian philosophy was permeated by the mathematical and logical spirit. The construction or analysis of an epic according to Le Bossu's scheme became a fascinating minor adventure for an age which, in its graver moments, demonstrated the reality of God with Malebranche or mapped out the Universe with Newton. That this ruling logical passion did not, in the case of the greater geniuses like Dryden, always pull very well with their instinctive feeling

---

[4] J. G. Robertson, *Studies in the Genesis of Romantic Theory in the Eighteenth Century* (Cambridge, 1923), pp. 243–244.

for poetic beauty is certain; but there is no reason for regarding either of these contending enthusiasms as unreal or forced.[5]

It was this spirit that led to an eager acceptance in many quarters of the view promulgated by Boileau and others, that nature and reason and the rules of Aristotle are one. It was, therefore, a principal support of neoclassicism in its most extreme phases as it appeared in the French formalists, in the English Rymer and Gildon, and, as it manifests itself on occasion, in Dennis. Herein Dennis found his justification for his strict adherence to the formulae of Le Bossu in the main body of his *Remarks on "Prince Arthur."*

But there was another phase of the new philosophy which pointed in a different direction. This was a searching scientific attitude which doubted all received rule and dogma until they could be proved by beginning anew with the facts of experience and following wherever these facts led. The initial skepticism of Descartes and Hobbes's scorn for opinion not subjected to the test of experience or scientific inquiry were manifestations of this side of rationalism. Such an approach was inherently opposed to the backward-looking, static elements in neoclassicism, which regarded the secrets of art as all discovered and the perfection of poetry as having been attained in the past. The new rationalism admitted nothing as settled. It was essentially progressive, eagerly anticipative of fresh discoveries and new insight. Its actuating spirit may be found in Hobbes's scornful animadversions on Greek and scholastic philosophy, for which he would substitute a true natural philosophy resting on scientific inquiry,[6] and in his theory that

---

[5] *Boileau and the French Classical Critics in England* (Paris, 1925), p. 250.

[6] "There walked in old Greece a certain phantasm, for superficial gravity, though full within of fraud and filth, a little like philosophy; which unwary men, thinking to be it, adhered to the professors of it, some to one, some to another, though they disagreed among themselves, and with great salary put their children to them to be taught, instead of wisdom, and, neglecting the laws, to determine every question according to their own fancies" ("Epistle Dedicatory," *The Elements of Philosophy*, in *The English Works of Thomas Hobbes of Malmesbury*, ed. by Sir William Molesworth [London, 1839–45], I, ix–x). In later times from a mingling of Christian doctrine there grew up a system which was "like that *Empusa* in the Athenian comic poet, which was taken in Athens for a ghost that changed shapes, having one brazen leg, but the other was the leg of an ass, and was sent, as was believed, by Hecate, as a sign of some approaching evil fortune" (*ibid.*, x).

there is felicity only in progress.[7] Such views and attitudes were manifestly inimical to neoclassical assumptions.

Unlike Dryden, Dennis was no agnostic. There was small skepticism in his mind regarding the sanctity of the rules or the infallibility of the ancients. He believed in an ordered world and in ordered works of art, if there was to be any value in them. When, therefore, he undertook, in his *Advancement and Reformation of Modern Poetry* and later in his *Grounds of Criticism in Poetry*, to present a theory of poetry and criticism, he was not in any sense presuming to discredit the traditions of neoclassicism; he was rather seeking an extension of them by offering new rules on matters that had been imperfectly covered by previous critics. That he saw these matters as psychological, relating to the passions and to facts of the creative and responsive phenomena of mind, may be attributed to the influence of the new philosophy as represented chiefly in Hobbes and his followers, reinforced by the example of Longinus, just as Dennis's method of attacking his problems was largely derived from these same sources.

Coming, therefore, not to destroy but to fulfil the law, Dennis approaches his scheme for an enlarged aesthetics by direct professions of loyalty to the rules and of belief in logic and order in all art. The *Oedipus* of Sophocles is to be preferred to *Julius Caesar* because it is "Just and Regular," whereas Shakespeare's play is "very Extravagant and Irregular"; and "writing Regularly is writing Morally, Decently, Justly, Naturally, Reasonably." [8] There is, indeed, no way really to please in poetry but by rules. It may be suggested that poets may please by chance. But this idea Dennis finds repugnant to the universal principle of rule and order which dominates nature and by virtue of which men live and move and have

---

[7] "Seeing all delight is appetite, and appetite presupposeth a farther end, there can be no contentment but in proceeding. . . . Felicity, therefore . . . consisteth not in having prospered, but in prospering" (*The Elements of Law*, ed. by Ferdinand Tönnies [Cambridge, 1928], I, vii, 7).

[8] "The Epistle Dedicatory," *The Advancement and Reformation of Modern Poetry* (London, 1701). I am using as texts for most of Dennis photostat copies from first editions of his various works in the British Museum. Unfortunately for me, this chapter was written before Professor Hooker's excellent edition of Dennis had appeared.

their being. He expresses himself on this point with the vigor of unswerving conviction:

> . . . Now Nature, taken in a stricter sense, is nothing but that Rule and Order and Harmony which we find in the visible Creation. . . . And the little World, which we call Man, owes not only his Health and Ease and Pleasure, nay, the continuance of its very Being to the Regularity of Mechanical motion, but even the strength too of its boasted Reason, and the piercing force of those aspiring thoughts, which are able to pass the bounds that circumscribe the Universe.[9]

And here follows one of the most remarkable of all Augustan statements of the principle of the equivalency of nature, reason, and order: "As Nature is Order and Rule and Harmony in the visible World, so Reason is the very same throughout the invisible Creation. For Reason is Order and the Result of Order. And nothing that is Irregular, as far as it is Irregular, ever was or ever can be either Natural or Reasonable." [10] Thus Dennis offers triumphant vindication of the principle of rationalized and inviolable rules in art.

The passage as a whole is an instructive example of the blending of traditional theory with ideas from the new philosophy. Nothing could better show how, in Dennis's case at least, the lately developed scientific theories with their emphasis on mechanical uniformity in nature had reinforced the neoclassic regard for law in poetry. In such a view these laws assumed infallible authority as manifestations of the inherent reason and order of a well-regulated universe. So Dennis declares of the "Renown'd masters among the Ancients, Homer and Vergil," that they

> had too much Capacity, and too much Discernment, not to see the necessity of knowing and practising the Rules which Reason and Philosophy have prescribed to Poets. . . . They wrote to their fellow Citizens of the Universe, to all Countries and all Ages. . . . They were clearly convinced that nothing could transmit their Immortal works to posterity, but something like that harmonious Order which maintains the Universe . . . .[11]

In *The Author's Apology for Heroic Poetry and Poetic Licence* Dryden had proposed a way for the modern poet by which he

[9] *Ibid.*   [10] *Ibid.*   [11] *Ibid.*

might "build a nobler, a more beautiful and more perfect poem, than any extant since the ancients." [12] His prescription included a very free play of fancy in ideal constructions surpassing the possibilities of nature, though still probable for the age in which they were written (that is, within the range of popular belief), and an expression heightened by figurative language to the end of flashing on the mind of the reader exciting and enthralling imagery, embellished and elegant, yet controlled by judgment. So may the poet, through "a propriety of thoughts and words elegantly adapted to the subject," achieve the effects of transport indicated by Longinus as the immediate end of heroic poetry. One may readily conceive that Dennis had pondered well this passage before he undertook his recipe for the advancement of modern poetry. He is apparently correcting Dryden. The end he proposes, Longinian enthusiasm, is the same as Dryden's, but the means to this end are to be more definite. Dryden had missed (so we may imagine Dennis arguing) an essential point: to wit, the *kind* of ideas that arouse transport. He had also been lax in his attitude toward the rules.

II

Dennis, as we have seen, permits no doubt as to his stand on the rules. And he is quite as decisive in his contention for the kind of ideas essential to the highest poetry. Accepting the general neoclassic assumption that the ultimate end of poetry is to delight and instruct, Dennis begins the formulation of his aesthetic with the postulate that this result can be best attained by exciting the passions.[13] "Passion is the Characteristical Mark of Poetry," [14] he declares. Again he says, "For therefore Poetry is Poetry because it is more sensual and passionate than Prose." [15] Harmony is important, but "Passion can please without Harmony." [16] Passion is essential to sublimity, and Dennis takes Longinus sharply to account for ad-

---

[12] *Essays of John Dryden*, ed. by W. P. Ker (Oxford, 1926), I, 190.
[13] *The Grounds of Criticism in Poetry* (London, 1704), pp. 9–10.
[14] *The Advancement and Reformation of Modern Poetry*, p. 25.
[15] *Ibid.*, p. 24.   [16] *Ibid.*, p. 25.

mitting the possibility of exceptions to this rule.[17] There are two kinds of passion in poetry, the "ordinary," or "vulgar," and the "enthusiastick." Ordinary passion is that "whose cause is clearly comprehended by him who feels it." [18] These same passions are "Enthusiasms when their cause is not clearly comprehended by him who feels them." [19] This is the distinction that Dennis makes in *The Advancement and Reformation of Modern Poetry*. Three years later in *The Grounds of Criticism in Poetry* he has changed the term "ordinary" to "vulgar," and he defines this passion as one raised by actual objects or events or ideas that occur in the ordinary course of common society in the everyday world. Thus anger is moved by an actual affront or by the ideas of an affront, pity by the sight of a mournful object or by the relation of one.[20] On the other hand, "Enthusiastick Passion or Enthusiasm, is a Passion which is moved by the Idea's in Contemplation or the Meditation of Things, that belong not to common Life." [21] More explicitly Dennis goes on to explain: "Now, the Enthusiastick Passions are chiefly Six, Admiration, Terror, Horror, Joy, Sadness, Desire, Caused by Idea's occuring to us in Meditation, and producing the same Passions that the Objects of those Idea's would raise in us, if they were set before us in the same Light that those Idea's give us of them." [22] Religious ideas are of course preëminently fitted to excite the enthusiastic passions.

In these definitions of the passions and in their implications, which appear more clearly in subsequent passages, Dennis is showing something of the influence of fifty years of psychological speculation upon English aesthetic thinking. He is focussing attention on the mind of the poet and his reader; his primary interest is *internal* causes and effects. This he thought had been lacking in previous criticism. Longinus, for instance, not only had neglected to give a definition for the sublime, "a very great fault," but had also failed to show causes. Longinus had indeed set before us the effects which

---

[17] *The Grounds of Criticism in Poetry*, pp. 71–72.
[18] *The Advancement and Reformation of Modern Poetry*, p. 26.
[19] *Ibid.*
[20] *The Grounds of Criticism in Poetry*, p. 20.
[21] *Ibid.*, p. 16.   [22] *Ibid.*, pp. 16–17.

the sublime produces,[23] but had gone no further. Dennis feels
that he himself has rectified this fault; for he has "endeavour'd
to shew what it is in Poetry that works these effects, so that
take the Cause and its Effects together, and you have the
Sublime." [24]   And in so doing, one can imagine, he rests
assured that he has added materially to what Dryden or any
other critic had said on the subject.

   In one most important respect Dennis has made a contribution which must already have struck the reader: that is,
the notion of meditation as a source for poetic emotion. Wordsworth was later to express in its most memorable form the
relation of poetry to meditation. Dennis is by no means anticipating the dictum that "poetry is emotion recollected in
tranquility"; indeed, his conception is far from including the
element of tranquility — poetic fury is a nearer equivalent for
his "Enthusiastick Passion." He is, nevertheless, calling attention to the fact that even the vulgar passions essential to poetry
may be aroused by reflection. The highest passions, hence the
highest poetry, can be traced almost entirely to reflection upon
ideas of lofty being and action, often beyond the reach of full
comprehension.

   Dennis shows in various places that imagery is the material
and stimulus for the reflection that leads to passion. It is
sense impression acted upon by the mind, not mere physical
imagery, however, which awakens the poetic passion. "Sacred
Poetry requires . . . a very warm and Strong Imagination," [25]
he writes. That this imagination is not limited to a mere power
to recall imagery or to invent fanciful creations, but is rather
a creative faculty in something of the later Wordsworthian sense,
is apparent from one of Dennis's most notable passages:

   . . . And here I desire the Reader to observe, that Idea's in Meditation, are often very different from what Idea's of the same Objects are,

---

   [23] *The Advancement and Reformation of Modern Poetry*, p. 47: ". . . as, for
example, that it causes in them admiration and surprize; a noble Pride, and a
noble Vigour, an invincible force transporting the Soul from its ordinary Situation,
and a Transport, and a fulness of Joy mingled with Astonishment."
   [24] *Ibid.*
   [25] *The Grounds of Criticism in Poetry*, p. 112.

in the course of common Conversation. As for Example, the Sun men-tion'd in ordinary Conversation, gives the Idea of a round flat shining Body, of about Two Foot Diameter. But the Sun occurring to us in Meditation, gives the idea of a vast and glorious Body, and the top of all the visible Creation, and the brightest material Image of the Divinity.[26]

Such an idea is attended with "Admiration and that Admira-tion I call Enthusiasm." A like enthusiasm, in this case char-acterized by the quality of terror, is aroused by our reflective response to thunder. The common idea of thunder is of a black cloud and a great noise: "But the Idea of it occurring in Meditation, sets before us the most forcible, most resistless, and consequently the most Dreadful Phænomenon in Nature." [27]

These two illustrations, particularly the second, contain in little Dennis's theory of sublimity. For to him a chief source of the sublime lies in objects which produce "terrible Ideas" — accompanied with admiration, surprise, astonishment. And in specific enumeration he ventures to lay before the reader the various ideas capable of producing this "Enthusiastick Terrour." They are: "Gods, Dæmons, Hell, Spirits and Souls of Men, Miracles, Prodigies, Enchantments, Witchcrafts, Thunder, Tempests, raging Seas, Inundations, Torrents, Earth-quakes, Volcanos, Monsters, Serpents, Lions, Tygres, Fire, War, Pestilence, Famine." [28] An impressive list.

But for our immediate purpose the more important point to these passages is the recognition on the part of Dennis that poetic emotion is engendered through a reflective imaginative process by means of which the original sense image is re-created into something quite new, thence to become the subject for enthusiastic contemplation. Dennis is here thinking in terms of considerable significance for future aesthetics. Wordsworth's theory of the imagination as a conferring, abstracting power through which the. poet's mind re-forms the objects of the material world into subjects for aesthetic delight; Coleridge's idea of the primary and secondary creative imagination; the general Wordsworthian-Coleridgean conception of lofty, sub-lime poetic experiences as having their origin in contemplative response to mighty scenes in nature — a Simplon Pass or a

[26] *Ibid.*, p. 17.   [27] *Ibid.*, pp. 17–18.   [28] *Ibid.*, pp. 87–88.

Vale of Chamouni: all contain a seminal kinship to the principle Dennis has here evolved. Nearer to Dennis in point of time are Shaftesbury's recognition of the enthusiastic emotions aroused in the contemplation of noble scenery, Addison's more developed idea of aesthetic response to nature, particularly his theory of sublimity as arising from the contemplation of mountain and ocean scenes and of wide-flung solar spaces, and Burke's whole notion of sublimity as a product of objects fitted to excite terror.

I do not wish to argue the point that these writers were directly influenced by Dennis, though Addison and Burke at least probably were. What I would emphasize, rather, is that all of them worked in a psychological tradition which included Dennis, and which in English criticism can be traced back for its most definite impulse to Thomas Hobbes. Some of Hobbes's predecessors and contemporaries, notably Bacon and Descartes, contributed; but Hobbes was the psychologist par excellence of the seventeenth century, and by a fortunate concurrence of individualities and circumstances his psychological approach, first quite generally applied in his own thinking on poetic problems, was rapidly caught up in the stream of the more independent aesthetic speculations of the next generation, to be transmitted in modified form to still later times. Its immediate effect was to direct attention in criticism to the subject rather than the object, hence to focus attention upon causes and effects in poetry, rather than upon form and convention; ultimately it was to prove a mighty factor in destroying the authority of the rules and in substituting for them an aesthetic which recognized conformity to facts of the mind as the only valid criterion in judging art.

The psychology upon which Dennis constructs his theory seems generally to be derived from Hobbes. -It is an adaptation not a direct borrowing, however, with some important modifications. With Dennis, as with Hobbes, ideas have their origin in sense impression. These ideas are of two sorts: those which come from ordinary objects and those which derive from the uncommon and the extraordinary. In the first case the ideas are full and clear; in the second, they are indefinite, somewhat beyond the realm of full apprehension. The first give rise to ordinary passions, the second to the enthusiastic passions. The ideas of the second class appear to include our conceptions of deity. And here Dennis diverges from Hobbes, who had insisted that, since we have not seen the Deity, or angels and devils for that matter, we can have no imaginations (or ideas) of deity or of anything else that is infinite: "And therefore the Name of *God* is used, not to make us conceive him; (for he is Incomprehensible . . . ;) but that we may honour him." [29] Dennis steers a middle course, extending application of the word "ideas" to the infinite beings who furnish the subjects for meditation in the highest religious poetry, but admitting a certain lack of clarity in our conception of them. Without making specific statement he saves himself from too great inconsistency with a basic sensationalist psychology by quite steadily assuming an anthropomorphic conception of deity. Moreover, Dennis could have found justification for his extension of ideas to deity in Hobbes's implicit defense of the use of supernatural agencies in the works of the ancients on the ground that poetical liberty may include the "conceived possibility of nature" in any given age.[30]

Dennis's notion that our ideas of any object may be different from the sense impression of the object (e.g. our idea of the sun or of thunder) again has its basis in Hobbes. For with Hobbes, as we have seen (Chapter III, *supra*), in perception the actual impression is modified by the intervention of judgment operating upon the incoming image and previous impressions re-presented by memory. . Memory, which upon occasion is regarded by Hobbes as the agent of both perceptive and creative acts, is also imagery, retained in the mind but growing dimmer as time recedes; for after some time, "wee lose . . . of Cities wee have seen, many particular Streets; and of Actions, many particular Circumstances." [31] Only the general idea rather than the specific image then remains, with what modifications the experience of all can easily witness.

[29] *Leviathan*, ed. by Ernest Rhys (London, Toronto, and New York, 1914), I, iii.
[30] *The Answer to Davenant*, in *Critical Essays of the Seventeenth Century*, ed. by J. E. Spingarn (Oxford, 1908), II, 62.   [31] *Leviathan*, I, ii.

Dennis's theory of the results of reflection in modifying
our ideas and in shaping the passions which accompany these
ideas is also contained in Hobbes. It is true that Hobbes is
not explicit on this point. He does, however, specifically recognize mental processes in the absence of objects of original
perception, the brain acting as intermediary between retained
"species of objects" and the animal spirits and the understanding.[32] Moreover, in his discussion of the passions in both
Leviathan and *The Elements of Law* he constantly implies reflective acts similar in kind to those which Dennis has in mind in
describing meditation. Thus the passion of "glory" is essentially a feeling of self-esteem and exultation arising from reflection upon our own power and worth; [33] the passion of "shame"
conversely comes from a discovery and reflection upon our
infirmities and errors.[34] Hobbes does not, it is true, use the
word "reflection" or "meditation"; but, in describing the
"Pleasures of the Mind" he speaks of the "joy" which, when
objects are absent from sense, arises from "expectation" and
"foresight of the End, or Consequence of things," [35] and he
considers at some length the problem of "deliberation" (with
particular application to doing and the consequence of alternative acts) and its effects on the passions.[36] From this it is
apparent that, assuming that he is basing his psychology on
the teaching of Hobbes, Dennis is again but making a logical
extension and application when he goes on to show that
meditation is the direct means of engendering the "Enthusiastick Passions" of lofty religious poetry, and may even be
employed in working up the vulgar passions which form the
substratum of the more ordinary works.

---

[32] This is perhaps best presented in Appendix I, Section iii, of *The Elements
of Law*. Hobbes resorts to a picturesque physical analogy to make his point:
"Though it may be doubted how the brayne can receive such power from the
externall obiect; yet it is no more, nor otherwise, than when steele, touchd
by the Loadstone, receiveth from it a Magneticall virtue, to worke the same
effects the Loadstone it self doeth."

[33] *The Elements of Law*, I, ix, 1; *Leviathan*, I, vi.

[34] *The Elements of Law*, I, ix, 3.

[35] *Leviathan*, I, vi.   [36] *Ibid*.

III

Dennis's theory of genius is corollary to his theory of the passions, and it likewise bears a certain relationship to general Hobbian doctrine. Hobbes had definitely taught that the way to both happiness and achievement lies in a certain capability for passion. "And therefore, a man who has no great Passion . . . ; but is as men terme it indifferent . . . cannot possibly have either a great Fancy, or much Judgement. . . . For as to have no Desire, is to be Dead: so to have weak Passions, is Dulnesse. . . ." [37]   When we recall that with Hobbes genius is wit, and that wit is marked by celerity of imagining in a mind stirred by lively appetites, we may assert with some assurance that to Hobbes the foundation of genius is passion. It is so with Dennis. It is not saying everything to state it thus briefly, but if one were seeking for the most concise possible definition, one could almost say that to Dennis genius is the capacity for great passion.[38] In *The Advancement and Reformation of Modern Poetry* Dennis states his definition succinctly. He here names three things which contribute to the perfection of poetry. The second of these is the rules, the use of which contributes to the raising of the passions; the third is the language of the country so used as adequately to convey the passions of the author. "The first is Nature, which is the foundation and basis of all. For Nature is the same thing with Genius, and Genius and Passion are all one. For Passion in a Poem is Genius, and the power of exciting Passion is Genius in a Poet; to the raising of which, Religion . . . gives a very great Advantage." [39] This is an idea to which Dennis, in one way or another, quite consistently adheres. It is necessary to add, of course, the corollary that genius is the capacity for great ideas — since lofty passions can come only from lofty thoughts.

As early as 1696, in his *Remarks upon "Prince Arthur,"* the

[37] *Leviathan*, I, viii.

[38] Like Hobbes, too, Dennis attributes the passions to egoism: "For all our Passions are grounded upon the Love of our selves," he remarks (*The Advancement and Reformation of Modern Poetry*, p. 68).   [39] *Ibid.*, p. 115.

Preface to which is largely a treatise on aesthetics, Dennis addresses himself to the task of explaining poetical genius. He promises much more than he fulfils, but his attempt is nonetheless weighted with suggestion:

> . . . and here I design'd to have inserted a Discourse concerning Poetical genius, of which no one that I know of has hitherto treated. I design'd to show that this extraordinary thing in Poetry which has been hitherto taken for something Supernatural and Divine, is nothing but a very common Passion, or a complication of common Passions. That felicity in writing has the same effect upon us that happiness in common Life has: That in Life when any thing lucky arrives to us, upon the first surprize we have a transport of Joy, which is immediately follow'd by an exaltation of mind: *Ut res nostræ sint ita nos magni atque humiles sumus;* and that both these, if the thing that happens be beyond expectation fortunate, are accompanied with astonishment: we are amazed at our own happiness: That the very same thing befalls us upon the conception of an extraordinary hint. The Soul is transported upon it, by the consciousness of its own excellence, and it is exalted, there being nothing so proper to work on its vanity; because it looks upon such a hint as a thing peculiar to it self, whereas what happens in Life to one Man, might as well have happen'd to another; and lastly, if the hint be very extraordinary, the Soul is amazed by the unexpected view of its own surpassing power.[40]

We readily perceive in this the influence of the naturalistic psychological approach. Dennis is at the outset disposing of the fallacy of divine fire from above. The inspired *vates* and seer becomes a man like other men, whose states of illumination and exaltation are to be regarded as demonstrable phenomena of the human mind and whose elevated expression is to be accounted for as a corollary to such mental states. Hobbes, it will be recalled, had condemned the idea of inspiration and professed to trace all extraordinary capacities to natural mental processes: to lively appetites, a quick fancy, a ready judgment, in general, to the mind's reactions to and use of experience.

Two pages later in the Preface Dennis essays a further definition of genius:

> . . . After that I had done this, I design'd to lay down this definition of genius, that it was the expression of a Furious Joy, or Pride or Astonishment, or all of them caused by the conception of an extraordinary hint.

---

[40] "The Preface," *Remarks upon "Prince Arthur"* (London, 1696), A2.

Then I intended to show, that a great many Men have extraordinary hints, without the foremention'd motions, because they want a degree of Fire sufficient to give their animal spirits a sudden and swift agitation. And these are call'd Cold-Writers. On the other side, if Men have a great deal of Fire and have not excellent Organs, they feel the foremention'd Motions in thinking without extraordinary hints. And these we call Fustian-Writers. When I had done this I intended to show that Mr. Blackmore had very seldom either the hints or the motions. In order to which I design'd to consider the several sorts of hints that might justly transport the Soul by a conscious view of its own excellency. And to divide them into hints of Thoughts and hints of Images. That the Thought which might justly cause these motions of Spirits were of three sorts, such as discover a greatness of Mind, or a reach of Soul, or an extent of Capacity. That Images were either of Sounds or of Things, that Images of Things were either Mighty or Vast ones.[41]

Here is further direct attempt to reduce the phenomena of aesthetic experience to the psychological plane. The Longinian idea of elevation and transport is present; but the method and the basis of this definition are to be found in Hobbes. Like Hobbes, Dennis is making the passions the mainspring of pleasure and productive effort. He is using Hobbes's term "joy" to express positive and vigorous operation of these passions, and his word "pride" appears to be a substitute for Hobbes's "glory," a legitimate self-esteem and sense of power, as opposed to the unreasonable imagining of power known as "Vaine-Glory." "Joy, arising from imagination of a man's own power and ability," declares Hobbes, "is that exultation of the mind which is called Glorying: which if grounded upon the experience of his own former actions, is the same with *Confidence:* but if grounded on the flattery of others, or onely supposed by himself, for delight in the consequence of it, is called Vaine-Glory." [42]

In later passages some of the ideas here only dimly adumbrated are more clearly set forth. The definition of genius as passion in *The Advancement and Reformation of Modern Poetry* (1701), quoted on page 233, is illustrative. In this same treatise Dennis further remarks (p. 66): "Everything that is great in Poetry must be great by the Genius that is felt in it, which

<hr/>

[41] *Ibid.*, A3–A4.   [42] *Leviathan,* I, vi.

is the chief thing in Poetry . . . . Now all Genius is Passion because it moves, and all Passion is either Enthusiasm or ordinary Passion."

It will be noted that in these definitions the term "passion" has supplanted the words "pride" and "joy" of the earlier treatise, though the meaning is virtually the same, with adaptations now to the more recently conceived premises of religion and "enthusiasm." Again, in the still later *Grounds of Criticism in Poetry* (1704), Dennis definitely clarifies the meaning he had evidently attached in the *Remarks* to such phrases as "extraordinary hints" and "furious joy," when, in an explanation of the inconsistency of Longinus in asserting that there may be sublimity without passion, he writes (p. 82): "The more the Soul is mov'd by the greatest Ideas, the more it conceives them, but the more it conceives of the greatest Ideas, the greater Opinion it must have of its own Capacity. By consequence the more it is mov'd by the Wonders of Religion the more it values it self upon its own Excellences. Again, the more the Soul sees its Excellences the more it Rejoyces." The cumulative cycle suggested here is, first emotion aroused by great ideas, secondly a heightened awareness of these ideas induced by emotion, thirdly an egotistic exultation over the possession of a soul that can feel and know so supremely. This, one may assume, is analogous to the "furious joy" from the "extraordinary hints" of the passage in the *Remarks*.

In the Preface to the *Remarks upon "Prince Arthur"* Dennis had listed three kinds of writers with respect to genius. The first have great ideas without great emotion, the second have great emotions without great ideas, the third have both great ideas and great emotions. The first are "cold writers," the second, "fustian writers," the third are men of genius. In *The Grounds of Criticism* Dennis has reduced his categories to two, which seem roughly to correspond to the fustian writer and the genius of the *Remarks*. Men are moved for two reasons, he says: either they have weak minds and souls, capable of being moved by little and ordinary things, or they have sufficient greatness of soul and capacity to feel and discern great ones. Dennis is here reasoning to the effect that religious ideas are the most proper ones for sublime poetry. But not all men are capable of perceiving the full significance of religious ideas. Only those who have the most comprehensive souls are able to apprehend the greatness of God and to feel the appropriate emotional response.[43] For,

the Enthusiastick Passions being caus'd by the Idea's, it follows, That the more the Soul is capable of receiving Idea's whose Objects are truly great and wonderful, the greater will the Enthusiasm be that is caus'd by those Idea's: From whence it follows, that the greater the Soul is, and the larger the Capacity, the more will it be mov'd by religious Idea's; which are not only great and wonderful, but which almost alone are great and wonderful to a great and wise Man.[44]

So we find that the highest poetical genius may belong only to the soul capable of experiencing the most exalted passions in contemplation of the most exalted ideas.[45]

---

[43] *The Grounds of Criticism in Poetry*, p. 21. This idea is quite eloquently expressed in a later passage: "Enthusiasm in Poetry is Wonderful and Divine, when it shows the Excellence of the Author's Discernment, and the largeness of his Soul; now all the Ideas of God are such, that the more large and comprehensive the Soul of a Poet is, and the more it is capable of Receiving those Idea's the more is it sure to be raised, and fill'd, and lifted to the Skies with Wonder" (*ibid.*, pp. 37–38).

[44] *Ibid.*, p. 21.

[45] Ideas of God and of the hierarchy of his angels are most suited to produce such emotions. But Dennis admits other causes for exalted passion: for instance, nature.

"The next Ideas that are most proper to produce the Enthusiasm of Admiration, are the great Phænomena of the Material World; because they too lead the Soul to its Maker, and shew, as the Apostle says, his Eternal Power and Godhead: As the Heavens and Heavenly Bodies, the Sun, the Moon, the Stars, and the Immensity of the Universe, and the Motions of the Heaven and Earth" (*ibid.*, p. 45).

In discussing Lucretius Dennis finds that a materialist can be sublime only by reflecting on the causes of great phenomena of nature:

"*Lucretius* is most Poetical and and [*sic*] Sublime where he is Religious. But where he is lofty in other places, we find him describing the great *Phænomena* of Nature, and the higher a man rises and the nearer he comes to the first infinite cause, the nearer he certainly comes to Religion. Besides, where *Lucretius* is lofty and Poetical in Describing the great *Phænomena* of of [*sic*] Nature, there we are sure to find him astonish'd for from whence comes his vehemence but from his astonishment, which may give us a Suspicion, that Lucretius was not so very assur'd of the truth of his opinion. For effects astonish no man. He who is astonish'd is moved deep for his comprehension" (*The Advancement and Reformation of Modern Poetry*, pp. 129–130).

But, as has been indicated, poetical genius implies a capacity for expressing and producing, as well as for experiencing passion. Dennis's expositions of this point come close to a pronouncement for spontaneity, and they are clearly a statement for a sort of organic writing. In the *Remarks upon "Prince Arthur,"* continuing his first definition of genius, Dennis writes:

> Now it is very certain that a Man in transport, and one that is lifted up with pride and astonish'd, expresses himself quite with another air, than one who is calm and serene. Joy in excess as well as rage is furious. And the pride of Soul is seen in the expression as well as in the mien and actions, and is the cause of that Elevation, which *Longinus* so much extolls, and which, he says, *is the image of the greatness of the mind.* Now it is certain that greatness of mind is nothing but pride well regulated. Now as Joy causes Fury, and pride elevation, so astonishment gives vehemence to the expression. [46]

The conception of style as born of emotion and thought recurs in even more decisive form in the later essays, where it appears as almost an integral part of Dennis's developed theory that poetry is the product of exalted passion. In *The Advancement and Reformation of Modern Poetry*, elaborating the idea that enthusiasm proceeds from great thoughts, that is meditation upon lofty images, Dennis at one point remarks: "But one thing we have omitted, that as thoughts produce the spirit, the spirit produces and makes the expression; which is known by experience to all who are Poets; for never any one, while he was wrapt with Enthusiasm, wanted either Words or Harmony; . . . the Expression conveys and shows the Spirit, and therefore must be produced by it." [47] At this point, in a new definition, Dennis places direct emphasis on expression as the hallmark of genius: "Poetical Genius in a Poem is the true expression of Ordinary or Enthusiastick Passion, proceeding from Ideas, to which it naturally belongs; and Poetical Genius in a Poet, is the power of expressing such Passion worthily and the sublime is a great thought exprest with the Enthusiasm that belongs to it . . . ." [48] In previous passages I have cited

---

[46] "The Preface," *Remarks upon "Prince Arthur,"* A3.
[47] *The Advancement and Reformation of Modern Poetry*, pp. 45–46.
[48] *Ibid.*, p. 46.

Dennis has identified genius with the capacity for great passion; now he is defining genius as the capacity for adequate expression of great passion. The two ideas are not inconsistent. Longinus had, quite correctly, made lofty conceptions and elevated expression natural corollaries. Our only quarrel with Dennis is that he seemed to forget the one when he talked of the other.

The power of expressing a passion "worthily" includes with Dennis, it should be remarked, the exercise of judgment. For all his fervid rhetoric when on his favorite subject of enthusiasm, Dennis in no sense forgets the necessity of judgment in art. Thus, very specifically, he writes: "Poetical Enthusiasm is a Passion guided by Judgment, whose cause is not comprehended by us . . . . That it ought to be guided by Judgment is indubitable. For otherwise it would be Madness, and not Poetical Passion." [49] Wherever he touches upon art and the rules — and the places where he does this are numerous — Dennis has in mind writing well ordered by judgment. Comparing Virgil with Lucan, Dennis praises Virgil for what he made of his subject — less great than Lucan's (in his *Pharsalia*) when he found it — through invention (imagination) and art (disposition and expression keeping with the rules). Virgil's art was commensurate with his genius and the magnitude of his subject; and therein lay his greatness: "For, tho 'tis by the Genius of a Writer, that is, by a Soul that has the power of expressing great Passions, whether ordinary or Enthusiastick, that we treat a Subject with Dignity equal to its greatness, yet 'tis Art that makes a Subject very great, and consequently gives occasion for a great Genius to shew it self." [50] Here the balance is tipped against spontaneity in favor of judgment in a work well disposed according to the rules of art.

Dennis's final view, we may assume, was that there should be a just proportion of enthusiastic passion and judgment in poetry. He would certainly agree with Hobbes that "without Steddinesse, and Direction to some End, a great Fancy is one kind of Madnesse," but he would also agree that without great passion there can be no poetry. For all his talk about art and

[49] *Ibid.*, p. 29.   [50] *Ibid.*, p. 64.

the rules, Dennis would not consistently put judgment above enthusiasm, any more than Hobbes would make judgment predominate over fancy. One of the most valuable accomplishments of Hobbes in aesthetics was to indicate a due balance between reason and fancy in poetry. He recognized the fact that fancy and emotional excitation must be chief, but steadily insisted on the restraining power of judgment. Dennis seeks a similar solution to this difficult problem, though his surcharged enthusiasm prevents the steadiness and direction to a single definite end in his own expressions on the matter that Hobbes would have praised.

Indeed, Dennis has a conception of a modern religious poetry in which there is achieved a complete reconciliation between the claims of enthusiasm (emotionalized imaginative contemplation) and reason. In the early history of man there was a complete harmony between the rational and the animal powers. "Man therefore constantly contemplated God, not so much by the force of Reason as of Intuition, or luminous lively Intelligence." [51] His happiness lay in the exercise of passions which were in agreement with these intuitions. Then came the Fall, and with it a wilful indulgence in unworthy passions which the reason could not approve. The original fine equilibrium between passion and reason was thus destroyed: "the Passions being natural and congenial to the Soul, could not be idle, and Man could not reduce them to their primitive object." [52] This discordance led not only to unhappiness, since there can be no pleasure outside the natural exercise of the passions under the approval of reason, but to a condition unfavorable to poetry. [53]

The Christian religion, however, bringing man again *en rapport* with deity, permits a reconciliation of reason and the passions, hence pleasure in the exercise of the passions. For this religion "exalts our Reason by exalting the Passions," and so restores the harmony of the human faculties. [54] Thus by in-

---

[51] *The Advancement and Reformation of Modern Poetry*, pp. 146–147.
[52] *Ibid.*, p. 150.
[53] *Ibid.*, pp. 154–155. Again recall Hobbes's insistence that active passions are essential to felicity.   [54] *Ibid.*, p. 159.

clining our affections to God we find desire and reason once more reconciled. Since the morality of the Christian religion is easily proved (by revelation), and when proved "is pursu'd with pleasure, because it is every part of it dictated by Love, the best and sweetest of the Passions," [55] reason and passion coöperate in producing the superlative reasonable passion requisite to move the modern genius to the highest poetry: "And as the Reason rouzes and excites the Passions, the Passions, as it were in a fiery vehicle, transport the Reason above Mortality, which mounting, soars to the Heaven of Heavens, upon the wings of those very affections that before repress'd the Noble Efforts that it made to ascend the Skies." [56] The greatest genius, then, we may infer, is one in whom is to be found this equilibrium (if equilibrium can be conceived in a state of emotional soaring to the skies) of reason and passion, and who is able to produce in his reader a similar state of balance. For to Dennis the best art has for its end a harmonious exercise of the human faculties: "So that that must be the best and noblest Art, which makes the best Provision at the same time for the satisfaction of all the Faculties, the Reason, the Passions, the Sences. But none of them provides in such a Soveraign manner as Poetry, for the satisfaction of the whole

[55] *Ibid.*, p. 163.
[56] *Ibid.*, p. 161. Despite the rhetoric of Dennis, and his limitation of such experience to the lofty ranges of religious subjects, reading this passage inevitably brings to mind Wordsworth's description of the generation of poetic substance through a reciprocal activity of thought and emotion. Well known as it is I quote it here for convenient reference:

"For all good poetry is the spontaneous overflow of powerful feelings: and though this be true, Poems to which any value can be attached were never produced on any variety of subjects but by a man who, being possessed of more than usual organic sensibility, had also thought long and deeply. For our continued influxes of feeling are modified and directed by our thoughts, which are indeed the representatives of all our past feelings; and, as by contemplating the relation of these general representatives to each other, we discover what is really important to men, so, by the repetition and continuance of this act, our feelings will be connected with important subjects, till at length, if we be originally possessed of much sensibility, such habits of mind will be produced, that, by obeying blindly and mechanically the impulses of those habits, we shall describe objects, and utter sentiments, of such nature, and in such connection with each other, that the understanding of the Reader must necessarily be in some degree enlightened, and his affections strengthened and purified."

man together." [57]   Thus it is that poetry, Dennis concludes, "by restoring the Harmony of the Human Faculties provides for the Happiness of Mankind, better than any other Human Invention whatever." [58]

It is instructive to find that Dennis at this point, though proceeding from quite different premises, has arrived at a conclusion similar in respects to that announced over a century later by Coleridge, when he declared in *Biographia Literaria*, Chapter XIV, that the poet "brings the whole soul of man into activity, with the subordination of its faculties to each other, according to their relative worth and dignity." Like Dennis, Coleridge finds that the poetic power reveals itself in a balance or reconciliation of opposite qualities: of the imagination with the will and understanding, of emotion with more than usual order, of judgment with enthusiasm profound or vehement. A great difference between the two is that, where Coleridge is building almost wholly from psychological principles, Dennis, working in a quasi-psychological mode, is seeking to reconcile neoclassic formalism with both the Hobbian mental philosophy and the newly discovered facts about poetry presented in the treatise of Longinus. It must be admitted, however, that he has achieved some very important implications for a definition of genius, hence for the mind of a poet and the ingredients that enter into poetic composition.

IV

Wherever Dennis discusses genius he is likely to touch upon the subject of poetic effects. The basis for his theory of effects is again a merging and adaptation of Longinian and Hobbian teaching. He constantly recommends the enthusiasm and transport of the *Peri Hupsous*, but his psychological explanations are in the Hobbes tradition. Hobbes's idea that felicity in life is to be had only in exercise of the passions seems to have made a strong appeal to Dennis. "For without Passion," he wrote, "there can be no Happiness, because there can be no

---

[57] *The Advancement and Reformation of Modern Poetry*, pp. 168–169.
[58] *Ibid.*, p. 171.

Pleasure."[59] And Dennis's interpretation of this principle for poetry was that pleasure lay in nothing less than in decisive, soul-shaking agitation.

In one of his interesting aesthetic digressions in the *Remarks upon "Prince Arthur,"* Dennis sets forth his fundamental principle for moving the mind through artistic representation:

> For the Mind does not care for dwelling too long upon an Object, but loves to pass from one thing to another; because such a Transition keeps it from languishing, and gives it more Agitation. Now Agitation only can give it Delight. For Agitation not only keeps it from mortifying Reflections, which it naturally has when it is not shaken, but gives it a Force which it had not before, and the Consciousness of its own Force delights it. Besides that every large incident gives fresh Surprize.[60]

"Agitation," with Dennis, is closely associated with the sense of novelty or surprise. Every incident in an epic poem must give a fresh surprise. "It is impossible," he asserts, "that any pleasure can be very great that is not at the same time surprizing. I speak of the Pleasures of the Mind.[61] Though what is said of them may be truly affirm'd of the rest too. If any one doubts of this, let him but have Patience till the next time that he is very much pleas'd, and upon Reflection he will be oblig'd to confess it."[62] Surprise in itself is not enough, however; it must be of a particular sort: "Now, that Surprize alone which is admirable, may be said to be proper to Epick Poetry. And Aristotle has formally declared, in the ninth Chapter of his Treatise of Poetry, that that Surprize is the

---

[59] *Ibid.*, p. 146.

[60] P. 145. It is to be noticed that this statement precedes both Addison's vigorous approbation of imagination and art as a foe to ennui, in his essay on the imagination (No. 411), and Du Bos's similar theory in his *Réflexions critiques sur la poësie et sur la peinture*, in 1719. Before Dennis, Rapin had said, in his *Reflections on Aristotle's Treatise of Poesie*, 1674, "some will have the end [of poetry] to be Delight, and that 'tis on this account it labours to move the Passions, all whose motions are delightful; because nothing is more sweet to the soul than agitation, it pleases itself in changing the Objects to satisfie the immensity of its desires" (vii, p. 141). Both Dennis and Addison may have been indebted to Rapin for suggestions here, but both, approaching the problem under the influence of the new psychology, went well beyond the French critic in elaborating the idea.

[61] Cf. Hobbes's phrases "Pleasures of the Mind" (*Leviathan*, I, vi), and "delight of the Mind" (*The Elements of Law*, I, vii, 9).

[62] *Remarks upon "Prince Arthur,"* p. 177.

most admirable, which flows from Incidents that spring from one another contrary to our Expectations." [63]   Dennis extends his principle of surprise, or novelty, to comedy, insisting that in every good comedy we are not only "diverted with the *Ridiculum*" but "we are entertained with Discoveries, which is very delightful." [64]   Modern comedy is superior to that of the ancients in that it has greater variety "both in the Incidents and in the Characters, and that variety must make it more delightful.   For a uniformity in this case takes away from the surprize, and without surprize the *Ridiculum* cannot subsist." [65]

Activity and pleasure are elsewhere explained as bearing a reciprocal relationship with passion as both a cause and a result in the process of their interaction.   In everything we do, Dennis asserts, "we are moved by Pleasure, which is Happiness."   Thus, as we may know from a little reflection, we are always incited by "some Passion or other, either to Action or to Contemplation"; but, conversely, "Passion is the result either of Action or Contemplation," and "as long as either of them please, and the more either of them please, the more they are attended with Passion." [66]   Dennis is here using "passion" in the dual sense, as Hobbes had done before him, of pleasure itself and of appetite, or desire created by a promise of good through pleasure.   This becomes clearer in the sentences that follow: "The satisfaction that we receive from Geometry it self comes from the joy of having found out Truth, and the desire of finding more.   And the satiety that seizes us upon too long a Lecture, proceeds from nothing but from the weariness of our Spirits, and consequently from the cessation or the decay of those two pleasing Passions." [67]   Thus we learn that pleasure itself is a condition to the activity which makes pleasure possible, since without original appetite (or passion) there is no incentive to activity; that in turn without activity there can be no pleasurable agitation, such as results from the discovery of new truth; and that when this circular

[63] *Remarks upon "Prince Arthur,"* p. 179.
[64] *The Advancement and Reformation of Modern Poetry*, p. 53.
[65] *Ibid.*, p. 52.
[66] *The Grounds of Criticism in Poetry*, pp. 10–11.
[67] *Ibid.*

process of mutual stimulation dies down the mind sinks into wearied apathy.

In the basic philosophy of pleasure which Dennis has here presented there is little or nothing not to be found in Hobbes, particularly in passages from Chapters VII and IX of *The Elements of Law* and Chapter VI of *Leviathan*. Here Hobbes had said that "As appetite is the beginning of animal motion toward something that pleaseth, so is the attaining thereof, the END of that motion"; [68] also that, "seeing all delight is appetite, and appetite presupposeth a farther end, there can be no contentment but in proceeding"; [69] that "Because curiosity is delight, therefore all novelty is so"; [70] that the "hope and expectation of future knowledge, is that passion which we commonly call ADMIRATION; and the same considered as appetite, is called CURIOSITY, which is appetite of knowledge." [71] He had also defined "CURIOSITY," which is "*Desire to know why and how*," as "Lust of the mind, . . . a perseverance of delight in the continuall and indefatigable generation of Knowledge"; [72] "Joy, from apprehension of novelty," as "ADMIRATION; proper to Man, because it excites the appetite of knowing the cause"; and "Joy, arising from imagination of a mans own power and ability," as "that exultation of the mind which is called Glorying." [73] Dennis has used his own language, but the logic and psychology are the logic and psychology of Hobbes. He is including the element of contemplation as a source of passion, but, as we have seen, this, too, is implicit in Hobbes.

A successful poem must then, according to Dennis, create agitation. To do this it must present incidents which are surprising and new. But novelty and sudden discoveries are not enough; it must also speak to the heart. Without the "pathetick" a poem is powerless to please. The greatest wit in the world, when he ceases to move the heart, is but "a Rhimer and not a Poet," for, in order to instruct, the poet must give all the delight that he can. To proceed with Dennis's own words:

[68] *The Elements of Law*, I, vii, 5.   [69] *Ibid.*, I, vii, 7.
[70] *Ibid.*, I, ix, 18.   [71] *Ibid.*   [72] *Leviathan*, I, vi.   [73] *Ibid.*

. . . Now nothing that is not pathetick in Poetry, can very much delight: For he who is very much pleas'd, is at the same time very much mov'd; and Poetical Genius, as we shall prove in another Place, is it self a Passion . . . . And it is for this reason, that Point and Conceit, and all that they call Wit, is to be for ever banish'd from true Poetry; because he who uses it, speaks to the Head alone. For nothing but what is simple and natural, can go to the Heart; and Nature (humanly speaking) can be touch'd by it self alone.

A Poet is so indispensably oblig'd to speak to the Heart, that the epick Poets have for that very reason, made Admiration their predominant Passion; because it is not so violent but that it may be lasting, and may be consequently diffus'd through the whole Poem. But as that Passion is not violent, it is not alone sufficient to give full Delight: For Admiration can only move and raise the Reader, whereas to give him the last pleasure, he must have the last Transport.[74]

Proceeding from such assumptions, Dennis ventures in his *Remarks* to analyze the sources of the "tender and terrible" in poetry. Such an excursion into the problem of the psychology of effects is the more interesting and instructive because it occurs in a treatise which has as its general design to show that Blackmore's failure in his *Prince Arthur* was to be traced to his ignorance of the rules as they had been laid down by Aristotle and were now interpreted once and for all by one Monsieur Le Bossu. It reveals the confusion that fell upon certain English critical minds when the new philosophy met neoclassic formalism in professions of friendly accord.

In *The Usefulness of the Stage* (1698) Dennis carries on his argument for passion as the source of delight, and for emotional agitation as the only cause of this passion. In language that must have sounded strange to Augustan ears, he proclaims the superiority of passion over reason in artistic works:

For reason may often afflict us, and make us miserable, by setting our impotence or our guilt before us; but that which it generally does, is the maintaining us in a languishing state of indifference, which perhaps is more remov'd from pleasure, than that is from affliction, and which may be said to be the ordinary state of men . . . .

Since nothing but pleasure can make us happy, it follows that to be very happy, we must be much pleas'd; and since nothing but passion

---

[74] *Remarks upon "Prince Arthur,"* pp. 186–187.

can please us, it follows that to be very much pleas'd we must be very much mov'd.[75]

Dennis goes even further: in the perfect future life reason will be a thing of the past; there will be only passion:

> And that very height and fulness of pleasure which we are promis'd in another life, must, we are told, proceed from passion, or something which resembles passion. At least no man has so much as pretended that it will be the result of Reason. For we shall then be deliver'd from these mortal Organs, and Reason shall then be no more. We shall then no more have occasion from premises to draw conclusions, and a long train of consequences; for, becoming all spirit and all knowledge, we shall see things as they are: We shall lead the glorious life of Angels, a life exalted above all reason, a life consisting of Extasie and Intelligence.
>
> Thus it is plain that the happiness both of this life and the other is owing to passion, and not to reason.[76]

To such an extent is Dennis able to go, in moments of enthusiasm, in the exaltation of passion as a source of pleasure.

Emphasis on passion and enthusiasm in response to poetry is prominent throughout the later *Advancement and Reformation of Modern Poetry* and *The Grounds of Criticism in Poetry.* Here again, in spite of the basic theory of these essays, that religious ideas are the source of the highest poetry and that such poetry is marked by a harmonious exercise of reason and passion, each reinforcing the other, Dennis seems at times to make the emotional quite submerge the rational elements. This appears in such passages as the following from *The Advancement and Reformation:*

> But these passions . . . are seldom so strong, as they are in those kind of thoughts which we call Images. For they being the very lively pictures of the things which they represent, set them, as it were before our very eyes. But Images are never so admirably drawn, as when they are drawn in motion; especially if the motion is violent. For the mind can never imagine violent motion, without being in a violent agitation it self; and the Imagination being fir'd with that agitation, sets the very things before our eyes; and consequently makes us have the same passions that we should have from the things themselves. For the warmer the Imagination, the more present the things are to us, of which we draw the Images,

---

[75] *The Usefulness of the Stage, To the Happiness of Mankind. To Government, and To Religion* (London, 1698), pp. 6–7. This again flavors strongly of Rapin. See note 60, p. 243.   [76] *Ibid.,* pp. 7–8.

and therefore when once the Imagination is so inflam'd as to get the better of the understanding, there is no difference between the Images and the things themselves; as we see, for example, in Fevers and Mad men.[77]

In *The Grounds of Criticism*, written three years later, this thought reappears in virtually the same form. Praising Homer and Virgil for their method of setting any absent or terrible object before our sight, Dennis points out that these great writers not only drew an "Image or Picture of it," but in order to present this image "so as to surprise and astonish the Soul," they drew it "in violent Action or Motion," and chose "Words and Numbers" which might best express this violence. Unless such action or motion is shown, Dennis reasons, the "Soul has leisure to reflect upon the Deceit";[78] moreover,

violent Motion can never be conceived without a violent agitation of Spirit, and that sudden agitation surprises the Soul and gives it less time to Reflect; and at the same time causes the Impressions that the Objects make to be so Deep, and their traces to be so profound, that it makes them in a manner as present to us as if they were really before us. For the Spirits being set in a violent emotion, and the Imagination being fir'd by that agitation; and the brain being deeply penetrated by those Impressions, the very Objects themselves are set as it were before us, and consequently we are sensible of the same Passion that we should feel from the things themselves.[79]

The warmer the imagination the less able we are to reflect, Dennis continues; "therefore when the Imagination is so inflam'd as to render the Soul utterly incapable of reflecting there is no difference between the Images and the things

[77] *The Advancement and Reformation of Modern Poetry*, pp. 32–33.
[78] *The Grounds of Criticism in Poetry*, pp. 90–91.
[79] *Ibid.*, pp. 91–92. These two passages reveal an instructive relationship between Dennis's conception of imaginative power and certain ideas advanced by Longinus, Cicero, Quintilian, and later by Hobbes. Imagination, they held, is the faculty for making and transmitting images. Writers achieve their supreme effects by ability to conceive and to set, as if before the very eyes of their readers, images of distant or past objects. A distinction between the observations of Dennis and those of Longinus and Quintilian, which at the same time identifies him with the Hobbian tradition, is the attempt to reduce the phenomena described to psychological explanation. Dennis is here making agitation a condition to imaginative activity, at the same time that he is saying, somewhat confusedly but perhaps not unpsychologically, that a quick imagination is requisite to agitation. Hobbes, it will be recalled, had admitted a good fancy only to those possessed of lively passions. Dennis, again like Hobbes, postulates novelty, or surprise, as a condition to intense emotional response.

themselves; as we may see for example by Men in Raging Feavours." [80]

There is only one possible justification for Dennis in his indulgence in the notoriously bad aesthetics of the conclusion of each of these passages. He was in both cases writing of the effect of sublimity in poetry depicting terrifying objects, and sublimity of this sort (if it is sublimity) is likely to be accompanied with little rationality. Even so, to admit, even tacitly, that good art reaches its culmination in complete deception, and to compare any sort of aesthetic experience with the delusions of fevers and madness seems inexcusably naïve. This view is, fortunately, inconsistent with Dennis's frequent assumption of a harmony of reason and passion in great poetry. It is likewise inconsistent with some of his more valid conclusions relative to aesthetic response.

Thus, speculating upon the phenomenon of pleasure in the ugly and terrible, Dennis notices that "those very Passions which plague and torment us in life, please us, nay transport us in Poetry." [81] His explanation of this paradox is illustrative of his penchant for analysis of causes. In such cases, he says, the reason is satisfied with the exact proportions and beautiful symmetry of the artistic presentation. The reason is also pleased with the "exact perpetual of Servance [sic] of Decorums," with perceiving itself "exalted by the exaltation of the Passions," and with seeing the passions confined to those bounds prescribed to them. Moreover, the "noble senses" are pleased not only with imagery but with the beauty and variety of the poet's numbers: "Nor is the Eye less satisfied than the Ear, For an Admirable Poet always Paints, and all his Pictures are always beautiful. Let the real objects be never so odious, let them be never so dreadful, yet he is sure to paint them Delightful." [82] Finally a realization though never so faint that this is all illusion contributes to our pleasure:

---

[80] *Ibid.*, pp. 92–93. Homer and Virgil were not satisfied to set the image before the eyes, and in violent motion, "but if their motions occasioned any Extraordinary Sounds that were terrifying; they so contriv'd their Numbers and Expressions, as that they might be sure to ring those sounds in the very Ears of their Readers" (*ibid.*).

[81] *The Advancement and Reformation of Modern Poetry*, p. 170.   [82] *Ibid.*, p. 171.

"For, tho sometimes a vigorous lively Imitation of Creatures that are in their Natures noxious, may be capable of giving us Terror, yet Nature by giving us a secret Intelligence that the Object is not real, can turn even that Tormenting Passion to pleasure." [83]

Let us add to this a remark which occurs in *The Grounds of Criticism in Poetry*, and we have a quite different description of aesthetic response from that suggested by the unreasoning confusion of representation with reality experienced in fevers and in madness: "and no Passion is attended with greater Joy than Enthusiastick Terrour, which proceeds from our reflecting that we are out of Danger at the very time that we see it before us." [84]   The illusion here implied suggests a willing and limited rather than an involuntary and irresponsible suspension of disbelief, with the rational self well in hand, ready to assume control at need.

The preceding explanation shows that to Dennis valid aesthetic effect implies both the delight of the senses — or imagination — and satisfaction of the reason: something of the same type of equilibrium between the rational and the emotional, we may assume, that is requisite for the production of the best poetry.   This point of view is far from an isolated one.   It represents, indeed, Dennis's accepted theory when he is really on guard.   Thus, arguing for the superiority of divine subjects, Dennis reaches the conclusion that "nothing is more certain than that the more the Sences are stirr'd, and the more the Reason at the same time is satisfied, the more strongly for the most part the Passions of Reasonable Creatures are mov'd." [85]   And he proposes to show that "true Divine poetry" can satisfy the reason more at the same time that it raises more passion, and entertains the senses, especially the eye,[86] more delightfully than pagan poetry.   Dennis's

---

[83] *The Advancement and Reformation of Modern Poetry*, p. 171.

[84] P. 86.   This recalls, of course, Hobbes's explanation of the pleasure to be had in seeing ships in distress at sea or armies in battle when the spectator is on shore or in a safe castle (*The Elements of Law*, I, ix, 9).

[85] *The Advancement and Reformation of Modern Poetry*, pp. 178–179.

[86] Dennis regards the eye as the most important of the senses in relation to imaginative effects.   This is expressed nowhere better than in a passage in *The*

thought is that contemplation of Christian subjects fills the mind with great ideas, which, exciting the imagination power-fully at the same time that they completely satisfy the rea-son, are presently converted into exalted imagery. Conveyed through the art of the poet, this imagery has in turn the ca-pacity of arousing imagery in the mind of the reader, thence ideas, and thence satisfaction of the reason, similar to that which had been originally experienced by the poet.

Comparing Christian and pagan poetry, Dennis finds that Milton's account of the Creation (Book VII) soars above any-thing in Virgil and Ovid. The cause is to be found not in Milton's greater genius nor in his greater art,[87] but in the fact that his Christian subject furnished nobler and more exalted ideas, hence nobler and more exalted images, than can be found in his pagan predecessors.[88] In a previous comparison Dennis had found the eighteenth Psalm finer than a given passage in Virgil because it better satisfies the reason, raises the passions more strongly, and entertains the senses the better: "the more amazing effects that we see of Divine displeasure, the more it answers our Idea of infinite wrath . . . David says, That the very Mountains seem'd to have a sense of the Indigna-tion of their Creator." [89] Such effects are conveyed through appeal to the imagination, "because all Reveal'd Religion whether true or pretended speaks to the Senses, brings the wonders of another World more home to us, and so makes the Passions which it Raises the greater." [90]

Advancement and Reformation of Modern Poetry in praise of Psalm 18: "How terribly is the Eye delighted here, which is a sence that the Poet ought chiefly to entertain; because it contributes more than any other to the exciting of strong Passion" (p. 186).

[87] "For it would be an easie matter to prove that none of the Moderns under-stood the Art of Heroick Poetry, who writ before *Bossu* took pains to unravel the Mystery" (*ibid.*, p. 201).

[88] *Ibid.*, pp. 201 ff.

[89] *Ibid.*, pp. 184–185. The harmonious relationship between the reason and passion and imagination is even more strongly put in a subsequent sentence: "And that which satisfies the Reason the more here [in Psalm 18], raises the Passion more strongly, and entertains the sences the better, because there are more, and more amazing effects of the Divine pleasure."

[90] *The Grounds of Criticism in Poetry*, p. 96.

Of the passage in Book VII of *Paradise Lost* beginning,

> The Earth was form'd but in the womb as yet,

Dennis declares, "What an Image is here?" [91]   Again quoting the passage beginning,

> The Earth obey'd, and strait
> Op'ning her fertile womb,

he exclaims:

> . . . What a number of admirable Images are here crowding upon one another? So natural and peculiar to the subject, that they would have been as absurd and extravagant in any other, as they are wonderfully just in this. And yet even in this subject nothing could have supply'd a Poet with them, but so Divine a Religion. So that at the same time that the eye is ravishingly entertain'd, Admiration is raised to a height, and the Reason is supremely satisfied. For are not these effects that are worthy of an infinite Cause? Can anything be more suprizingly strong than this energetick Image?

> > Now half appear'd
> The Tawny Lyon, pawing to get free
> His hinder parts, then springs as broke from bonds,
> And Rampant shakes his brinded Mane.

Is not the following one great and wonderful?

> > The Ounce,
> The Libbard and the Tyger, as the Moale,
> Rising, the Crumbling Earth about them threw
> In Hillocks.

And how admirable is the next?

> > The swift Stag from under ground
> Bore up his branching head.[92]

In such fashion Dennis asserts the power of imagery in poetry, and reaffirms his theory that the highest aesthetic effects are achieved when reason and the emotions are in harmonious accord. And in such fashion, it may also be remarked, he helps to establish in English criticism a method of attention to specific passages for their essential aesthetic quality, a method which was to be greatly advanced by Addison, who, likewise, even more than Dennis, was to show interest in imaginative effects secured through concrete pictorial presentation.

---

[91] *The Grounds of Criticism in Poetry*, p. 209.   [92] *Ibid.*, pp. 215–216.

V

The evidence presented in the preceding discussion reveals to what extent Dennis realized that any true explanation of poetry and genius can be made only through an analysis of relevant mental activities. His contention that the qualities of a literary work are to be traced to the content and state of the mind creating it has great significance for all who are concerned with the evolution of modern aesthetic theory. Precisely to the extent that he has made use of the scientific approach of Bacon, Descartes, Hobbes, and Locke, Dennis shows progress over Longinus, with whose ideas he so often began. In focussing attention upon the mind and its processes Dennis is again preceding Addison in the psychological approach in aesthetics, and is anticipating by half a century some of the achievements of eighteenth-century thinkers in defining the elusive quality of genius.

Altogether, we find in Dennis the most elaborate and, may we say, the most adequate attempt so far made to reduce the phenomena of poetic creation to a sound psychological basis. We have only to read the literally hundreds of vague references to genius and inspiration in Restoration and Augustan criticism, to realize how far Dennis has advanced beyond the current generalities. It is in the perception of the problem involved, and the seriousness of the attempt to solve it, that the value of such criticism often lies. There was, moreover, a core of sound truth in Dennis's theory. "All knowledge," Coleridge once said, "is a species of revelation," meaning not at all that such knowledge comes down like fire from above, but that when the mind through the imagination has isolated and focussed its relevant materials to a single point, new perceptions burst on the understanding like a flash of light from the sky. So Dennis would explain apparent inspiration: it is merely the mind at work under its natural laws, stretching itself, under the influence of emotional excitation to responses and performances that appear superhuman, yet which are such as under certain conditions might happen to anyone.

Nevertheless, for all Dennis accomplished, he did not

create a revolution in critical theory. The reasons are not difficult to find. We have already noticed that he was unfortunately inconsistent within his theories. That this inconsistency was more apparent than real, and that much of it was inherent in his attempt to bring two opposing modes of approach into harmony does not alter the fact that any first reading of Dennis is almost certain to leave the impression of a muddleheaded thinker who now emphasizes one thing, now another, and whose enthusiasms and reasoned arguments get sadly tangled. He reveals, moreover, even greater inconsistency in applying his theories in practical criticism. Thus, promising passages about genius, with their suggestion of a psychological approach, in the opening to the *Remarks upon "Prince Arthur"* prove but a deceptive preface to a barren formalistic critique devised in obvious emulation of Le Bossu. Dennis, unfortunately, had a mind that could discourse well in the abstract, but could easily forget its worthy maxims in practice. He came the nearest to successful application of his own original theories of passion and imaginative effects in his criticism of Milton. But even here he was unable to escape the shackles of the rules. Milton possessed to a high degree both original genius and the poetical art, including the "true use that ought to be made of Religion in Poetry"; yet of Milton's achievement in the latter respect the best Dennis will allow is that "he happen'd upon it," [93] and he is ever ready to point to Milton's lapses from true art.

Shakespeare gave Dennis infinite trouble in applying in practical criticism his principles of genius — according to rules. Addison, writing against rule-by-thumb critics, was to declare that "our inimitable Shakespeare is a Stumbling-block to the whole tribe of these rigid Criticks." [94] Dennis was more than a rule-by-thumb critic, but Shakespeare was nonetheless a stumbling block to him. The difference between his attitude

[93] "And ev'n of those rare ones who have apply'd themselves hardly one of the Moderns has known the true use that ought to be made of Religion in Poetry. Milton, indeed happen'd upon it, in his Paradise Lost, I say happen'd upon it, because he has err'd very widely from it in his Paradise Regain'd, as shall be shown in its proper place" (*The Grounds of Criticism in Poetry*, pp. 112–113).

[94] *The Spectator*, ed. by G. Gregory Smith (London, 1897), No. 592.

toward Shakespeare and that of Addison may roughly be taken as a measure of the advance Addison shows over Dennis in the psychological approach to criticism, and in the consequent subordination of the rules to effects. These little critics, Addison asserts, are ignorant of the fact that "1st., there is sometimes a greater Judgement shown in deviating from the Rules of Art, than in adhering to them; and 2dly, That there is more Beauty in the Works of a great Genius who is ignorant of all the Rules of Art, than in the Works of a little Genius, who not only knows, but scrupulously observes them." Who is there, challenges Addison, that would not rather read one of Shakespeare's plays, "where there is not a single Rule of the Stage observed, than any Production of a modern Critick, where there is not one of them violated?" [95]

Dennis definitely recognized the genius of Shakespeare, but he was profoundly troubled by his neglect of the rules. "*Shakespear* was one of the greatest Genius's that the World e'er saw for the Tragick Stage," [96] Dennis declares. Lacking the advantages of his successors, he nevertheless excelled them all in beauties, and what adds luster to his name is that these beauties were his own. He had natural judgment, a true talent for distinguishing character and raising the passions, his thoughts are usually noble and just, his imagery powerful, his expression harmonious, bold, and graceful. His faults are the faults of ignorance and the age in which he lived. Dennis's words to this effect are quite worth the quotation:

... One may say of him as they did of *Homer*, that he had none to imitate, and is himself inimitable. His Imaginations were often as just, as they were bold and strong. He had a natural Discretion which never cou'd have been taught him, and his Judgment was strong and penetrating. He seems to have wanted nothing but Time and Leisure for Thought, to have found out those Rules of which he appears so ignorant. His Characters are always drawn justly, exactly, graphically, except where he fail'd by not knowing History or the Poetical Art. He has for the most part more fairly distinguish'd them than any of his Successors have done, who have falsified them, or confounded them, by making Love the predominant

---

[95] *Ibid.*

[96] *Letters on the Genius and Writings of Shakespear*, in *Original Letters, Familiar, Moral and Critical* (London, 1721), II, 371.

Quality in all. He had so fine a Talent for touching the Passions, and they are so lively in him, and so truly in Nature, that they often touch us more without their due Preparations, than those of other Tragick Poets, who have all the Beauty of Design and all the Advantage of Incidents. His Master-Passion was Terror, which he has often mov'd so powerfully and so wonderfully, that we may justly conclude, that if he had had the Advantage of Art and Learning, he wou'd have surpass'd the very best and strongest of the Ancients. His Paintings are often so beautiful and so lively, so graceful and so powerful, especially where he uses them in order to move Terror; that there is nothing perhaps more accomplish'd in our *English* Poetry. His Sentiments for the most part in his best Tragedies, are noble, generous, easie and natural, and adapted to the Persons who use them. His Expression is in many Places good and pure after a hundred Years; simple tho elevated, graceful tho' bold, and easie tho' strong. He seems to have been the very Original of our *English* Tragical Harmony; that is the Harmony of Blank Verse, diversified often by Dissyllable and Trissyllable Terminations. For that Diversity distinguishes it from Heroick Harmony, and bringing it nearer to common Use, makes it more proper to gain Attention, and more fit for Action and Dialogue.   Such Verse we make when we are writing Prose; we make such Verse in common Conversation.[97]

There is a good deal of Dryden in this, particularly in the sentences about distinguishing the characters and raising the passions;[98] but Dennis is in general simply acknowledging how superbly Shakespeare fits into his pattern for genius.   With, however, one constant qualification: Shakespeare lacked the rules of art; hence perforce fell short of the highest requirements for genius.   Dennis's advances and withdrawals, as he alternately confesses to Shakespeare's genius and deplores his defects, bear eloquent testimony to his inability to effect a reconciliation between the psychological and the formalistic approaches in criticism:

If *Shakespear* had these great Qualities by Nature, what would he not have been, if he had join'd to so happy a Genius Learning and the Poetical Art. For want of the latter, our Author has sometimes made gross Mistakes in the Characters which he has drawn from History, against the Equality and Convenience of Manners of his Dramatical Persons.[99]

[97] *Letters on the Genius and Writings of Shakespear*, in *Original Letters, Familiar, Moral and Critical*, II, 372–373.
[98] See particularly *The Grounds of Criticism in Tragedy*, Ker, I, 217–221, 224, 226–228.
[99] *Letters on the Genius and Writings of Shakespear*, in *Original Letters, Familiar, Moral and Critical*, II, 373–374.

. . . But indeed Shakespear has been wanting in the exact Distribution of Poetical Justice, not only in his *Coriolanus*, but in most of his best Tragedies, in which the Guilty and the Innocent perish promiscuously; as *Duncan* and *Banquo* in *Mackbeth*, as likewise *Lady Macduffe* and her Children; *Desdemona* in *Othello; Cordelia, Kent,* and King *Lear,* in the Tragedy that bears his Name; *Brutus* and *Porcia* in *Julius Caesar* and Young *Hamlet* in the Tragedy of *Hamlet*.[100]

Thus have we endeavour'd to shew, that for want of the Poetical Art, *Shakespear* lay, under very great Disadvantages. At the same time we must own to his Honour, that he has often perform'd Wonders without it.[101]

Such criticism is neither flesh nor fowl. Dennis is plainly in a logical difficulty. His inability to take a firm position on the basis of reason and the rules, as did Rymer, or to ignore the rules in view of Shakespeare's inimitable power to produce effects, as Addison was to do, leaves him in a distinctly equivocal position, his conclusions uncertain, and his principles obscured.

A further evidence of weakness in Dennis is to be observed in his frequent failure to follow a line of thought through to a conclusion. His best ideas frequently fail to come to a head. In the first definition of genius in the *Remarks upon "Prince Arthur,"* in case, there is actually no word to show how a genius is to be distinguished from a non-genius; having described the manifestations, Dennis, eager to support Hobbes in denying inspiration, merely says that "whereas what happens in Life to one Man might as well have happen'd to another," and lets his case rest there. Wordsworth, writing on the same subject in words at times similar to those of Dennis, does better: "What is a Poet? . . . He is a man speaking to men: a man, it is true, endowed with more lively sensibility, more enthusiasm and tenderness, who has a greater knowledge of human nature, and a more comprehensive soul than are supposed to be common among mankind . . . . To these qualities he has added a disposition to be affected more than other men." The gap between Dennis's approximations and Wordsworth's lucid statement is obvious. Dennis no doubt meant to say that the poet is uniquely susceptible to the states

[100] *Ibid.*, p. 379.   [101] *Ibid.*, p. 380.

of mind he describes, and is thereby a genius. It is true that in a subsequent paragraph in the same essay he does point out that in the best writers there is a combination of "extraordinary hints" and "Furious Joy, or Pride or Astonishment"; and in later treatises, as we have seen, he quite definitely identifies genius with a capacity for great passion inspired by great conceptions. We can now put such statements together, and find in them significant materials for a definition of genius. But Dennis himself did not so unite them. He made many good starts, but few good finishes. Most of the best things he said came in isolated passages, as if in brilliant flashes of illumination rather than in sustained ratiocination.

His argument for the religious-sublime in *The Advancement and Reformation of Modern Poetry* and in *The Grounds of Criticism in Poetry* is his most consistent performance. And though his ideas on these points are not clearly developed, his emphasis on a balance of reason and passion and on imaginative quality in poetry, his attention to effects and the causes of effects, his recognition of the place of contemplation in generating poetic ideas and images, his general interest in the psychological bases for aesthetic phenomena, are all indications of a mind alert to vital problems in poetry, and have value not only for the partial solutions offered but for the suggestions they must have furnished to his readers, Addison for example, in speculations on the same problems. They show Dennis definitely in the Hobbian psychological tradition.

The attempt of Dennis to combine the aesthetic of Longinus with the materialistic psychology of Hobbes is interesting and significant: it shows clearly the diversity of the ingredients seething in the critical caldron of the day. But it is not a successful attempt. Dennis himself, haphazard logician though he was, must have seen the difficulty in accepting both Longinus and Hobbes. Hobbes and Longinus had, it is true, certain things in common. Both, for example, dignified the passions, Longinus in poetry, Hobbes both in poetry and in life. Yet they differed materially in their fundamental approach to the poetic problem. For, while it was true Longinus had explained the elevation of soul in the poet as an "image of greatness in the mind," he had also talked of this exaltation as "heaven-sent" and of the writers who displayed it as "super-human." Hobbes, with his naturalistic bias, could, of course, have none of this. Neither would Dennis. Dennis's way is to accept the Longinian theory of elevation and transport as requisite to the poet, but to substitute for any suggestion of the super-natural an explanation based on Hobbes's psychology, ascrib-ing this state to a natural operation of the mind. The result is at best an unsatisfactory compromise. An even more pro-nounced compromise marks the attempt to bring a method of psychological inquiry into accord with accepted neoclassical dogma. Dennis is still inclined to side with those neoclassic critics who refuse to recognize the merits of a work until they have ascertained that it conforms to the dictates of traditional theory; he has not yet reached the stage represented by Addi-son and Samuel Johnson, and oftentimes by Dryden, who refused to accept dogma if it conflicted with their own instinctive feeling for what was good. Even so he made some advances toward liberating himself and his age through a freshly ra-tionalized aesthetic of creation and emotional response. And though he did not wholly succeed, he must be praised for his effort, and even more for the occasional flashes of light by which he helped mark the way for some of his more fortunate successors.

CHAPTER IX

Evidences of Hobbes's Influence on Cowley and Others

I

WITHOUT assuming to trace with anything like completeness the influence of Hobbes I wish before leaving the subject to note a few additional examples of acceptance of his ideas in seventeenth-century aesthetics. Of the names to be mentioned perhaps that of Cowley deserves most prominence. Cowley's favorable response to the new philosophy led him to enthusiastic encomiums upon Bacon and Hobbes and eventuated in the notable pamphlet *A Proposition for the Advancement of Experimental Philosophy*, 1661, which is usually regarded as having furnished the immediate impulse for the formation of the Royal Society. His attitude here is related to a general scorn for and independence of the scholastic and ancient philosophies, and to a frequent advocacy of nature as the source of truth. His acceptance of definite principles is further witnessed by his adoption of certain terminology from Hobbes and by the fact that in his declining years he spent much labor on his remarkable *Six Books of Plants*, in which he turned his attention from fancied mistresses and other conventional subjects to the affectionate poetic delineation of growing things in the out-of-doors world.

The most obvious evidence of Cowley's reception of Hobbes is to be found in the notable "To Mr. Hobs," published in the *Pindarique Odes* in 1656. Here Cowley exalts Hobbes as one who, after the old regions occupied by Aristotle and the Scholastics had proved barren, had both discovered and cultivated into glorious fruitfulness the golden lands of the new philosophy. He is in part indulging youthful enthusiasm no doubt, but he is also revealing an attitude that is highly significant. The best comment upon this poem is the poem itself:

To Mr. Hobs

1

Vast *Bodies* of *Philosophie*
I oft have seen, and read,
But all are *Bodies Dead*,
  Or *Bodies* by *Art fashioned;*
I never yet the *Living Soul* could see,
    But in thy *Books* and *Thee.*
  'Tis onely *God* can know
Whether the fair *Idea* thou dost show
Agree intirely with his *own* or no.
    This I dare boldly tell,
'Tis so *like Truth* 'twill serve our turn as well.
Just, as in *Nature* thy *Proportions* be,
As full of *Concord* their *Varietie,*
As *firm* the parts upon their *Center* rest,
And all so *Solid* are that they at least
As much as *Nature, Emptiness detest.*

2

Long did the mighty *Stagirite* retain
The *universal Intellectual reign,*
Saw his own Countries short-lived *Leopard* slain;
The stronger *Roman-Eagle* did out-fly
Oftner *renewed* his *Age,* and saw that *Dy.*
Mecha it self, in spite of *Mahumet* possest,
And chas'ed by a wild *Deluge* from the *East,*
His *Monarchy* new planted in the *West.*
But as in time each great imperial race
Degenerates, and gives some new one place:
    So did this noble *Empire* wast,
    Sunk by degrees from glories past,
And in the *School-mens* hands it perisht quite at last.
    Then nought but *Words it grew,*
    And those all *Barba'rous* too.
  It *perisht,* and it *vanisht* there,
The *Life* and *Soul* breath'd out, became but empty *Air.*

3

The *Fields* which answer'd well the *Ancients Plow*,
Spent and out-worn return no *Harvest* now,
In barren *Age* wild and unglorious lie,
    And boast of *past Fertility*,
The *poor relief* of *Present Poverty*.
    Food and *Fruit* we now must want
    Unless new *Lands* we *plant*.
We break up *Tombs* with *Sacrilegious hands;*
    Old *Rubbish* we remove;
To walk in *Ruines*, like vain *Ghosts*, we love,
    And with fond *Divining Wands*
      We search among the *Dead*
      For Treasures *Buried*,
    Whilst still the *Liberal Earth* does hold
So many *Virgin Mines* of *undiscover'ed Gold*.

4

The *Baltique*, *Euxin*, and the *Caspian*,
And slender-limb'ed *Mediterrean*,
Seem narrow *Creeks* to *Thee*, and only fit
For the poor wretched *Fisher-boats* of *Wit*.
Thy nobler *Vessel* the vast *Ocean* tries,
    And nothing sees but *Seas* and *Skies*,
    Till unknown *Regions* it descries,
Thou great *Columbus* of the *Golden Lands* of *new Philosophies*.
    Thy task was harder much than his,
    For thy learn'd *America* is
    Not only found out first by Thee,
And rudely left to *Future Industrie*,
    But thy *Eloquence* and thy *Wit*,
Has *planted*, *peopled*, *built*, and *civiliz'd* it.

5

    I little thought before,
    (Nor being my *own self* so *poor*
    Could comprehend so vast a *store*)
That all the *Wardrobe* of rich *Eloquence*,
    Could have afforded half enuff,
    Of *bright*, of *new*, and *lasting* stuff,
To cloath the mighty *Limbs* of thy *Gigantique Sence*.
Thy solid *Reason* like the *shield* from heaven
    To the *Trojan Heroe* given,
Too strong to take a mark from any mortal dart,
Yet shines with *Gold* and *Gems* in every part,

And *Wonders* on it grav'd by the learn'd hand of *Art*,
    A *shield* that gives delight
    Even to the *enemies* sight,
Then when they're sure to *lose* the *Combat by't*.

6

Nor can the *Snow* which now cold *Age* does shed
    Upon thy reverend Head,
Quench or allay the noble *Fires* within,
    But all which thou hast *bin*,
    And all that *Youth* can *be* thou'rt yet,
    So fully still dost Thou
Enjoy the *Manhood*, and the *Bloom* of *Wit*,
And all the *Natural Heat*, but not the *Feaver* too.
So *Contraries* on *Aetna's* top conspire,
Here hoary *Frosts*, and by them breaks out *Fire*.
A secure *peace* the *faithful Neighbors* keep,
Th'emboldned *Snow* next to the *Flame* does *sleep*.
    And if we weigh, like *Thee*,
    Nature, and *Causes*, we shall see
    That thus it *needs must be*,
To things *Immortal Time* can do no wrong,
And that which never is *to Dye*, for ever must be *Young*.[1]

As an addendum to this splendid — perhaps somewhat
extravagant — encomium, Cowley offers, in the form of a
footnote to Stanza 5, a still more explicit statement of his
position: "The meaning is, that his *Notions* are so *New*, and
so *Great*, that I did not think it had been possible to have
found out *words* to express them clearly; as no *Wardrobe* can
furnish *Cloaths* to fit a *Body* taller and bigger than ever any was
before, for the *Cloaths* were made according to some *Measure*
that then was."

After this one might well expect in Cowley almost any
kind and degree of obeisance to the ideas of Hobbes. The
evidence, though convincing, is not, however, always as easy
to detect as one might suppose. The problem is further complicated by the fact that Cowley admired Bacon with a fervor
almost equal to that which he accorded Hobbes. "To the
Royal Society" (1663) contains what is probably the most ful-

---

[1] *Pindarique Odes* (1656), in *The Works of Mr. Abraham Cowley* (London, 1693),
pp. 26–28.

some eulogy of Bacon ever written. Hobbes must share with
Bacon first place in turning the attention of Cowley to the
riches of the new philosophy. When he thought of experimental science, indeed, it seems to have been Bacon more than
Hobbes who was in Cowley's mind. From both he learned
his skepticism of the old philosophic systems, which, having
degenerated through the centuries,

> Sunk by degrees from glories past,
> And in the *School-mens* hands it perisht quite at last.

In "To Mr. Hobs" Cowley gives the Malmesbury philosopher
full credit for rescuing the world from the barren wastes of
outmoded thought and for leading it to a new land which his
wit had *"planted, peopled, built,* and *civiliz'd."* But in "To
the Royal Society" it is Bacon, among the "few exalted Spirits
this latter Age has shown," who deserves the palm for putting
to rout the authority of the Schools:

> Autority, which did a body boast,
> Though 'twas but Air condens'd, and
>   stalk'd about;
> Like some old Giant's more Gigantick Ghost,
>   To terrifie the learned Rout
> With the plain Magick of true Reasons Light,
> He chac'd out of our sight,
> Nor suffer'd Living *Men* to be misled
> By the vain shadows of the Dead.[2]

It is possible that in the intervening years between the writing
of the ode to Hobbes and the address to the Royal Society [3]
Cowley, in view of attacks discrediting some of Hobbes's
scientific speculations and imputing atheism to his teachings,
had grown cautious in voicing his enthusiasm for his erstwhile
master in philosophy, or it may be that later reading had
converted him to the belief that Bacon, not Hobbes, merited
credit for the victory of modern over ancient thought; whatever the reason, Cowley now assigns to Bacon achievements
for which he had formerly praised Hobbes:

---

[2] "To the Royal Society," Stanza 3. The text is from *Verses Written on Several
Occasions,* in the 1669 edition of the *Works.*
[3] "To the Royal Society" was finished in 1667.

> From Words, which are but Pictures of the Thought,
> . . . .
> To things, the Mind's right Object, he it brought,
> Like foolish Birds to painted Grapes we flew;
> He sought and gather'd for our use the True.[4]

And again:

> In Desarts but of small extent,
> Bacon, like *Moses*, led us forth at last,
> The barren Wilderness he past
> Did on the very Border stand
> Of the bless'd promis'd Land,
> And from the Mountains Top of his Exalted Wit,
> Saw it himself, and shew'd us it.[5]

The figure for discovery in "To Mr. Hobs" was Columbus, and the new land of philosophy was America. The terms of the comparison are changed, the idea remains the same. It is not easy to disentangle, then, in Cowley, the influence of Hobbes from that of Bacon. This is particularly true where Cowley expresses a general attitude of independence of traditional authority or of preference for truth to be had from first-hand acquaintance with nature. The championship of Harvey is a case in point. Harvey is extolled for his courage, his willingness to stand alone, his determination to look for truth in God's own creation rather than in men's ideas of it:

> Thus *Harvey* sought for Truth in Truth's own Book
> The Creatures, which by God himself was writ;
>   And wisely thought 'twas fit,
> Not to read Comments only upon it,
> But on th'Original it self to look.
> Methinks in Arts great Circle others stand
>   Lock't up together, hand in hand,
>   Every one leads as he is led,
>   The same bare path they tread,
> A Dance like Fairies a Fantastick round,
> But neither change their motion, nor their ground:
> Had *Harvey* to this Road confin'd his wit,
> His noble Circle of the Blood, had been untrodden yet.

---

[4] "To the Royal Society," Stanza 4.
[5] *Ibid.*, Stanza 5.

> Great Doctor! Th'Art of Curing's cur'd by thee,
>   We now thy patient Physick see,
> From all inveterate diseases free
>   Purg'd of old errors by thy care,
> New dieted, put forth to clearer air,
>   It now will strong and healthful prove,
> Itself before Lethargick lay, and could not move.[6]

This, however, is not aesthetics. In aesthetic matters it is likely to be Hobbes rather than Bacon that appears in Cowley. The evidence is, as I have said, sometimes obscure. His use of relevant terms is far from exactly analogous to Hobbes's own; it is at times nevertheless such as to suggest that it would have been different had it not been for Hobbes. And when he praises Davenant for following nature by bringing "Men and Manners" into his poem, we recognize an undeniable echo of Hobbes. Cowley, indeed, seems to have followed Hobbes, and even to have gone beyond him, in a theory of nature as the subject of poetry.

The terms "reason," "judgment," "fancy," and "wit" occur frequently in Cowley's writings. In his "Reason" (*Miscellanies*, 1656), he vigorously condemns reliance on visions and inspiration and the practice of setting fancies above reason.

> In vain, alas, these outward Hopes are try'd;
>   *Reason* within's our only *Guide*
> *Reason*, which (God be prais'd!) still *Walks*, for all
>   It's old Original *Fall*.

The disparagement of inspiration is reminiscent of Hobbes. Cowley is writing of religion, not poetry, and he at this point gives reason a more important place with relation to fancy than is his wont. For Cowley, like Hobbes, shows himself generally tolerant of fancy in poetry. Thus in "To Sir William Davenant" he appears to identify fancy with wit in its better sense. In Davenant's verse he declares eulogistically, "ancient *Rome* may blush . . . to see her *Wit* o'recome." Davenant's superiority appears in his original fancy:

[6] "Ode upon Dr. Harvey," Stanza 4, in *Verses Written on Several Occasions*, ed. cit., p. 13.

> Some men their *Fancies* like their *Faith* derive
> And think all ill but that which *Rome* does give.

Davenant, however, has not only found his own paths but has made new ones for others to follow:

> Since Time does all things change, thou think'st not fit
> This latter *Age* should see *all New but Wit.*
> Thy *Fancy* like a *Flame* its way does make,
> And leave bright *Tracks* for following pens to take.[7]

Here, twice within a few lines, fancy and wit are used as virtual equivalents, and each has to do with the inventive powers and activities of the poet. Hobbes, it will be recalled, had said in *Leviathan* that by a *"Good Wit* . . . in this occasion, is meant a *Good Fancy,"* [8] and in *The Answer to Davenant* had made fancy the primary agent in poetic creation.

Hobbes had, indeed, always insisted on judgment. Cowley, too, celebrates judgment, though not with the consistency nor yet with the same specific discrimination in its relationships that we find in Hobbes. In the Preface to *Miscellanies* (1656), Cowley names judgment with fertility of invention, wisdom of disposition, and proper numbers as the requisites to either a profane or a divine poem.[9] Elsewhere he praises the judicious hand of Bacon in all that he writes; [10] he speaks of the judgment and wit in the harmoniously blended nature of Brutus; [11] and, as we shall presently see, makes judgment one of the steeds which in "The Muse" draw the chariot of poesy.

Cowley often uses wit, in a common seventeenth-century sense, as a general term to denote an active intellect, as in "To Mr. Falkland" (*Miscellanies*) and "To Mr. Hobs" (*Pindarique Odes*). In Stanza 4 of the latter poem we find, for example, such lines as,

> But thy *Eloquence* and thy *Wit*,
> Has *planted, peopled, built,* and *civiliz'd* it.

---

[7] *Miscellanies,* in *The Works of Mr. Abraham Cowley* (London, 1693), p. 25.
[8] *Leviathan,* ed. by Ernest Rhys (London, Toronto, and New York, 1914), I, viii.
[9] "Memorial Introduction," Appendix C, in *The Complete Works in Verse and Prose of Abraham Cowley,* ed. by A. B. Grosart (Edinburgh, 1881), I, cxxxi.
[10] "To the Royal Society," Stanza 9, *Verses Written on Several Occasions,* ed. cit., p. 42.   [11] "Brutus," Stanza 5, *Pindarique Odes,* ed. cit., p. 34.

Again Cowley bids Hobbes enjoy the manhood and the bloom, but not the fever, of wit (Stanza 6). But on occasion, again in accord with a popular use of his day, he makes wit an equivalent for conceits, striking similitudes, or general glitter of expression. This is his meaning in the lines in "Of Wit," when, severely condemning wit in the sense in which he is momentarily using it, he declares,

> *Jewels* at *Nose* and *Lips* but ill appear;
> Rather than *all things Wit*, let none be there.[12]

He uses the term in a more specifically Hobbian sense, however, when in this same ode "Of Wit" he seems to regard true wit as the sum of imaginative activities. Wit is not a tale nor a jest, it is not mere verse nor adornment; nor is it a bold similitude, nor an anagram nor acrostic, nor clever ribaldry, nor empty bombast. Rather, in it,

> All ev'ry where, like *Mans*, must be the *Soul*,
> And *Reason* the *Inferior Powers* controul.[13]

> In a true piece of *Wit* all things must be,
>   Yet all things there *agree*.
> As in the *Ark*, joyn'd without force or strife,
> All *Creatures* dwelt; all *Creatures* that had Life.[14]

Cowley here leaves the "all things" which must be present and must agree without specific designation. What these "all things" are may perhaps be inferred from the enumeration in "The Muse" of elements operative in a work of poetry. In this poem the spirit of poetry is apostrophized as a glorious queen who takes the air in a chariot to which are "harnest," ready for the "winged race," a diversified team of "unruly phansie," "strong Judgment," "nimble-footed Wit," [15] "smooth-pac'd Eloquence," "sound Memory," and "young Invention." The postilion is "Nature" and the coachman "Art." Alongside runs a footman who seems to represent rhetoric and incidental

---

[12] "Ode. Of Wit," Stanza 5, *Miscellanies*, ed. cit., p. 3.
[13] *Ibid.*, Stanza 4, p. 3.   [14] *Ibid.*, Stanza 8, p. 4.
[15] Cowley is, at this point, obviously using "wit" in one of his narrower designations — as ingenuity of phrase perhaps — in lieu of his larger meaning, a harmonious unity of the various factors that must coöperate in art.

invention. When all is ready the queen mounts her airy throne
and is away, to explore, in smooth, harmonious motion, the
ethereal spaces of the realms of art:

> Where never *Foot* of *Man*, or *Hoof* of *Beast*,
>   The passage prest,
>   Where never *Fish* did *fly*,
> And with short silver *wings* cut the low liquid *Sky*.
>   Where *Bird* with painted *Oars* did nere
> *Row* through the trackless *Ocean* of the *Air*.
>   Where never yet did pry
>   The busie *Mornings* curious *Ey*:
> The *Wheels* of thy bold *Coach* pass quick and free;
>   And all's an *open Road* to *Thee*.
>   Whatever *God* did *Say*,
> Is all thy plain and smooth, uninterrupted *way*.
> Nay ev'n beyond his *works* thy *Voyages* are known,
>   Thou'hast thousand *worlds* too of thine *own*.
> Thou speakst, great *Queen*, in the same *stile as He*,
> And a *New world* leaps forth when *Thou* say'st *Let it Be*.[16]

Here is metaphoric exposition of the boldness, and elevation, and enthusiasm, and withal the freedom, of poetic genius
— one should also add of its omniscience and its omnipotence.
The instruments of its achievements, let us recall, are fancy,
judgment, wit,[17] memory, invention, and eloquence. By representing fancy, judgment, memory, and all as working in
harmonious activity in poetic creation Cowley is revealing a
conception of poetry as a product of the whole mind of man
that is very near Hobbes's own, and one, incidentally, that
would have been difficult to find outside of Hobbes.

For the rest, it must be admitted that "Of Wit" and "The
Muse" are not very Hobbes-like. It is true that the picture
of the excursions of the queen of poetry into all known things
of the earth is in part reminiscent of Hobbes's description of
fancy as seeming to fly from "one Indies to the other," to search
out materials for poetic construction, but there is in Cowley
no explicit indication as in Hobbes that the airy realm traversed
by the well-attended muse is within the mind of the poet

---

[16] "The Muse," Stanza 2, *Pindarique Odes*, ed. cit., p. 23.

[17] Cowley has here again slipped into the narrower, more conventional use
of wit, as adornment or whatnot, in contrast with his larger conception of it as
that in which "all things must be."

himself, the internal world of stored experience. Moreover, though he names judgment and art, Cowley is less severe
than Hobbes in limitation to the probabilities, at the same
time that he gives more latitude for fanciful creation.

On this issue Cowley is nearer to Hobbes when, in the
Preface of 1656, he virtually repeats Hobbes's qualifying statement about probability in *The Answer to Davenant*. Cowley
is speaking for new themes and characters in poetry as opposed
to continued repetition of the old. The flavor is gone from
these old dishes, he says: "They are but the Cold-meats of
the Antients, new-heated and new set forth." Even so we must
recall in extenuation that "though those mad stories of the
Gods and *Heroes* seem in themselves so ridiculous, yet they were
then the *Whole Body* . . . of the *Theologie* of those times. They
were believed by all but a few *Philosophers* and perhaps some
Atheists . . . ." [18] Cowley's argument is against copying the
ancients whose beliefs we no longer share; in the passage in
which the original of this idea occurred Hobbes was making
a case for such deference to the probabilities as never to go
beyond the "conceived possibilities of nature." The similarity
is nonetheless striking.

Elsewhere, speaking more emphatically against the traditional machinery of epic, Cowley shows that he has in mind
this closer adherence to nature advocated by Hobbes. In
"To Sir William Davenant" [19] he praises Davenant for finding
the true way of writing epic poetry and so marking a new
track for others. For the gods, devils, nymphs, witches, and
giants of the old epic Davenant has substituted "Men and
Manners"; he deserves thanks for giving men the work of a
"Poet's Fury" rather than that of a "*Zelot's Spirit*," that is,
for products of wit and fancy, rather than of inspiration. He
has raised up human emperors and real empires, representing
them as better than their originals, yet the same:

> So *God-like Poets* do past things reherse
> Not *change*, but *Heighten* Nature by their Verse.

---

[18] *Works* (Grosart ed.), p. cxxx. See pp. 159–160 of this book for Hobbes's
remark and the evidence for the adoption of his idea by Dryden and Addison.
[19] *Miscellanies*, ed. cit., pp. 24–25.

The general trend of this argument is in accord with Hobbes's emphasis on the known world as a subject for the poet's study. Cowley is following the Hobbes-inspired Davenant in renouncing the fabled impossibilities of the ancient epics in favor of the realities, and his commendation of the "Men and Manners" with which Davenant deals specifically recalls Hobbes's statement that the proper subject of poetry is the "manners of men." [20]

II

In a number of other critics of the last half of the seventeenth century it is possible to find evidence of Hobbes's thought, particularly in conceptions of wit, fancy, and judgment and of truth to nature, verisimilitude, and style. It must be admitted that definite relationship, even where the reader quite certainly detects Hobbian intonation, is sometimes difficult to prove. The influences that entered into the critical thought of the period are many and varied, and to say with assurance that this element came from Hobbes, that from Descartes, another from Aristotle, Bacon, or the French critics is hazardous, often unscholarly. Even so, I venture in the following pages to indicate traces of Hobbian theory in the writings of such minor figures of the time as Flecknoe, Shadwell, Sprat, and Tate, critics who were individually of small importance perhaps, yet who collectively contributed much to the sum of the thought of their generation. In some cases the evidence I shall offer seems definite, in others it is, admittedly, slight and tenuous.

An instance of the tenuous sort is to be found in Richard Flecknoe's *A Short Discourse of the English Stage*. Comparing Jonson with Fletcher, Flecknoe finds that the difference in them is between wit and judgment, Fletcher displaying wit,

---

[20] *The Answer to Davenant*, in *Critical Essays of the Seventeenth Century*, ed. by J. E. Spingarn (Oxford, 1908), II, 56. In "On the Death of Sir Henry Wotton" (*Miscellanies*, ed. cit.) Cowley uses the same phrase in a similar commendatory sense:

"In whatever land he chanc'd to come,
He read the Men and Manners, bringing home
Their *Wisdom*, Learning, and their Pietie."

Jonson judgment: "Wit being an exuberant thing, like *Nilus*, never more commendable than when it overflowes; but Judgement, a stayed and reposed thing, always containing it self within its bounds and limits." [21]   Beaumont and Fletcher, though excellent in their kind, often sinned against decorum, Flecknoe points out:

. . . Besides, *Fletcher* was the first who introduc't that witty obscenity in his Playes, which like poison infused in pleasant liquor is always the more dangerous the more delightful. And here to speak a word or two of Wit, it is the spirit and quintessence of speech, extracted out of the substance of the thing we speak of, having nothing of the superfice, or dross of words, as clenches, quibbles, gingles, and such like trifles have: it is that, in pleasant and facetious discourse, as Eloquence is in grave and serious, not learnt by Art and Precept, but Nature and Company. 'Tis in vain to say any more of it; for if I could tell you what it were, it would not be what it is; being somewhat above expression, and such a volatil thing, as 'tis altogether as volatil to describe. [22]

Flecknoe has set wit against judgment, implying the same desirability of a balance of the two that we find in Hobbes's treatment of fancy and judgment.   Flecknoe's definition of wit is not Hobbian, however: the witty "obscenity" of Fletcher is rather of the Restoration order.   Yet, even here there is a suggestion of Hobbes in that part of the definition which declares wit to be "extracted out of the substance of the thing we speak of," with nothing of the superficialities "or dross of words, as clenches, quibbles, gingles . . . have."   For Hobbes had required that acceptable language should be drawn from its subject, and in *Leviathan*, I, viii, he had used the word "gingles" in condemning equivocal significations and unseemly play with sound. [23]

---

[21] *A Short Discourse of the English Stage* (appended to *Love's Kingdom* [1664]), Spingarn, II, 94.

[22] *Ibid.* Flecknoe's similarity to Hobbes in his distinction between wit and judgment and in his ascription of functions to each has been pointed out by Ustick and Hudson ("Wit, 'Mixt Wit,' and the Bee in Amber," *The Huntington Library Bulletin*, No. 8 [1935], p. 112).

[23] Ustick and Hudson (*op. cit.*, p. 112) have quoted from Flecknoe's "Of Wit," in *A Farrago of Several Pieces* (1666), a passage which, as these authors point out, is "prophetic of Coleridge's and Shelley's idea of the imagination as a spiritualizing force." Yet it, too, contains phrases — those about the soaring and elevated

A more obvious instance of borrowing from Hobbes is to be found in Robert Boyle's *Occasional Reflections* (1665). Hobbes's definition in *Leviathan*, I, viii, of natural wit as *"Celerity of* Imagining (that is swift succession of one thought to another)" and his further statement that those who have this virtue "will be easily fitted with similitudes, that will please" not only by illustrating their discourse and adorning it with "new and apt metaphors, but also by the rarity of their invention," finds echo in Boyle's characterization of wit as "that nimble and acceptable faculty of the mind, whereby some Men have a readiness and subtilty in conceiving things, and a quickness and neatness, in expressing them." [24] To Boyle the virtue of quickness and neatness in expression includes the ability of a writer so to exercise his invention as to "surprise his hearers . . . one of the most endearing circumstances of the productions of wits," and to coin "various and new expressions" to suit a "variety of unfamiliar subjects." Surprise should not be purchased at the expense of naturalness, however; for that expression, no matter how novel and elaborate, is best which is derived "from the very nature of the thing" of which the writer speaks.[25] Boyle may be making a concession to rare expression in dealing with the unfamiliar that Hobbes would not grant, but otherwise he is in accord with the general tenor of *Leviathan*, I, viii, and with the passage in *The Answer to Davenant* in which Hobbes advocates, in the drawing of varied and novel metaphors and similitudes, "a variety and change-

---

quality of wit and about nature as the source of wit — that seem to show the intermingling of Hobbian influence: "Wit, like Beauty, has somewhat in it of *Divine* . . . . It is the spirit and quintessence of speech, extracted out of the substance of things; and a spiritual fire that rarefies, and renders every thing spiritual like it self; it is a soaring quality, that just like *Dedalus* wings, elevates those who have it above other men . . . . In fine, it is some what above expression; and easier to admire, than tell you what it is: not acquir'd by Art and Study, but Nature and Conversation . . . ." The addition of "Conversation" to nature here for the acquisition of wit, as that of "Company" to nature in the passage cited from the Preface, is, Ustick and Hudson acutely show, "a new note, prophetic of the coffee-house and its influence, and a very early expression of the view which stresses urbanity."

[24] "A Discourse *touching* Occasional Meditations," premised to *Occasional Reflections*, in *The Works of the Honourable Robert Boyle* (London, 1744), II, 153.
[25] *Ibid.*

able use of words," in new and "significant translation to our purposes."

Boyle finds that apt similitudes have the advantage of adding both charm and persuasiveness to discourse: for "lucky comparisons make the strongest impressions upon the mind, as they leave the deepest on memory." [26] Aptitude in finding likenesses for such comparisons Boyle identifies with wit, as aptitude in finding dissimilitudes is judgment: "And since, as the being able to find the latent resemblances betwixt things seemingly unlike, makes up a great part of what we are wont to call wit; so the being able to discern the unobvious disparities of things manifestly resembling, is one of the chief things, that displays the faculty, men call judgment." [27] In this definition, as Ustick and Hudson have pointed out,[28] although he has substituted "wit" for Hobbes's "fancy" — in no way a far-fetched substitution, since on occasion Hobbes makes a "good fancy" equivalent to a "good wit" — Boyle is in substantial agreement with Hobbes.[29]

Thomas Shadwell's discussion of Jonson in his Preface to The Humorists (1671) contains further evidence of debt to Hobbes. Shadwell is obviously replying to Dryden's thesis that Jonson wrote from judgment rather than from wit. "I cannot be of their opinion who think he wanted wit," Shadwell writes, and proceeds to argue that Jonson had not only judgment but "more true wit than any of his contemporaries." He sees a fallacy in the assumption that in the writing of his humors Jonson needed only judgment and not wit. Those who believe this "speak as if judgment were a less thing than wit." [30]

> But certainly it was meant otherwise by nature, who subjected wit to the government of judgment, which is the noblest faculty of the mind. Fancy rough-draws, but judgement smooths and finishes; nay, judgment does in deed comprehend wit, for no man can have that who has not wit.

---

[26] Boyle, op. cit., II, 154.
[27] Ibid., II, 155.   [28] Op. cit., p. 112.
[29] Such evidence of agreement on these points is the more remarkable when we recall that Boyle was not in general friendly to Hobbes and on occasion took it upon himself to refute Hobbian theory, as in his Animadversions upon Mr. Hobbes's Problemata de Vacuo in Works, ed. cit., III, 476 ff.
[30] "Preface to The Humorists," Spingarn, II, 158–159.

In fancy mad men equal if not excel all others; and one may as well say that one of those mad men is as good a man as a temperate wiseman, as that one of the very fancyful Plays, admired most by Women, can be so good a Play as one of *Johnson's* correct and well-govern'd Comedies.

Shadwell has accepted the theory that to write well one must write from the materials of experience. To the argument that "humor is the effect of observation, and observation the effect of judgment," he replies that observation is as necessary in all other plays as in the comedy of humor.

> For, first, even in the highest Tragedies, where the scene lies in Courts, the Poet must have observed the Customs of Courts and the manner of conversing there, or he will commit many indecencies, and make his Persons too rough and ill-bred for a Court.
> Besides, Characters in Plays being representations of the Vertues and Vices, Passions or Affections of Mankind, since there are no more new Vertues or Vices, Passions or Affections, the Idea's of these can no other way be received into the imagination of a Poet, but either from the Conversation or Writings of men. After a Poet has formed a Character (as suppose of an Ambitious Man) his design is certainly to write it naturally, and he has no other rule to guid him in this, but to compare him with other men of that kind, that either he has heard of or conversed with in the world, or read of in Books (and even this reading of Books is conversing with men); nay, more; besides judging of his Character, the Poet can fancy nothing of it but what must spring from the Observation he has made of Men or Books. . . .
> . . . Besides, wit in the Writer, I think, without any Authority for it, may be said to be the invention of remote and pleasant thoughts of what kind soever; and there is as much occasion for such imaginations in the writing of a Curious Coxcomb's part as in writing the greatest Hero's; and that which may be folly in the Speaker may be so remote and pleasant to require a great deal of wit in the Writer.[31]

One cannot read such a passage without being impressed with the extent to which the ideas of Hobbes have permeated the critical thought of the writer. Shadwell is here in part restating the Hobbian postulate that a poet should write of the manners of men; that he must draw from nature as he has had occasion to study it and as his imagination has been filled with impressions from it; and that his fancy, or invention, and his judgment are primarily limited to such experience as he has had from observation. Shadwell admits books to a place of

[31] *Ibid.*, II, 159–160.

greater importance than does Hobbes, and in his last sentences he appears to give — without authority — some latitude to wit beyond the scope of experience. In fundamentals, however, he runs close to Hobbian theory.

Edward Phillips writes of those who have pretended to "Poetical fancy or judgement" equal to any who have achieved fame, yet "have contented themselves to be wise, ingenuous [ingenious], or judicious only to themselves." Again, he declares, in a statement for *poeta nascitur*, that "it is not in the power of mortal Man to discover that Wit, Judgment, Fancy, or Industry, with which he never was endow'd, and without most of which, if not all, a good Poem cannot be written." [32] Warton thought, not without reason, that Phillips owed some of the best sentiments in *Theatrum Poetarum Anglicanorum* to his uncle John Milton. And in such statements as the preceding there is probably as much of Milton as of Hobbes. Certainly Hobbes could have had no part in the notion of special innate endowment,[33] though his hand is probably evident in the expressions on wit, fancy, and judgment. A similar integration of ideas from Milton and Hobbes may be inferred in Phillips's exposition of verisimilitude. The well-management of invention, says Phillips, is no other than decorum, and consists of a kind of truth even in fiction:

. . . and circumstances, the more they have of verisimility, the more they keep up the reputation of the Poet, whose business it is to deliver

---

[32] "Preface to *Theatrum Poetarum Anglicanorum*" (1675), Spingarn, II, 260, 261, 262.

[33] Hobbes occasionally ventures a suggestion for the causes of the difference in the wits of men. The cause is in the difference in the passions, he says, both in *The Elements of Law* and in *Leviathan*, and in each case he seems to be mildly accepting Huarte's view that the basis for divergence lies in physical quality. "But . . . men differ much in constitution of body, whereby, that which helpeth and furthereth vital constitution in one . . . hindereth it and crosseth it in another. The difference therefore of wits hath its original from the different passions, and from the ends to which their appetite leadeth them" (*The Elements of Law*, ed. by Ferdinand Tönnies [Cambridge, 1928], I, x, 2). Again, "The causes of this difference of Witts, are in the Passions: and the difference of Passions, proceedeth partly from the different Constitution of the body, and partly from different Education. . . . It proceeds therefore from the Passions; which are different, not onely from the difference of mens complexions; but also from their difference of customes, and education" (*Leviathan*, I, viii).

feign'd things as like to truth as may be, that is to say, not too much exceeding apprehension or the belief of what is possible or likely, or positively contradictory to the truth of History. So that it would be absurd in a *Poet* to set his Hero upon Romantic actions (let his courage be what it will) exceeding Human strength and power, as to fight singly against whole Armies and come off unhurt, at least if a mortal Man, and not a Deity or armed with Power Divine.[34]

This is in general accord with Hobbes's theory of probability, though Hobbes would not himself have added, as a principle for a modern poet, the qualification about a deity.

Phillips goes on to say, in terms that suggest both Milton and Hobbes, that

Heroic Poesie ought to be the result of all that can be contrived of profit, delight, or ornament, either from experience in human affairs or from the knowledge of all *Arts* and *Sciences*, it being but requisite that the same Work which sets forth the highest Acts of Kings and Heroes should be made fit to allure the inclinations of such like Persons to a studious delight in reading of those things which they are desired to imitate.[35]

The reference to knowledge of "all *Arts* and *Sciences*" has a Miltonic intonation, but the emphasis on "experience in human affairs" seems to hark back to Hobbes.

There is a further interesting passage in Phillips that in part echoes Hobbes, in part appears to be a direct refutation. Writing of style, Phillips observes:

There is also a *Decorum* to be observ'd in the style of the H. Poem, that is, that it be not inflate or gingling with an empty noise of Words, nor creepingly low and insipid, but of a Majesty suitable to the Grandeur of the subject, — not nice or ashamed of vulgarly unknown or unusual words, if either tearms of Art well chosen or proper to the occasion, for fear of frighting the Ladies from reading, as if it were not more reasonable that Ladies who will read Heroic Poem should be qualified accordingly, then that the Poet should check his fancy for such, either Men or Ladys, whose capacities will not ascend above *Argalus* and *Parthenia*.[36]

Hobbes, it will be recalled, had remarked in *Leviathan* (I, viii) upon the impropriety in a serious subject of a "Gingling of words" and he had consistently advocated in the heroic poem a majesty of style suited to the subject. But he had also, in

[34] "Preface to *Theatrum Poetarum Anglicanorum*," Spingarn, II, 267–268.
[35] *Ibid.*   [36] *Ibid.*, II, 269.

his quietly realistic fashion, advised against the introduction of foreign and other unusual words in poems which are to be read by "Women no less than Men . . . though their skill in Language be not so universal." [37] Phillips is in agreement about the "gingling of words," but he is obviously taking a potshot at Hobbes's — perhaps to him very amusing — qualification in favor of the ladies.

Thomas Sprat held, in common with Hobbes, a great respect for science and the species of truth to be derived through science. His writings show that, whether directly or indirectly, he had absorbed some of the Hobbian ideas of wit, fancy, and judgment and of the principles of acceptable style. Thus he writes of Cowley: "His Fancy flow'd with great speed, and therefore it was very fortunate to him that his Judgment was equal to manage it. He never runs his Reader nor his Argument out of Breath. He perfectly practices the hardest secret of good writing, to know when he has done enough." [38] Sprat admits that some parts of the "Davideis" show "youthfulness and redundance of Fancy," but he excuses this as an error of immaturity which his "riper Judgment" would not have allowed.[39] Whenever we encounter in late seventeenth-century criticism such an expression of tolerance of fancy with at the same time a demand for sufficient judgment to keep the fancy within bounds, we have reason to suspect the influence of Hobbes.

In his ideas of style and form Sprat seems even nearer to Hobbes. Praising Cowley's manner of writing, Sprat declares: "In the particular expressions there is still much to be Applauded, but more in the disposition and order of the whole. From thence there springs a new comeliness, besides the feature of each part. His Invention is powerful and large as can be desir'd. But it seems all to arise out of the Nature of the subject, and to be just fitted for the things of which he speaks." [40] In another place Sprat remarks that the "true perfection of

[37] *The Virtues of an Heroic Poem*, Spingarn, II, 68.
[38] Thomas Sprat, *An Account of the Life and Writings of Mr. Abraham Cowley. Written to Mr. M. Clifford*, Spingarn, II, 130. The date is 1667.
[39] *Ibid.*, p. 133.   [40] *Ibid.*, p. 130.

Wit is to be plyable to all occasions, to walk or flye according to the Nature of every subject." [41] Sprat is in this latter instance speaking of Cowley's late essays, the prose of which, he says, contains "little Curiosity of Ornament," but is "written in a lower and humbler style than the rest," appropriate to an unfeigned image of soul "without Flattery."

Hobbes, it will be recalled, had urged orderly arrangement and a style drawn from the subject. Sprat's remarks are quite in the spirit of *Leviathan* (I, viii), where Hobbes had indicated the desirable proportions of fancy and judgment in the different forms of discourse — poetry, history, sermons, and so forth — and of the paragraphs in *The Answer to Davenant* which have to do with clearness and propriety in expression.

Sprat has much to say in *The History of the Royal Society* in favor of the plain style. His advocacy there of plain undeceiving expressions and his irritation at inappropriate ornament also link him with Hobbes. Such sentiments, it is true, place him in a tradition in English letters that goes back as far as Chaucer and includes Wilson, Gascoigne, Ascham, Jonson, and Bacon. Some of these preached far better than they practiced, but all, nevertheless, were in sympathy with the sentiments that inspired Jonson in his condemnation of the "vast and tumorous" effects of overwrought language and Bacon in his vigorous indictment of the cloudy verbiage of the Scholastics. Sprat therefore could have had other English precedent for his anger at "all these seeming Mysteries" upon which writers "look so big . . . this vicious abundance of Phrase, this trick of Metaphors, this volubility of Tongue, which makes so great a noise in the World," [42] and for his desires to have "Reason set out in plain undeceiving expressions." [43] He need have gone no further than Hobbes, however; and some of his phrasing suggests that he did not. This is apparent in his argument that of all the products of men's "Wit and Industry" scarcely any could be more useful than civil history, "if it were written with that sincerity and majesty,

---

[41] *Ibid.*, p. 138.
[42] *From the History of the Royal-Society of London* (1667), Spingarn, II, 117.
[43] *Ibid.*, p. 112.

as it ought to be, as a faithful Idea of humane Actions," [44]
and in his commendation of those writers of the time who,
as a remedy against extravagance, show "A constant Resolution to reject all amplifications, digressions, and swellings of
style; to return back to the primitive purity and shortness,
when men deliver'd so many *things* almost in an equal number
of words." [45]   While this is no mere repetition of Hobbes, it
readily recalls his insistence on propriety and perspicuity, particularly his disparagement of the use of words "that though
of a magnifique sound, yet (like the windy blisters of a troubled
water) have no sense at all," and his advice against adding
to the "palpable darkness" so achieved by an "ambitious obscurity of expressing more than is perfectly conceived" or by
attempting to express a "perfect conception in fewer words
than it requires." [46]

Writing in praise of Cowley's *Six Books of Plants*, Nahum
Tate uses the terms "wit," "fancy," and "judgment" in a quite
Hobbian manner.   He finds in Cowley "the utmost force of
Judgment and Invention in most happy Conjunction." [47]   He
notes with particular admiration the descriptive parts of
Cowley's poem "divested of that imaginary Life which might
beautifie the Work."   "*Hic labor, hoc opus*, it is there it seems
worth our while to observe the sagacious Methods of his Fancy,
in finding Topicks for his Wit, and Instances of amiable Variety." [48]   These topics existed largely in the circumstances of
the places and occasions of the life and flowering of his plants,
all of which he has introduced with admirable play of fancy,
but always with judgment.

[44] *From the History of the Royal-Society of London*, Spingarn, II, 114.

[45] *Ibid.*, pp. 117–118.

[46] *The Answer to Davenant*, Spingarn, II, 63.   Locke was later to speak vigorously against the abuse of rhetorical figures (*Of Human Understanding*, III, x, 34, in
Vol. I of *The Works of John Locke* [London, 1867]), as Spingarn has pointed out
(note to Sprat, II, 338), and Dryden had much to say of the impropriety of
bombastic and swollen expression, but both of them wrote too late to have
influenced Sprat in 1667, the date of the *History*.

[47] *The Works of Mr. Abraham Cowley*, Eighth Edition (London, 1693).   Tate's
remarks are "To the Reader" and form the second item of the third section of
the book.   They had previously appeared in the first printing of the *Six Books of
Plants* in 1689.

[48] *Ibid.*

. . . Yet in all this liberty, you find him nowhere diverted from his Point, Judgment . . . being never carried too remote by the heat of his Imagination and quickness of his Apprehension. His Invention exerts its utmost Faculties, but so constantly over-rul'd by the Dictates of Sense, that even those Conceits which are so unexpectedly started, and had lain undiscover'd by a less piercing Wit, are no sooner brought to light, but they appear the result of a genuine Thought, and naturally arising from his Matter.[49]

Such sentences readily bring to mind Hobbes's notion of wit as a *"Celerity* of Imagining," and of a good fancy well balanced with judgment. Tate's use of "Conceits" as a product of wit suggests the discoveries of resemblances by fancy. As in Hobbes, these discoveries are of truth not easily discerned; and, likewise as in Hobbes, they have poetic value because the expression seems to arise naturally from the thought, is not laid on from the outside.[50]

Similarities to Hobbes in the teachings of Locke have been often noted. Ustick and Hudson have lately emphasized the importance of Locke's restatement of and elaboration upon the distinction between "fancy" and "judgment" previously made

[49] *Ibid.*

[50] There are similar reminiscences of Hobbes in Sir William Temple's *Of Poetry* (1690). Perhaps the most striking of these is contained in the following: "There must be a spritely Imagination or Fancy, fertile in a thousand Productions, ranging over infinite Ground, piercing into every Corner, and by the Light of that true Poetical Fire discovering a thousand little Bodies or Images in the World, and Similitudes among them, unseen to common Eyes, and which could not be discovered without the Rays of that Sun . . . . Besides the heat of Invention and liveliness of Wit, there must be the coldness of good Sense and soundness of Judgment, to distinguish between things and conceptions which at first sight or upon short glances seem alike . . ." (Spingarn, III, 81).

Thomas Rymer also may be mentioned as one who recognized the Hobbian principle that there must be coöperation between fancy and judgment in good poetry. In *The Tragedies of the Last Age* (London, 1678) he writes: "Say others, *Poetry* and *Reason*, how come these to be Cater-cousins? Poetry is the *Child* of *Fancy*, and is never to be school'd and disciplin'd by *Reason;* Poetry, say they, is *blind* inspiration, is pure *enthusiasm*, is *rapture* and *rage* all over.

"But Fancy, I think, in Poetry, is like *Faith* in Religion; it makes for discoveries, and soars above reason, but never clashes, or runs against it. *Fancy* leaps, and frisks, and away she's gone; whilst *reason* rattles the chains, and follows after. Reason must Consent and ratify what-ever by *fancy* is attempted in its absence; or else 'tis all *null* and void in law. . . . Those who object against reason, are the *Fanaticks* in Poetry, and are never to be saved by their good works" (p. 8).

by Hobbes and some of his successors, notably Boyle and Flecknoe. There are many other points of likeness between Locke and Hobbes. Locke's insistence on the origin of ideas through the senses, his theory of pleasure and pain, his idea of the function of memory, even the basis for his notion of secondary qualities of matter, were all anticipated in Hobbes. Occasional passages distinctly call to mind ideas from *Leviathan* or *The Elements of Law*. Such, for example, is Locke's comment on the dull mind. The memory of the dull man is slow; such ideas as he may have are of little value, for they are not ready at hand when need calls for them. Almost as well be entirely ignorant. "It is the business therefore of the memory to furnish to the mind those dormant ideas which it has present occasion for; in the having them ready at hand on all occasions, consists that which we call invention, fancy, and quickness of parts." [51] We have here only another version of Hobbes's description of wit as a " *Celerity* of Imagining" and of the quick ranging mind of the man of fancy and judgment in contrast with the slow and immobile spirits of those who are dull.

Locke's remarks on aesthetic pleasure to be derived from poetry are highly general, ending in little more than statements for bare entertainment as the chief end of all works of fancy. His remarks on the basis of such effects are, however, more specific. These occur in his discussions of the phenomena of pleasure and pain. Paralleling Hobbes closely, Locke points out that, just as in the body there is bare sensation in itself, or "sensation accompanied with pain or pleasure; so the thought or perception of the mind is simply so, or else accompanied also with pleasure or pain, delight or trouble." [52] Like Hobbes, Locke associates pleasure and pain with the passions: "Pleasure and pain . . . are the hinges upon which our passions turn: and if we reflect on ourselves, and observe how these, under various considerations, operate in us; what modifications or tempers of mind, what internal sensations (if I may call them) they produce in us, we may thence form to ourselves the ideas of our passions." [53] Locke's exposition of the pas-

---

[51] *Of Human Understanding*, II, x, 8.
[52] *Ibid.*, II, vii, 3.   [53] *Ibid.*, II, xx, 3.

sions might, in general, be taken from Hobbes. His use of the term "internal sensations" in this paragraph, however, invites particular comparison with a sentence in *The Elements of Philosophy*, where Hobbes writes: "But there is another kind of sense, of which I will say something in this place, namely, the sense of pleasure and pain, proceeding not from the heart outwards, but from continual action from the outermost part of the organ towards the heart." [54] As I have elsewhere shown, the attribution by Hobbes and Locke of pleasure and pain to a sort of sixth sense, or to "internal sensations," [55] foreshadows the later ideas of an "internal sense" of beauty (as well as of virtue — since Hobbes and Locke also associate pleasure and pain with ideas of good and evil) — developed by Shaftesbury and Hutcheson. [56]

But the part of Locke that most directly challenges comparison with Hobbes is the famous definition of wit. This passage is well known and has been much quoted, but, because I wish to make certain specific comments upon it, I venture to cite it once again:

> . . . If in having our ideas in the memory ready at hand consists quickness of parts; in this, of having them unconfused, and being able nicely to distinguish one thing from another, where there is but the least difference, consists, in a great measure, the exactness of judgment, and clearness of reason, which is to be observed in one man above another. And hence perhaps may be given some reason of that common observation, that men who have a great deal of wit, and prompt memories, have not always the clearest judgment or deepest reason; for wit lying most in the assemblage of ideas, and putting those together with quickness and variety, wherein can be found any resemblance or congruity, thereby to make up pleasant pictures and agreeable visions in the fancy; judgment, on the contrary, lies quite on the other side, in separating carefully, one

---

[54] *The Elements of Philosophy*, IV, xxv, 12, in *The English Works of Thomas Hobbes of Malmesbury*, ed. by Sir William Molesworth (London, 1839–45).

[55] It will be recalled that in another place Hobbes also virtually uses the term, when in *The Elements of Law*, explaining the phenomenon of our taking notice when a conception of the same thing comes again that we have had this conception before — "which is as much as to imagine a thing past" — he declares: "This therefore may be accounted a sixth sense, but internal, not external, as the rest, and is commonly called REMEMBRANCE" (I, iii, 6).

[56] In "Addison and Hutcheson on the Imagination," *A Journal of English Literary History*, II (1935), 215 ff.

from another, ideas wherein can be found the least difference, thereby to avoid being misled by similitude and by affinity to take one thing for another. This is a way of proceeding quite contrary to metaphor and allusion, wherein for the most part lies that entertainment and pleasantry of wit, which strikes so lively on the fancy, and therefore is so acceptable to all people; because its beauty appears at first sight, and there is required no labour of thought to examine what truth or reason there is in it. The mind, without looking any further, rests satisfied with the agreeableness of the picture and the gaiety of the fancy; and it is a kind of affront to go about to examine it by the severe rules of truth and good reason, whereby it appears that it consists in something that is not perfectly conformable to them.[57]

This is obviously close to Hobbes, but it reveals difference in two important particulars, which difference, it seems fair to say, may be taken as the measure of the gap which lies between Hobbes and Locke as aestheticians. Hobbes had ascribed to fancy quickness in perceiving *unexpected* similitudes and to judgment the ability to discern "*suddenly* dissimilitude in things that *otherwise appear the same.*" In the words which I have italicized Hobbes indicates the acuteness characteristic of a good fancy and a good judgment, contrasting this (by implication) with the ordinary undistinguished perception of expected and obvious similitudes and dissimilitudes. Boyle follows Hobbes in noting this difference, as his words, "latent resemblances betwixt things seemingly unlike" and "unobvious disparities," quite clearly show. Locke fails to make this all-important distinction. Addison, a few years later, quoting Locke's definition and accepting it in main outline, was to correct Locke by insisting that only those resemblances of ideas can be called wit which give "delight and surprise to the reader." The element of surprise is especially important, he says, and goes on to show that resemblances become wit only when the ideas do not in the nature of things lie too close to each other. Thus, "To compare one Man's Singing to that of another, or to represent the Whiteness of any Object by that of Milk or Snow, or the Variety of its Colours by those of the Rainbow, cannot be called Wit, unless, besides this obvious Resemblance, there be some further Congruity dis-

[57] *Of Human Understanding*, II, xi, 2.

covered in the two Ideas, that is capable of giving the Reader some Surprise." [58] Hobbes, Boyle, and Addison are all in this respect showing their superiority to Locke, for all are noting what Locke neglects, the principle of novelty, of that experience of things coming upon the mind with a pleasant recognition of truth before unperceived, which is so important an element in aesthetic effect.

Another item in Locke's definition which sets him apart from Hobbes is his implied distinction between works of wit (or fancy) and of truth. Hobbes found that works of fancy might upon occasion take the philosopher's part onto themselves. The writer of a great heroic poem is not only "the Poet . . . but also the Philosopher." He is this by virtue of fancy operating in the field of experience under the control of judgment. Works of fancy have therefore assumed an important rôle in the evolution of civilization, Hobbes maintains. Locke, on the contrary, sees no value in the fancy except its capacity to entertain. He sharply differentiates truth-giving judgment from pleasure-giving wit. This is true not only of this passage but of his remarks on the subject in general. His concessions to wit, or fancy, as he sometimes calls it, are habitually to discourse with a capacity to tickle men's lighter sensibilities; he constantly sets off dreams and fancies from the realities of things; he is even capable of going so far as to charge fancy with unwholesome deception: "There are so many ways of fallacy, such arts of giving colours, appearances, and resemblances by this court-dresser, the fancy, that he who is not wary to admit nothing but truth itself . . . cannot but be caught." [59]

So it turns out that where Hobbes was tolerant to works of fancy, Locke inclined toward intolerance; where Hobbes pointed to products in which rare inventive genius brings together elements of experience to be welded under the direction of judgment into meaningful patterns of philosophic truth, Locke regarded the results of fancy as separate from truth, even at enmity with it. Those who find tendencies in

[58] *The Spectator*, ed. by G. Gregory Smith (London, 1897), No. 62.
[59] *Of the Conduct of the Understanding*, in Vol. I of *The Works of John Locke* (London, 1867), 33.

Augustan England to regard art as a plaything for men's lighter moments, having no traffic with the serious concerns of life may therefore look to Locke rather than to Hobbes as the villain in the piece. For Hobbes envisaged a union of fancy and judgment in poetry and a *rapprochement*, not a divorce, between pleasure and truth.

CHAPTER X

Conclusion: Hobbes's Contributions to the Psychological Method

WHAT, one may ask, has Hobbes accomplished? Professor Spingarn declares that he was the originator of a "new aesthetic." And there are reasons for such a judgment.[1] Perhaps, however, in view of all the facts, it is enough to say that, rather than originating, he made valuable contributions to a new aesthetic. Many of his ideas, something of his method, may be found in his predecessors, from Aristotle to Bacon. Nevertheless, for his own time, both his theory and his method were new, and he gave impulse to a type of thought that for his age was different. More definitely than Descartes, more completely than Bacon even, he represents a break from the scholastic tradition. He stood at the crossroads between scholastic and modern thinking, and he chose with unmistakable decision the modern way. In so doing he was in a large measure but going back to the Aristotelian mode of searching for fundamentals.

But Aristotelianism and Scholasticism had become almost inextricably confused, and it is not strange that both Hobbes and his admirers felt that he was rejecting Aristotle as well and was replacing with something quite new a philosophy

---

[1] This is not an isolated view. An English scholar, not inclined to enthusiasm, corroborates Spingarn's judgment in finding that, though Hobbes "had not a poetic soul nor even unfaltering literary judgment," he is in his aesthetic views "in front of his contemporaries and is yet the recognized founder of the school of poetical criticism which first distinguished fancy and judgment, insisted on experience and realism, and based aesthetic on a rudimentary psychology" (George E. G. Catlin, *Thomas Hobbes as Philosopher, Publicist, and Man of Letters* [Oxford, 1922], p. 13).

287

that in "the *School-mens* hands" had "perisht quite at last."
So that because of what he taught and because of the manner
in which he taught it Hobbes became not only to Cowley but
to many others of his own and succeeding generations the
"*Columbus* of the *Golden Lands* of *new Philosophies*," who was
to be eagerly followed in voyages of fresh exploration. It is
of prime importance to take into account Hobbes's part in
awakening this spirit of bold adventure. Hobbes's doctrine
turned out to be the kind of thing calculated to stir the imaginations of good Englishmen, as Davenant promptly showed by
his proud, rather boastful, acknowledgment that, in venturing
in new tracks beyond the old "Sea-marks" of Homer, Virgil,
and others, he had but followed the example of Hobbes:
"because you move not by common Mapps, but have . . .
made your own prospect." One may say without too much
exaggeration that what the discovery of America and renewed
acquaintance with the Classics had done for the early Renaissance imagination in the way of opening new world views and
in giving impetus to fresh literary endeavors, Hobbes, aided
by Bacon and Descartes and the new science, in general, did
for the end of the Renaissance in the field of English thought
and letters. One could well conceive of Davenant, for instance,
picturing himself as something of the Sir Francis Drake of the
literary world of his day. Cowley, Dryden, Dennis, and Addison, likewise, were all to a greater or less degree actuated by
the spirit of adventure and discovery. In all new movements
such a spirit is of vast importance. Had Hobbes done nothing
more than to help engender it he would have been a great
force in the history of aesthetics.

But Hobbes, of course, did more. Through his analyses
and definitions he set patterns of thought for others to follow,
and he gave them a method which when adopted led to the
enlargement and completion of these patterns.

Hobbes's tendency to place a high value upon passion as a
means to the good life would have made his researches in the
emotional side of man's nature important to aesthetics even
had he made no specific applications to literature. Previous
writers on the subject in English had been chiefly concerned

with recipes for holding the passions under control, some of them to be subdued entirely, others to be subjected to reason. Such, roughly, were the interests of Thomas Wright [2] and Edward Reynolds.[3] Hobbes, on the contrary, finding the passions the mainspring of human activity, without the lively exercise of which a man can have neither a strong intellect nor a good fancy, encouraged a more tolerant attitude toward the emotional life and the pleasures related to it. He restricted this tolerance to passions of the mind, rather than to merely sensual ones, to be sure, but at a time when strong forces were at work toward quelling the emotions entirely, it was no small thing for a man of his stature to speak in their favor, with whatever qualifications. When he went further, however, and made applications to literature, the significance of his theory for aesthetics was greatly enhanced. By frankly admitting delight through emotional excitation as the immediate end in literature — though moral teaching might be the ultimate objective — and by seriously setting himself to the problem of analyzing specific sources of aesthetic pleasure, such as novelty, he furnished a powerful precedent for emphasis on effects by such psychologically inclined critics as Dryden, Dennis, Addison, and Burke.

Hobbes did much to make the emotions respectable; he also helped to make them understood. His aim was to uncover first principles. His findings had in consequence both depth and universality, and in addition a persuasive rationality. His ideas on novelty may be taken as an example.

Hobbes's approbation of novelty is rooted in his developed conception of the natural craving of the human spirit for an extension of experience. "Knowing much" is the basis for novelty, because the writer whose wide observation and ranging curiosity has carried him beyond the ordinary reaches can open to the minds of his readers previously undiscerned vistas. He has discovered relationships before unperceived, has seen more, has seen more clearly and deeply than others; he is therefore able to express similitudes which are fresh and new and which

[2] *The Passions of the Minde in Generall* (London, 1601).
[3] *A Treatise of the Passions and Faculties of the Soul of Man* (London, 1640).

strike with pleasant surprise, with a sense of strangeness, and with a delightful satisfaction in a perception of added knowledge. This is essentially a romantic principle. "It is the addition of strangeness to beauty," says Pater, "that constitutes the romantic character in art; . . . it is the addition of curiosity to . . . desire of beauty that constitutes the romantic temper." [4] Hobbes can hardly by any stretch of the term be called a romanticist. It is a testimony to his perspicacity, however, that he should so clearly discern and so accurately evaluate this permanent trait in human nature as a source of pleasure in art and a motivating force in man's advance toward broadened horizons of perceived experience. Hobbes was not the first to recognize the principle, but he was the first of the moderns to give it a full and rational exposition. It is not strange, therefore, that his statement made strong appeal to succeeding critics who had an eye to fundamentals.

Among the results of Hobbes's teachings we may include, without overworking the case too much, I believe, encouragement and reinforcement to the tendency which began in the late seventeenth, and gained momentum during the eighteenth, century, to set emotional effect above formal quality in judging a piece of literature, a tendency which included both the remarkable development of interest in sublimity and the vitiated taste for excitement at any price manifested in the Gothic romance. Longinus is traditionally given credit for the growth of interest in sublimity and for much of the paradoxical tolerance for emotion in art in a period prevailingly rational. If all the facts are taken into consideration, however, it would appear that Longinus must share honors in this influence with the new philosophy, Hobbes's contribution to it in particular.

Mr. Monk quite properly points out that Longinus was gladly received because eighteenth-century England was ready for him. English literary thought had, after the Restoration, ostensibly settled down to the comfortable orthodoxy of neoclassic principles of form and correctness. Underneath, however, was an uneasy feeling that "the true destiny of English

---

[4] "Postscript," *Appreciations* (London, 1889).

letters lay with Shakespeare and not with Horace and Boileau."
For those who in answer to this feeling sought "a freer, more
individualistic, and consequently more native theory of art,"
hence a type of criticism aimed to "combat and destroy the
rules," Longinus became, throughout the eighteenth century,
"a sort of *locus classicus*," whose word was quoted as impeccable
authority for a new critical approach to literature.[5]   It is true
that the time was ready for Longinus.   But it seems equally
true that one of the great forces which contributed to this
readiness was Hobbes, who through his treatment of the
passions, particularly in giving them a firm psychological *raison
d'être*, had helped prepare the English mind for the Longinian
theory of emotional intensity as a proper effect of literature.
Before the name of Longinus began to figure importantly in
English writings Hobbian theories of emotion and the Hobbian
method of analysis had made themselves distinctly felt.   Thus
before the Bolivan translation of *Peri Hupsous* Dryden had said
in one way or another substantially all that he was to say,
even after he had begun to cite Longinus, on the subject of
emotional appeal.   He had, moreover, shown a disposition
toward a more distinctly psychological approach than he
could have derived from the Greek critic.   No one would
be so naïve as to assume that Hobbes alone was responsible for
these tendencies in Dryden; yet, on evidence presented earlier
in this book, logic requires that we attribute to Hobbes an
important share in the whole.   This also is true in the case
of other critics of the period whose theories of effects we have
been considering.

A significant result of the Hobbian approach was the development during the following century of, first, skepticism,
then, complete distrust of rules and conventions which were
in obvious conflict with the methods of poets and dramatists
whose works had proved successful.   Cases in point were Dryden's doubts as to the applicability of the rules to English
drama, Addison's condemnation of critics who would place
dogma above genius, and Samuel Johnson's flat denial of the

⁵ Samuel H. Monk, *The Sublime: A Study of Critical Theory in XVIII-Century
England* (New York, 1935), pp. 26–27.

sanctity of the conventions when they seemed to him inconsistent with nature and with his own best judgment of what was
excellent in Shakespeare.

No part of Hobbes's aesthetic seems to have made deeper
imprint on the minds of his contemporaries and successors than
his speculations on wit, fancy (or imagination), and judgment.
The pertinent details of his theory here center about two main
points: his conception of fancy as a generally impetuous
creative faculty and as a capacity for seeing likenesses not
easily discerned, and his theory of judgment as a discriminating
and corrective agency to direct and control the fancy.   A lively
fancy and a good judgment, impelled by appetite, operating
harmoniously to a desired end, gathering and arranging the
materials of experience from the stores of memory, constitute
a good wit.   Some of these ideas were not basically and individually new.   The notion that judgment should restrain the
inventive fancy, for instance, had been frequently expressed
before Hobbes: by the Stoics, by Plotinus, by half the neoclassic critics of Italy and France.   But Hobbes's unique
formulation, based as it was on a psychology which lent firm-
ness and authenticity to his views, came upon his age as a
fresh discovery, and, as we have seen, was widely accepted by
critics who were deeply interested in explanations and standards
but found the traditional formulae inadequate to their purposes.

In an earlier chapter I have pointed out the analogy between Hobbes's statements about the peculiar ability to discern
difficult likenesses and Wordsworth's ascription to the imagination of power to observe "affinities" not perceived by ordinary
minds.   Addison was to follow Hobbes (through Locke) in
describing wit as such a "resemblance and congruity of ideas"
as "gives delight and surprise to the reader." [6]   He was also
to point out that the man of good imagination sees the world
in a different way from the person not so gifted.   Such a man
looks upon a beautiful scene, or a novel or a great one, with
quickened animal spirits and aroused apprehensions.[7]   The

[6] *The Spectator*, ed. by G. Gregory Smith (London, 1897), No. 62.
[7] *Ibid.*, No. 411.

Abbé du Bos, who seems to have been a good deal influenced by Addison and other English thinkers, carries this idea a few years later to its logical conclusion in maintaining that the "man of genius sees nature which his art imitates, with other eyes than persons without genius. He discovers an infinite difference between objects which to other men's eyes appear alike, and makes this difference felt in his imitation, so that the most hackneyed subject becomes new under his pen or brush." [8] So he varies his treatment of men and their emotions in infinite ways without ever departing from nature. Hobbes's theory leads quite naturally to this view. Since the man of a good fancy or wit (that is, the genius) sees relations and qualities of which the ordinary mind is oblivious, the uniqueness of his presentation will, perforce, be conditioned by his special difference in perceiving. This is an idea that, developing gradually through the eighteenth century, under the direction of Addison, Shaftesbury, Hutcheson, Hume, Burke, Gerard (particularly in the *Essay on Genius*), and others was to reach its culmination in Coleridge's theory, according to which the Primary Imagination becomes a specific esemplastic, or shaping, agency in the quite complicated reconciliation of subject and object in the re-creation into mind stuff of the impressions daily received from the physical world.

Similarly, Hobbes's notions of the fancy as creating new forms through a reconstruction of the materials of experience — the precise nature of which activity is left unaccounted for, since, unfortunately, Hobbes fails to attribute with any clearness the anterior powers of mind necessary to make such a process explicable [9] — are to be modified and perfected into full-bodied maturity in Coleridge's view of the Secondary Imagination as re-creation, through permanent laws of intellect, from the dissolved and diffused materials stored in the subconscious mind.

[8] *Réflexions critiques sur la poësie et sur la peinture* (1719), Seventh Edition (Paris, 1770), I, 231–232.
[9] I am accepting the contention of Coleridge that a theory of mechanical association is inadequate to explain creative processes. As we have seen (pp. 94 ff. of this book), Hobbes's own descriptions of the operations of fancy *imply* more than can be accounted for by his theory of association.

It must not be supposed that I am claiming for Hobbes fully developed theories of the sort held by Coleridge. I am only indicating significant foreshadowings. Hobbes, more definitely than anyone up to his time, brought the whole creative process indoors. He did as much as any other single person in the history of aesthetic speculation to transfer the *object* of poetic creation from the external world to the mind of man. It was no small thing to substitute for the traditional neoclassic theory which regarded the external object as a source for imitation (guided though the artist might be by an *idea* of beautiful form by which to fashion his ideal) a conception of creation by powers of mind from its own stored experience made available through memory. Hobbes deserves high credit for his great part in bringing about this change.[10]

As I have previously indicated, Hobbes's skepticism of traditional authority and his example in reasoning on literary matters assume a place of great significance in evaluating his influence on later theory. One of his undoubted services to future aesthetics was to set up a principle both for a method in reasoning and for evaluating the conclusions achieved through reasoning as compared with conclusions reached through other methods, as through common sense or intuition — he himself uses the term "natural prudence." To Hobbes the only infallible road to truth is reasoning. But reasoning is valid only when the evidence and premises are certain; reasoning based on false or even dubious assumptions is worse than no reasoning at all:

> But yet they that have no *Science*, are in better, and nobler condition, with their naturall Prudence, than men, that by mis-reasoning, or by trusting them that reason wrong, fall upon false and absurd generall rules. For ignorance of causes and of rules does not set men so farre out of their way as relying on false rules, and taking for causes of what they aspire to those that are not so, but rather causes of the contrary.[11]

"As much Experience is *Prudence;* so is much Science *Sapience*," Hobbes goes on to explain. The Latins called one

---

[10] In this he was, we may believe, pretty much one with Aristotle, to whom poetry appears to have been "philosophic" in proportion to its "ideal" character.

[11] *Leviathan*, ed. by Ernest Rhys (London, Toronto, and New York, 1914), I, v.

prudentia, the other *sapientia*, ascribing the one to experience, the other to science. To make clear their relative value, Hobbes uses the analogy of a man with a "naturall use and dexterity" of arms as compared with a man who adds to such natural skill an acquired science of combat: "The ability of the former would be to the ability of the later as Prudence to Sapience, both usefull; but the latter infallible." Suppose, however, a man has acquired faulty rules of combat; his incorrect science would be more dangerous than none. And here Hobbes delivers a stinging rebuke to pseudo-authoritarians: "But they that, trusting onely to the authority of books, follow the blind blindly, are like him that, trusting to the false rules of a master of Fence, ventures præsumptuously upon an adversary, that either kills or disgraces him." [12] Prudence can never be certain; it is always liable to error. Even so it is a much safer guide than a presumptuous, pretending science, unable to teach its truth perspicuously: "But in any businesse, whereof a man has not infallible Science to proceed by; to forsake his own naturall judgement, and be guided by generall sentences read in Authors, and subject to many exceptions, is a signe of folly, and generally scorned by the name of Pedantry." [13]

Could there have been a more cogent statement of principle for literary critics to follow in dealing with the science of aesthetics formulated by neoclassic minds? In this attitude of a judicious, discriminating evaluation of traditional knowledge of any sort before we accept it, in lieu of our own best judgment — our "natural prudence" acquired through experience — lies the foundation for the distrust of dogmatism and tradition that grew up in England during the next century; and in such emphasis on the superiority, over uncertain science, of what is in effect individual intuitive judgment, is authority for the whole later school of taste.

Hobbes's intended emphasis is, it is true, upon strict scientific procedure in which judgments resting on empirical data and logical process should prevail. His continued attack on reasoning and argument derived from received authority rather

[12] *Ibid.*   [13] *Ibid.*

than from observation and true knowledge served, however, to call into question most of what passed in his day for scientific and philosophic discussion, and hence tended to create a skeptical attitude toward all such discussion and the theory from which it proceeded. Bacon had previously fostered such skepticism when he had argued the folly of the speculative subtleties of the Scholastics, who had wasted their effort on words rather than turning their attention to "things or nature." All discursive efforts of the mind are preposterous, he had said, except "when experiment is to be weighed and axioms to be derived from it." [14]   Bacon's plan for science was to discard the prevailing foolish reverence for antiquity and to make a fresh start, building our knowledge little by little on the secure foundation of the ascertainable facts of observation and experiment. Thus he declares that "the reverence for antiquity, and the authority of men who have been esteemed great in philosophy, and general unanimity, have retarded men from advancing in science, and almost enchanted them." [15]   And even more to the point, in applicability to literary matters, Bacon points out the danger of paying too great deference to the "miracles of art" of past ages:

> For there is some danger, lest the understanding should be astonished and chained down, and as it were bewitched, by such works of art, as appear to be the very summit and pinnacle of human industry, so as not to become familiar with them, but rather to suppose that nothing of the kind can be accomplished, unless the same means be employed, with perhaps a little more diligence, and more accurate preparation.
>
> Now, on the contrary, it may be stated as a fact, that the ways and means hitherto discovered and observed, of effecting any matter or work, are for the most part of little value, and that all really efficient power depends, and is really to be deduced from the sources of forms, none of which have yet been discovered.[16]

The way to advancement lies in striking out into new paths: "It is in vain to expect any great progress in the sciences by the superinducing or engrafting new matters upon old. An

[14] *Novum Organum*, I, Aphorism CXXI, in *The Physical and Metaphysical Works of Lord Bacon*, ed. by Joseph Devey (Bohn ed., London, 1872), p. 440.
[15] *Ibid.*, I, Aphorism LXXXIV (Bohn ed.), p. 417.
[16] *Ibid.*, II, Aphorism XXXI (Bohn ed.), p. 498.

instauration must be made from the very foundations, if we do not wish to revolve forever in a circle, making only some slight and contemptible progress." [17]

Hobbes, who was once Bacon's favorite amanuensis, may have been influenced by his sometime master in his uncompromising condemnation of argument from words rather than from things and of the general practice of blindly falling into the lockstep of tradition. It is difficult to believe that he was not. This, however, is a matter less important than that he held such opinions and expressed them clearly and forcefully for all to read.

Thus in a continuation of the passage about true versus false teaching quoted a few pages back he strikes out vigorously at the whole tribe of *dogmatici*, who by definition are those "that take up maxims from their education, and from the authority of men, or of custom, and take the habitual discourse of the tongue for ratiocination." [18] These men are "imperfectly learned, and with passion press to have their opinions pass everywhere for truth" [19] without demonstration from experience or other uncontroverted source.[20] In contrast to the *mathematici*, or the true teachers, to whom we owe all our advances in the arts of civilization, who, working from education and experience, proceed according to the steps of science from the known to the unknown, from fact to proposition, from proposition to larger principles, the *dogmatici* hand down nothing which has not been believed in the past, contribute nothing but controversy and doubt.

It is obvious that in his scornful castigation of the traditionalists Hobbes, so far as he was accepted, must have contributed materially to the growth of the skeptical attitude of the later seventeenth century which reached its climax in the

[17] *Ibid.*, I, Aphorism XXXI (Bohn ed.), p. 388.
[18] *The Elements of Law*, ed. by Ferdinand Tönnies (Cambridge, 1928), I, xiii, 4.
[19] *Ibid.*
[20] Cf. Bacon: "Axioms determined upon in argument can never assist in the discovery of new effects; for the subtilty of nature is vastly superior to that of argument. But axioms properly and regularly abstracted from particulars easily point out and define new particulars, and therefore impart activity to the sciences" (*Novum Organum*, I, Aphorism XXIV [Bohn ed.], p. 387).

literary criticism of John Dryden. Hobbes, to be sure, does not name literature as one of the favorite subjects of the dogmatists, confining himself to "moral philosophy," "government," and "laws"; but at a time of canting reverence for so-called Aristotelian ideas application of his general theory to the aesthetic field would be so easy and natural as to be almost inevitable.

Mr. Basil Willey has summarized the effect upon poetry of the "new philosophy" in general, of Descartes in particular, as being inimical to serious purpose:

> Cleavage began to appear between 'values' and 'facts'; between what you *felt* as a human being or as a poet, and what you *thought* as a man of sense, judgment and enlightenment. Instead of being able, like Donne or Browne, to think and feel simultaneously either in verse or in prose, you were now expected to think prosaically and to feel poetically. Prose was for conveying what was felt to be true, and was addressed to the judgment; poetry was for conveying pleasure and was addressed to the fancy.[21]

These developments, Mr. Willey argues, inevitably lowered the status of poetry, an activity by which truth could not be reached. Hence we find that, "After Descartes, poets were inevitably writing with the sense that their constructions were *not true*, and this feeling robbed their work of essential seriousness." [22]

However much truth this judgment may contain for Descartes — and its broad application even to Descartes may be seriously challenged — it could not be extended to Hobbes.[23] The sum of Hobbes's thinking is distinctly in another direction. By insisting upon the element of judgment in the works of fancy and by making the basic impulse toward artistic creation and aesthetic enjoyment, that is, appetite and pleasure in mental activity, almost identical with the impulse toward truth, Hobbes, as had Aristotle before him, goes far toward justifying works of the imagination (fancy) as normal and

---

[21] *The Seventeenth Century Background; Studies in the Thought of the Age in Relation to Poetry and Religion* (London, 1934), p. 88.   [22] *Ibid.*

[23] Mr. Willey does not in fact so apply it, except that, since Descartes and Hobbes were contemporaries and were engaged in the same type of philosophic research, his sweeping generalization must by implication include the effects of Hobbes as well as of Descartes. He is, however, particularly in view of the subtitle of his book, strangely silent on Hobbes's aesthetic.

dignified products of the human spirit. No one can read *The Answer to Davenant* and the Preface to the *Iliad* and believe that Hobbes regarded poetry as opposed to the essentially true and serious. On the contrary, he specifically extends the sphere of the same fancy that is the activating principle in poetry to all those works of man that have marked his progress from barbarism to civilization.[24]

It will aid in appreciating the extent of Hobbes's concession to the worth of fancy in *The Answer to Davenant* (quoted on pages 107–108) to supplement what he says there with a statement on valid philosophic method and achievement which appears in the earlier *Elements of Law*. It will be recalled that in his reply to Davenant Hobbes ascribes to fancy not only poetry but the various inventions and discoveries that have raised man from savagery to civilization. Poetry is itself an instrument of civilization in that at its best it "traces the way of true philosophy," may, indeed, even surpass the best that philosophy has so far achieved. In the section in *The Elements of Law* of which I speak Hobbes has been discoursing on the ways of true "teaching" as opposed to mere "persuasion." True teachers "know what they teach." He that teaches uses only conceptions that begin "from experience," but he that persuades begins and ends with untried assumptions. The one, speaking words that carry their own evidence of truth, begets belief and understanding; the other begets mere opinion. From the truths enunciated by the teacher, there is no appeal; but the words of the practitioner of persuasion lead only to controversy. This is manifest if we examine the writings of those who have exercised their pens on divers subjects:

. . . For those men who have taken in hand to consider nothing else but the comparison of magnitudes, numbers, times, and motions, and their proportions one to another, have thereby been the authors of all

[24] It would be easy to accumulate evidence to show that Restoration and Augustan critics and poets who were influenced by Hobbes were far from resigning themselves to a conception that poetry has no traffic with truth. One need only cite Cowley's deep and abiding seriousness, Dryden's comprehensive definition of drama, Addison's purpose in writing his *Cato*, the insistence of Dennis that the greatest poetry derives its sublimity from high religious ideas, to indicate the falsity of Mr. Willey's generalization.

those excellences, wherein we differ from such savage people as are now the inhabitants of divers places in America; and as have been the inhabitants heretofore of those countries where at this day arts and sciences do most flourish. For from the studies of these men hath proceeded, whatsoever cometh to us for ornament by navigation; and whatsoever we have beneficial to human society by the division, distinction, and portraying of the face of the earth; whatsoever also we have by the account of times, and foresight of the course of heaven; whatsoever by measuring distances, planes, and solids of all sorts; and whatsoever either elegant or defensible in building: all which supposed away, what do we differ from the wildest of the Indians? Yet to this day was it never heard of, that there was any controversy concerning any conclusion in this subject; the science whereof hath nevertheless been continually amplified and enriched with conclusions of most difficult and profound speculation. The reason whereof is apparent to every man that looketh into their writing; for they proceed from most low and humble principles, evident even to the meanest capacity; going on slowly, and with most scrupulous ratiocination (viz.) from the imposition of names they infer the truth of their first propositions; and from two of the first, a third; and from any two of the three a fourth; and so on, according to the steps of science, mentioned chap. 6, sect. 4. On the other side, those men who have written concerning the faculties, passions, and manners of men, that is to say, of moral philosophy, or of policy, government, and laws, whereof there be infinite volumes have been so far from removing doubt and controversy in the questions they have handled, that they have very much multiplied the same; nor doth any man at this day so much as pretend to know more than hath been delivered two thousand years ago by Aristotle. And yet every man thinks that in this subject he knoweth as much as any other; supposing there needeth thereunto no study but that it accrueth to them by natural wit; though they play, or employ their mind otherwise in the purchase of wealth or place. The reason whereof is no other, than that in their writings and discourses they take for principles those opinions which are already vulgarly received, whether true or false; being for the most part false. There is therefore a great deal of difference between teaching and persuading; the signs of this being controversy; the sign of the former, no controversy.[25]

It is hardly to be supposed that between the writing of *The Elements of Law* in 1640 and *The Answer to Davenant* in 1650 Hobbes had rejected scientific ratiocination in favor of poetry as a way to truth. The *Leviathan* (1651) and *The Elements of Philosophy* (1655) stand to refute such a view. It is more reasonable to assume that his thinking had led him to see that the activities of fancy and judgment in artistic creation may

[25] *The Elements of Law*, I, xiii, 3.

eventuate in truth quite as valuable as the activities of fancy
and judgment in strictly logical processes. It will be noted
that the materials and the results of poetry and science are
the same. Both the poet and the teacher begin with experience; both end, each in his own way, with truth. Writing
of scientific teaching, Hobbes declares: "The first use of
language is the expression of our conceptions, that is the begetting in another the same conceptions that we have in ourselves; and this is called TEACHING; wherein if the conceptions
of him that teacheth continually accompany his words, beginning at something from experience, then it begetteth the
like evidence in the hearer that understandeth them . . . ." [26]
Writing of the foundations of poetry, Hobbes asserts that
"time and education begets experience" and that experience
begets all the rest. And he further points out that the two
things which give a "Poem the true and natural Colour" are
"*To know well*, that is to have images of nature in the memory
distinct and clear, and *To know much*." [27]

The bases for science and poetry are then alike, and, as
we have seen, their ends, so far as they are of practical benefit
to mankind, as in inventions, discoveries, and the general arts
of civilization which distinguish "the civility of Europe from
the barbarity of the *American* savages," are similar and of
equal merit. Indeed, if anything, poetry seems to have something of the edge in beneficial effects. For where the precepts
of philosophy fail, "as they have hitherto failed in the doctrine
of Moral virtue, there the Architect, *Fancy*, must take the
philosopher's part upon herself."

The methods of poetry are, however, clearly different from
those of science. Hobbes reveals no tendency to confuse the
two. If poetry has shown man the path to truth, she has done
it in her own way, through pleasant fictions, through novelty
and liveliness of idea and expression, in appeal to the imagination through apt descriptions and striking metaphors, in general

[26] *Ibid.*, I, xiii, 2. Elsewhere Hobbes writes of two kinds of knowledge
"which we call SCIENCE, the first 'Experience of fact,' the second 'evidence of
truth'" (*ibid.*, I, vi, 4).

[27] *The Answer to Davenant*, in *Critical Essays of the Seventeenth Century*, ed. by
J. E. Spingarn (Oxford, 1908), II, 63.

through elevation of fancy. "For men more generally affect and admire Fancie than they do either Judgment, or Reason, or Memory. . . . For in Fancie consisteth the sublimity of a Poet, which is that Poetical Fury which the Readers for the most part call for." [28]   The scientific teacher works in a different mode, on a quieter, more humble plane, putting two and two together, proceeding from facts to propositions, from propositions to general conclusions.   What the philosopher attains by slow and laborious steps, the poet reaches quickly — by virtue of a nimble fancy which, swiftly and with unerring movement, pursues to their hiding places the innumerable items of stored experience, seeks out their inherent relationships, and, aided by a ready judgment which is at hand to "furnish and square" the matter according to the dictates of truth and the requirements of artistic composition, brings them together in new and pleasing structures.[29]

Poetry thus becomes not mere byplay, not a diversion from profitable mental pursuits, but one of the legitimate and highly reputable modes of mind by which man finds his way to, and expresses, truth.   Believing such things Hobbes naturally contemns inspiration, and holds suspect extravagance in fanciful creation.   The idea of speaking by inspiration seems to him "a reasonless imitation of custom," and why a man should love to be thought to speak so, "like a Bagpipe," when he is

[28] *The Answer to Davenant*, Spingarn, II, 60.

[29] *Ibid.* Bacon gives to the imagination and the arts dependent on the imagination a less dignified position.   Hobbes nowhere suggests that the works of fancy are any more the result of chance than are the works of science.   But Bacon consistently regards the useful inventions and discoveries that have aided in civilization the produce of lucky accidents.   Logic, says Bacon, "professes not, nor pretends to invent, either mechanical or liberal arts."   Experience is the mother of invention.   "Hence," he declares, "those who write upon the first inventors of things, and the origin of the sciences, rather celebrate chance than art" (*On the . . . Advancement of Learning*, V, ii [Bohn ed.], p. 184).   Again he writes, "And if we should, according to the traditions of the Greeks, ascribe the first invention of arts to men, yet we cannot say that Prometheus studied the invention of fire; or that when he first struck the flint he expected sparks, but that he fell upon it by accident, and, as the poets say, stole it from Jupiter. So that as to the invention of arts, we are rather beholden to the wild goat for chirurgery, to the nightingale for music, to the stork for glysters, to the accidental flying off of a pot's cover for artillery, and, in a word, to chance, or anything else, rather than to logic" (*ibid.*, p. 185).

"enabled to speak wisely from the principles of nature and his own meditation," Hobbes cannot imagine.[30] Inspiration is but a form of madness, he says elsewhere, commonly but "some lucky finding of an error generally held by others," for holding which the inspired ones "presently admire themselves, as being in the special grace of God Almighty." [31] Writers by inspiration, one may then infer, are to true poets what those who write to persuade — the *dogmatici* — are to the *mathematici*, or true teachers. In each case the one proceeds from opinion only, the other from a store of experience. The first works by chance and from received belief, the second by judgment and from prudence founded on wide and close observation of men and nature.[32] That is, the poet, like the scientist, must derive his materials from experience, constructing forms that will stand the test of actual knowledge, or of probability founded in knowledge.

This is Hobbes's central theory of verisimilitude. It is a doctrine based upon respect for truth and it is related to an independent psychological approach to the problem of poetry. Following its dictates, the poet writes not according to principles laid down by the ancients, nor yet according to their example, fine as it may be, but according to the natural working of his own mind — fancy controlled by judgment operating in the field of memory, wherein are lodged exact and true images of the world in which he lives. Only so may the poet carry a conviction of truth to the heart of his reader and perform his unique function of taking the "Philosopher's part" upon himself, thus instructing man, where formal philosophy has failed, in "a doctrine of Moral virtue." [33]

In all this insistence on experience as the source of poetic material Hobbes is definitely registering progress over such

[30] *The Answer to Davenant*, Spingarn, II, 59.
[31] *Leviathan*, I, viii. By inference it *may* be truth that is lighted upon: Hobbes's further words are, "though it be many times an untruth they light on" (*ibid.*).
[32] "As much Experience is *Prudence;* so is much Science *Sapience*" (*ibid.*, I, v). Hobbes is somewhat tolerant here, however, granting the poet the right to use in his compositions that which is received as true in any given age. (See p. 159 of this book.)
[33] *The Answer to Davenant*, Spingarn, II, 60.

ideas of fanciful creation as we find expressed in Shakespeare's description of the poet who, "as imagination bodies forth | The forms of things unknown . . . gives to airy nothing | A local habitation and a name." For "airy nothing" Hobbes substitutes the substantial forms (phantasms) of actual experience, integrated through the coöperative agencies of fancy and judgment (impelled and directed to given ends by appetite) into new and delightsome creations.

So it comes about that, so far from contributing to any such future division between poetry and truth as Mr. Willey ascribes to the new philosophy, Hobbes is, on the contrary, going far toward a reconciliation of apparently conflicting elements — an accommodation of the claims of the poetic and the imaginative with those of the rational, of the pleasurable with the serious — similar to that attempted by the great Romanticists a century and a half later. So far from depreciating the works of the imagination Hobbes exalts them, just as, in spite of his fondness for rationality, he gives to the emotions dignity and integrity as an essential element in the good life. It was fortunate for subsequent English poetry and criticism that so influential a personage as Hobbes held such views.

Reflection upon such facts leads one to an appreciation of something of the complexity of the effects of Hobbes on subsequent critical attitudes. In so far as he emphasized rationality and insisted on judgment and restraint in poetry he may be reckoned on the side of the rationalistic neoclassic thought of the Restoration and Augustan periods; but to the extent that he taught men to hold authoritarianism suspect and to strike out on new courses for themselves, charting their way by experience, reason, and even natural prudence, he was undermining the very props on which neoclassicism stood. By introducing anew, after Aristotle and Longinus and Bacon, the spirit of free philosophical inquiry into the study of literary problems, and by upholding in good English fashion the integrity of individual judgment as opposed to rules and formulae of questionable validity, he was opening the way not only to emancipation from the rules and their accompanying traditions, but to a mode of independent aesthetic speculation which was to characterize much of the best thought of the next two centuries.

It would be too much to say that Hobbes's theory is complete. It does, indeed, contain valuable contributions to a new aesthetic. Hobbes made additions where they were vitally needed, and which if better understood would have cleared subsequent English criticism of much of the accumulating mists of neoclassic dogmatism. He set out to determine psychological facts. His suggestions of the assimilative processes of the perceiving mind and his description of the complex nature of the activities of the fancy in poetic creation show definite advances over previous thought. It was no small thing that he asserted the dignity and integrity of the fancy in human affairs. He did not, however, perceive the fallacies of the mechanical approach. And, much as he achieved in directing attention to the activities of mind concerned in literary production, he left the question of the imagination still in a nebulous state. His whole theory of knowledge, hence his theory of imaginative creation, falters at the most crucial point: for he is not able to offer a satisfactory solution to the problem of how the mind makes use of its materials; how it comes about that individual minds differ; how, in short, inner reality is built out of outer reality.

We can be quite certain that Hobbes never fully recognizes the true nature of the psychological processes later described by Coleridge.[34] His emphasis is upon consciously manipulated faculties rather than upon the unified, inevitable workings of a creative intelligence. He does not yet see the fancy (imagination) in the Coleridgean way as a sort of reagent in a process of spiritual digestion. In other words, he fails to take fully

[34] Hobbes's contemporary Peter Sterry, Cambridge Platonist, comes nearer the Coleridgean view. To Sterry the imagination, the "*first* and *highest* faculty of the *sensitive Soul* where it is in its *perfection*, is as ample as the *universal object* of *sense*, the whole *Corporeal world* . . . . It not only takes in and *enjoys* the sensitive forms of all the *objects* of *sense, uniting* and *varying* them according to its own pleasure, but also . . . it *espouseth* in itself the *spiritual* and *corporeal world* to each other, receiving the *impressions*, the *similitudes*, the *illapses* of the *invisible Glories* as the *Originals* into their *sensitive Image*, and *heightning* the *sensitive Image* to a greatness and glory *above* it self by this communion with its invisible patterns" (Vivian de Sola Pinto, *Peter Sterry, Platonist and Puritan* [Cambridge, 1934], p. 103). Sterry here

into account the mysterious alchemy through which materials dropped into the deep well of the subconscious take organic form through the power of the imaginative activity.

Similar qualifications may be made of Hobbes's theory of effects. It is neither complete nor entirely satisfactory. It revolves too nearly about the axle of self-interest. His theory of tragic effect represents a divergence from rather than a fulfilment or complement of Aristotle's view of equilibrium through purgation. Even so Hobbes's pronouncements on effects are an event in literary criticism; they are in many respects fundamental, and they came at a time when they were much needed.

Whether or not, in reading Hobbes, we accept his account of the causes and nature of pleasure, we must in fairness acknowledge that he is shifting emphasis in literary criticism. His approach *is* new. However bound by certain of the neoclassic conventions he may appear to be, his chief interest is not in rules and external form; he is instead vitally concerned with what a poem, or an action, does to a man; and, taken all in all, he makes an attempt, really elaborate and fruitful, to discover the why of these effects.

Hobbes certainly made further progress toward an analysis of the mental processes related to poetry than had anyone before him, or than anyone was to do after him up to Addison and Hutcheson. He laid bare problems which were to be main issues in criticism from his day to ours: the nature of imagination, or "fancy"; the relation of imagination to judgment, of imagination to memory; the place of experience in art. He was immensely productive of thought, and set in motion streams of ideas which, having passed through the middle stages in Dryden, Dennis, Shaftesbury, Addison, Burke, Blair, and others, were to eventuate in the profound formula-

---

introduces an element with which Hobbes, whose philosophy had no place in it for the supersensible, would have shown small patience. In making the imagination the agency for the fusion of mind stuffs from the corporeal and the spiritual worlds, Sterry is, however, as I. A. Richards has noticed, going far toward anticipating an important phase of Coleridge's psychology. Coleridge was here to leave Hobbes and his kind to join hands with the Platonist.

tions of Kant and Coleridge, were indeed to continue their influence, among better critics, to our own day. And though one cannot go quite all the way with Mr. Spingarn in declaring that "Hobbes's aesthetic is consistent and logical throughout," for there are certainly lapses in consistency, it is still possible to say it is the nearest approach to such an aesthetic up to this time in English literature.

BIBLIOGRAPHY

I. PRIMARY SOURCES

ADDISON, JOSEPH, *The Spectator*, eight volumes, edited by G. Gregory Smith; with an Introductory Essay by Austin Dobson. London: J. M. Dent and Co., 1897.

ARISTOTLE, *A Briefe of the Art of Rhetorique. Containing in Substance all that Aristotle hath written in his Three Bookes of that Subject Except onely what is not applicable to the English Tongue*, by Thomas Hobbes. London: Printed by Tho. Cotes for A. Crook, 1637 (?).

—— *De Anima*, with Translation, Introduction and Notes by Robert Drew Hicks. Cambridge: At the University Press, 1907.

—— *The Ethics of Aristotle*, illustrated with Essays and Notes by Sir Alexander Grant. London: J. W. Parker and Sons, 1857–58.

—— *The Metaphysics*, two volumes, with an English Translation by Hugh Tredennick. Loeb Classical Library. Cambridge: Harvard University Press; London: William Heinemann, 1936.

—— *The Nicomachean Ethics of Aristotle*, translated, with an Analysis and Critical Notes, by J. E. C. Welldon. London: Macmillan and Co., 1897.

—— *The Poetics*, edited, with Critical Notes and a Translation, by S. H. Butcher. Fourth edition. London: Macmillan and Co., 1922.

—— *La Poétique d'Aristote, contenant les règles les plus exactes pour juger du poëme héroïque, et des pièces de théâtre, la tragédie et la comédie*, traduit en François par André Dacier. Paris: C. Barbin, 1692.

—— *The Rhetoric of Aristotle, a Translation by Sir Richard Claverhouse Jebb*, edited, with an Introduction and with Supplementary Notes, by John Edwin Sandys. Cambridge: At the University Press, 1909.

AUGUSTINUS, AURELIUS, *The Works of Aurelius Augustine, Bishop of Hippo*, fifteen volumes, translated by Marcus Dods, J. F. Shaw, and others, edited by Marcus Dods. Edinburgh: T. and T. Clark, 1872–78.

BACON, FRANCIS, *The Works of Francis Bacon*, fifteen volumes, collected and edited by James Spedding, Robert Leslie Ellis, and Douglas Denon Heath. New York: Hurd and Houghton, 1869.

—— *The Physical and Metaphysical Works of Lord Bacon*, edited by Joseph Devey. Bohn edition. London: Bell and Daldy, 1872.

BACON, FRANCIS, *Of the Advancement of Learning*, edited by William Aldis Wright. Oxford: At the Clarendon Press, 1920.

BOYLE, ROBERT, *The Works of the Honourable Robert Boyle*, five volumes. London: A. Millar, 1744.

BURTON, ROBERT, *The Anatomy of Melancholy*. London: B. Blake, 1838.

CHARLETON, WALTER, *The Darkness of Atheism Dispelled by the Light of Nature, a Physico-Theological Treatise*. London: Printed by F. G. for William Lee, 1652.

—— *Enquiries into Human Nature, in VI. Anatomic Prælections in the New Theatre of the Royall Colledge of Physicians in London*, published by order of the most learned President. London: Printed by M. White for Robert Boulter, 1680.

—— *Epicurus's Morals: Collected, and Faithfully Englished*, with an Introductory Essay by Frederic Manning. London: Printed for P. Davies, Publisher, 1926.

—— *The Immortality of the Human Soul Demonstrated by the Light of Nature*, in two dialogues. London: Printed for Richard Wellington . . . and Edmund Rumbold, 1699.

—— *Natural History of Nutrition, Life, and Voluntary Motion, Containing all the New Discoveries of Anatomists, and Most Probable Opinion of Physicians, concerning the Oeconomie of Human Nature*. London: Printed for Henry Herringman, 1655.

—— *Natural History of the Passions*. London: Printed by T. N. for James Magnes in Russell Street, near the Piazza in Convent Garden, 1674.

—— *Two Discourses. I. Concerning the Different Wits of Men: II. Of the Mysterie of Vintners*. London: Printed by R. W. for William Whitwood, 1669.

CICERO, *The Orations of Marcus Tullius Cicero*, four volumes, translated by C. D. Yonge. Bohn edition. London: Bell and Daldy, 1870. Volume IV contains the rhetorical works of Cicero.

COLERIDGE, SAMUEL TAYLOR, *Anima Poetæ*, edited by E. H. Coleridge. Boston and New York: Houghton, Mifflin and Co., 1895.

—— *Biographia Literaria*, two volumes, edited by J. Shawcross. Oxford: At the Clarendon Press, 1907.

COWLEY, ABRAHAM, *The Complete Works in Verse and Prose of Abraham Cowley*, two volumes, edited by A. B. Grosart. Chertsey Worthies' Library. Edinburgh: University Press, 1881.

—— *The Works of Mr. Abraham Cowley*. London: Printed by J. M. for Henry Herringman, 1669.

COWLEY, ABRAHAM, *The Works of Mr. Abraham Cowley*, two volumes. Eighth edition. London: Printed for Henry Herringman, 1693.

—— *Poems: Miscellanies, The Mistress, Pindarique Odes, Davideis, Verses Written on Several Occasions*, edited by A. R. Waller. Cambridge: At the University Press, 1905.

CUDWORTH, RALPH, *The True Intellectual System of the Universe Wherein All the Reason and Philosophy of Atheism Is Confuted and Its Impossibility Demonstrated, with an Account of the Life and Writings of the Author*, by Thomas Birch. First American Edition. New York: Andover, Gould, and Newman, 1837–38.

DACIER, ANDRÉ, *Aristotle's Art of Poetry*. Translated from the original Greek, according to Mr. Theodore Goulston's Edition. Together with Mr. D'Acier's Notes translated from the French. London: Printed for Dan. Browne and Will. Turner, 1705.

DAVENANT, SIR WILLIAM, "Preface to *Gondibert*," in Vol. II of *Critical Essays of the Seventeenth Century*, three volumes, edited by J. E. Spingarn. Oxford: At the Clarendon Press, 1908.

DENNIS, JOHN, *The Advancement and Reformation of Modern Poetry. A Critical Discourse in Two Parts*. London: Printed for Rich. Parker, 1701.

—— *A Defense of Sir Fopling Flutter, a Comedy written by Sir George Etheridge*. London: Printed for T. W. Warner, 1722.

—— *An Essay on the Genius and Writings of Shakespeare with Some Letters of Criticism to the Spectator*. London, 1712.

—— *The Grounds of Criticism in Poetry, Contained in some New Discoveries never made before, requisite for the Writing and Judging of Poems surely*. London: Printed for Geo. Strahan, 1704.

—— *The Impartial Critick: or Some Observations on a Late Book entituled A Short View of Tragedy, written by Mr. Rymer*. London: R. Taylor, 1693.

—— *Miscellanies in Verse and Prose*. London: J. Knapton, 1693. (Imprimatur, Edmund Bohun, 1692.)

—— *Original Letters, Familiar, Moral and Critical*, two volumes. London: W. Mears, 1721.

—— *Remarks upon "Cato, a Tragedy."* London: Printed for B. Lintott, 1713.

—— *Remarks upon "Prince Arthur."* London: Printed for R. Sare, 1696.

—— *The Usefulness of the Stage, To the Happiness of Mankind. To Government, and To Religion*. London: Printed for Rich. Parker, 1698.

DESCARTES, RENÉ, *The Philosophical Works of Descartes*, two volumes, translated by Elizabeth S. Haldane and G. R. T. Ross. Cambridge: At the University Press, 1911–12.

DRYDEN, JOHN, *The Works of John Dryden*, eighteen volumes, edited by Sir Walter Scott and George Saintsbury. Edinburgh and London: William Paterson and Co., 1882–93.

—— *Essays of John Dryden*, two volumes, selected and edited by W. P. Ker. Oxford: At the Clarendon Press, 1926.

DU BOS, JEAN BAPTISTE, *Réflexions critiques sur la poësie et sur la peinture*, three volumes. Paris: Pissot, 1770.

DU FRESNOY, C. A., *The Art of Painting*, translated by John Dryden (1695), in Vol. XVII of *The Works of John Dryden*, eighteen volumes, edited by Sir Walter Scott and George Saintsbury. Edinburgh and London: William Paterson and Co., 1882–93.

FIRENZUOLA, AGNOLO, *Of the Beauty of Women;* Dialogue by Messer Agnolo Firenzuola, translated from the Italian by Clara Bell, with an Introduction by Theodore Child. London: J. R. Osgood, 1892.

FLECKNOE, RICHARD, "A Short Discourse of the English Stage," appended to *Love's Kingdom* (1664), in Vol. II of *Critical Essays of the Seventeenth Century*, three volumes, edited by J. E. Spingarn. Oxford: At the Clarendon Press, 1908.

GRACIÁN Y MORALES, BALTASAR, *The Art of Prudence: or A Companion for a Man of Sense*, written Originally in Spanish by that Celebrated Author Baltazar Gracián, now made English from the best Edition of the Original, and Illustrated with Sieur *Amelot de la Houssare's* Notes, by Mr. Savage. London: Printed by Daniel Brown . . . and T. Benskin, 1702.

—— *The Compleat Gentleman or A Description of the Several Qualifications, Both Natural and Acquired, That Are Necessary to Form a Great Man*, translated by T. Saldkeld. London: Printed for T. Osborne, 1730. (This is the second edition. The original was first published, under the title *El Descreto*, in 1646.)

—— *The Courtiers Manual Oracle, or The Art of Prudence*, written Originally in Spanish by Baltazar Gracián, and now done into English. London: Printed by M. Flesher, for Abel Sevalle, 1685. (The original was first published in 1653.)

—— *The Critick, written Originally in the Spanish by Lorenzo Gracián, One of the Best Wits of Spain*, . . . translated into English by Paul Rycaut, Esq. London: Printed by T. N. for Henry Brome, 1681. (This work was first published in Spain in 1657.)

—— *The Hero, from the Spanish of Baltasar Gracián, with Remarks Moral, Political, and Historical, of the Learned Father J. de Courbeville*, by a Gentleman of Oxford. London: Printed for T. Cox, 1726.

GRACIÁN Y MORALES, BALTASAR, *The Heroe of Lorenzo, or The Way to Eminence and Perfection*, translated by Sir John Skeffington. London: Printed for John Martin and James Allestrye, 1652. (This was Gracián's first work, originally published in 1639.)

—— *L'Homme d'etrompé, ou le Criticon de Baltazar Gracián*, traduit de l'Espagnol en François. Paris: Chez Jacques Collombat, 1696. (*El Criticon* was first published in three parts, in Madrid and Huesca, 1650–53.)

—— *Oráculo Manual y arte de prudencia, sacada de los aforismos*, . . . (1653), translated by Martin Fischer under the title *A Truthtelling Manual and the Art of Worldly Wisdom*. Lancaster, Pennsylvania: The Science Press Printing Company, 1934.

HOBBES, THOMAS, *The English Works of Thomas Hobbes of Malmesbury*, eleven volumes, collected and edited by Sir William Molesworth. London: J. Bohn, 1839–45.

—— *The Answer to Davenant*, in Vol. II of *Critical Essays of the Seventeenth Century*, three volumes, edited by J. E. Spingarn. Oxford: At the Clarendon Press, 1908.

—— *The Elements of Law Natural and Politic*, edited by Ferdinand Tönnies. Cambridge: At the University Press, 1928.

—— *Leviathan*, edited by Ernest Rhys, with an Introduction by A. D. Lindsay, Everyman's Library. London and Toronto: J. M. Dent and Sons; New York: E. P. Dutton and Co., 1914.

—— *Leviathan*. Reprinted from the edition of 1651, with an essay by the late W. G. Pogson Smith. Oxford: At the Clarendon Press, 1909.

—— *The Metaphysical System of Hobbes in Twelve Chapters from Elements of Philosophy Concerning Body, together with Briefer Extracts from Human Nature and Leviathan*, selected by Mary Whiton Calkins. Chicago: The Open Court Publishing Company, 1913.

—— *Opera Philosophica Quae Latine Scripsit Omnia*, in unum corpus nunc primum collecta, quinque volumina, studio et labore Gulielmi Molesworth. Londini: Apud Joannem Bohn, 1839–45.

—— *Tracts* . . . . *Containing I. Behemoth, the History of the Causes of the Civil Wars of England* . . . . *II. An Answer to Arch-Bishop Bramhall's Book, called The Catching of the Leviathan* . . . . *III. An Historical Narration of Heresie, and the Punishment thereof* . . . . *IV. Philosophical Problems, dedicated to the King* . . . . London: Printed for W. Crooke, 1682.

—— *The Virtues of an Heroic Poem*, in Vol. II of *Critical Essays of the Seventeenth Century*, three volumes, edited by J. E. Spingarn. Oxford: At the Clarendon Press, 1908.

HUARTE, JUAN DE DIOS, *Examen de ingenios para las sciencias. Donde se muestra la differencia de habilidades que ay en los hombres, y el genero de letras que à cada uno responde en particular.* Compuestra par el doctor Iuan Huarte naturel de sant Iuan del pie del Puerto. En Pamplono, con Licencia, par Thomas Porralis, 1578.

—— *Examen de ingenios. The Examination of Men's Wits, in which, by discovering the varietie of natures, is showed for what profession each one is apt, and how far he shall profit therein,* by John Huarte, translated out of the Spanish tongue by M. Camillo Camilli, Englished out of his Italian by R. C. Esquire. London: Printed by Adam Islip for Richard Watkins, 1594.

—— *Examen de ingenios: or the Tryal of Wits among Men, and what sort of Learning suits best with each Genius.* Published Originally in Spanish by Doctor Juan Huartes. And made English from the most Correct Edition by Mr. Bellamy. Useful for all Fathers, Mothers, Tutors, &c. London: Printed for Richard Sare, at Grays-Inn-Gate in Holborn, 1698.

KANT, IMMANUEL, *Kant's Critique of Judgement,* translated by J. H. Bernard. London: Macmillan and Co., 1914.

LE BOSSU, RENÉ, *Treatise of the Epick Poem,* translated by "W. J." London, 1695.

LESSING, GOTTHOLD EPHRAIM, *Laokoon and How the Ancients Represented Death,* translated by E. C. Beasley and Helen Zimmern. Bohn edition. London: G. Bell and Sons, 1914.

LOCKE, JOHN, *Of the Conduct of the Understanding,* in Vol. I of *The Works of John Locke,* two volumes, with a Preliminary Essay and Notes by J. A. St. John. London: Bell and Daldy, 1867.

—— *Of Human Understanding,* in Vol. I of *The Works of John Locke,* two volumes. London: Bell and Daldy, 1867.

LONGINUS, *On the Sublime,* translated by W. Rhys Roberts. Cambridge: At the University Press, 1907.

LUCRETIUS, *De Rerum Natura. On the Nature of Things,* translated by H. A. J. Munro. Bohn edition. London: G. Bell and Sons, 1914.

PATER, WALTER HORATIO, *Appreciations: with an essay on Style.* London and New York: Macmillan and Co., 1889.

PHILLIPS, EDWARD, "Preface to *Theatrum Poetarum,*" in Vol. II of *Critical Essays of the Seventeenth Century,* three volumes, edited by J. E. Spingarn. Oxford: At the Clarendon Press, 1908.

PHILOSTRATUS, *The Life of Apollonius of Tyana,* two volumes, with an English Translation by F. C. Conybeare. Loeb Classical Library. London: Macmillan and Co., 1912.

PLOTINUS, *The Ethical Treatises*, Vol. I; *Psychic and Physical Treatises*, Vol. II; *On the Nature of the Soul*, Vol. III; *The Divine Mind*, Vol. IV; *On the One and Good*, Vol. V: translated by Stephen Mackenna and B. S. Page. The Library of Philosophical Translations. London: The Medici Society, 1917–30.

PUTTENHAM, GEORGE, *The Arte of English Poesie* (1589), in Vol. II of *Elizabethan Critical Essays*, two volumes, edited by G. Gregory Smith. Oxford: At the Clarendon Press, 1904.

—— *The Arte of English Poesie*, edited by Gladys Doidge Willcock and Alice Walker. Cambridge: At the University Press, 1936.

QUINTILIAN, *The Institutio Oratoria*, four volumes, with an English translation by H. E. Butler. Loeb Classical Library. London: William Heinemann; New York: G. P. Putnam's Sons, 1921–22.

RAPIN, RENÉ, *Reflections on Aristotle's Treatise of Poesie*, in Vol. II of *The Whole Critical Works of Monsieur Rapin*, two volumes, translated by "Several Hands." London: Printed for H. Bonwicke . . . T. Goodwin, M. Wotton, B. Tooke . . . S. Manship, 1706. (Thomas Rymer first translated Rapin's *Reflections* in 1674.)

REYNOLDS, EDWARD, *A Treatise of the Passions and Faculties of the Soul of Man* (London, 1640). London: Printed by F. N. for Robert Bostock and George Badger, 1650.

RYMER, THOMAS, *The Tragedies of the Last Age Consider'd and Examin'd by the Practice of the Ancients and by the Common Sense of all Ages, in a Letter to Fleetwood Shepheard, Esq.* London: Printed for Richard Tonson, 1678.

SCALIGER, J. J., *Select Translations from Scaliger's Poetics*, translated by F. M. Padelford. New York: Henry Holt and Company, 1905.

SHADWELL, THOMAS, "Preface to *The Humorists*" (1671), in Vol. II of *Critical Essays of the Seventeenth Century*, three volumes, edited by J. E. Spingarn. Oxford: At the Clarendon Press, 1908.

SIDNEY, SIR PHILIP, *An Apology for Poetry* in *English Critical Essays (Sixteenth, Seventeenth, and Eighteenth Centuries)*, edited by Edmund D. Jones. London: Humphrey Milford, Oxford University Press, 1922.

SMITH, D. NICHOL, *Eighteenth Century Essays on Shakespeare*. Glasgow: James MacLehose and Sons, 1903.

SPRAT, THOMAS, *An Account of the Life and Writings of Mr. Abraham Cowley. Written to Mr. M. Clifford* (1667), in Vol. II of *Critical Essays of the Seventeenth Century*, three volumes, edited by J. E. Spingarn. Oxford: At the Clarendon Press, 1908.

—— *From the History of the Royal-Society of London* (1667), in *ibid.*

TATE, NAHUM, "To the Reader," *The Third Part of the Works of Mr. Abraham Cowley*, in *The Works of Mr. Abraham Cowley*, two volumes. Eighth edition. London: Henry Herringman, 1693.

TEMPLE, SIR WILLIAM, *Of Poetry*, in Vol. III of *Critical Essays of the Seventeenth Century*, three volumes, edited by J. E. Spingarn. Oxford: At the Clarendon Press, 1908.

THOMAS AQUINAS, SAINT, *Summa Theologica*, twenty-two volumes, literally translated by Fathers of the English Dominican Province. London: Thomas Baker, 1911–17; Burns, Oates and Washburne, 1922–25.

—— *Somme de la foi catholique contre les gentils, par Saint Thomas d'Aquin*, traduction avec le texte Latin, par M. l'Abbé P. F. Écalle. Paris: Le Vives, 1854–56.

WORDSWORTH, WILLIAM, *Poetical Works*, edited by Thomas Hutchinson. London and New York: Oxford University Press, 1917.

—— *The Prelude, or Growth of a Poet's Mind*, edited from the manuscripts, with Introduction and Notes, by Ernest de Selincourt. London: Oxford University Press, 1933.

—— *Wordsworth's Literary Criticism*, edited with an Introduction by Nowell C. Smith. London: Humphrey Milford, 1905.

WRIGHT, THOMAS, *The Passions of the Minde in Generall* (London, 1601). London: Printed by M. Flesher . . . to be sold by Robert Davolman, 1630.

II. SECONDARY MATERIALS

These are works cited or otherwise used in this study.

AUBREY, JOHN, *'Brief Lives,' Chiefly of Contemporaries, set down . . . between the Years 1669 and 1696*, edited from the author's MSS. by Andrew Clark, two volumes. Oxford: At the Clarendon Press, 1898.

BALDWIN, JAMES MARK, *History of Psychology*, two volumes. New York and London: G. P. Putnam's Sons, 1913.

BALZ, ALBERT GEORGE ADAM, *Idea and Essence in the Philosophies of Hobbes and Spinoza*. New York: Columbia University Press, 1918.

—— "The Psychology of Ideas in Hobbes," *Studies in the History of Ideas*, I, 127–148. New York: Columbia University Press, 1918.

BLANCHET, LÉON, *Campanella*. Paris: Librairie Félix Alcan, 1920.

BOND, DONALD F., "The Neo-Classical Psychology of the Imagination," *A Journal of English Literary History*, IV (1937), 247–264.

BORINSKI, KARL, *Baltasar Gracián und die Hoflitteratur in Deutschland*. Halle: Max Niemeyer, 1894.

BOSANQUET, BERNARD, *A History of Aesthetics*. London: Swan Sonnenschein and Company, 1892; New York: The Macmillan Company, 1892.

BOUILLIER, VICTOR, *Baltasar Gracián et Nietzsche.* Paris: Librairie ancienne, Honoré Champion, 1926.

BRAY, RENÉ, *La Formation de la doctrine classique en France.* Lausanne-Genève: Librairie Payot et Cⁱᵉ, 1931.

BREDVOLD, LOUIS I., *The Milieu of John Dryden*, University of Michigan Publications, Language and Literature, Vol. XII. Ann Arbor: University of Michigan Press, 1934.

—— "The Tendency toward Platonism in Neo-Classical Esthetics," *A Journal of English Literary History*, I (1934), 91–119.

BRETT, GEORGE SIDNEY, *A History of Psychology, Ancient and Patristic.* London: George Allen and Company, 1912.

—— *A History of Psychology*, Vol. II ("Mediaeval and Early Modern Period"). London: George Allen and Unwin; New York: The Macmillan Company, 1921.

—— *A History of Psychology*, Vol. III ("Modern Psychology"). London: George Allen and Unwin; New York: The Macmillan Company, 1921.

BROAD, CHARLIE DUNBAR, *The Philosophy of Francis Bacon.* Cambridge: At the University Press, 1926.

BUCK, PHILO M., JR., *Literary Criticism.* New York and London: Harper and Brothers, 1930.

BUNDY, MURRAY WRIGHT, *The Theory of Imagination in Classical and Mediaeval Thought*, University of Illinois Studies in Language and Literature, Vol. XII. Urbana: University of Illinois Press, 1927.

—— "Bacon's True Opinion of Poetry," *Studies in Philology*, XXVII (1930), 244–264.

—— " 'Invention' and 'Imagination' in the Renaissance," *Journal of English and Germanic Philology*, XXIX (1930), 535–545.

BURT, BENJAMIN C., *A History of Modern Philosophy*, two volumes. Chicago: A. C. McClurg and Co., 1892.

CALLAHAN, LEONARD, *A Theory of Aesthetic according to the Principles of St. Thomas Aquinas.* Washington, D.C.: The Catholic University of America, 1927.

CARR, H., "The Function of the Phantasm in St. Thomas Aquinas," *Philosophical Essays Presented to John Watson*, pp. 179–203. Kingston, Ontario: Queen's College, 1923.

CATLIN, GEORGE E. G., *Thomas Hobbes as Philosopher, Publicist, and Man of Letters: An Introduction.* Oxford: Basil Blackwell, 1922.

CLARENDON, EDWARD HYDE, *A Brief View and Survey of the Dangerous and Pernicious Errors to Church and State, in Mr. Hobbes's Book, entitled Leviathan.* Oxford: Printed at the Theatre, 1676.

CLARK, A. F. B., *Boileau and the French Classical Critics in England (1660–1830).* Paris: Librairie ancienne, Édouard Champion, 1925.

CLARKE, FRANCIS PALMER, *The Intellect in the Philosophy of St. Thomas.* Philadelphia: University of Pennsylvania, 1928.

COADY, MARY ANASTASIA, *The Phantasm according to the Teaching of St. Thomas.* Washington, D.C.: The Catholic University of America, 1932.

CROCE, BENEDETTO, *Aesthetic as Science of Expression and General Linguistic,* translated from the Italian by Douglas Ainslie. Second edition. London: Macmillan and Co., 1929.

DAVIDSON, WILLIAM LESLIE, *The Stoic Creed.* Edinburgh: T. and T. Clark, 1907.

DEWEY, JOHN, "An Empirical Survey of Empiricisms," *Studies in the History of Ideas,* Vol. III. New York: Columbia University Press, 1935.

DOWLIN, CORNELL MARCH, *Sir William Davenant's Gondibert, Its Preface, and Hobbes's Answer: A Study in English Neo-Classicism.* Philadelphia: University of Pennsylvania, 1934.

FISCHER, KUNO, *Francis Bacon und seine Nachfolger. Entwicklungsgeschichte der Erfahrungsphilosophie.* Leipzig: F. U. Brockhaus, 1875.

—— *Geschichte der neuern Philosophie,* six volumes. Heidelberg: F. Bassermann, 1865–69.

—— *History of Modern Philosophy: Descartes and His School,* translated by J. P. Gordy, edited by Noah Porter. London: T. Fisher Unwin, 1887.

FRYE, P. H., *Dryden and the Critical Canons of the Eighteenth Century,* University of Nebraska Studies, Vol. VII. Lincoln, 1907.

GAYLEY, C. M., AND SCOTT, FRED NEWTON, *An Introduction to the Methods and Materials of Literary Criticism.* Boston and New York: Ginn and Company, 1899.

GILBY, THOMAS, *Poetic Experience; an Introduction to Thomist Aesthetic.* New York: Sheed and Ward, 1935.

GILSON, ÉTIENNE HENRY, *The Philosophy of St. Thomas Aquinas,* translated by Edward Bullough, edited by G. A. Elrington. Cambridge (England): W. Heffer and Sons, 1924.

GUARDIA, JOSÉ M. M., *Essai sur l'ouvrage de J. Huarte: Examen des aptitudes diverses pour les sciences.* Paris: Auguste Durand, 1855.

GUIBELET, JOURDAIN, *Examen de l'examen des esprits.* Paris: Chez la Veufue Jean de Heuqueville, et Louys de Heuqueville, 1631.

HAMELIUS, PAUL, *Die Kritik in der englischen Literatur des 17. und 18. Jahrhunderts*. Leipzig: T. Grieben, 1897.

HAZLITT, WILLIAM, "On the Writings of Hobbes," "On Liberty and Necessity," "On Locke's Essay on the Human Understanding," in *Literary Remains of the Late William Hazlitt*, two volumes, edited by E. L. Bulwer and Sergeant Talfourd. London: Saunders and Otley, 1836.

HOBHOUSE, LEONARD TRELAWNEY, *The Theory of Knowledge*. London: Methuen and Co., 1896.

HOWARD, WILLIAM GUILD, *"Ut Pictura Poesis," Publications of the Modern Language Association of America*, XXIV (1909), 40–124.

HUGHES, MERRITT Y., "Dryden as a Statist," *Philological Quarterly*, VI (1927), 335–350.

JOYCE, GEORGE HAYWARD, *Principles of Logic*. New York: Longmans, Green, and Co., 1929.

KLEMM, OTTO, *A History of Psychology*, translated by Emil Carl Wilm and Rudolph Pintner. New York, Chicago, and Boston: Charles Scribner's Sons, 1914.

KRANTZ, ÉMILE, *Essai sur l'esthétique de Descartes*. Paris: G. Baillière, 1882.

LAIRD, JOHN, *Hobbes*. London: Ernest Benn, 1934.

LEWES, GEORGE HENRY, *The History of Philosophy from Thales to Comte*, two volumes. London: Longmans, Green, and Co., 1871.

LOISEAU, JEAN, *Abraham Cowley's Reputation in England*. Paris: Henri Didier, 1931.

LORD, HERBERT G., "The Attempt of Hobbes to Base Ethics on Psychology," *Studies in the History of Ideas*, Vol. I. New York: Columbia University Press, 1918.

LYON, GEORGES HENRI JOSEPH, *La Philosophie de Hobbes*. Paris: F. Alcan, 1893.

McCORMICK, JOHN F., *Scholastic Metaphysics*. Chicago: Loyola University Press, 1928.

MAHAFFY, JOHN PENTLAND, *Descartes*. Philadelphia: J. B. Lippincott Company, 1887.

MAHER, MICHAEL, *Psychology: Empirical and Rational*. London and New York: Longmans, Green, and Co., 1908.

MARITAIN, JACQUES, *Art and Scholasticism, with Other Essays*, translated by J. F. Scanlan. New York: Charles Scribner's Sons, 1935.

MARLING, JOSEPH M., *The Order of Nature in the Philosophy of St. Thomas Aquinas*. Washington, D.C.: The Catholic University of America, 1934.

MONK, SAMUEL H., *The Sublime: A Study of Critical Theory in XVIII-Century England*. New York: Modern Language Association of America, 1935.

MORRIS, GEORGE S., *British Thought and Thinkers*. Chicago: S. C. Griggs and Company, 1880.

PARKER, DEWITT HENRY, *The Principles of Aesthetics*. Boston and New York: Silver, Burdett and Company, 1920.

PAUL, HARRY GILBERT, *John Dennis, His Life and Criticism*. New York: Columbia University Press, 1911.

PAULSEN, FRIEDRICH, *Introduction to Philosophy*, translated by Frank Thilly, with a Preface by William James. New York: Henry Holt and Co., 1895.

PINTO, VIVIAN DE SOLA, *Peter Sterry, Platonist and Puritan, 1613–1672, a Biographical and Critical Study with Passages Selected from His Writings*. Cambridge: At the University Press, 1934.

RICHARDS, I. A., *Coleridge on the Imagination*. New York: Harcourt, Brace and Co., 1935.

—— *Principles of Literary Criticism*. New York: Harcourt, Brace and Co., 1928.

ROBERTSON, GEORGE CROOM, *Hobbes*. Edinburgh and London: Wm. Blackwood and Sons, 1886.

—— "Hobbes," *Encyclopaedia Britannica*, eleventh edition.

ROBERTSON, J. G., *Studies in the Genesis of Romantic Theory in the Eighteenth Century*. Cambridge: At the University Press, 1923.

ROUSSELOT, PIERRE, *The Intellectualism of Saint Thomas*, translated, with a Foreword, by Father James E. O'Mahony. New York: Sheed and Ward, 1935.

RUGGIERO, GUIDO DE, *Modern Philosophy*, translated by A. Howard Hannay and R. G. Collingwood. London: George Allen and Unwin; New York: The Macmillan Company, 1921.

SAINTSBURY, GEORGE, *A History of Criticism and Literary Taste in Europe*, three volumes. Third edition. Edinburgh and London: William Blackwood and Sons, 1908.

SETH, JAMES, *English Philosophers and Schools of Philosophy*. London: J. M. Dent and Sons; New York: E. P. Dutton and Co., 1912.

SMITH, G. GREGORY, *Elizabethan Critical Essays*, two volumes. Oxford: At the Clarendon Press, 1904.

SORLEY, WILLIAM R., *A History of English Philosophy*. New York: G. P. Putnam's Sons, 1921.

SORLEY, WILLIAM R., "Hobbes and Contemporary Philosophy," *Cambridge History of English Literature*, Vol. VII, Chap. XII. New York: G. P. Putnam's Sons; Cambridge: At the University Press, 1911.

SPINGARN, J. E., *Critical Essays of the Seventeenth Century*, three volumes. Oxford: At the Clarendon Press, 1908.

—— *A History of Literary Criticism in the Renaissance.* New York: Columbia University Press, 1925.

—— "Jacobean and Caroline Criticism," *The Cambridge History of English Literature*, Vol. VII, Chap. XI. New York: G. P. Putnam's Sons; Cambridge: At the University Press, 1911.

STEPHEN, LESLIE, *Hobbes.* London: Macmillan and Co., 1904.

TAYLOR, ALFRED EDWARD, *Thomas Hobbes.* London: Archibald Constable and Co., 1908.

THORPE, CLARENCE D., "Addison and Hutcheson on the Imagination," *A Journal of English Literary History*, II (1935), 215–234.

—— "Addison and Some of His Predecessors on 'Novelty,'" *Publications of the Modern Language Association of America*, LII (1937), 1114–1129.

—— "Addison's Theory of the Imagination as 'Perceptive Response,'" *Papers of the Michigan Academy of Science, Arts, and Letters*, XXI (1936), 509–530.

TÖNNIES, FERDINAND, *Hobbes Leben und Lehre.* Stuttgart: F. Frommann, 1896.

USTICK, W. LEE, AND HUDSON, HOYT H., "Wit, 'Mixt Wit,' and the Bee in Amber," *The Huntington Library Bulletin*, Number 8 (1935), pp. 103–130.

VAN DEUSEN, NEIL C., *Telesio: The First of the Moderns.* New York: Columbia University Press, 1932.

VAN DOREN, MARK, *The Poetry of John Dryden.* New York: Harcourt, Brace and Howe, 1920.

WARD, LEO, "Natural Tendency in the Thought of St. Thomas," unpublished paper read before the Michigan Academy at Ann Arbor, March, 1938.

WILLEY, BASIL, *The Seventeenth Century Background; Studies in the Thought of the Age in Relation to Poetry and Religion.* London: Chatto and Windus, 1934.

WOOD, ANTHONY À, *Athenæ Oxonienses, an Exact History of all the Writers and Bishops who have had their education in the University of Oxford*, four volumes. London, 1813. (First published in two volumes in 1691–92, with a third volume in 1721.)

INDEX

Particular works are entered by title rather than by author.

293; and Gerard, 293; on history, 153; and Hume, 293; and Hutcheson, 293; idea of aesthetic pleasures in, 22; on imagery, 134, 135; on imagination, 79, 80 ff., 82 n., 83 n., 91 n., 104 n., 107, 108, 109 n., 110 n., 113, 145 n., 163, 177 n., 202 n., 281 n., 283 n., 305, 306; on imitation, 158; importance of aesthetics of, v–vi; importance for Romantic psychology of, 88; independence in aesthetics of, 150–151, 156; and inductive approach, 10 ff., 190 ff.; dual influence of, 123; influence of Puttenham on, 53; influence of Renaissance thought on, 298; insight into psychological phenomena, 84 n.; on inspiration, 302, 303; on internal sensation, 124 n.; introspection in, 84; and Johnson, 291; on judgment, 84, 85, 91, 94, 95, 96, 98, 99, 100, 179, 281 n., 292, 298, 300, 301, 302, 303, 304, 305; and Kant, 307; on laughter, 145 ff., 161; as literary man, 3–6; and Locke, 86 n., 89 n., 97–98 n., 187 n., 282, 283, 284, 285; and Longinus, 290, 291, 304; and Lucretius, 143 n.; materialism of, 8; on memory, 80–82, 92, 152, 302, 303; on mental processes, Bacon and, 70 n.; on metaphor, 141 n.; and neoclassicism, 6–7, 150, 151, 156, 161, 162, 295, 304, 305; and new aesthetic, 287, 288, 289, 304, 305; on novelty, 137 ff., 289; on passions, 20, 91 ff., 97, 119 ff., 144 n., 146, 172 n., 288; on perception, 80, 81, 82, 83, 84 ff., 114; on persuasion and truth, 299–300; on pleasure and pain, 119–120, 123, 124; on "pleasures of the mind," 125, 126, 127, 128; on poetry, 101, 102, 104, 105, 106 ff., 147,

158 ff., 287, 300 ff.; on poets, 100, 158, 159 n., 302; on probability, 142, 159 ff.; on "prudence," 99, 100, 294–295; psychological approach in, 7, 25, 149, 150, 291, 304; psychology of, 79 ff.; on reason and science, 195, 294, 302; and Romanticism, 169 n., 290, 304; on the Scholastics and Scholasticism, 79, 79 n., 287, 288, 296; science defined by, 11–12, 99–100; sensationalism of, 10, 16–17; on sense, 79, 80; on sensual pleasure, 125 ff.; and Shaftesbury, 306; and Shakespeare, 304; on similitudes, 97, 97 n., 98, 98 n., 99, 107; on speech, 11, 155 n.; spirit of approach to study of faculties and passions, 21; on style, 154, 155, 155 n., 161, 162, 164–169; and the sublime, 290; on taste, 122, 123; terms variously used by, 116–117; on Thucydides, 151 ff.; Thucydides' influence on, 21–22; tolerant attitude toward passions and imagination in, 24, 118; on unity, 161–162; on verisimilitude, 156, 159 ff., 303; on wit, 80, 96, 98 ff., 161, 177, 178, 276 n., 291 n.; and Wordsworth, 292; "Vita Tho. Hobbes" by, 4 n.

Homer: 76 n., 249 n., 288; Davenant on, 171; Dryden on, 201, 218 n.; Rapin on, 218 n.

Hooker, Edward Niles, 224 n.

Horace: 109, 192, 198, 201; Dryden on, 192, 198, 201, 218 n.

Howard, William Guild, 35 n.

Huarte, Juan de Dios: 39, 42–48, 42 n., 61, 115, 116, 146 n., 163; on imagination, 43–48, 44 n., 61, 110 n., 115, 124–125 n.; influence of, 47; on memory, 43–44, 44 n.; psychology of, 43–48; on the understanding, 43, 44, 44 n., 45, 47

DATE